Lives   of the Caesars

D0012358

Lives of the Caesars

Edited by Anthony A. Barrett

Blackwell
Publishing

© 2008 by Blackwell Publishing Ltd

BLACKWELL PUBLISHING
350 Main Street, Malden, MA 02148-5020, USA
9600 Garsington Road, Oxford OX4 2DQ, UK
550 Swanston Street, Carlton, Victoria 3053, Australia

First published 2008 by Blackwell Publishing Ltd

1   2008

Library of Congress Cataloging-in-Publication Data
Lives of the Caesars / edited by Anthony A. Barrett
     p. cm.
  Includes bibliographical references and index.
  ISBN 978–1–4051–2754–7 (hardcover : alk. paper)—ISBN 978–1–4051–2755–4 (pbk. : alk. paper) 1. Emperors—Rome—Biography. 2. Rome—History—Empire, 30 B.C.–476 A.D. I. Barrett, Anthony, 1941–

  DG274.L56 2008
  937'.060922—dc22

                        2007043478

A catalogue record for this title is available from the British Library.

Set in 10.5/13pt Minion
by Graphicraft Limited, Hong Kong
Printed and bound in Singapore
by Markono Print Media Pte Ltd

The publisher's policy is to use permanent paper from mills that operate a sustainable forestry policy, and which has been manufactured from pulp processed using acid-free and elementary chlorine-free practices. Furthermore, the publisher ensures that the text paper and cover board used have met acceptable environmental accreditation standards.

For further information on
Blackwell Publishing, visit our website at
www.blackwellpublishing.com

Contents

Illustrations

Notes on Contributors

Anthony A. Barrett is Emeritus Professor and Distinguished University Professor at the University of British Columbia, Vancouver. He is a Fellow of the Royal Society of Canada. He has written extensively on the ancient world and is the author of biographies of Caligula, Agrippina the Younger, and Livia. Most recently he co-authored, with John Yardley, the Oxford World's Classics edition of *The Annals* of Tacitus. Since retirement he is studying Anglo-Saxon, Norse, and Celtic at Sidney Sussex College, Cambridge.

Anthony R. Birley was Professor of Ancient History at the universities of Manchester, from 1974 to 1990, and Düsseldorf, from 1990 to 2002. His publications include biographies of the emperors Hadrian, Marcus Aurelius, and Septimius Severus. He is Chair of the Trustees of the Vindolanda Trust.

Mary T. Boatwright is Professor of Ancient History in the Department of Classical Studies at Duke University. She has published widely on the Roman world, and her works include *Hadrian and the City of Rome* (Princeton, 1987) and *Hadrian and the Cities of the Roman Empire* (Princeton, 2000). With Daniel Gargola and Richard J. A. Talbert she has co-authored *The Romans: From Village to Empire* (Oxford, 2004) and *A Brief History of the Romans* (Oxford, 2005).

Simon Corcoran is Senior Research Fellow in the Department of History at University College London. He is currently working on Roman law and its legacy in late antiquity and the early middle ages as part of the Volterra Roman law projects. His book *The Empire of the Tetrarchs: Imperial Pronouncements and Government AD 284–324* (Oxford, 1996) won a silver medal in the IV Premio romanistico internazionale Gérard Boulvert (1998).

Werner Eck is Professor of Ancient History at Cologne University, and one of the world's leading historians of the Roman empire. His books include

    Notes on Contributors

Die Verwaltung des römischen Reiches in der Hohen Kaiserzeit, 2 vols (Basel, 1995, 1998), *Das senatus consultum de Cn. Pisone patre* (with A. Caballos and F. Fernández; Munich, 1996), *Tra epigrafia, prosopografia e archeologia: scritti scelti, rielaborati ed aggiornati* (Rome, 1996), *Köln in römischer Zeit* (Cologne, 2004) and *The Age of Augustus* (2nd edn Oxford, 2007).

James Allan Evans was until retirement Professor of Classics at the University of British Columbia, Vancouver, and is a Fellow of the Royal Society of Canada. He has published widely on Hellenistic economic history, Herodotus and the Persian Wars, and the proto-Byzantine period. His latest book is *The Beginnings of History: Herodotus and the Persian Wars* (Campbellsville, Ont., 2006); forthcoming are *Everyday Life in the Hellenistic World from Alexander the Great to Cleopatra* (2008) and *The Power Game in Byzantium: Antonina and the Empress Theodora* (London, forthcoming).

Miriam Griffin is Emeritus Fellow of Somerville College, Oxford, having served as Tutor in Ancient History for thirty-five years. She is the author of *Seneca, a Philosopher in Politics* (Oxford, 1992), *Nero, the End of a Dynasty* (London and New Haven, 1984), and (with E. M. Atkins) *Cicero: On Duties* (Cambridge, 1991). She is also co-editor with Jonathan Barnes of *Philosophia Togata I* and *II* (Oxford, 1989 and 1997). She is currently working on a study of Seneca's *De Beneficiis*.

Donna W. Hurley has taught at Columbia, Princeton, and Rutgers universities. She is the author of a number of articles on Roman history and of two commentaries on Suetonius: *An Historical and Historiographical Commentary of Suetonius' Life of C. Caligula* (Atlanta, 1993) and *Suetonius: Divus Claudius* (Cambridge, 2001).

Noel Lenski is Associate Professor of Classics at the University of Colorado at Boulder, specializing in late antiquity. He is the author of *Failure of Empire: Valens and the Roman State in the Fourth Century AD* (Berkeley, 2002) and editor of *The Cambridge Companion to the Age of Constantine* (Cambridge, 2005).

Barbara Levick, Emeritus Fellow and Tutor in Literae Humaniores at St Hilda's College, Oxford, is the author of *Claudius* (London and New Haven, 1990), *Vespasian* (London and New York, 1999), and *Tiberius the Politician* (2nd edn, London and New York, 2000), and co-editor with Richard Hawley of *Women in Antiquity: New Assessments* (London, 1995). She is now working on a book about Augustus.

David Potter is Arthur F. Thurnau Professor of Greek and Latin in the Department of Classical Studies at the University of Michigan. His recent books include *The Roman Empire at Bay* (London, 2004), *A Companion to the Roman Empire* (editor; Oxford, 2006), and *Emperors of Rome* (London, 2007).

Greg Rowe is Associate Professor of Greek and Roman Studies at the University of Victoria, Canada. He is the author of *Princes and Political Cultures: The New Tiberian Senatorial Decrees* (Ann Arbor, 2002).

Acknowledgments

The task of completing this book was made much lighter by the generous help afforded by a number of individuals. In a collaborative venture like this it would perhaps be odious to single out individuals, since each of the contributors has been able to call on the generosity of colleagues, friends, and family members, but the cheerful, patient, and persistently helpful role of the editorial staff at Blackwell should not go unrecorded.

Abbreviations

Standard abbreviations are used for ancient texts and modern collections and journals. The following abbreviations for modern authorities are also used throughout the book:

McCrum and Woodhead 1961	M. McCrum and A. G. Woodhead, *Select Documents of the Principates of the Flavian Emperors, including the Year of Revolution* AD *68–96* (Cambridge, 1961)
Oliver 1989	J. H. Oliver, *Greek Constitutions of Early Roman Emperors from Inscriptions and Papyri* (Philadelphia, 1989)
Sherk 1988	R. K. Sherk, *The Roman Empire: Augustus to Hadrian* (Cambridge, 1988)
Smallwood 1966	Smallwood, E. M., *Documents Illustrating the Reigns of Nerva, Trajan and Hadrian* (Cambridge, 1966)
Smallwood 1967	Smallwood, E. M., *Documents Illustrating the Principates of Gaius, Claudius and Nero* (Cambridge, 1967)
Syme 1958	Syme, R., *Tacitus* (Oxford, 1958)

Timeline

The following list shows the sequence of Roman emperors from Augustus to the Severan dynasty, and (with omissions) through to Justinian. The subjects of individual essays in this volume are shown in bold type.

After the death of the last member of the Severan dynasty in 235 the picture becomes very complicated; hence the full list of emperors after that date is not given.

27 BC–AD 19	**Augustus**
AD 19–37	**Tiberius**
37–41	**Caligula**
41–54	**Claudius**
54–68	**Nero**
68–9	Galba
69	Otho
69	Vitellius
69–79	**Vespasian**
79–81	Titus
81–96	Domitian
96–8	Nerva
98–117	Trajan
117–38	**Hadrian**
138–61	Antoninus Pius
161–80	**Marcus Aurelius**
161–9	Lucius Verus
177–92	Commodus
193	Pertinax
193	Didius Julianus
193–211	**Severus**

211–17	Caracalla
211	Geta (joint emperor)
217–18	Macrinus
218–22	Elagabalus
222–35	Alexander Severus
[. . .]	
284–311/12	**Diocletian**
[. . .]	
306–37	**Constantine**
[. . .]	
527–65	**Justinian**

Family Trees

The Julio-Claudians

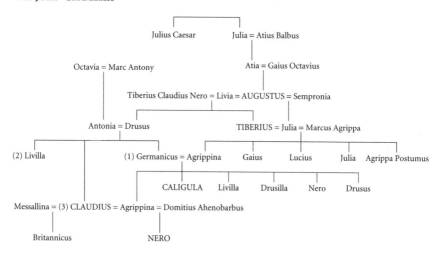

Trajan and Hadrian

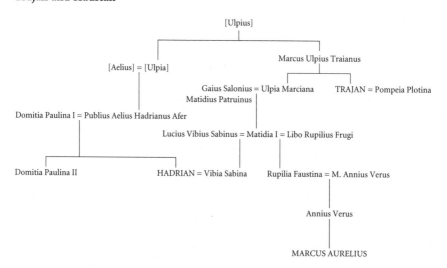

Marcus Aurelius

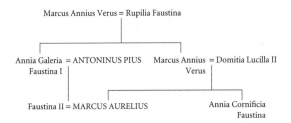

Marcus Annius Verus = Rupilia Faustina

Annia Galeria = ANTONINUS PIUS   Marcus Annius = Domitia Lucilla II
Faustina I   Verus

Faustina II = MARCUS AURELIUS   Annia Cornificia
                                           Faustina

Maps

North Sea

GERMANIA
● Kalkriese
Rhine ● Haltern
Cherusci
Oberaden
Oppidum Ubiorum ●
Ubii ● Waldgirmes
Moguntiacum ●
Marktbreit ●
Marcomanni

Atlantic Ocean

Elbe

Seine

Loire

Mosel

Neckar

Main

Danube

Camunturn ●
RHAETIA NORICUM

GALLIA
COMATA

LUGDUNUM   Arausio ●

Drau

PANNONIA

VENETIA
ET HISTRIA

GALLIA
TRANSPADANA

Save

GALLIA
NARBONENSIS

LIGURIA

1

2 ● ● 3

ILLYRICUM
(DALMATIA)

Astures *Cantabri*

HISPANIA TARRACONENSIS

Duero

Ebro

Massilia ●

Forum
Iulii ●

Rubicon

ETRURIA

4 ●

A
d
r
i
a

UMBRIA

Roma ◉
5 ●

SAMNIUM
CAM

LUSITANIA

Barcino ●

Tarraco ●

CORSICA

6 PANIA
9 ●

● 7
● 8

10 ● 11 ●

Tajo

Emerita ●

BAETICA

SARDINIA

● Gades

Tingis ●

M e d i t e r r a n e a n   S e a

12 ●
13 ●

MAURETANIA

Cirta ●

SICILIA

Gaetuler

AFRICA PROCONSULARIS

1 Mantua
2 Mutina
3 Bononia
4 Perusia
5 Velitrae
6 Circei
7 Beneventum

8 Nola
9 Misenum
10 Tarentum
11 Brundisium
12 Naulochos
13 Mylae

500 km

Garamantes

The Roman empire in the time of Augustus

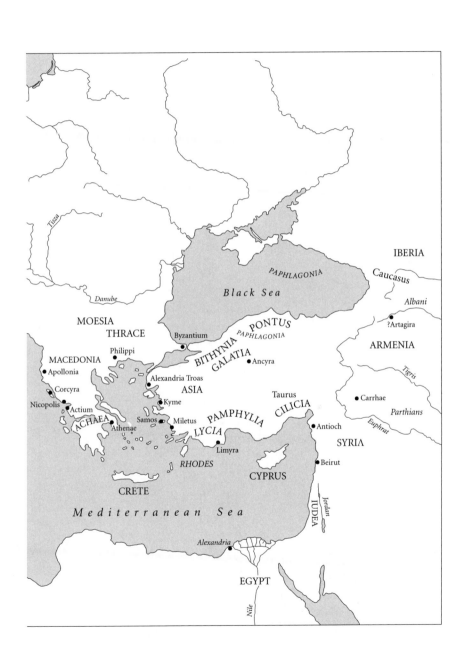

IBERIA

Caucasus

PAPHLAGONIA

Black Sea

Albani

?Artagira

MOESIA
THRACE

Tissa

Danube

Byzantium

PONTUS
PAPHLAGONIA

ARMENIA

Philippi

MACEDONIA

BITHYNIA
GALATIA

Ancyra

Tigris

Apollonia

Corcyra

Alexandria Troas

ASIA

Taurus

Carrhae

Parthians

Nicopolis
Actium

Kyme

CILICIA

Euphrat

ACHAEA

Samos

PAMPHYLIA

Antioch

Athenae

Miletus

LYCIA

SYRIA

Limyra

Beirut

RHODES

CYPRUS

Jordan

CRETE

M e d i t e r r a n e a n   S e a

IUDEA

Alexandria

EGYPT

Nile

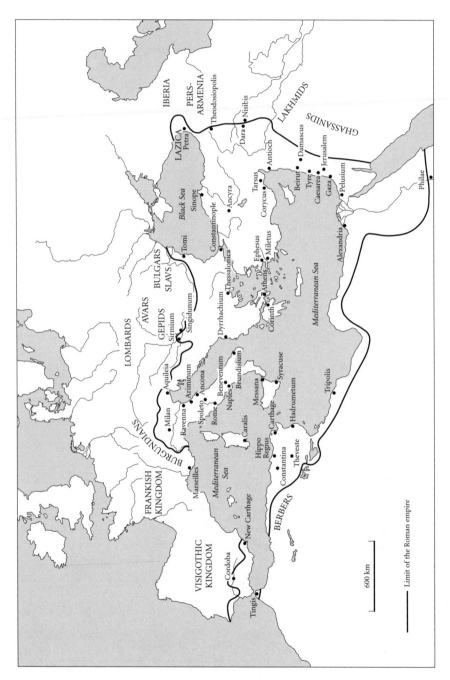

The Empire in the Time of Justinian

IBERIA
PERS-
ARMENIA
Theodosiopolis
Nisibis
Dara
LAKHMIDS
GHASSANIDS
LAZICA
Petra
Damascus
Antioch
Jerusalem
Tarsus
Beirut
Tyre
Caesarea
Corycus
Gaza
Pelusium
Black Sea
Sinope
Ancyra
Constantinople
Alexandria
Tomi
Philae
BULGARS
SLAVS
Ephesus
Miletus
Thessalonica
Athens
Mediterranean Sea
AVARS
Corinth
GEPIDS
Sirmium
Singidunum
Dyrrhachium
LOMBARDS
Aquileia
Ariminum
Ancona
Spoleto
Milan
Ravenna
Rome
Beneventum
Naples
Brundisium
Syracuse
Messana
Tripolis
Hadrumetum
Caralis
Carthage
BURGUNDIANS
Hippo
Regius
Theveste
FRANKISH
KINGDOM
Marseilles
Mediterranean
Sea
Constantina
BERBERS
New Carthage
VISIGOTHIC
KINGDOM
Cordoba
Tingis

600 km

—— Limit of the Roman empire

Introduction

Anthony A. Barrett

Since at least the time of Edward Gibbon the Roman empire has always seemed to represent the quintessential imperial enterprise. Other great empires may rise and fall, but when they do they somehow follow a preordained course that this archetypal model laid down for them. So it is, that when doomsayers predict that our civilization is teetering on the brink of collapse, they more often than not point out that it is the *Romans*, specifically, who teach us that such a fate is inevitable. While we continue to be intrigued by almost every aspect of this remarkable institution, what holds our attention most firmly is undoubtedly the succession of individuals who stood at its centre, the emperors. The last decade or so has seen a surge of books, both popular and academic, on the lives of these individuals, a trend that has flourished in the teeth of considerable opposition from those classical scholars who harbor a deep suspicion about the biographical approach to history. The late Oxford historian Sir Ronald Syme argued that emphasis on individual emperors distorted historical analysis, and that once the system had been put in place it made little difference who was emperor, especially by the second century AD. Fergus Millar, who was later appointed to the same Oxford chair that Syme held, similarly sees the emperor as defined essentially by the institution and does not attach great significance to the personalities of individual emperors. Both viewpoints have considerable merit, but it is possible to make a very strong case that individuals can, under certain circumstances, influence, if not determine, the course of history in a profound way, and that those circumstances existed in imperial Rome. In fact, it is arguable that there are few topics potentially more rewarding to the student of history than the lives of the Roman emperors. They can surely teach us better than most the relationship between humans and power, and the ends, sometimes good but more often malign, to which arbitrary power can be directed.

The title of this collection of essays on the most significant (or, in one or two cases, the most familiar) emperors is undoubtedly reminiscent of Suetonius' *Lives of the Caesars*, written in the second century AD, and the fact that we have similarly included twelve lives might, to some small degree, be seen as an unconscious homage to Suetonius' great classic. It is also fair to say that we aim for a similar, non-specialist readership. But the parallelism goes no further. If we concede that Suetonius was a seeker after the truth, we would want at the same time to point out that he shared with other authors of his age a more flexible concept of the truth than we now consider acceptable in historical writing. The ancient historian would, for instance, without fear of contemporary censure, make up a speech where none existed in the record or blithely ascribe motives based on nothing more than supposition. The twelve essays of this collection are written by individuals who, as a matter of routine, subject the available evidence to rigorous scrutiny, and who are professionally committed to the ideal of objective historical truth, in so far as it is humanly attainable. The authors have all published extensively on their subjects and each can lay claim to considerable expertise in the period on which they write; indeed, it is no exaggeration to say that most of them are the recognized world authorities on their chosen emperors.

Each chapter is self-contained, although for the first eleven we have tried to provide enough linkage to enable them to be read consecutively as a reasonably coherent narrative. The last emperor, Justinian, reigned much later than the others, and in a way stands alone; but his inclusion is clearly justified as a link between the Roman empire and the Byzantine empire that followed, or, one might argue, into which it metamorphosed. While all the essays adhere to broad guidelines, and there is a degree of consistency in some of their mechanical aspects (such as citations and terminology), there has been no attempt to impose a rigid conformity. Hence there is no uniformity of approach. These chapters will introduce readers to the changing dynamics of the Roman empire, and they will also introduce them to the different ways in which modern scholars approach their subjects. As a result, while each chapter reflects the idiosyncrasy of the emperor being studied, it also reflects the individual methodology (as well, perhaps, as a little of the idiosyncrasy) of the scholar writing on him. Thus, while it is hoped that there will be no jarring contradictions, it is felt to be healthy for the reader to be exposed to differing conclusions. A good case in point is the interpretation of the period marking the end of Caligula's reign and the beginning of Claudius', where it will be seen that the confused testimony of the ancients can legitimately be interpreted in more than one way.

Perhaps what distinguishes the Roman empire above all else is the way it combined, within a single institution, both revolution and conservatism. Romans were not innovators; the principle they most zealously upheld was that of *mos maiorum*, "the tradition of our ancestors." So when toward the end of the first century BC the Roman republic collapsed under the weight of ambitious warlords and civil conflicts, it was not replaced by a radical new system. Instead, the republican constitution was refined and modified, in such a way that it remained in form a republic although it was in reality a monarchy. This set the pattern for the following centuries. Remarkably, although by the time of Justinian the system had in many ways been transformed, in others it still preserved the essence of Augustus' great contribution to history at the birth of the empire. It will be useful to provide an outline of that Augustan system, as a background against which the essays might be read.

The main deliberative and legislative body in Rome was the senate, consisting of some 600 former magistrates (in Roman times, the word means simply "officials") of the rank of quaestor or above. Arguably, it was initially not *strictly* legislative, since in a narrow technical sense the senate could not pass legislation during the Augustan period or, it seems, for a century or so after his death. For a senatorial decree (*consultum*) to have the force of a law (*lex*) it had to be ratified by the popular assemblies, although this ratification tended to be little more than a formality. Through a process that is not fully understood, by the second century AD senatorial decrees had acquired the force of law. Membership of the senate was usually permanent, but subject to the approval of the censor. This official maintained the citizen list and had the power to remove senators either on moral grounds or if their financial assets fell below the necessary property qualification. Membership of the body required, as a result of Augustus' reforms, a property qualification of 1,000,000 sestertii. It might be noted that Romans normally expressed monetary amounts in sestertii (abbreviated HS), the highest denomination of the common coins, made of brass (an alloy of copper and zinc) and valued at four to one silver denarius. It is impossible to cite precise monetary equivalence, but we do know that in the Julio-Claudian period the legionary soldiers were paid HS900 (225 denarii) each year, before deductions.

The first significant event in the life of a Roman male occurred usually around the age of fourteen, when he underwent the formal ceremony that marked his entry into manhood. At this point he exchanged his purple-edged toga (*toga praetexta*) for a plain white one, the *toga virilis* or "toga of manhood." If he aspired to a senatorial career (such aspirations were not harbored by young Roman women, since, with the exception of certain priestly

positions, public offices were not open to them), he might hope to enter the
quaestorship when he had reached at least his twenty-fifth year. Twenty
quaestors were elected annually; they were concerned with a variety of duties,
financial and other, and, by virtue of holding the office, granted entry into
the senate. The quaestorship might be followed by one of two offices. The
position of aedile brought responsibility for certain aspects of municipal
administration in Rome. The alternative, that of the tribune of the plebeians,
had originally been meant for the protection of the interests of the plebeians,
and in Augustus' time the office was still reserved for plebeians; but the old
principle by which each Roman belonged to either the lower-class plebeians
or the upper-class patricians was by now largely a relic with few practical
implications, and the tribune was primarily concerned with minor legislative
matters. The quaestor could, however, bypass the tribunate or aedileship,
and pass straight to the next office in the hierarchy, the first major one: the
praetorship. Under Augustus, twelve praetors were elected annually. They
had responsibility for the administration of justice, and could afterwards
compete for one of the two consulships, the most prestigious and much
sought-after senior offices in the state. Strictly speaking, consular rank could
be attained only after the candidate had reached the age of forty-two, but
family background could enable an individual to seek the office much sooner,
possibly by thirty-two, while members of the imperial family were able to
achieve it even earlier. From 5 BC it became common for consuls to resign
during the course of the year. Their replacements were called 'suffect' consuls
(*suffecti*). There was a certain cachet to being appointed one of the first pair
of the year, in part no doubt because the year was officially identified by their
names. The consul first appointed was known as *ordinarius*, the Latin term
usually still employed in preference to the misleading "ordinary."

The magistrate's sphere of action was known as his *provincia*. By the
Augustan period this term tended to be applied to Rome's external possessions.
The victory over the Carthaginians in the late third century BC had led to the
control of much of Spain, beginning a process by which more and more
territories fell to Rome. These acquisitions came about usually through warfare,
but they could be voluntary, as in the case of the province of Asia, organized
from a kingdom bequeathed to Rome by Attalus III of Pergamum on his
death in 133 BC. During the republican period, praetors and consuls governed
these provinces after their regular terms of office had expired. They consequently exercised their power, their *imperium*, in the capacity of the offices
previously held, as *propraetors* or *proconsuls*. In 27 BC, Augustus handed the
territories he controlled over to the senate and people. They for their part
granted him an enormous "province" (its precise extent varied over time),

made up basically of provinces in Gaul, Syria, and Spain, for a term of ten years, with the option of renewal. In these "imperial" provinces, by and large where the Roman legions were stationed, the governors (*legati Augusti*) and the legionary commanders (*legati legionis*) were appointed by the emperor, so that in effect he was commander of the Roman armies. As a consequence, the culminating achievement of a military campaign, the splendid parade or "triumph" that followed a major victory in the field, was the prerogative of the emperor and his family. Less well-connected commanders had to remain content with triumphal *insignia*. The remaining "public" provinces (sometimes misleadingly referred to in modern sources as "senatorial") were governed by senators appointed by lot (competence was maintained in the "lot" system by a strict process of regulating who would be eligible to put his name into the hat). The most desirable of these public provinces were Africa and Asia. Generally this class of province did not house legionary troops; Africa, with one legion, was the most notable exception to this principle (and only until the time of Caligula). The Augustan provincial arrangements remained virtually unchanged until the very end of the third century AD, when Diocletian broke up the provinces into smaller units and organized them into twelve "dioceses," each headed by a deputy (*vicarius*). The terminology of this arrangement has survived in ecclesiastical language.

Egypt became a Roman possession under Augustus. Like some of the smaller districts, it was governed by an imperial appointee from the equestrian order, the "knights": broadly, a social rank with a lower property qualification (HS400,000), whose members engaged openly in commercial business. A man could not be knight and senator simultaneously (different sets of offices were open to them), although he could be transferred from one order to another, to match the upward, or downward, change in his fortunes. The governor of Egypt held the rank of prefect, and most of the other prefectures were the prerogative of the equestrian class, the most significant being those of the *annona* (corn supply), of the *vigiles* (fire and police service), and, most importantly, of the imperial or praetorian guard, the elite cadre of troops stationed in the city itself, and initially elsewhere in Italy, enjoying special pay and privileges. There was a small number of senatorial prefectures, the most noteworthy being the ancient office of prefect of the city (*praefectus urbi*), largely ritual by the late republic but given real functions by Augustus and charged with maintaining order in Rome. It had originally been held by a senator of consular rank and continued to be so. This city prefect held powers of summary justice in dealing with minor criminal cases and through time assumed responsibility for more serious cases. In the later empire he became an individual of considerable importance.

Augustus acquired two of the constitutional rights of the plebeian tribunes, without holding the actual office (one of the fictions that allowed the republic to function as a monarchy). They were in turn inherited by his successors. Tribunician *sacrosanctitas* made an assault on his person sacrilegious, while his tribunician *potestas* gave him a number of rights, including those of convening the senate and the popular assemblies, and of initiating or vetoing legislation. This special authority was a potent symbol of the principate – indeed, in many ways it lay at its heart. Emperors dated their reigns from the point when their *tribunicia potestas* was assumed. In the later period covered by this collection the emperor Diocletian introduced a government innovation that was in many ways radical, but in a very Roman way continued the institutions that had been laid down since Augustus. To deal with the complexities of empire, he instituted the principle of two *Augusti*, each taking a share of the responsibilities. Each *Augustus* was to be assisted by a successor in waiting, a *Caesar*. This fourfold arrangement is known generally by the Greek term tetrarchy (not used in antiquity). The reform marked an important stage in the ultimate evolution of the empire into a western and an eastern division, the latter with its capital in Byzantium/Constantinople. By virtue of the shared origin of the Roman and Byzantine empires the institution created by Augustus in 27 BC endured in a very real sense for almost fifteen centuries, until 1453, when the last Byzantine emperor was defeated by the Ottoman Turks.

I

Augustus

Werner Eck

On March 15, 44 BC, a cataclysmic event stunned the people of Rome. In the senate chamber inside the Theater of Pompey, Gaius Julius Caesar lay in a pool of his own blood. He had been assassinated. During the previous disastrous civil wars he had been opposed by his arch-rival Pompey and by most of the senators, but he had prevailed, and gone on to establish autocratic rule. The precise nature of this rule had not yet been clearly defined, but he had made it clear that he had no intention of relinquishing control of Rome or of allowing supreme authority to slip out of his hands. After all, what else could the title *dictator perpetuo*, "dictator for life," as proclaimed on his coins, mean? The frustration of many of his enemies, among them highly respected men like the two senators Brutus and Cassius, was understandable. They saw no real place for themselves in this political scheme. This is why the conspiracy to assassinate him was able to succeed.

For a brief moment the conspirators seemed to have achieved their aim: freedom for Rome, which of course meant freedom for the ruling senatorial aristocracy. Soon, however, it became evident how little they had in fact achieved. They had attributed the crisis of the republic to a single man. They had not recognized that the crisis went much deeper and that there were many others striving for the same goals as Caesar. Confronted by popular anger and the astuteness of Marc Antony, who as consul represented legal authority, the conspirators were obliged to retreat from the city. There were many reasons why Antony, a long-time follower of Caesar, now had the best chance in the looming battle to succeed him.

Emergence of Octavian

From the town of Velitrae, however, a nineteen-year-old, born during the consulship of Cicero on September 23, 63 BC, entered the Roman political arena – an arena he would not quit until his death on August 19, AD 14, almost fifty-seven years later. In April 44 he had just returned to Rome from the province of Macedonia, beyond the Adriatic, where he had spent time with Caesar's troops as they prepared to go to war against the Parthians. Until then he had borne the name of his senatorial father Gaius Octavius; but shortly after his return from Macedonia he began to use the name Gaius Julius Caesar. His great-uncle Julius Caesar had adopted him in his will as his nearest male relative, the grandson of his sister Julia, and had bequeathed to him a three-quarter share of his estate. Normally an adoption was a private legal transaction, but not when it was made by a man like Julius Caesar. The decision meant that the young Caesar would also be his great-uncle's political heir. Perceptive observers would have recognized that the course to monarchy on which Julius Caesar had earlier embarked would be pursued. Indeed, they would have recognized that Octavian, as we call him after his adoption, although he himself never used the name, could do no other than pursue it. A short while later he made this intention very clear in a public speech in Rome (Cic. *ad Att.* 16, 15, 3).

Even before Octavian arrived in Rome, he had left no room for doubt that he was a force to be reckoned with. Without authorization from the senate or the people, he attempted to raise an army on his own initiative. In the *Res Gestae*, the summation of his reign he wrote in AD 14, he stated this clearly: "At nineteen years of age, by my own decision and at my own expense, I raised an army, with which I freed the republic oppressed by the tyranny of a faction" (*Res Gestae* 1). It is no accident that the *Res Gestae* begin with this sentence. His association with the army was the basis not only for his initial rise to power; he also depended on it on later occasions, as did all of his successors.

All the same, in the year 44 the young Octavian was only one of the actors on the political and military stage. At first he was also one of the weakest, because his name was a reminder that he was not Caesar's blood relative, but only his adopted son. Yet he soon managed, through tactical finesse and unabashed switches of loyalty, to strengthen his position. At first the consul Antony seemed to be his main adversary. So Octavian associated himself with all those senators opposed to that man's growing power. Their leader was Cicero, who saw the opportunity to play the decisive role of his life at the republic's helm (*rector rei publicae*). Cicero actually believed he could use Octavian to further his own ambitions against Antony. But Octavian outdid Cicero both in tactics and in ruthless determination. He had the senate assign to himself an official position that enabled him legally to raise an army and to take part in the senate and public assemblies. Together with the consuls of 43, Hirtius and Pansa, long-standing supporters of Caesar, Octavian embarked on a campaign against Antony, who was using his army to build a power-base in northern Italy. In the resulting conflict, at Mutina, in April 43 BC, Antony's army was defeated by Octavian and the consuls. The two consuls fell in the battle and, without troubling to offer a justification, Octavian took over their legions. The senate and its leader Cicero had thus lost their own military prop. Octavian grasped the initiative. A contingent of his centurions appeared in Rome and promoted his case for the consulship, the highest legal office obtainable. When the senate rejected him, Octavian returned, this time with the legions. Neither the senate nor the people (to the extent that they participated in the elections) could hold out against the might of his armies. On August 19, 43 BC, Octavian, not yet twenty years old, was elected consul for the first time. Never before had someone so young attained this position. Decades later, when he set about nominating his own successors, the similar conferment of an early consulship was a clear signal of his dynastic intentions, as will later be demonstrated by the premature advancement of his adopted sons Gaius and Lucius, and of his nephew Marcellus.

The first consulship proved to be only a short episode for the new young Caesar. Antony had recovered from his defeat and, with the support of the governors of the Gallic and Spanish provinces, had established himself in northern Italy. Among the notable allies of Antony were Aemilius Lepidus and Munatius Plancus, men who, like him, had had close ties to the late Caesar (they would both play an important role also in Octavian's future career). Octavian could not have held his ground against such a united military force. But he was not to be put to the test, since there was an incentive for both camps to come to an agreement, if they wanted to keep the upper hand in both the political and the military spheres. Caesar's murderers had to be defeated. They had established a stronghold in the eastern provinces, from where they threatened the Caesarians, Antony as well as Octavian. Many in the senate, especially Cicero, placed their hopes in Brutus and Cassius and their armies. It was with good purpose that these put on their coins the date of Caesar's assassination: Eid(us) Mart(iae) = 'the ides of March' (15 March), thus identifying themselves as the collective enemy of the Caesarians.

Triumvirate

Antony, Lepidus, and Octavian met on an island in the Reno river, not far from Bologna. Deeply mistrustful of one another, they negotiated for three days before reaching an agreement. Their first and most important goal was to secure their own positions of power. They agreed to a triple rule, a triumvirate. Since Antony had officially abrogated the position of dictator, which would have been inappropriate in a triumvirate in any case, they chose the title of *triumviri rei publicae constituendae* ("board of three men entrusted with the organization of the state"). It seemed a harmless designation at first glance. Yet, just forty years earlier, Sulla had used the same expression, only in his case the first word had been "dictator." This should have been a grim warning. No one had forgotten the horror of that time. Indeed, the new allies decided, just as Sulla had, to rid themselves of their enemies by proscriptions. By this means approximately 300 senators and 2,000 equestrians were identified as opponents of the regime and proscribed – effectively, sentenced to death. Whoever killed one of them received a portion of the victim's property as compensation; the remainder was collected for the state treasury, that is, for the use of the triumvirs. Octavian apparently argued against including among the intended victims Cicero, a man who had so decisively aided the young man's rise while so seriously underestimating his abilities. But Antony had a deep hatred for Rome's greatest orator. After Caesar's death Cicero seemed to have snatched away from Antony an almost guaranteed succession, and Antony insisted on including him on the list. In the end, Octavian acceded to his murder. Nor did he show mercy toward others. All these proceedings were perfectly legal. The position of the triumvirs, and the absolute power that resulted from it, was confirmed for a period of five years through a law carried in the popular assembly on November 27, 43 BC. Theirs was a legalized, albeit arbitrary, power.

The triumvirs divided among themselves the task of regaining enemy-held territories. Initially Antony seemed to be the strongest member of the coalition. He accordingly received as his province northern Italy and the part of Gaul annexed by Caesar, along with all its resources. Lepidus received the provinces of Gallia Narbonensis and Spain. Octavian was given the two islands of Sardinia and Sicily, as well as Africa. All these areas were under the direct or indirect control of anti-Caesarians, who had powerful fleets at their disposal.

Before a new state order could be initiated, the power of Caesar's murderers had to be broken. Octavian enacted a law to have them declared enemies of the Roman people. But legal measures were insufficient. The problem had to be finally settled by weapons. In October and November 42 BC, at Philippi in northern Greece, the republican armies, under the leadership of Brutus and Cassius, were defeated in two bloody massacres, in which both leaders died. There was no one left to mount an effective defense of the old republic. This should have opened the way to a new political order. But none of the three allies was aiming for that goal: what mattered more to them was which one would prevail in the subsequent power struggle. Neither Antony nor Octavian considered sharing power. Again, Antony was set to build up the strongest position. His mandate was to secure the east, where he was to find the means to pay for the huge armies – almost forty legions had fought at Philippi. The soldiers saw their service for the triumvirate in terms of hard cash, and many army veterans wanted to retire and settle down. The triumvirs deemed meeting these wishes a top priority, and since the soldiers were all Roman citizens with homes mainly in Italy, this inevitably meant settling them in Italy. Octavian was given this task. No matter how he carried it out, he would make enemies. There was no more free land available in Italy for settlement, so the only way to acquire it was to seize it, by whatever means necessary. The people of eighteen cities were driven from their homes and their property was handed over to the veterans. Octavian later boasted that to settle former soldiers in Italy and the provinces he paid for the land from his own funds, but in fact no such payments were made after Philippi.

The hatred felt for Octavian by the displaced populace knew no bounds. Lucius Antonius, Marc Antony's brother and one of the consuls of 41, gathered the dispossessed and attempted to eliminate him. It is difficult to imagine that Lucius did this without his brother's permission. From the outset the unity between the two key members of the triumvirate, Octavian and Antony, was very fragile; Lepidus no longer counted at all. As it turned out, Antony's strategy failed, and it was Octavian who prevailed. Perusia (modern Perugia), where his opponents had sought refuge, was forced to surrender. Lucius' life was spared, but countless other opponents were sacrificed at an altar dedicated to Caesar. Octavian never fully lost his reputation as the butcher of Perugia. Even today the theme of Perusine savagery continues to resonate in the poetry of Propertius (1. 22). That said, in the long term the thankless task of providing settlements in Italy for the veterans paid off for Octavian. In contrast to the fury of the dispossessed, the soldiers considered Octavian their bene-factor, and gave him their loyalty, since from now on he alone could guarantee their hard-won gains. Many thought of him in the same terms as had the young Virgil, a native of Mantua, who at first was dispossessed, but later had his family property restored. "He will always be a god for me," declares a shepherd in one of Virgil's *Eclogues*, in praise of Octavian (Verg., *Ecl.* 1. 45).

And it was from Italy that, ten years later, Octavian drew his main support in his final battle against Antony.

But for the moment Octavian's position was still very precarious. He had from the outset considered his first task to be to establish a firm territorial stronghold. After the death of Antony's appointee for governor of Gaul, Octavian had taken over this province without consulting the other two members of the triumvirate. Antony could not accept this, and was even tempted to form an alliance between himself and Sextus Pompeius, son of Caesar's great foe, Pompey. With his fleet, Sextus Pompeius was still virtually unchallenged in the western Mediterranean. The Italians suffered from his attacks and from the precarious state of their supply lines, since his ships often interrupted the shipments of grain. A long-term alliance between Antony and Sextus would have proved exceptionally dangerous for Octavian. After Antony's landing at Brundisium in lower Italy, his legions, committed Caesarians, were loath to fight against Octavian's troops. Moreover, an alliance with the "republican" Sextus Pompeius was abhorrent to them. So through their troops, especially the powerful centurions, Antony and Octavian were forced to conclude the pact of Brundisium, by which the Roman world was divided more or less in two: the east fell to Antony, the west mainly to Octavian. Lepidus would have to content himself with Africa. Italy would remain open to all three, especially for the purpose of recruiting legionaries. A public display of harmony between the two rivals was created by a "dynastic" union: Octavia, younger sister of Octavian, was wed to Antony.

However, even family ties did not guarantee a lasting harmony of interests, given that the conflict with Sextus Pompeius continued. Pressed by the ever-menacing cooperation between Antony and Sextus Pompeius and public disquiet over Sextus' unfettered activities, Octavian was finally obliged to come to terms with the ruler of the seas, whose position was at last officially recognized. The most notable consequence was that those members of the senatorial aristocracy who had fled to Pompeius when threatened with elimination by the triumvirate were now permitted to return to Italy. One of them was Tiberius Claudius Nero, a man of old patrician stock. His wife Livia Drusilla, also of the old nobility, was pregnant with their second child. A little earlier Octavian had separated from his wife Scribonia, who had borne him a single daughter, Julia. Now Livia entered his life. The mutual attraction was so strong that the newly pregnant Livia left her husband and, even before the birth of her child, married Octavian. She bore her second son, Drusus, in his house. The priests had given exceptional permission for this marriage. Livia also brought her first son, Tiberius, into Octavian's home. Both stepsons would play a key role in his plans after he achieved sole rule.

Octavian never lost sight of this goal. Sextus Pompeius was operating on Italy's doorstep. If Octavian were to stabilize his power in Italy and in the western empire, this troublesome rival would have to be dealt with. This could be achieved only by a strong fleet of his own. Marcus Vipsanius Agrippa, Octavian's closest ally since 44 BC, provided the fleet and, after some initial setbacks, succeeded in decisively defeating their dangerous adversary off the Sicilian town of Naulochos. Sextus was forced to retreat to the east, where he met a sordid end. To prevent this war from looking like a civil conflict, Octavian later defined it as a "slave war" (*Res Gestae* 25). He returned 30,000 slaves who had fled to Pompeius and fought at his side to their original masters to be punished; 6,000 slaves whose masters could not be located were crucified along the Appian Way. Everyone could see that the merciless triumvir upheld the traditional rights of the property owners. Human suffering of slaves meant nothing to Octavian, or to most of the population.

In the turbulent aftermath of these events Lepidus, the weakest member of the triumvirate, tried to reassert his position. His attempt led to his total eclipse. He lost his army and his provinces in Africa, retaining only the position of chief pontiff. Even this one remaining office was seen as a concession, since Octavian later claimed that Lepidus had usurped the post after Caesar's death. But priests were appointed for life, and Octavian's gesture was further proof of his respect for republican tradition, something he increasingly emphasized in his program as long as it did not conflict with his broader plan. That plan was to hold sole power in the Roman world. The only obstacle now was Antony.

Conflict with Marc Antony

Antony's sphere was the provinces of the eastern Mediterranean, most notably Egypt. Despite his marriage to Octavian's sister Octavia, he began an intense love affair with Cleopatra, Queen of Egypt, following their very first meeting in 41 BC. Their passion would serve the political goals of both. Cleopatra sought to extend her sphere of power for herself and for her children by both Caesar and Antony. For his part, Antony needed to bolster his leadership within the Roman world. He could best achieve this if he defeated the Parthians, the great power beyond the Euphrates. Caesar had already wanted to punish them for the destruction of the Roman army at Carrhae in 53 BC. The prestige Antony might gain would make up for his repeated political misjudgments. During the early years of the Roman civil war the Parthians had overrun most of the eastern provinces, thus making clear the danger they posed for Roman dominance. Antony needed soldiers for the campaign, and could find them only in Italy. He had made significant concessions to Octavian, and had even placed 120 ships at his disposal for his final action against Sextus Pompeius. Octavian was supposed to reciprocate, with 20,000 legionnaires, as part of the deal; but he delivered only a small fraction of what had been promised, sending only 2,000 men to the east. Antony must have seen this as a profound insult. But this does not in itself explain the failure of his Parthian campaigns. The initial announcements of victory from the east proved to be little more than empty words, and handed Octavian the opportunity to undermine Antony's reputation as a great commander. More seriously, Antony had transferred to Cleopatra and her children portions of Roman provinces. Word of this spread, and was represented as a sell-out of Roman interests in the east. The charge made a powerful impact on Italy, in particular on many of the senators. This was all the more significant because a number of them had up to now felt that the distant Antony could be better trusted than Octavian to restore the republic, or at any rate to exercise a less ruthless leadership. Octavian was there, in person, and people inevitably experienced his ruthless political maneuverings at first hand, despite his efforts to present himself as a respecter of tradition and bringer of freedom. After the victory over Sextus Pompeius, Octavian even officially declared the end of the civil wars. Not everyone believed him. Antony's blunders accordingly helped Octavian to distinguish himself from his opponent, as the defender of Roman and Italian interests. All he needed was the excuse to take on Antony in open combat. But whoever took that first step would brand himself as destroyer of peace.

At the end of 34 BC Antony presented his plans for the eastern provinces in a public ceremony in Egypt. Cleopatra's children would receive various territories as personal domains, including some that had been subject to Rome for a considerable time; Cleopatra would be elevated to the rank of 'queen of queens', *regina regum*, all thanks to Antony, a Roman. This would have been seen by Romans as an attack on Rome. What must have appeared the most dangerous development of all in the struggle between the Caesarian loyalists was the fact that Antony had officially recognized Caesarion, Caesar's son by Cleopatra, and had given him a place in the new order. As a result, a natural son of the deified Caesar stood in opposition to Octavian, who was only his adopted son, even if Octavian did refer to himself as *divi filius*, "son of deified Caesar." Octavian responded to what he saw as Antony's provocations with bitter attacks in the senate. Above all, it was now clear that Antony must not set foot in Italy. Octavian would not even allow him to raise recruits. This meant, in effect, that Antony was henceforth banned from

Rome. That city, and Italy, now "belonged" exclusively to Octavian. In political if not strictly legal terms, this was a declaration of war against Antony. Sure enough, Antony then took a concrete step toward war, just as Octavian had hoped he would. Even though Antony was eyeing a new military venture in Armenia and Parthia in 33 BC, he interrupted this campaign in response to the changing general situation in Italy. He now prepared his armies and fleets for an attack on Octavian and the west.

At the beginning of 32 BC the conflict was still limited to verbal jousts in the senate. The two new consuls for that year, Gaius Sosius and Domitius Ahenobarbus, attacked Octavian in the chamber. An important issue was the question of whether the authority of the triumvirs, which had been renewed for a further five years in 37 BC, still provided a legal basis for the roles played by the two rivals. Doubts raised on this point in the senate posed a threat to Octavian, who was present, but not to the absent Antony. The imminence of this threat made Octavian respond all the more energetically. In the next session he assumed the offensive, protected by armed followers, and made it clear that he no longer thought the matter needed to be debated. He announced that at the next meeting he would present explicit charges against Antony and against Sosius. Rather than wait, Sosius and Domitius left the city and fled to Antony. More than 300 senators joined them. The issue would be now settled by weapons alone.

Antony drew closer to Italy. Athens became his military and political base, and it was there that the fugitive senators assembled. Cleopatra was also in Athens, and stood conspicuously at Antony's side when both political and military questions were addressed in public. Many of his Roman followers found this unacceptable, partly because of their deeply felt sense that women should stay out of such matters, but more importantly because they felt that such ostentatious appearances of Antony alongside the Egyptian queen could only undermine his role, as well as their own position, in Italy, in a society that saw such behavior as a mark of social disintegration. And of course Octavian let it be known to the Romans that a queen from the east aspired to reign on the Capitol. When Antony failed to respond to the urgent concerns of his followers, many of the senators abandoned him. Two of them, Munatius Plancus and his nephew Marcus Titius, returned to Rome and crowned their shift of allegiance with a choice gift for Octavian. They had been witnesses to the sealing of Antony's will and knew its explosive details. Also, they knew where it was kept: in the Temple of Vesta, in Rome. Although unauthorized access to a will was considered a sacrilege in Rome, as was simply entering the sacred domain of the Vestal Virgins, Octavian could not let this opportunity slip away. He forced the chief Vestal to deliver the will to him and he read aloud in the senate those parts of it that served his purpose. Among other things, Antony had confirmed the award of eastern territories to Cleopatra's children. But most strikingly he solemnly avowed that in the event of his death he should be buried beside Cleopatra in Alexandria. He, a Roman, wanted his final resting place to be in the decadent capital of the east. Any Roman who wanted that could surely not be master of his own decisions. When Antony sent Octavia, who was still officially his wife, her divorce letter, this was the final proof that he had been bewitched by the sorceress of Egypt. Who could now still dare to support him? Thus, without any opposition in the senate, Antony's consulship for the following year was withdrawn, along with all his other public functions. Politically, he had been annihilated. By contrast, Octavian openly began the construction of his own enormous mausoleum on the Campus Martius, emphasizing beyond any possible doubt that Rome was the center of not only his political, but also his personal, world.

The threat looming over Italy was now officially blamed on Cleopatra. No one could hesitate to take up arms against her. For this reason, when war was declared it was against her, a foreign queen, not against Roman citizens. The *civil* wars had ended long ago, according to Octavian's propaganda. All Italy took an oath to Octavian as *dux*, leader in the fight against the threat from the east, as he later described it (*Res Gestae* 25). The western provinces similarly gave him their allegiance. Now Octavian reaped the rewards, especially in Italy, of his investment over the recent years. Through their oath the veterans ensured him the political backing of the Italian cities, as well as military support. In return he had to ensure that Italy would not once again suffer in the civil war, which, despite the pretence to the contrary, is what was really being fought.

In late 32 BC Antony and Cleopatra stationed a portion of their troops along the west coast of Greece and Epirus, while the main contingent ended up at Actium. In terms of nominal battle capability, their forces must have seemed superior to Octavian's. This would certainly have been the impression they created at sea, because of their enormous fleet. Thus there was a danger that an attack from the Adriatic might succeed. But this was balanced by the fact that Agrippa was by far the better strategist. Octavian succeeded in transporting his land forces from Italy without heavy casualties. At Actium, quarters were established opposite the main enemy force. In a series of sea battles, ranks of enemy flotillas were defeated, outmatched by the smaller, more mobile, ships under Agrippa's inspired tactical leadership. As a consequence, reinforcements from Egypt were cut off. On land, Antony was unable to draw Octavian into a decisive battle. The enforced idleness weakened

Antony's troops especially, since they could not be resupplied. With increasing frequency whole units deserted. In the end this meant that a major encounter on land was not an option for him, since Octavian had gained the upper hand. The battle at sea finally came to a conclusive outcome on September 2, 31 BC. Whether this was through deliberate planning or because Antony tried to flee the trap he had fallen into is an open question. In any event, for Antony the result was military disaster; Cleopatra fled and Antony along with her. After negotiations, the leaderless land forces surrendered. Octavian attributed his victory at Actium to Apollo, from now on one of the great divine protectors of the new leader. He had a magnificent temple built to the god, closely linked to his own house on the Palatine hill.

What followed Actium was little more than the closing act of the internal Roman conflict. The eastern provinces surrendered without resistance. The client kings also came over to Octavian, among them Herod of Judea, who thus not only saved his kingdom, but even managed to expand it. Octavian used the system of client rulers extensively. In many regions it was they who maintained the security of the frontiers. In the summer of 30 BC Octavian finally stood at the threshold of Egypt, where Antony had followed Cleopatra. Defeated at Actium, in his desperation Antony hoped for a final military victory before the walls of Alexandria. But most of his supporters had abandoned him, and his only escape was suicide. He died in Cleopatra's arms. She had indeed become the center of his life.

The queen may well have hoped to come to some arrangement with the victor, just as she had earlier with Caesar and Antony. But Octavian was not interested. He just wanted to preserve her as choice booty for his triumphal procession in Rome. She evaded this final humiliation with a snakebite. Thus she escaped Octavian, though Egypt and the treasures of the Ptolemaic royal household did fall to the victor. Together these spoils enabled him to provide Romans with the tangible signs of victory. Egypt was to be subject to the authority of the Roman people, as Octavian himself wrote in the *Res Gestae* (27): the land of the Nile now became a Roman province. This arrangement would survive until the seventh century AD.

Octavian was thus the sole victor, and supreme power was now his, with no serious contender on the horizon. Immediately after the fall of Alexandria, he put to death Caesarion, Cleopatra's son by Caesar. There was to be absolutely no doubting his claim to be Caesar's political heir. Again, he was confronted with the question of how to define his own role in the future Roman state. This time he had to come up with an answer. One thing was certain: never again would he relinquish his hold on the political leadership. But the precise form this leadership should take would still need to be worked out.

The Augustan Settlement

For three consecutive days in August, 29 BC, Octavian paraded his victories over Illyricum, over Cleopatra at Actium, and over Egypt, before the Roman people; never before had there been such a powerful display of military conquest. Even before the triple triumph he had begun to direct the political debate toward his own future role in the *res publica*. This process reached a provisional conclusion in January, 27 BC, formally confirmed by two carefully staged spectacular sessions of the senate, on January 13 and 16. The new form of government did not emerge through a single event, despite the common perception created by the one remaining historical narrative of this period by Cassius Dio, written early in the third century (Dio 53. 2–12). Octavian himself states in his record that, in his sixth and seventh consulships, that is, in the years 28 and 27 BC, he returned the state, the *res publica*, to the people and the senate, even though by general consensus he had been declared "in control of the entire state" (*potens rerum omnium*: *Res Gestae* 34).[1] Exactly how the details of this process were worked out we do not know. There is also uncertainty about the exact proposals and who the main players were. There is no dispute that within Octavian's circle various models of government were discussed. Later Dio summarized these discussions in two speeches supposedly delivered to Octavian: by Agrippa, in support of a return to the republic, and by his close friend and advisor Maecenas, in support of an overtly monarchic form of rule (Dio 52, 1–40). The debates are fictitious; but no doubt thinking at the time must have wavered between these two extremes. The extremes themselves, a free republic or a direct monarchy, were both ruled out from the outset.

Throughout, Octavian adopted the fundamental premise that he would never again relinquish control of the body politic. But it was just as evident that an open monarchy, such as Caesar had begun to form, was impossible, since there would be no proper role in such a scheme for those who had hitherto wielded political power, the senators. Even now, after nearly twenty years of civil war, they would hardly be willing to be set aside completely. At the very least the appearance that they would have their appropriate share of power was a necessity. The senate (along with the people) constituted the *res publica*. It was essential for Octavian to acknowledge this without at the same time compromising his own position. The power that he sought to exercise would have to be handed over to him voluntarily by the senate and the people in a form that would be fundamentally unassailable in future. Octavian had therefore to succeed in establishing in the eyes of the public, or at least of the senate, a degree of confidence that this restoration of power and authority was not merely symbolic. In any case he had already made known on a coin of 28 BC that he had returned *iura et leges* ("law and statutes") to the Romans. The official institutions of the state, the courts and public meetings, would resume their traditional form, one almost forgotten during the period of civil war.

On January 13 and 16, 27 BC, the final act of the restoration of the state was played out in the senate. Perhaps Octavian had actually announced to the senators that he wanted to retire from all public duties. If so, it was of course never really his intention. Rather, he had a deliberate purpose in mind: to be urged openly to assume responsibility for the *res publica*, so that no one could accuse him of having seized power illegally. Most likely, at least some of the senators were made privy to the plan. The result was as expected. The senate urgently pressed Octavian to remain at the disposal of the state, and he finally acquiesced. It was not even necessary to transfer any new legal authority, since he was consul, together with his trusted friend Agrippa. Thus, in exact accordance with the principles of the republic, he already held the highest magisterial authority, *imperium*. It remained only to define what this position would encompass.

Octavian's solution was brilliant. Alongside the duties of consul, based on his consular *imperium*, the senate transferred to him certain provinces of the empire to govern: both Spanish provinces, all of Gaul, Syria, Cilicia, Cyprus, and Egypt. With the provinces came control of the legions stationed in most of them. Thus the bulk of the army was under his command. Formally this corresponded to republican procedures, as long as the mandate had a specific time limit, which was until such time as the provinces could be deemed peaceful, in any case not longer than ten years. Temporary power could not be officially construed as monarchical power. To the end of his life Augustus observed this time limit, even if eventually its extension was barely a formality. Symbolically the limit was enormously significant. He could later maintain that he never had at his disposal more power than did his colleagues in office. Only in authority and influence, *auctoritas*, did he supersede everyone (*Res Gestae* 34). This was a huge oversimplification of the true terms by which he exercised power.

The official act of returning power to the senate and Roman people could be celebrated in the senate as the restoration of the *res publica*. The man who had allowed this to come about freely was rewarded for his service by expressions of universal gratitude. Special and distinctive honors had to be devised. The approach to his house on the Palatine hill was decorated with laurel; over the entrance they affixed the *corona civica*, the civic crown, granted to a man who had rescued Roman citizens from mortal danger. Coins of this period appeared bearing this wreath and the words: *ob cives servatos* "for rescuing the citizens." Some remembered the citizens for whom Octavian had meant not rescue, but ruin. But no one spoke openly about them. How could anyone have dared to speak up against someone honored for so many services? These were so great that only a new name could express them. At the suggestion of Munatius Plancus the senate voted to give this man at the center of the state the name Augustus, elevating him to the sphere of the gods. From this time on his full name became Imperator Caesar divi filius Augustus. It was unique. Early on Octavian had dropped his adopted name Gaius Julius Caesar and had called himself Imperator Caesar. The first name, Imperator, expressed, at least as an ideal, the power of the military commander; out of the name Caesar he created a new family name, one that belonged to no one else. Thus the new dynasty of the Caesars had been born. Also, his claim to a deified father, *divi filius*, elevated him above all mortals. And now these names were joined by the extraordinary *cognomen* Augustus, which in itself sufficed to show how exceptional was its bearer. His qualities were publicly proclaimed on a golden shield in the chamber of the senate, the Curia: his military vigor (*virtus*), his clemency (*clementia*), his integrity (*iustitia*), and his sense of duty to gods and men (*pietas*).

This novel form of government had to prove itself. Because so many provinces had been officially handed over to Augustus to maintain peace, they clearly demanded his early attention. Soon after the new system was in place he left Rome and headed first to Gaul, then to Spain, where the north of the country still resisted Roman domination. He could have exercised direct personal command there. But Spain was not the only region transferred to him. Others had been too. Each of them required someone to represent in person the man who had legally been given the authority to exercise governing power. To this end Augustus appointed *legati* ("legates") as his representatives. These were men of the senatorial order and thus able to participate directly in the government of the empire, no longer mandated by the senate and people, of course, but answering to Augustus. Logically, therefore, each one held the title *legatus Augusti*, legate of this one specific man, Augustus. So that they might not seem to be ranked as equal to Augustus, who was consul, that title was further qualified as *pro praetore*, which meant that they held the rank of praetor; in the republic, the governing power of a consul, in the case of disagreement, was superior to that of a praetor. In the last years of Augustus' life, only a minority of governors were not his representatives, but remained legally independent governors: just ten, in fact, a number that had shrunk since 27 BC. But even the disproportionately small number of governors not directly depending on Augustus does not tell the whole story of his actual power. These governors, officially independent of him, held office with the title *proconsul*, intended ideally for provinces that were already considered at peace and in which only few, if any, legionary units were stationed. In 27 BC there were still at least three such proconsular provinces with legions: Africa, Illyricum, and Macedonia. Their governors possessed full *imperium* and nominally were equal to Augustus, but their actual power could in no way match his. Four decades later, when Augustus died in 14 AD, only the proconsul of Africa commanded troops, and then only a single legion. No one in the intervening years had introduced any official modifications to the powers of the governors; the change had evolved simply by placing a province under Augustus' authority, such as Illyricum, or by transferring troops to the provinces controlled by him in times of war. Thus the balance of power gradually redefined itself even further in Augustus' favor.

The senatorial aristocracy had to adjust to this obvious concentration of power. They still had to learn how to deal with the new legalized position of the "first man" in the state, the *princeps*, as Augustus called himself. Above all, each individual aristocrat had to determine what level of prestige and participation this new system allowed him. The first governor assigned to the rich province of Egypt in the year 30 BC, Cornelius Gallus, provided a cautionary example. Contrary to tradition he was not a senator, but an equestrian, and in command of legions. He apparently behaved in Egypt as though he himself was master of the land, rather than representative of a master in Rome. Augustus dismissed him and withdrew his friendship, which meant political death. The senate passed judgment on him, and Gallus evaded the consequences only by taking his life. Not even he, a very close friend of the princeps, had understood how far he could go. He provided a lesson to others.

Augustus also had to learn to compromise and agree to moderate changes, in order to strike a balance with the interests of other powerful families, and not least with the demands of his own followers, the Caesarians. The rank of an individual and his family was still measured by the standards established during the republic: participation in the *res publica* was marked by being entitled to wear the garb of the highest magistrates, the consuls. During much of the period of the triumvirate several consuls had been appointed in the course of each single year (they then at least nominally belonged to this elite group and could behave as men of consular rank in public). The return to the rules of the republic after the end of the civil wars had meant a return to consulships that lasted the whole year. The consulship was the foundation of Augustus' own position, and he held one from 31 to 23 BC without interruption. The continuous consulship was quite at variance with a *res publica* that was republican in character. Also, it meant that in any given year only one of the many aspirants could hold this coveted position as his colleague, a cause of considerable dissatisfaction.

In addition, Augustus made it clear that he wanted to pass on authority within his own family, along blood lines. The son of his sister Octavia by her first marriage, Claudius Marcellus, born 42 BC, was Augustus' closest male relative. He arranged for him to marry his only daughter, Julia. Marcellus had not yet achieved anything of significance and had held only the office of aedile, but was permitted by a senatorial decree to seek the consulship ten years before the legal term. Everyone must have seen this as a clear indication that Augustus intended Marcellus to succeed him one day. This created tension even in his own camp, with Agrippa in particular, who had always deferred to Augustus but now apparently turned his back on him and left the city. Moreover in 23 BC Augustus' fellow consul joined a conspiracy against the princeps and a crisis erupted that left Augustus seriously ill. Although the events are clouded in obscurity, we do know that after his recovery in June 23 BC Augustus gave up his consulship.

This was a modest retraction, but there was no change in his control of the provinces that had been assigned to him, along with their legions, in 27 BC. The *imperium* that Augustus had until then exercised as consul he exercised from 23 BC as proconsul. An edict dating to 15 BC, found at Bierzo in northern Spain, leaves no doubt on this score.[2] It seems further that after his resignation from the consulship, his *imperium*, which he exercised as proconsul, was extended to cover his dealings with the other provinces, so that in the event of conflict he had greater power than the governor. Agrippa also was given *imperium*, as proconsul, admittedly for only five years and at first only in the east. In this way Augustus both sidestepped conflict with his closest supporter and received some compensation for the loss of the consulship. In Rome, however, his resignation from the highest republican office meant that he lost all the mechanisms for conducting business inherently associated with it. These he could not relinquish if he intended to maintain the political initiative. A partial substitute was found by bestowing on him all the legal power of the tribune of the plebeians; he had already possessed an element of the rights inherent in this office, namely personal immunity (*sacrosanctitas*), since 36 BC. He also had the *ius auxilii ferendi*, the right to offer assistance, from 30 BC; through this he could present himself as the ideological protector of the ordinary people. From now on, through possession of *tribunicia potestas*, he could exploit the full authority of the office to summon the popular assemblies; he even had the right to convene the senate. On top of this he was granted special privileges in the senate, so that here too he was unchecked in the conduct of business. But control of the elections to the consulship, the political nerve center of the state, was not included.

The consequences of Augustus' retraction from the consulship soon became evident in Rome. The ordinary people seemed to be unhappy with the decision. When problems arose in the grain supply, they tried to force Augustus to assume the dictatorship. In a dramatic public gesture he openly rejected their demands. He did assume the task of ensuring the provision of grain (*cura annonae*), without yet defining the institutional nature of his responsibility. This would not happen until 8 AD, when he appointed a prefect (of equestrian rank) who would henceforth permanently oversee the proper delivery of grain from outside Italy. In the next three years, from 22 to 19 BC, Augustus spent time in the east dealing with the problems between Rome and Parthia, along with his stepson Tiberius. In the meantime final efforts were being made in Rome to create a political scenario where ambitious candidates might engage in genuine competition. The first experiment involved the elections to the consulship, which resulted in scenes of chaos. Over and over it proved impossible to restore order, or it proved possible for only one consul to function. To what extent the system was manipulated to ensure that Augustus could still control it we cannot know. In any case it was once again demonstrated that unless he had the powers to impose order, the survival of the restored *res publica* could be in jeopardy. This was no doubt what he had hoped for. It was therefore possible, after his return from the east in 19 BC, to effect another change in his legal position, one that led to the extension of his *imperium* to include Rome and Italy. It was the same *imperium* he had previously exercised in the provinces as proconsul, only now there was no territorial restriction on his authority. As a sign that his *imperium* was now operative in the center of his domain also, he was permitted henceforth to display the *fasces*, the bundle of rods, as a symbol of total magisterial power also in Rome, and to sit in the chair of office, the *sella curulis*, like a consul. From this point we hear no more of disturbances during consular elections. From now on Augustus exercised his power in Rome and Italy on the basis of his *imperium*, like a consul, and in the provinces on the same basis, like a proconsul.

With this new ruling, the role of the princeps had essentially reached its legal definition. There was, however, a further development in 12 BC. It was perhaps not significant in terms of political power, but it did help Augustus to present himself more than ever as the representative of the Roman state in its broadest sense. This followed the death of Aemilius Lepidus, the least important of the triumvirs of 43 BC. Despite having been stripped of power in 36, Lepidus had retained the office of pontifex maximus, as the senior Roman official in religious matters. Now this office too passed on to Augustus. It is emphasized in the *Res Gestae* (10) that more people flocked in from all over Italy for this election than on any previous occasion. The involvement of so many people confirmed his extraordinary position as *princeps*, "leading man," of all the citizens. As a consequence, Augustus was able to effect changes in the religious colleges, which had responsibility for the relations between gods and Romans. A visible manifestation of this was the nomination of a new sacrificial priest of Jupiter, the *flamen Dialis*. This post had been dormant for many decades, because no senator had been willing to live by its numerous restrictive rules. Augustus now intervened, in his role of pontifex maximus: in the restored *res publica* nothing must be spared in the worship of the gods.

Legislation

Augustus' public self-image was of someone who linked his contemporary policies to the past, and pursued them within traditional Roman guidelines. The old ways had proven their worth, and must be respected. In his *Res Gestae* he prided himself on not only maintaining but even reinforcing traditional laws. At the same time he referred to the many new laws introduced as a model for future generations (*Res Gestae* 8). Moreover, this link was emphasized in the galleries that celebrated the renowned men of the past, erected by him in the porticos of the forum that would come to be called the Forum of Augustus. Its central temple was dedicated to Mars Ultor, Mars the Avenger, preserving the memory of the victory over Caesar's murderers. The succession of distinguished men who had made Rome great led from Romulus directly to Augustus, and confirmed that he indeed stood at the zenith of Roman history, just as Virgil had described in the *Aeneid*. Furthermore, Augustus' image stood in the Forum on two quadrigas erected by a decree of the senate, when, with the consensus of the equestrians and the people, they honored him in 2 BC with the title *pater patriae*, father of the fatherland. This role, like that of the father of a family, encompassed contradictory traits: fatherly concern and necessary firmness. Augustus' responsibility was the state as a whole, and he was thus obliged to take firm action when necessary. He involved himself in the daily, and the private, lives of the citizens as no one ever had before in Roman history. These citizens no longer even had full control over decisions about their own personal behavior. He deemed it particularly crucial to preserve moral values, which included marriage and childbearing. The moral disintegration of the civil war period

Forum of Augustus, Rome

had eroded these values, especially in the higher levels of society, among senators and equestrians. Through a number of laws he established new rules that significantly affected lifestyle. Marriage was obligatory at a certain age for both men and women, as was the production of offspring. Whoever failed to meet these requirements could expect not outright punishment but considerable restrictions on the holding of office and especially on the rights of inheritance. In a society like the Roman, with a high death rate, valuable legacies were passed on quite rapidly from one generation to the next. An individual might also be bequeathed certain sums in the wills of friends. The sanctions must have been thought arduous at the time, but the legislation did not apparently enjoy long-lasting success.

Other laws addressed the emancipation of slaves, a practice that, especially in Rome proper and in Italy, had a considerable effect on the social structure. Before this time, every emancipation by a Roman citizen automatically led to the creation of new Roman citizens. Testamentary emancipations not infrequently reduced an inherited estate considerably, since slaves represented an important economic asset. Such emancipations were henceforth severely restricted, and subjected to certain conditions. Allegedly, Augustus aimed to minimize the dilution of Roman blood by foreigners; the slaves originated from all ethnic groups, inside and outside the empire.

There was considerable opposition to many of these laws, but most of all to the law by which inheritances would, for the first time, be taxed. The revenues were to go into the newly founded military compensation fund (*aerarium militare*). The tax would consist of only 5 per cent of the value of the estate left, and would not apply to next of kin. All the same, the majority of senators in particular maintained a long and persistent protest against it. Still, Augustus won. At stake was the social welfare of the veterans, and with that the long-term maintenance of his power, and of internal peace.

After the civil wars Augustus had to discharge and find land for many tens of thousands of soldiers, not just from his own armies but also from Antony's. These settlements (*coloniae*) were established partly in Italy, but more extensively in the provinces: in this respect he followed the lead of Caesar. In the *Res Gestae* (28) he cites Africa, Sicily, Macedonia, the two Spanish provinces, Achaea, Asia, Pisidia, Syria, and Gallia Narbonensis. These settlements belonged mainly to the early period of his rule, when larger military units or at least sections of legions were discharged all at once. Since an army of about twenty-six to twenty-eight legions had to be maintained to protect the borders and to support Augustus' imperial policy, he had to find a way to prevent such an army from being used in political conflicts, as it had been in the late republic. This would be best achieved if Augustus himself could guarantee that he would take care of the soldiers' central concern, which had been the key factor in the politicization of the armies: a fixed period of service, with the date of retirement clearly established, along with an appropriate settlement. Augustus guaranteed both, even if it meant drawing on his own resources (*Res Gestae* 16). But after a time, even the tremendous wealth of the princeps was insufficient to meet this commitment. That is why he needed new sources of funds, to be derived mainly from the estates of the Roman citizens. Under Augustus the majority of Romans still lived in Italy, but this region had not been subjected to any regular form of taxation since the civil wars. Romans, as masters of the world, were supposed to be free of it. On the other hand, veterans who as Roman citizens had served in the legions received compensation. Augustus evidently felt it was ideologically and economically right that the burden for the support of these soldiers after active service should fall on Roman citizens. The provinces should not be expected to take care of Roman veterans. Therefore only Romans were obliged to pay the 5 per cent inheritance tax, earmarked, as noted, for the military compensation fund.

The Frontiers

The soldiers had definitely earned the special attention Augustus bestowed on them. Not only had they enabled him to take power; they had contributed to his policy of expanding the empire. He achieved more in this respect than anyone before. On almost every frontier he extended the dominion of the Roman people and took over new provinces, all of which remained under his direct control. Contrary to the plans of Caesar and Antony, he did not extend the *imperium romanum* eastward by direct military intervention. He did, however, establish provinces. Besides Egypt, these included the kingdom of Galatia in central Anatolia, which was incorporated into the empire after the death of King Deiotarus. Judea also was provincialized in the year 6 AD, when the inhabitants could no longer endure the rule of Herod's son Archelaus. The prefect representing Roman authority there was not, however, a provincial governor; rather, he managed Judea as part of the province of Syria and was subordinate to its *legatus Augusti*. But, contrary to Roman expectations, Augustus did not wage war against the Parthians, despite all the tensions that could have served as grounds for war. His stepson Tiberius in 19 BC negotiated successfully to recover the legionary eagles and the surviving prisoners of war who had fallen into enemy hands at Carrhae in 53 BC and in later engagements. In Rome this achievement was fêted as a victory; a triumphal arch celebrated the return of the legionary standards. Nearly twenty years later Augustus' grandson Gaius was obliged to travel to the east on a further diplomatic mission. Yet Augustus considered it neither opportune nor necessary to widen his direct authority in the east. The early expeditions of two prefects from Egypt to Arabia and the Sudan passed without major consequence.

The focus of his expansionist strategy was directed to the Rhine and the Danube. Up to Augustus' time there were persistent security problems in those districts of northern Italy that bordered immediately on non-Roman territory. These, and the land route over the Balkans, demanded his attention, quite apart from the impulse to extend Roman (and his own) power until Rome mastered the world. He writes in his *Res Gestae* (26) that he had enlarged the territory of all the provinces that shared borders with peoples not yet under Roman rule. Virgil's famous phrase *imperium sine fine*, "empire without any limit [of time or space]," reflects similar thinking. Shortly after the consolidation of his power, Augustus launched an expedition against the independent regions in the northern Iberian peninsula. No fewer than six legions were involved in the campaign. When the conquest was completed, in 19 BC, not all the legions were needed there. Many of these units found themselves eventually on the Rhine frontier. All our evidence suggests that Augustus and Agrippa developed the grand strategy of advancing the empire to the Danube and actually beyond the waters of the Rhine. Until this was done, the already conquered tribes under Roman control could easily rope in neighboring kinfolk who inhabited the still unsubjugated regions on the far side of the Sava and the Rhine and threatened the security of Roman territory.

The urgent need for action became even clearer when two invading Germanic tribes, the Usipeti and Tencteri, defeated Augustus' legate Marcus Lollius in Gaul in 16 BC, with the loss of a legionary eagle. This occurred only a short time after the dramatic and widely publicized return of the captured standards from the Parthians. But the defeat was not the rationale for the plan of conquest. That policy was far more grandiose and had been in gestation for a long time. After the conquest of the entire Alpine region in 16 and 15 BC (still recalled today in the La Turbie victory monument near Monaco), a dual attack against the Danube and the Rhine was thought to promise a quick victory. Agrippa, the experienced strategist, was to defeat the Pannonians, while Augustus' two stepsons would move into action on the Rhine. The division of tasks shows that in the plan of conquest priority was given to the Balkans. When Agrippa died unexpectedly in the spring of 12 BC, Tiberius took over command in Illyricum, and his brother Drusus on the Rhine. The conquest of Pannonia seemed assured in 9 BC. In the late summer of 12 BC Drusus had begun his assault on the Germans and had in 9 BC just reached the Elbe, when he fell from his horse and met a sudden death, his mission incomplete. Tiberius took over and conquered at least as far as the Weser, and more likely even the Elbe. On January 1, 7 BC, he could celebrate victory over the Germans in Rome.

It has often been assumed that Germania on the right bank of the Rhine was never a true province for Augustus, just a place where the expansion became bogged down. But this assumption is based essentially on its later loss. Immediately after the victory of 7 BC actual settlements were established in those Germanic regions east of the Rhine that were under Roman military administration, as was proved a few years ago when surviving traces of such a settlement were discovered at Waldgirmes. Far to the east of the Rhine lead mines owned by Augustus were leased out, and in the oppidum Ubiorum, today's Cologne, a provincial cult of the *dea Roma* and Augustus was established embracing Germanic districts on both sides of the river. This all shows that Germania was regarded as a province, just as was Illyricum. Both regions were in some respects precarious possessions. Admittedly, Tiberius was able to stamp out an uprising in Illyricum that began in AD 6, albeit with enormous effort; but only a few days after the announcement of the victory in Rome in AD 9 came the news of Quinctilius Varus' catastrophic defeat in north-west Germany. Remains of slaughtered Roman troops were found in the 1990s in the vicinity of the town of Kalkriese. A coalition of Germanic tribes, under the leadership of the Cheruscan Arminius, had virtually annihilated an essential part of the Roman army: three legions and numerous auxiliaries. The shock ran deep, but Augustus did not entertain the idea of giving up the annexed Germanic lands. Tiberius quickly stabilized the situation, and his late brother's son, Germanicus (who had inherited that honorific name from his father), achieved an immediate success over the Germans, which earned Augustus his final acclamations as victor, his twentieth and twenty-first. In the meantime the Romans had already begun reconstruction in Waldgirmes, which had been destroyed by the Germans. Germanic territory east of the Rhine was totally lost only after Augustus' successor Tiberius abandoned the idea of re-annexation in AD 16. This was the only province that was lost. It had been held for almost two decades, which made its loss more painful for the Romans.

Despite some setbacks, Augustus extended the empire further than any other Roman leader before or after him. Most notably, his generals won for him nearly the entire region of the Danube. Only in the fifth century did major population migrations bring Roman authority there to an end.

Toward the close of Augustus' life the new *imperium Romanum* created by him encompassed twenty-five distinct provinces, fifteen of which were under his direct control. The remaining ten were provinces of the Roman people (wrongly called "senatorial" provinces), governed by proconsuls. Augustus made no radical change to the system of provincial administration. It did not occur to him to introduce an administrative system that covered the whole province. The authority of the governors remained essentially the same as before. Under him the provinces flourished, thanks to almost universal peace and the protection against the excesses of individual governors that he had been able to guarantee since 30 BC. The welfare of an entire province was fundamentally more important to Augustus than the private interests of aristocratic governors. The collection of taxes was still carried out through the tax-leasing system that had aroused much resentment against the Roman government in the late republic. But the *publicani* ("tax collectors") had lost their political backing, and they now had to deal with the Master of the World. It was in his interest also that the provinces should prosper. In his own provinces Augustus created new officials to supervise tax collection, procurators, who answered to Augustus alone. Their staff consisted exclusively of slaves and freedmen of Augustus. But even they did not personally collect the taxes; they merely provided local supervision of the leasing corporations and the tax collectors appointed by the cities. When necessary, Augustus could call his procurators directly to account. His governors of senatorial rank had no involvement in tax collection.

After 27 BC Augustus spent at least twelve years in the provinces. This fact alone indicates how important they were for him, and how much attention he gave them. It is no wonder, then, that in several of them he was regarded as a savior and that cults for his worship were even established. Already in 29 BC, in the provinces of Asia and Pontus et Bithynia, a provincial cult was created in which Octavian, as he was still called then, was worshiped along with the goddess Roma. Other provinces followed, to demonstrate clearly that they too were loyal subjects. Several cities eagerly imitated this model, in the Greek east as well as the Roman west. Only in Rome itself and to some extent in Italy was the overt cult of Augustus impossible. In all the regions of Rome, nonetheless, sacrifices could be made to honor Augustus' genius. This was basically just a public manifestation of customs observed in private Roman households. But the public nature of the practice and the scale on which it was observed lent the whole tradition a new character.

Rome and Italy

Although Augustus spent a considerable time in nearly all regions of the empire, Rome and Italy remained his undisputed focus. It was important to proclaim this through the magnificent appearance of the capital. According to Suetonius, Augustus claimed to have found Rome a city of brick, and left it a city of marble (Suet. *Aug.* 28. 3). That he adopted a deliberate policy of enhancing the physical appearance of the buildings to suit their position at the center of the world is demonstrated by the way he tallies the individual structures that he built or restored in the city (*Res Gestae* 19–21). He gave his attention to numerous temples that had been neglected in the late republic. During his sixth consulship (28 BC) alone Augustus had eighty-two temples restored, as he himself records. These were mostly smaller shrines. But in addition he rebuilt others on a more splendid scale: the temples of the Capitoline Triad, of Jupiter Feretrius, and of Jupiter Tonans on the Capitoline hill; the shrines of Minerva, of Juno Regina, and of Jupiter Libertas on the Aventine; and many more. The assembly building of the senate, the Curia, and the Theater of Pompey were renovated by him, as were many more functional structures such as the aqueducts and the extensive road network in Italy. Agrippa built other structures in line with arrangements agreed with Augustus: not only the Pantheon, in whose entrance hall stood a monumental statue of Augustus, but also the first thermal baths for the people of Rome, and the many fountains that made access to water easier all over the city. This significantly raised the quality of life for the inhabitants. The free distribution of grain for the urban masses was continued and consolidated, and protection from the frequent fires was improved with the creation of seven fire brigades, one for every two districts of Rome. The public games also were held in ever grander style and extended by many days. Numerous occasions brought inescapable reminders of the princeps' achievement in festivals and games in the circus, amphitheater, and theater. All of this brought home to Romans how important they were to him, even if politically they now had hardly any say. Annual elections were held all the same, and Augustus ensured that the members of the voting units he belonged to could not be bribed. From the outset he paid out enough to them to discourage corruption. That said, only those senators Augustus had recommended to the consulship were elected.

Since the end of the civil wars Augustus had represented the focal point of Roman political life. Yet there was little evidence of this in the buildings from where he exercised this power. During his lifetime there was no emperor's palace in Rome. His house on the Palatine hill was replete with symbolism, differing from ordinary residential structures in the approach lined with laurel trees and in its temple-style gable. Directly linked to the house was a temple to Apollo of Actium, built of white Carrara marble. The senate often convened in its portico, especially as Augustus grew older. But still, the buildings did not resemble those of a monarch; in fact they seemed fairly modest, relative to the power of the inhabitant. The house was one of the *res publica*. As elected pontifex maximus, Augustus should strictly have moved to the *regia*, the official residence of the chief priest, at the edge of the Forum Romanum. Since he did not wish to do so, he transferred a portion of that house to the public domain. Here his wife Livia created a sanctuary to Vesta, in which she acted as priestess. The realm of the private life of the princeps and his wife took on a public aspect. The identification of Rome and its destiny with the first man progressed considerably after 12 BC. Everything associated with him had repercussions for Rome and for the entire world.

Succession

Augustus' early opponents often mocked his feeble physique. Indeed, he had never enjoyed a strong constitution. Few who knew him in 42 BC, as he lay ill in his tent during the slaughter of Philippi, would have foreseen that he would survive for another fifty-five years. In fact he outlived nearly all those there at the time. Death was, of course, a constant threat for him as for every other citizen in Roman times. Accordingly, from an early stage he gave thought to what would happen when he was gone. In typical Roman manner, he thought of Rome and his own achievements there in familial terms. Since earliest times it had been assumed in Rome that the son would follow in his father's footsteps in the political sphere. When Octavian heard in 44 BC of his testamentary adoption by Caesar, he understood at once that accepting the inheritance and agreeing to be Caesar's son meant taking on the political aspirations of his adoptive father, despite the warnings of his mother and his stepfather, the highly regarded former consul Marcius Philippus.

Once the power struggle was over and he had been entrusted as princeps with the welfare of all Romans and the empire, Augustus had to think of the future if he wanted to avoid jeopardizing his entire achievement. What form should the direction of the state take after his death? Two basic considerations underlay all his thoughts. He did not doubt for a moment that his power should stay within his own family. All the great families of the republic had thought this way. If there was no son in the family, they had recourse to adoption, which played a highly significant role in Roman life. Augustus believed firmly in the tradition of transmitting power within the family. He himself had only one child, and that no son but only a daughter, Julia. His wife Livia had brought two sons to the marriage, first Tiberius, born in 42 BC, then Drusus, born in 38 BC. In planning for the future, however, Augustus believed strongly in the importance of the blood line where feasible, and even when it might not at first sight seem feasible. For this reason his closest male relative, Claudius Marcellus, son of his sister Octavia, was prominently marked out soon after 27 BC. When Marcellus married the only daughter of the princeps, many assumed that Augustus looked to him one day to take over his role.

How would such arrangements be presented? During the crisis of 23 BC, in order to suppress all speculation, Augustus had offered to read out his will. He most likely could have done this without creating problems. Bequeathing his official position in his will was ruled out. All his power had been transferred to him formally by the senate and the people. It was not his to pass on. In the will he could dispose only of his private wealth, which was certainly considerable and was urgently needed to finance numerous "public" ventures. The *Res Gestae* provide many examples. Whoever inherited these resources would on that basis alone be able to exercise massive influence. But the transfer of the political leadership of the *res publica* could not be achieved in this way; Augustus had to find other means.

After the death of Marcellus it soon became clear who would "succeed" Augustus, in the case of his sudden demise. Augustus' loyal companion Agrippa received *imperium*, as he himself had done, at first for five years; this he could exercise as proconsul, which placed him in an advantageous position should he be challenged by other holders of *imperium*. More importantly, he married Augustus' daughter, Julia, and thus became a member of her family. When two sons Gaius and Lucius were born in 20 and 17 BC, the future looked especially bright. In 17 BC Augustus adopted his grandsons, making a political statement that could be misunderstood by no one. From then on their names were Gaius Julius Caesar and Lucius Julius Caesar. At first, being too young to play any direct role, they could represent only future hopes; hence their father Agrippa became all the more prominent. Aside from his *imperium* he had already, five years earlier, received *tribunicia potestas*, this also restricted in his case to a five-year period. His position was subordinate to that of Augustus, but all the same he had at his disposition the two most important political tools possessed by his superior: *imperium* and *tribunicia potestas*. If the princeps should die unexpectedly, the senate and people would have no choice but to entrust him with the continuation of his mission. The alternative would have been civil war. When Agrippa's sons, legally Augustus' sons, came of age, the question would be answered by a two-generation formula.

But before such broader considerations could come into play, Agrippa died suddenly in the spring of 12 BC. Gaius was in his eighth, Lucius in his fifth year. A third son, Agrippa Postumus, was born, as his name suggests, posthumously. All three were still too young for political life. Yet Augustus could not make political certainty his priority; he was too committed to succession by a blood relative. Livia most likely presented her oldest son Tiberius as the most appropriate heir, in that he had accumulated military and political experience: if so, Augustus certainly grasped the opportunity, but only partially. He arranged for Agrippa's widow, his daughter Julia, to marry Tiberius, who in the following years achieved spectacular victories in the Danube and Rhine areas. But the young adopted sons were ushered into the political limelight with increasing frequency. For instance, during his last stay in Gaul in 8 BC, Augustus distributed a special payment in Gaius' name to the armies at the Rhine, at the very time when Tiberius successfully completed his conquests. The sons were presented as "first among the [equestrian] youth" (*principes iuventutis*); everyone was obliged to acknowledge the intended parallelism with Augustus as *princeps senatus*, "the first of the senators." Obviously Augustus refused to acknowledge that a strong personality like Tiberius would find this unacceptable, especially given the stormy relations that quickly developed with his wife Julia. Tiberius was unwilling to wait for a long time as stop-gap for the two still very young sons of his stepfather, even though in 6 BC he was at last granted tribunician authority, similar to that of Augustus. He retired to the island of Rhodes and thus abandoned politics. Undaunted, Augustus persevered with his goal of preparing his "sons" one day to take his place. The senate granted them the right when they became twenty to seek the consulship, still the highest office in Rome. This was prominently inscribed for everyone to see on major monuments in the Forum Romanum. The young men still lacked military experience and the aura of a victorious leader (in Latin: *virtus*), which only military conquest can bestow on someone. For this reason Gaius was sent to the east, to achieve success against the Parthians through a mixture of military threats and diplomacy. Lucius was to go to the armies in Spain to gain his first experience. On the way there, however, he died, in AD 2 in Massilia. His brother died two years later in the east. Once again Augustus stood alone. He was now sixty-six years old. Time was pressing.

Finally, Augustus was prepared to accept his stepson as successor, even though by now Tiberius had already been divorced from Julia for two years. She was no longer important to her father, being too much at variance with certain aspects of his policies. She was exiled to the island of Pandateria. Augustus now adopted Tiberius, and at the same time obliged him to adopt the eighteen-year-old Germanicus, who was directly related to the princeps through his mother Antonia, Augustus' great-granddaughter. Tiberius' future prospects were thus burdened by an irksome condition; after all, his own son Drusus was nearly the same age as Germanicus. Augustus also adopted Agrippa Postumus, the much younger brother of Gaius and Lucius. The drive to find blood relations became a kind of obsession for him. Immediately after Tiberius' acceptance into Augustus' family, the senate and people bestowed on him *tribunicia potestas* and *imperium*, which he exercised as proconsul. Thus Tiberius found himself in the position once occupied by Agrippa. The senate and the people could no longer bypass him. This was how Augustus designated his successor, even though in strictly legal terms he had no authority to do so. There was no escaping the implications of Augustus' actions.

After adopting Tiberius, Augustus remained firmly in public life, as the true focal point of Roman politics, even though his "son" exercised influence through political decisions and the selection of office-holders. Many laws were passed in the final decade of Augustus' life. He constantly strove to strengthen the demography of the Roman people, especially of the upper classes. This led to further dissatisfaction over the legislation of 18 BC, which had entrenched the obligation to marry. Additions to this legislation were agreed upon in the year AD 5, including new age limits for the holding of office. Finally in AD 9 important new legislation, the *lex Papia Poppaea*, was introduced, which completed and strengthened the earlier law. A reform of the elections of magistrates was also concluded in AD 5. The preliminary choice of candidates to be put forward for election was now left to a select group of senators and equestrians. The new election committees were named after the deceased Gaius and Lucius Caesar. Thus the monarchical reality became ever more publicly evident, even if the changes still respected republican forms. In AD 13 the long established fifteen-man committee of the senate, with which Augustus used to discuss pending issues, was transformed into an inner circle of twenty. Now that he was too old to appear in the senate as often as before, Augustus could reach binding decisions with this body as if the entire senate were in agreement. This could have had serious consequences if Tiberius had not abrogated the new rule.

Death

Augustus gave much thought to his own end and to the world that would come after him. On April 3, AD 13, he composed his will. Tiberius and Livia were named as his principal heirs, and both would carry his name Augustus (Augusta in the case of Livia). He bequeathed a large sum to the people of Rome, as well as to the Roman soldiers: to the members of the imperial guard, the praetorians, 1,000 sestertii each; to the urban cohorts, 500 each; and to the legionaries, 300 each. These Roman citizens were to remember him with gratitude. To his daughter Julia, whom he had banned through the senate to the island of Pandateria for her unconventional life choices, Augustus denied burial in the mausoleum on the Campus Martius, in which so many family members were interred (Suet. *Aug.* 101).

He also wrote of his services to the Roman people in his 'Achievements' (*Res Gestae*), an account of his deeds and his expenditures (*impensae*). We know that he was still working on it after June 26, AD 14 (*Res Gestae* 4). The report was to be displayed after his death on bronze pillars erected in front of his mausoleum, all arranged in his will. The impressions left by those pillars can still be seen today in the paving at the entrance. The inscriptions themselves have been lost, but the text through which Augustus directly addressed posterity was found in modern Ankara and two other cities in the province of Galatia, Antiochia and Apollonia. Through them, he conveys to us today his vision of the times and especially of his own personality. Thus even beyond the grave he remains the great public communicator that he had been in life.

Shortly after finishing the *Res Gestae*, Augustus died, on the nineteenth day of August (the month named after him) in AD 14, in Nola in Campania. He had reached almost the end of his seventy-sixth year. His body was carried to Rome, at first by officials of the communities through which the procession passed, in the latter stages by members of the equestrian order. There the official funeral celebrations took place. The last part of the journey led from his house on the Palatine hill to the Forum Romanum. Once again the close link between the deceased and the Roman people and its past was made clear. The bier carrying the corpse was followed not only by members of the Julian family and their relatives, as was customary in an aristocratic burial procession, but also by all the previously deceased great figures of the Roman past, from Romulus to Augustus' own time, played by actors wearing death masks and the appropriate cloak of office. This display was intended to reinforce the idea that Augustus had brought the past to completion. Tiberius and his son Drusus gave the funeral orations in the Forum. Then the procession continued on to the Campus Martius and the mausoleum, which had been ready since 28 BC. Augustus had buried many of his hopes there. The body was cremated on a funeral pyre, from which rose an eagle as symbol of his immortality. A senior magistrate, a praetor, claimed he had seen Augustus ascend to the gods; Livia rewarded his testimony with a payment of a million sestertii. Thus the senate could, just a few days later, announce on September 17 the reception of the deceased among the gods, with the attribute *divus*. A temple was built for him and a special priesthood established. The founder of the Roman monarchy would maintain a presence in future state affairs as an official god. The political transition to Tiberius proceeded without legal problems. Augustus had planned ahead.

One of the maxims that shaped Augustus' life consisted of two words: "hasten slowly" (*festina lente*). In keeping with this injunction his driving ambition was combined with calm rationality. He followed this principle over and over again. His long-term success relied on the clever, gradual steps that allowed the people as a whole time to get accustomed to a new situation. He did not create a monarchical form of government from the outset; rather, he let it grow over the decades. This was how he ensured its stability. He made no direct or radical break with the past. Instead he emphasized continuity, which cast a softer light on what were really dramatic changes in the political system of government. He realized his clear goal to become and remain the first individual in the *res publica* albeit sometimes with brutal effect: the substantial number, including some even from his own family, who refused to be subjected to him became victims of his ambition. He did, however, bring widespread stability and security to the government and the empire. The Augustan peace, the *pax Augusta*, was not merely a showy propaganda slogan. Rather, for the majority of people it represented a symbol of liberation after decades of civil war and military chaos. Most were willing to settle for security; even most of the Roman upper class came to terms with curtailments to their freedom, if security could be guaranteed. This was not too difficult under Augustus, in contrast to some of his later successors, since he observed a code of restraint. The principate founded and developed by him provided a solid foundation for the lengthy era of Roman imperial rule.

Translated by Ruth Tubbesing

Notes

1 *Zeitschrift für Papyrologie und Epigraphik* 154 (2005), 232–3.
2 *AE* 2000, 760.

Further Reading

J. Bleicken, *Augustus. Eine Biographie* (Berlin, 1998)
J. A. Crook, "Political History, 30 BC to AD 14," *Cambridge Ancient History*, vol. 10 (Cambridge, 1996), 70–112
W. Eck, *The Age of Augustus*, 2nd edn (Oxford, 2007)
D. Kienast, *Augustus. Princeps und Monarch*, 3rd edn (Darmstadt, 1999)
K. A. Raaflaub and M. Toher (eds), *Between Republic and Empire: Interpretations of Augustus and his Principate* (Berkeley, Los Angeles and London, 1990)
D. Shotter, *Augustus Caesar*, 2nd edn (London, 2005)
R. Syme, *The Roman Revolution* (Oxford, 1939)
P. Zanker, *The Power of Images in the Age of Augustus* (Ann Arbor, Mich., 1988)

II

Tiberius

Greg Rowe

The poet Ovid was in exile on the island of Tomi in the Black Sea when he learned that Tiberius had succeeded Augustus as Roman emperor. He refers to the event in his poetry, once prophetically – "Hence the grandson and son of a god, though he may himself refuse, will carry his father's burden with celestial mind" (*F.* 1. 529–36) – and once retrospectively: "Offered the reigns of empire, Tiberius took them after frequent refusal" (*Ex Ponto* 4. 13). The historian Velleius Paterculus, present in Rome, also refers to Tiberius' accession. Tiberius, he writes, "refused the principate almost longer than others have fought to seize it" (Vell. Pat. 2. 124. 2). Ovid would die three years after Tiberius' accession, in AD 17. Velleius would complete his universal history, dedicated to the consul of AD 29, before the fall of Sejanus in AD 31. Ovid describes Tiberius' accession in monarchical terms. For Ovid, he is the latest in a dynastic succession of divine, omnipotent rulers. Velleius describes Tiberius' accession in more republican terms. For Velleius, he is the latest in a line of leading men (*principes*), and his peaceful coming to power contrasts with the violence of the past. But Ovid and Velleius agree on one point: that, at the moment of his accession, Tiberius hesitated.

This life of Tiberius will highlight the perspectives offered by contemporary writers like Ovid and Velleius, as well as the surviving coins, inscriptions, papyri, and artwork of the period. Later writers, such as Tacitus, Suetonius, and Cassius Dio, knew that, after his accession, Tiberius would go on to rule for twenty-three years; that he would be succeeded by his grandson Caligula; and that the Julio-Claudian emperors would be followed by the Flavians, the Antonines, and the Severans. These later writers regarded Tiberius' hesitation as hypocrisy. But contemporary writers knew only their hopes and fears for the future. They were uncertain about the new emperor and the way he would rule. And they perceived that Tiberius himself also had doubts.

Ancestry and Childhood, 42–31 BC

Tiberius was descended from three of the most illustrious houses of the Roman republic: on the side of his father, Tiberius Claudius Nero, from the Claudii Nerones; on the side of his mother, Livia Drusilla (58 BC–AD 29), from the Claudii Pulchri; and, because Livia's father, Tiberius' grandfather, had been adopted by Livius Drusus (tribune of the plebeians, 91 BC), also from the Livii Drusi. Even after Tiberius had been adopted by Augustus, thereby becoming a member of the Julian family, contemporaries still recalled his other, Claudian, ancestors. Thus Valerius Maximus, writing his *Memorable Deeds and Sayings* after the fall of Sejanus in AD 31 and before the death of Tiberius in AD 37, called Tiberius and his brother Drusus "once the glory of the Claudian clan, now also of the Julian" (Val. Max. 5. 5. 3). Tiberius, too, was conscious of his distinguished Claudian ancestry, and produced a gladiatorial show in honor of his maternal grandfather. Tiberius' ancestors, including both stalwarts of the republic and radicals like Clodius Pulcher (tribune of the plebeians in 58 BC), offered no single political line for him to follow. But from them Velleius singles out Livius Drusus for special praise: "It was his aim to restore the senate to its ancient prestige . . . But in the very measures that Livius undertook on behalf of the senate he had an opponent in the senate itself." Assassinated on his way from the Roman Forum to the Palatine, he exclaimed as he died: "O my relatives and friends, will the republic ever have another citizen like me?" (Vell. Pat. 2. 13. 1–2, 14. 2). Velleius' praise of Livius Drusus reflected Tiberius' own character and predicament: his devious and paradoxical methods, his unappreciated championship of the Roman senate, and his consequent sense of martyrdom.

Tiberius was lucky to survive his infancy. His father Tiberius Claudius Nero had been a Caesarian, commanding Caesar's fleet at Alexandria and founding the Caesarian colonies at Narbo and Arelate. But at the meeting of the senate on March 17, 44 BC, he proposed rewarding Caesar's assassins. When his wife Livia gave birth to their son Tiberius on November 16, 42 BC, Claudius Nero held the praetorship. Retaining his praetorian insignia in the following year, he defended Perusia during the siege laid by Octavian, escaped, and tried to raise a slave revolt in Campania, which Octavian quashed. He then decided to flee with his family to Sicily, to Octavian's enemy Sextus

Pompeius, a flight in the course of which they were nearly betrayed by his infant son's crying. In Sicily, the father met with disappointment. He was rebuffed by Sextus Pompeius. The infant Tiberius got a warmer reception, and was given a Greek military cloak, a brooch, and golden amulets by Pompeius' sister; these gifts were later put on display at Baiae, where many years later they were seen by Suetonius. Fleeing once more, to Marc Antony in Greece, the family briefly sought refuge with the Spartans, ancestral clients of the Claudii. But yet again they were forced to take flight, and Tiberius "almost lost his life as he was leaving by night, when the woods suddenly took fire all about them, and the flames so encircled the whole company that part of Livia's robe and her hair were scorched" (Suet. *Tib.* 6). Velleius reflected on the vicissitudes of fortune:

> Take for example Livia. She, the daughter of the brave and noble Drusus Claudianus, most eminent of Roman women in birth, in sincerity, and in beauty, she whom we later saw as the wife of Augustus, and as his priestess and daughter after his deification, was then a fugitive before the army and forces of the very Caesar who was soon to be her husband, carrying in her bosom her infant of two years, the present emperor Tiberius Caesar, destined to be the defender of the Roman empire and the son of the same Caesar. (Vell. Pat. 2. 75)

Finally, in 38 BC, Octavian allowed Claudius Nero and his family to benefit from an amnesty and return to Rome. Once there, Tiberius' mother Livia, then six months pregnant, divorced her husband and married Octavian. When the child Drusus was born, Octavian returned him to Claudius Nero, to be raised with his brother Tiberius. And when the father died in 33 or 32 BC, Octavian allowed him a public funeral, in which Tiberius delivered a eulogy from the Rostra in the Forum, his first formal public appearance.

Civil and Military Career, 31–7 BC

Tiberius received an education that would make him markedly different from Octavian, studying Greek philosophy with the Academic Nestor, Greek rhetoric with Theodorus of Gadara, and Latin oratory with Marcus Valerius Messalla Corvinus. After his father's death, he was drawn closer to Octavian. Though not adopted by him, he was raised alongside Octavian's nephew Marcellus (42–23 BC). In 31 BC he was betrothed to Vipsania, the daughter of Octavian's second-in-command Marcus Agrippa. She would bear him his only son, Drusus. In his obituary of Agrippa, Velleius remarks: "Though a new man, he had by his many achievements brought distinction upon his obscure birth, even to the extent of becoming father-in-law to Nero" (Vell. Pat. 2. 96. 1). Two years later, when Octavian entered Rome in triumph after defeating Marc Antony, Tiberius rode alongside his chariot on the left, while Marcellus rode in the favored position on the right. After Octavian had reached his first settlement with the senate and had "restored" the *res publica* and received the name "Augustus," Tiberius donned the toga of manhood, and Augustus, as his guardian, led him into the Forum to have his name inscribed in the citizen rolls. Tiberius soon began his career as an advocate, representing eastern kings and communities before Augustus and the senate, and, in 23 BC, prosecuting Fannius Caepio, who "had entered into a plot to assassinate Caesar" with the consul Lucius Murena, according to Velleius' authorized version (Vell. Pat. 2. 91. 2). A year before, the senate had decreed that Tiberius could stand for office five years before the legal age, and he was elected quaestor. As quaestor he purged the workhouses of Italy, the infamous *ergastula*, of kidnapped travelers and men seeking to avoid military service. Velleius wrote "that it was apparent from his execution of this commission how great he was destined to become" (Vell. Pat. 2. 94. 3). But in fact, at this stage Tiberius' position was ambiguous. He was set apart from his contemporaries and aligned with the imperial house, but he had not yet been adopted into it.

Tiberius then embarked on a series of military commands, the most glorious phase of his career, for which he did not receive due credit. Augustus' policy was to push inland from the Mediterranean shore to natural frontiers: to the Alps in the north, in the Spanish peninsula to the Pyrenees, in Germany to the Elbe, and in the Balkans to the Danube. These campaigns were led by Augustus in person or by legates under his auspices. The most important commands were reserved for those attached to the imperial family: Agrippa and Marcellus, Tiberius and Drusus. Tiberius and Marcellus first served as military tribunes in Spain while Augustus and Agrippa subdued the province. In 20 BC Tiberius led two legions into Armenia, crowned a new king, and received from the Parthians hostages and previously captured Roman standards. Horace addressed two poetical epistles to members of Tiberius' staff (*Epist.* 1. 3 and 1. 8), and a third to Tiberius himself, recommending a certain Septimius as "one worthy of the mind and house of Nero, who esteems uprightness" (*Epist.* 1. 9). In a fourth letter, Horace reported that Armenia had fallen before Tiberius (*Epist.* 1. 12). In the following years, Tiberius governed Gaul, imposing Roman taxation (19–18 BC); conquered the Alps with his brother Drusus (16–15 BC); assumed command in Pannonia and

Dalmatia after Agrippa's death (12–9 BC); and took command in Germany after Drusus' death (9–7 BC).

These were savage campaigns. In Gaul, Tiberius was credited with eliminating the Druids. During the Alpine campaign, the Rhaetians were said to have killed all their male captives, even the unborn, whose sex they discovered by divination; Tiberius retaliated by deporting nearly all men of military age. He disarmed Pannonia and sold the men of military age into slavery. From Germany he expelled 40,000 prisoners of war, resettling them on the western side of the Rhine. Velleius exaggerated Tiberius' role, yet understated his achievements: "after traversing every part of Germany in a victorious campaign, without any loss of the army entrusted to him – for he made this one of his chief concerns – he so subdued the country as to reduce it almost to the status of a stipendiary province" (Vell. Pat. 2. 97). In fact, his brother Drusus had been the first to reach the Elbe. But Tiberius did leave Germany a stipendiary province, which it remained for fifteen years, until Augustus realized that he could not maintain it. Tiberius' connection with the imperial family had served him well, but ironically he received less recognition than he would have done under the republic, because in the imperial system he was fighting not as an independent commander, but under Augustus' auspices. In 12 BC the senate voted Tiberius a full triumph, but Augustus allowed only the triumphal insignia. In 9 BC the senate voted Tiberius an ovation, a lesser triumph. Augustus, in his record of the campaigns in the *Res Gestae*, sometimes mentions Tiberius as his instrument, but sometimes omits him altogether.

Tiberius earned a reputation for selfless devotion (*pietas*) toward Augustus and his family. At celebrations for the emperor's return to Rome in 13 BC, Tiberius brought the seven-year-old Gaius Caesar, son of Agrippa and Augustus' daughter Julia (Augustus had adopted both Gaius and his brother Lucius), to the front of the box to receive the crowd's applause. When Agrippa died in 12 BC, Tiberius consented to divorce Vipsania and marry Julia. When his brother Drusus took a life-threatening fall from a horse in Germany in 9 BC, Tiberius rode to his side. Valerius Maximus writes: "How swift and headlong his journey, snatched as it were in a single breath, is evident from the fact that after crossing the Alps and the Rhine, traveling day and night and changing horses at intervals, he covered at full stretch two hundred miles through a barbarous country recently conquered" (Val. Max. 5. 5. 3). The trip was said by Pliny the Elder to be the longest single-day ride on record (*NH* 7. 84). In the event he was too late. At Drusus' subsequent funeral, Tiberius delivered a public eulogy, described by the unknown author of a *Consolation* written for Livia: "We beheld Nero dazed by his brother's death, and weeping pale-faced with disheveled hair, unlike himself in his grief-proclaiming countenance, alas, how that grief was shown in every line!" (*Consolatio ad Liviam*, 85–8).

Retirement, 6 BC–AD 1

After the German campaigns, Tiberius finally won due recognition. But his *pietas* now came into conflict with his ambition, and he retired from Rome. In 7 BC he attained the summit of republican aspiration: the consulship, with Gnaeus Calpurnius Piso as his colleague, and a full triumph. After the triumph, Livia gave banquets to the women while Tiberius gave banquets to the men and joined his mother in dedicating in Rome a splendid monument that bears her name, the double-colonnaded Portico of Livia. In 6 BC Tiberius transcended republican possibilities when he was granted a share in the tribunician power of Augustus and *imperium* (military command) greater than all save Augustus, each for a five-year term. A second mission to Armenia was planned. Velleius scarcely exaggerates when he says that Tiberius was now "the most eminent of Roman citizens save one (and that because he wished it so); the greatest of generals, attended alike by fame and fortune, the second light and the second head of the *res publica*" (Vell. Pat. 2. 99. 1). Yet the situation was much more complicated than this suggests. The imperial family of the time included (besides Augustus, Livia, and Tiberius) Gaius and Lucius Caesar, the sons of the late Agrippa who had been adopted by Augustus, and their mother, Augustus' daughter Julia. In Germany, the year before, Gaius had been allowed to exercise with the troops, and the troops had been given a donative in his name. Gaius' introduction to the armies was commemorated on a coin: Tiberius had never received that distinction. Tensions had by now arisen between him and Julia, who wrote a letter to Augustus attacking her husband; Tiberius may have feared that she wished to promote her son ahead of him. In any event, instead of going to Armenia, he announced that he would retire. In the senate, Augustus complained that he was being forsaken, and, to reassure him and Livia of his attachment to them, Tiberius asked them to read his will. Then, leaving Rome and Julia, he characteristically hesitated. Hugging the shore off Campania, he heard that Augustus had taken ill, and contemplated returning to Rome; but he decided that to do so would suggest that he had been waiting for the emperor's demise, and continued his journey. Stopping at Paros along the way, he compelled the Parians to sell their statue of Vesta, goddess of hearth and family, and sent the statue back to be dedicated at the Temple of Concord in Rome, possibly as an ironic comment on the state of his household. In later

years, Tiberius would say that in leaving he merely wished to make room for
Gaius and Lucius, and this is the version repeated by Velleius, who adds:
"This man, moved by some strangely incredible and inexpressible feeling of
devotion [*pietas*] toward Augustus, sought leave from him who was both
his father-in-law and stepfather to rest from the unbroken succession of his
labors" (Vell. Pat. 2. 99. 2).

In retiring to Rhodes, Tiberius also sought, after his "unbroken succession
of labors," the leisure (*otium*) appropriate to a Roman aristocrat. He purchased
a town house and a modest villa, took exercise in the gymnasium without
attendants, greeted the locals "almost as equals," and attended the philosophers' and sophists' debates. Yet his position was ambiguous, and caused
confusion. He was still a Roman magistrate, and was shown all the deference
appropriate to that station. Once, for example, when he inquired after someone
who was ailing, the Rhodians brought all who were ill out under a portico,
classified them by illness, and presented them to an embarrassed Tiberius.
But at times he could not forget his own status. When on one occasion he
weighed into a dispute among sophists and one of the sophists addressed
him sharply, Tiberius backed off home, returned with his lictors, summoned
the sophist before a tribunal, and condemned him to jail. Roman officials
traveling east deferred to him, according to Velleius (Vell. Pat. 2. 99. 4).

But his status in the imperial scheme was declining. His name had been
omitted from a series of provincial oaths. Already in 6 or 5 BC, the magistrates,
council, and people of Conobaria in Spain pledged eternal allegiance to
Augustus, Gaius, and Lucius, and to their brother Marcus Agrippa (born
posthumously to Agrippa, and bearing the *cognomen* Postumus, not yet
adopted by Augustus), but omitted Tiberius. Rome's subjects recognized that
Rome was now ruled by a dynastic house, and that Tiberius was no longer
part of it. Thus in 5 BC, when Samos swore an oath to Augustus and his
descendants, or in 3 BC, when the inhabitants of Gangra in Paphlagonia,
along with resident Romans, swore allegiance to Augustus, his children, and
their descendants, there was no mention of Tiberius. Then, in 2 BC, Tiberius'
wife Julia fell from grace. Charged with adultery, she was condemned to exile
on Pandateria, while her lovers were put to death. By letter, Tiberius had
tried unsuccessfully to reconcile Augustus and his daughter. Soon he received
notice of divorce "by Augustus' authority." Finally, Augustus dispatched Gaius
to lead the Armenian campaign. Ovid, who, as a Roman knight, participated
in Gaius' ceremonial departure, recognized that Gaius, "now the leader
[*princeps*] of youths," would "soon be leader of seniors" (*AA* 1. 194). Dio
(55. 10. 18) says that Tiberius traveled to Chios to throw himself at Gaius'
feet. Velleius, an officer on Gaius' staff, tells the story the other way around:

"On his way to Syria, Gaius met with Tiberius Nero, whom he treated with all honor and as his superior" (Vell. Pat. 2. 101. 1). Yet even Velleius could not hide his wonder at seeing Gaius exchange diplomatic courtesies with the Parthian king at the Euphrates. In late AD 1 or early 2, Augustus would write to Gaius: "I pray the gods that I may pass however much time is left to me with all of us safe and well, with the *res publica* in a most prosperous condition, and with you two playing your parts as men and succeeding to my position [*statio*]" (Aul. Gell. *NA* 15. 7. 3).

Now, in 1 BC, Tiberius' formal powers were expiring. Livia petitioned Augustus to have her son named legate. But he reacted badly to rumors that Tiberius was sending messages to the legions through centurions formerly under his command. To accommodate the emperor, Tiberius gave up armed exercises and volunteered to be put under watch. At the same time, however, his ambition was reawakened. On Rhodes he had befriended the Greek philosopher and astrologer Thrasyllus, who told him that Lucius and Gaius would soon die and that Tiberius would hold supreme power. Portents of future power occurred – an eagle perched on Tiberius' roof; his tunic seemed to blaze when he changed clothes – and these portents were publicized by the Greek epigrammatist Apollonides:

I, the holy bird, in former days no visitant of Rhodians – the eagle, in former days a mere fable to the sons of Cercaphus – just then arrived, borne aloft on high-flying wings through the broad sky, when Nero held the island of the Sun. And in his house I lodged, tame to the ruler's hand, not shrinking from the future Zeus. (Apollonides 23 [Gow–Page])

Tiberius and Livia now petitioned Augustus to permit Tiberius to return to Rome. Augustus consulted Gaius, and Gaius consented. At the moment when the ship recalling him arrived at Rhodes, Tiberius was said to have been walking on the ramparts with Thrasyllus. Tiberius, having divulged his secrets to his companion, contemplated pushing him off. But when Thrasyllus said that he sensed imminent personal danger, and that the ship on the horizon was bringing the news the other had hoped for, Tiberius was impressed by his mantic powers, and spared him.

When Tiberius returned to Rome in AD 1, no one – except Tiberius, Thrasyllus, and possibly Livia – could have foreseen that he would return to Augustus' good graces and re-enter public life, still less that he would succeed Augustus as emperor. He was a private citizen, with no public responsibilities, and he resided away from the Palatine in a house in the former Gardens of Maecenas. His only public appearance was to lead his son

Drusus into the Forum to receive the toga of manhood. But circumstances
changed quickly. First, in AD 2, Lucius died. (Tiberius composed a poem
lamenting his loss.) Then, the following year, Gaius was wounded in Armenia.
Gaius asked Augustus permission to retire from public life and live in Syria;
Augustus communicated his wishes to the senate, asking only that he return
to Italy. When Gaius died early in AD 4, grief and panic seized all who had a
stake in the regime. The colony of Pisae issued a commemorative decree
beginning:

> When the news was brought to us that Gaius Caesar . . . was snatched by cruel
> fate from the Roman people, having already been designated princeps, as
> being most just and most like his father in virtues, and the sole defense of
> our colony, this renewed and multiplied [our] grief . . . at a time when the
> mourning the colony had collectively undertaken immediately after the death
> of his brother Lucius Caesar had not yet ceased. (*ILS* 140)

Adoption and Co-Regency, AD 4–14

The Augustan principate was by now an acknowledged dynastic monarchy,
and Augustus needed a dynastic successor. On June 26, AD 4, he fully reha-
bilitated Tiberius. Persuaded by Livia, he asked the senate to extend his
tribunician power for ten years, "in spite," Velleius writes, "of Tiberius' continued objections both in private and in the senate" (Vell. Pat. 2. 103). That
same day, the 65-year-old Augustus adopted the 44-year-old Tiberius, their
respective ages making the event remarkable even within the Roman tradition of political adoptions. At the same time Augustus also adopted Agrippa's
only surviving son, the fourteen-year-old Agrippa Postumus, and obliged
Tiberius to adopt his nineteen-year-old nephew Germanicus. This son of
Tiberius' late brother Drusus was now married to Augustus' granddaughter
Agrippina, and possibly seen as providing ultimate successors in Augustus'
line. Germanicus thus took his place alongside Tiberius' own son, the
seventeen-year-old Drusus. "In the case of [Tiberius] Nero," Velleius reports,
"an addition was made to the formula of adoption in Caesar's own words: 'I
do this for the sake of the *res publica*'" (Vell. Pat. 2. 104). Senatorial moneyers
issued coins bearing the motto "tranquility, greater than which it would not
have been possible to hope for"; the senate declared an annual holiday and
commissioned an *ara providentiae augustae*, "Altar of Augustan Foresight,"
to take its place among the other Augustan monuments in the Campus
Martius.

Once adopted, Tiberius immediately returned to the field. But the situation had changed since his earlier commands. Now events had reached the level of crisis, and Tiberius was obliged to suppress revolts and avenge defeats: to maintain the empire, not to expand it. From AD 4 to 6 he campaigned in Germany. By AD 5 he had reached the Elbe, where Velleius witnessed an old German man paddle over in a canoe and ask for permission to touch Tiberius, a god manifest (Vell. Pat. 2. 107). In Pannonia, where he campaigned in AD 6–9, a rebellion had broken out. The rebels, Augustus told the senate, were ten days from Rome; according to later accounts, they represented the worst threat since Hannibal. Tiberius required fifteen legions – more than half the Roman army – to restore order. In Germany, three Roman legions were lost in the Teutoberg Forest under the command of Quinctilius Varus (AD 9). Tiberius spent the following three years campaigning there, but when he left Germany in AD 12 the frontier was 400 miles to the west, on the Rhine. Varus' mistake, Velleius says, had been to treat the region between the Rhine and the Elbe as pacified. Velleius spoke with some authority, for, as he writes, "It was at this time that I became a soldier in the camp of Tiberius Caesar . . . and for nine continuous years, as prefect of the cavalry or as commander of a legion, I was spectator of his celestial achievements, and further assisted him to the extent of my *mediocritas*" (2. 104). Velleius' language – his contrast between the celestial commander and his own mediocre self – reflects the consciousness not of a citizen, but of a monarch's subject.

By the end of these campaigns there had been further constitutional developments. Tiberius was by AD 12 recognized as Augustus' co-regent, if not yet his equal. On his way to Germany in AD 4 he had received a Parthian embassy that Augustus had redirected from Rome, and another from the Aezani in central Anatolia, to whom he replied: "I have now most gladly received from your ambassadors the outstanding decree from your city of your goodwill toward me. I shall endeavor as far as I am able to advance your interests in all times when you ask for help" (*ILS* 9463). Yet in Roman art and ceremonial, Tiberius remained Augustus' subordinate. On entering the city during his German triumph, in AD 12, he dismounted and fell at Augustus' feet. The same subordination is conveyed in two contemporary artistic commemorations of the triumph. The first is a pair of silver cups from Boscoreale in Campania, one showing Tiberius sacrificing as he departs for war, and riding in a triumphal chariot as he returns, the eagle scepter and laurel branch in his hands, a slave holding the laurel crown above his head, but the other showing Augustus with the globe that signified world domination in his right hand. The second is the 23-centimeter-wide sardonyx intaglio known as the Gemma Augustea. In the gem's lower register, Roman soldiers are seen raising a trophy while Germans look on. In the upper register, Augustus holds the scepter and is being crowned with laurel, while off to the side Tiberius descends from the triumphal chariot. The message becomes unmistakable when we notice that Augustus is holding a *lituus*, the curved staff of the augurs that symbolized Augustus' auspices, under which Tiberius campaigned.

Eventually, in AD 13 Tiberius became Augustus' formal peer: "At the request of his father that he should have in all provinces and armies a right equal to his own, the senate and Roman people so decreed" (Vell. Pat. 2. 121). Even so, Velleius can still complain that Tiberius had received less than his due. He was the "avenger and guardian of the empire" (*vindex, custos*: 2. 104); he was its "perpetual protector" (*perpetuus patronus*: 2. 120); and he showed "restraint" (*moderatio*) in being satisfied with three triumphs (Velleius counts the 9 BC ovation) "although he unquestionably earned seven" (2. 122).

Emperor in Rome, AD 14–25

When Augustus died on August 19, AD 14, Tiberius acted promptly. He learned very quickly that the senate did not share his vision of his new role, and his reign was to be marked by confusion and mistrust for all its twenty-three years. He used his *imperium* to give the watchword to the urban cohorts and to write to the legions. He used his tribunician power to convene the senate to consider honors for Augustus. In the senate, Drusus read out Augustus' will, naming Tiberius heir to a two-thirds share of his estate and Livia heir to a one-third share, and adopting Livia into the Julian family as Julia Augusta. Before the senate's meeting, the consuls had sworn an oath of loyalty to Tiberius, and they were followed by the equestrian prefects, the senators, the soldiers, and the people. At the meeting, Valerius Messalla proposed renewing the oath annually. "Did I prompt this?" Tiberius asked. "No," Valerius responded.

Before Augustus' death had been made public, Tiberius' only rival, Agrippa Postumus, had been put to death in murky circumstances. After his adoption, Agrippa had been given a command briefly; but he had eventually been sent into exile on the island of Planasia, suspected of being insane. There were rumors of a reconciliation with Augustus in the months before the latter's death. It is not known whether Agrippa was killed on the order of Augustus or of Livia; Tiberius for his part denied any knowledge.

At a second meeting of the senate, Tiberius proposed sharing power with the senate and was forcibly rebuffed. The senators asked him to succeed to his father's *statio* – the same vague and all-encompassing term that Augustus had used to define his own role in a letter some years ago to Gaius Caesar:

> There was, however, in one respect what might be called a struggle in the state, as, namely, the senate and the Roman people wrestled with Caesar to induce him to succeed to the position of his father [*ut stationi paternae succederet*], while he on his side strove for permission to play the part of a citizen on a parity with the rest [*aequalis civis*] rather than that of princeps. (Vell. Pat. 2. 124)

The ensuing debate is recounted by Tacitus, who clearly derived his account from the official minutes. Tiberius protested that "only the mind of Divus Augustus was equal to such a burden," and proposed that "in a state which had the support of so many eminent men, they ought not to devolve the entire duties on any one person; the business of government would be more easily carried out by the joint efforts of a number" (*Ann.* 1. 11). Senators objected, and Tiberius produced a document in Augustus' own hand that listed the numbers of citizens and auxiliary troops; the dependent kingdoms, provinces, indirect and direct taxes, and regular and occasional payments. Tiberius said that he would assume whatever part of all this was mandated to him. "What part of the *res publica* do you want mandated to you?" asked Asinius Gallus. Tiberius hesitated and said that he did not want to choose. Gallus said that he had asked only to show that the *res publica* could not be divided, and Lucius Arruntius concurred. Then Quintus Haterius demanded: "How long will you allow the *res publica* to lack a head?" to which Tiberius responded with invective. Mamercus Scaurus asked: "Since Tiberius has not used his tribunician power to veto the consuls' motion [confirming Tiberius' powers], does he agree?" and Tiberius responded with silence. During the debate, Tiberius maintained that old age and near-sightedness would soon force him to resign, and made it clear that he accepted the position only until the senators saw fit to grant him repose.

The understanding that Tiberius would rule briefly and then give way to Germanicus and/or Drusus was in fact widely shared. As the reign wore on, references to Tiberius' unexpected longevity became current even among loyalists like Valerius Maximus, who, under the heading "On Old Age," asked that "the safety of our princeps and savior be prolonged to the longest limits allowed to the human condition" (Val. Max. 8. 13 *praef.*). At the time, Tiberius' reluctant accession was greeted with confusion and doubt. The people of Palaipaphos on Crete, for example, apparently did not know whether the new emperor would be called "Imperator," or, if so, whether he would use it as a first name or a title. So, in their oath to him, they left spaces before and after his name (*EJ* 105b). The legions on the Rhine and the Danube demanded to know whether Tiberius would abide by Augustus' commitments regarding pay, bonuses, and length of service. The troops were treated as mutinous, and the mutinies were suppressed by Germanicus (Rhine) and Drusus (Danube). The former officer Velleius was indignant: "They tried to fix for themselves the amount of their pay and their period of service!" (Vell. Pat. 2. 235). The people of Gytheion in southern Greece thought it wise to offer the new emperor divine honors. Tiberius replied:

> I praise you and believe it fitting that in general all men and in particular your city should hold in reserve – because of the magnitude of the benefits of my father to all the world – the honors that are appropriate for gods; I myself am content with more moderate honors, as befit men. My mother will give you her answer, when she learns from you what decision you have made about honors to her. (*EJ* 102b)

Still, the Gytheians hedged their bets and looked to the future, decreeing divine honors to Augustus, Tiberius, Livia, Germanicus, and Drusus.

At the start of the reign, Tiberius had insisted that senators were his masters: "I say now and have often said before, fathers of the senate, that a well-disposed and helpful princeps, to whom you have given such great and unrestrained power, ought to be the servant of the senate, often of the citizens as a whole, and sometimes even of individuals" (Suet. *Tib.* 29). He seems accordingly to have made an effort to collaborate with the senatorial order. In fact, he tried to augment the dignity and responsibility of both of Rome's senior orders, the senators and the knights. Following Augustus' instructions, he transferred the key electoral power from the people to the senate. Henceforth, Tiberius would commend certain candidates for office, the senate would fill out the electoral list, and the people would ratify the list. Among the first candidates commended by Augustus and presented to the senate by Tiberius were Velleius and his brother (Vell. Pat. 2. 124). Tiberius was also credited with giving the order of equestrians new shape. Equestrians had traditionally been the part of the landed aristocracy that did not hold public office, but Augustus had given them a role in government. As a corporate body, they were loosely defined by various privileges, such as the right to sit in the first fourteen rows of the theater behind the senators. Confusion and usurpation reigned until Tiberius imposed order and "the equestrian order achieved unity," according to one equestrian, Pliny the Elder (*NH* 33. 32). The Tiberian senate also passed a decree forbidding senators and knights to appear on stage. The decree "pertained to those who, contrary to the dignity of their social order, had appeared on the stage or in the games or had agreed to enter the arena . . . and thus had committed an offence by which they had diminished the dignity of the senate." Those who had given up equestrian seats in order to appear in the arena or on stage would be prohibited proper burial (Levick 1983). It was in the same spirit that Tiberius allowed the senate to try its own. Already under Augustus, the senate had begun to sit as a court, and to treat insults to the emperor as treason against the Roman people. But the practice deteriorated under Tiberius, as senators revived old rivalries and used the forum and the treason charge to attack each other. Tiberius had wished to remove himself from cases by deferring them to the senate. Instead, because of the treason charge, he was directly implicated, and senators did not hesitate to draw him in further. When, in AD 16, Granius Marcellus was charged with placing his own statue above those of the Caesars and with spreading tales about Tiberius, Tiberius expressed his wish to vote as one senator among others. His former consular colleague Gnaeus Piso pointedly demanded, "I would ask you, sir: when are you going to vote? If first, you set me an example to follow; if last, I am afraid that I may un-intentionally disagree with you" (Tac. *Ann.* 1. 74). When, in the same year, Scribonius Libo Drusus was charged with conspiring against Tiberius, it was understood that Tiberius and Livia were settling a score with a descendant of Octavian's first wife, Scribonia. The senate decreed a holiday to mark Libo Drusus' conviction "because on this day the evil schemes regarding the health of Tiberius Caesar, his children, and other leading men [*principes*] of the city, and regarding the *res publica*, initiated by Marcus Libo were condemned in the senate" (*F. Amit.*). When Gaius Silius was convicted of conspiracy in AD 21, his property was transferred not to the public treasury, but to the imperial estates. Over the course of Tiberius' reign, senatorial trials ran through three phases: first, senators prosecuting senators in Tiberius' name; second, senators prosecuting senators on the instructions of Sejanus, the commander of the praetorian guard; third, senators prosecuting senators on Tiberius' instructions. On leaving sessions of the senate, he was often heard to mutter about "men rushing into slavery." But it was Tiberius who was held responsible for the trials and prosecutions; and Tacitus would claim that he killed off the leading families of the republic.

Tiberius also earned the mistrust and enmity of the urban plebs. The plebeians had come to have a very personal relationship with the imperial family, a relationship reflected in a story from Pliny about a raven that "every morning used to fly off to the Rostra that faces the Forum and salute Tiberius and then Germanicus and Drusus Caesar by name," and whose "funeral

Tiberius

was celebrated with a vast crowd of followers, the draped bier being carried on the shoulders of two Ethiopians and in front of it going in procession a flute-player and all kinds of wreaths right down to the pyre" (*NH* 10. 60). But despite Velleius' attempts to portray him as a man with a kinship to the people ("How often did he honor the people with largesses!" 2. 129–30), Tiberius commissioned few public buildings, stayed away from spectacles produced by others, and even refused New Year's gifts from the plebeians. The popular aspect of the principate did not interest him.

The breach in Tiberius' principate opened with the deaths of Germanicus and Drusus. Following Augustus' practice, Tiberius had sent the two into the field. Following Augustus' counsel, his intention was to pursue a policy of maintaining the peace. But Germanicus, remaining in Germany during AD 15–16 after the mutinies, led the legions across the Rhine, staying in the field for another season, even after he had been awarded a triumph, until he was ordered home to accept the award in May AD 17. Drusus was now sent to a military command in Illyricum, and Germanicus given a special commission in the east, to deal with a number of problems, but primarily to mediate with Parthia over the controversial status of Armenia. He was also charged with sorting out the status of the kingdom of Cappadocia, whose king Archelaus III died in captivity in Rome not long before Germanicus' departure. While in the east Germanicus exceeded his authority by visiting Egypt without the emperor's permission, earning the emperor's reprimand. In Egypt, he was offered divine honors, which he refused in an edict: "odious to me are your shouts to me as godlike, and I decline them in every way. They are fitting for the true savior only and the benefactor of the entire race of men, my father and his mother (who is) my grandmother" (*EJ* 320). Returning from Egypt to Syria in AD 19, Germanicus fell ill and died. On his deathbed, he accused the Syrian legate Gnaeus Piso (Tiberius' fellow consul in 7 BC), of poisoning him and ordered him out of the province.

When news of Germanicus' death reached Rome, the city went into mourning. A false rumor that he had recovered began to circulate, and the ordinary people stormed the temples to fulfill vows taken on behalf of his health, waking Tiberius by chanting: *Salva Roma, salva patria, salvus est Germanicus* "Rome is safe, the fatherland is safe, Germanicus is safe!" (Suet. *Cal.* 6). Yet when Germanicus' remains were returned to Rome, Tiberius and Livia failed to appear in public. Tiberius even published an edict ordering the plebeians back to work: "For the conduct was not becoming . . . to leaders of the state and to an imperial people . . . Statesmen were mortal, the *res publica* eternal. Let the people return, therefore, to their usual occupations and – as the Megalesian Games would soon be exhibited – resume even their pleasures!" (Tac. *Ann.* 3. 6). So the senate stepped in, issuing a decree publishing Tiberius' muted eulogy for Germanicus ("this most intimate document of Tiberius Caesar Augustus contained less praise of his son Germanicus Caesar than an account of his whole life and a true witness to his valor") and testifying to the "consensus of all citizens in honoring the memory of Germanicus Caesar" (*T. Siar.*).

When Piso returned to Rome the following spring (AD 20), the people demanded that he be tried for murder. Accusers approached Tiberius, and Tiberius referred the case to the senate. During the trial, both Tiberius and Piso refused to disclose their correspondence. Hearing this, the plebeians threw down Piso's statues and threatened to take the law into their own hands. Piso, realizing he had lost the support of both Tiberius and his own wife Plancina, committed suicide, and was convicted posthumously. In the published verdict, the senate struck a note of consensus and tried to reinforce the cohesion of society, including both the soldiers, whose "loyalty and devotion displayed to the Augustan house the senate hopes that they will forever demonstrate, since they know that the safety of our empire reposes in the guardianship of that house" (*SCPP* 159–62), and the plebeian populace, which, "although it was fired with the most exuberant enthusiasm for carrying out the punishment of Gnaeus Piso senior itself, nevertheless . . . allowed itself to be controlled by our princeps" (*SCPP* 155–8).

But the senate could scarcely hide the fractures, for instance those between itself and Tiberius and those between Tiberius and Livia revealed in a remarkable passage of the verdict sparing Piso's widow:

> As regards the case of Plancina, against whom a great many extremely serious charges were brought, because she admits that all her hope resides in the mercy of our princeps and the senate, and because our princeps has often and zealously requested from this order that the senate, content with punishing Gnaeus Piso senior, spare his wife as it is sparing his son Marcus and himself pleaded for Plancina at the request of his mother and accepted the very just reasons which had been put to him by her for his mother wanting to secure her request, the senate thinks that support and indulgence should be accorded to Julia Augusta – who has served the state supremely not only in giving birth to our princeps but also through her many great favours toward men of every order and who, although she rightly and deservedly ought to have supreme influence in making a request of the senate, yet uses that influence most sparingly – and to the supreme devotion of our princeps towards his mother; and it is (the senate's) pleasure that Plancina's penalty be waived. (*SCPP* 109–19)

All the senate could do was urge the ageing emperor to think of the succession:

> The senate asks and urgently requests that he turn all the care that he had divided between his two sons toward the one whom he still has; and the senate hopes that the surviving son will have all the more care from the immortal gods for their realization that all hope for the continuation of his father's *statio* over the state falls back on this one son. (*SCPP* 123–31)

Immediately after Piso's funeral, Drusus was granted an ovation. In the following years he served as consul with Tiberius and received the tribunician power. He may well have represented Tiberius' hopes for the future; but in AD 23 he fell ill and died.

Emperor on Capri, AD 26–37

After the deaths of Germanicus and Drusus, as Tacitus saw it, Tiberius went into a phase of mixed good and evil, during the lifetime of his mother Livia.

It was a period of increasing frustration for the emperor, who in 26 decided to retire to Campania and Capri, from where most people assumed he would never return. Tiberius had withdrawn himself before: besides his seven years on Rhodes, he had gone to Campania early in AD 21, after Piso's trial, leaving Drusus alone in the consulship. Different reasons were given for his final retirement. He was unsightly: balding, stooped, prone to skin outbreaks, his face covered in plasters. He wished to escape his domineering mother. He wished to avoid crowds – in the year of Germanicus' death, there had been an outbreak of *mentagra* ('chin disease'), forcing Tiberius to issue an edict forbidding kissing (Pliny *NH* 26. 3). Most of all, Tiberius craved *otium*, in the traditional manner of Roman aristocrats. This meant Greek studies. Tiberius took Thrasyllus with him into his seclusion, and was visited by scholars, whom he would interrogate: "Who was Hecuba's mother? What name did Achilles assume among the virgins? What was it that the Sirens used to sing?" (Suet. *Tib.* 70). *Otium* also meant the pursuits of the gentleman farmer. Pliny writes:

> The cucumber . . . was a wonderful favorite with the Emperor Tiberius, and, indeed, he was never without it; for he had raised beds made in frames upon wheels, by means of which the cucumbers were moved and exposed to the full heat of the sun; while, in winter, they were withdrawn, and placed under the protection of frames glazed with mirror-stone. (Pliny *NH* 19. 23/64)

Tiberius' tastes are embodied in the decor of Sperlonga, a grotto for dinner parties that he had decorated with statues of Odysseus, where he stopped on his way to Campania. The statues show the hero recovering Ajax's body, stealing the Palladium, fighting Scylla, and, in the culminating composition, blinding Polyphemus. They reflect the emperor's philhellenism, and suggest how Tiberius saw himself, as another Odysseus: crafty, having first few companions, then none, and finally winning his rest only ten years after he had left the battlefield. On Capri, Tiberius endured for eleven more years. But he almost did not make it there. While he was dining at Sperlonga the entrance collapsed, killing several guests and attendants. Tiberius himself was saved by his praetorian prefect, Lucius Aelius Sejanus, who threw himself over the emperor and shielded him.

Sejanus was to become the most infamous figure of Tiberius' principate. He first enters the record in an unspecified capacity on the staff of Gaius Caesar. He was appointed joint prefect of the praetorian guard with his father in AD 14, then sole prefect in 16–17. By then he had the attention of Tiberius, whose insecurities he exploited during Germanicus' campaigns in

Germany in the early days of the reign. He is given a vague role in the Piso affair, in seeing to the suppression of incriminating documents. Sejanus was someone who worked well behind the scenes. Despite his very brief appearances in the historical record, he had by AD 20 become the emperor's right-hand man, described by Tiberius as the "partner of his labors" (*socius laborum*). He also built up a power base in both the army and the senate. He sought support widely and would reputedly seek to enlist Livia, among others, as his ally. In 23 he had further strengthened his position by concentrating the cohorts of the praetorian guard into a single set of permanent barracks at the Porta Viminalis. The main obstacle to his growing influence over the emperor was removed in September of the same year, when Drusus died, perhaps murdered through Sejanus' agency.

On Capri, Tiberius sought to retain authority, while leaving responsibility for day-to-day governance to others: to the senate, the magistrates, and Sejanus. Tiberius corresponded with the senate, but neglected to commend candidates for office, to dispatch governors to their provinces, or to replace governors once there (for instance, Pontius Pilate, the prefect of Judea, stayed in office for ten years, AD 26–36). Early on, his negligence led to disaster. Because he had failed to produce spectacles at Rome, Roman crowds flocked to neighboring Fidenae to see a gladiatorial show. In AD 27 the amphitheater there collapsed, killing 20,000, and Tiberius was forced to return to the mainland to meet the grieving families.

Tiberius' acknowledged representative at Rome was Sejanus. Velleius writes that "Sejanus was induced to assist the emperor with his burdens, and that brought the senate and the Roman people to the point where they were ready to summon for the preservation of its security the man whom they regarded as the most useful instrument" (2. 128). Because of his relationship with the emperor, Sejanus moved in senatorial circles; one senator bought one of his eunuchs for HS50 million (Pliny *NH* 7. 39). He seduced Livilla, the wife of the younger Drusus, while her husband was still alive, and sought to marry her (although Tiberius refused). He also influenced the senate as a whole, guiding prosecutions of his perceived enemies, especially the circle around Germanicus' widow Agrippina and her son Nero. In AD 29 he persuaded Tiberius to write to the senate denouncing Agrippina and Nero directly and ordering their arrest. As the consul made the appropriate motion, the plebeians gathered in their support of the accused, brandishing their effigies and declaring Tiberius' letter a forgery. Sejanus gave the senate a dressing-down; Tiberius addressed the people in an edict and restated the charges to the house; and the senate duly sent the two into exile. A year later the senate ordered the arrest of Drusus, who had backed Sejanus against his brother Nero. More arrests followed.

What were Sejanus' motives? As Velleius saw the situation, he had a position like that of Marcus Agrippa in Augustus' day, but, unlike Agrippa, was refused entry into the imperial house through marriage by a Tiberius who was perhaps more conscious of senatorial dignity than his predecessor had been. Probably Sejanus hoped that, by clearing away adult princes, he would be left to guide the hand of a child-emperor, like the younger Drusus' son Tiberius Gemellus, after Tiberius had died.

In AD 29, before Sejanus had moved against Agrippina and her sons, Livia had died. Tiberius had resented his debts to her and her continuing power and independence; now he allowed her only a modest funeral, and failed to execute her will, to erect a memorial, or to approve her deification. A contemporary poet would regret the loss of her moderating influence: "Augusta, who can boast of two divine sceptred Caesars, set light to twin porches of Peace; fit company for the Heliconian Muses, a choir mate of wise counsel, her wisdom was the whole world's savior" (Helicon no. 21 [Gow–Page]).

Sejanus' unchecked reign lasted a mere two years, and was brought to a sudden end. After the arrest of Germanicus' son Drusus, Sejanus was elected consul and given proconsular *imperium*. Now he expected to receive the tribunician power. Instead, a letter from Tiberius to the senate denounced his former ally and closed with instructions for his arrest (the *vigiles* were used, in view of the uncertain loyalties of the guard). He was immediately replaced as praetorian prefect by the old commander of the *vigiles*, Macro, and put to death. In his autobiographical notes, Tiberius claimed cryptically that he had acted because of what Sejanus had done to the children of "his son" Germanicus. In a speech to fellow members of his electoral tribe, an old man, perhaps Tiberius himself, condemned Sejanus' consular election:

> But now, since the criminal incitement and irregular assemblies which took place on the Aventine, where Sejanus was made consul – and I, feeble friend of the useless cane, was made a suppliant – now with all my heart I ask you, good fellow-tribesmen, if I have always seemed good to you, a useful member of the tribe, if I have never abandoned my duty . . . (*EJ* 53)

The municipal calendar of Ostia marked the deaths of Sejanus and his family matter-of-factly, recording that between October 18 and 26, AD 31, Sejanus and his son were strangled, his former wife killed herself, and his daughter and son-in-law were cast down the Gemonian steps (*F. Ost.*). But some of the violence of Sejanus' official condemnation is preserved in Valerius Maximus' rhetoric:

> But why do I upbraid these [outrageous words and criminal deeds] or dwell on them when I see all crimes surpassed by the thought of a single parricide? . . . For who with words of due execration sufficiently effectual could drive into the abyss an attempt to bury the human race in bloody darkness, extinguishing the loyalty of friendship? . . . If you had achieved your madness, would the world have stayed in place? Rome captured by the Gauls, the river Cremera disfigured by the slaughter of three hundred warriors of a famous clan, the day of the Allia, the Scipios destroyed in Spain, Trasimene lake, Cannae, the blades of civil wars streaming with domestic blood: all these you wished to manifest and surpass by the crazy designs of your delirium. But . . . the author and guardian of our safety saw to it in his divine policy that his most excellent benefactions should not collapse amid the ruins of the whole world. (Val. Max. 9. 11 *ext.* 4)

Around the empire, subjects praised Tiberius. In a dedication along the Via Flaminia, a magistrate's attendant wished him long life (*ILS* 159, AD 31). Elsewhere, a freedman from Interamna in Italy commemorated "the foresight of Tiberius Caesar Augustus, born to the eternity of the Roman name, a most dangerous enemy of the Roman people having been suppressed" (*ILS* 157, AD 32).

The fall of Sejanus coincided with the rise of Germanicus' last remaining son Gaius, better known as Caligula (AD 12–41). Tiberius was said to have been tipped off against Sejanus by Germanicus' mother Antonia, with whom Gaius had lived after Livia's death. In any case, after the prefect's fall Gaius moved to Capri, where Tiberius gave him the toga of manhood, betrothed him to Junia Claudilla, and made him pontifex and quaestor. The "foresight" that Tiberius' subjects had honored (see p. 46 above) was undoubtedly provision for the imperial succession. Even before Sejanus fell, Velleius had closed his history with a prayer for worthy successors:

> Guard, preserve, protect the present state of things, the peace which we enjoy, the present emperor, and when he has fulfilled his *statio* – and may it be the longest granted to mortals – grant him successors until the latest time, but successors whose shoulders may be as capable of sustaining bravely the empire of this world as we have found his to be: foster the pious plans of all good citizens and crush the impious designs of the wicked. (Vell. Pat. 2. 131)

But this was for the future. Against all probability, Tiberius endured for another six years. In Rome, the senate vigorously prosecuted Sejanus' alleged accomplices. On Capri, Tiberius was the subject of speculation and dark rumors: he held orgies; alone among men, it was said, he possessed night-vision; his superstitions had become such that he only had his hair cut before the new moon and he wore laurel during thunderstorms as protection against lightning. In his last days, Tiberius crossed to Misenum to attend games. To demonstrate his vigor he threw darts from his box at a wild boar in the arena. Collapsing, he died soon after, on March 16, AD 37. Vacillating to the end, he had said that he was preparing to return to Rome. In his will, he named Gaius and Tiberius Gemellus equal heirs, "each to be sole heir in the event of the other's death." Within the year, Gemellus would be executed on Gaius' orders.

Conclusion

Ovid, Velleius Paterculus, and Valerius Maximus had all expected that Tiberius would be deified after his death. Valerius had dedicated his *Memorable Deeds and Sayings* to Tiberius in the following terms:

> Therefore I invoke you to this undertaking, Caesar, surest salvation of the fatherland, in whose charge the unanimous will of gods and men has placed the governance of land and sea, by whose celestial providence the virtues of which I shall tell are most kindly fostered and the vices most sternly punished . . . For the other gods we have received, the Caesars we have bestowed. (Val. Max. 1 *praef.*)

But when the emperor died, the Roman plebeians shouted, "Tiberius into the Tiber!" and prayed to Mother Earth and the Manes that Tiberius' soul be allowed no repose except among the damned. In the senate, Gaius proposed deification, but the senators declined, and limited themselves to validating Tiberius' acts. Thus Tiberius became the only Roman emperor who was neither damned nor deified.

Further Reading

M. T. Griffin, "The Senate's Story," *Journal of Roman Studies* 87 (1997), 249–63
B. M. Levick, *Tiberius the Politician*, 2nd edn (London, 1999)

Greg Rowe

B. M. Levick, "The *Senatus Consultum* from Larinum," *Journal of Roman Studies* 73 (1983), 97–115

R. Seager, *Tiberius*, 2nd edn (Malden, 2005)

D. Shotter, *Tiberius Caesar*, 2nd edn (London, 2004)

A. F. Stewart, "To Entertain an Emperor: Sperlonga, Laokoon and Tiberius at the Dinner-Table," *Journal of Roman Studies* 67 (1977), 76–90

R. Syme, "History or Biography: The Case of Tiberius Caesar," *Historia* 23 (1974), 481–96, repr. in A. R. Birley (ed.), *Roman Papers* (Oxford, 1984), 937–61

A. J. Woodman, *Velleius Paterculus: The Tiberian Narrative, 2. 94–131* (Cambridge, 1977)

III

Caligula

Anthony A. Barrett

With the possible exception of Nero, no Roman emperor has made a more lasting impression on the popular imagination than Gaius Caligula. His reputation as the archetype of the depraved autocrat was acquired despite his reigning for a meager four years, and the impact that he has made is all the more remarkable for the fact that we have relatively little trustworthy information about him. Tacitus' accounts of Caligula's reign and the first half of Claudius' are missing, and we are obliged to turn mainly to the racy biography by Suetonius and the much later and often unreliable history of Cassius Dio, supplemented by information from two signally hostile contemporary witnesses: the philosopher Seneca and the prolific Jewish writer Philo of Alexandria, who met Caligula when heading a deputation to Rome.

Despite the widespread jubilation that greeted the death of Tiberius in March 37, more thoughtful Romans would have tempered their celebratory mood with concerns about the unprecedented constitutional situation. When Augustus died in AD 14 there had been an experienced administrator waiting in the wings: Tiberius, who had been associated in office with the emperor and marked out unmistakably as his successor. No clear candidate was available in 37. Tiberius had two grandsons. Tiberius Gemellus had not yet reached the formal age of manhood. Gaius Caligula, his grandson by adoption, was older but still only twenty-four, and politically inexperienced. Beyond designating both as his joint heirs in his will, Tiberius had given no hint of who should succeed, presumably intending that any such choice should be made by the senate. The resolution of this question had a profound effect on the subsequent course of Roman history.

Early Years

Caligula was the son of Tiberius' nephew and adopted son, Germanicus, and of Agrippina (the Elder), granddaughter of Augustus. Born in AD 12 in the imperial villa at Antium, he was taken as an infant to join his father in the Rhine district. His mother dressed him in a miniature uniform and he became a mascot of the legionaries, who gave him the name by which he is familiarly known, a diminutive of *caliga* (leather military boot). From the Rhine the young Caligula traveled with his father to the east in AD 17, enchanting audiences with his precocious speeches.[1] The happiness of the trip would have been shattered for Caligula by the death of Germanicus in Syria in late 19, and the return with his mother to Rome could have provided little solace, since the atmosphere of the imperial court was heavy with political tension. Germanicus had left three daughters and three sons. Caligula was the youngest of the sons, which was lucky for him, since the two older ones fell victim to Sejanus, the ruthless commander of the praetorian guard. Along with their mother Agrippina, they were imprisoned and eventually died in captivity. Presumably too young to be considered a serious threat, Caligula was in 31 summoned by Tiberius away from the corrupting influence of the capital to Capri (Tac. *Ann.* 1. 41. 3, 69. 5; Suet. *Cal.* 8. 1, 9. 1; Dio 57. 5. 6).

Despite the lurid tales of sexual excess and decadent parties, Caligula's time on Capri would have been largely devoted to his preparing for the responsibilities expected of an adult member of the imperial family. In 33 Tiberius arranged a quaestorship for him, holding out the possibility of higher office ultimately, but prudently asking the senate not to vote unwarranted honors that might turn the young man's head. Also in 33 Tiberius made one of his rare visits to the mainland, to participate in the wedding ceremony of Caligula and Junia Claudilla, daughter of a member of a prominent aristocratic family, Marcus Junius Silanus. This was a marriage of some distinction and a sign that Tiberius was far from hostile toward his adopted grandson. Junia died not longer after, in childbirth. The child did not survive.

Two individuals are recorded as being on close terms with Caligula during this Capri period. He was a friend of one of the grandsons of Herod the Great of Judea, Agrippa (popularly known as Herod Agrippa), a colorful and slightly unscrupulous individual, but also an engaging character of considerable charm and ability. Caligula also caught the attention of Macro, the commander of the imperial guard, an ambitious man who previously, as commander of the *vigiles*, had played a part in bringing down Sejanus. Macro recognized that Caligula was likely to be the successor to Tiberius and went to great pains to ingratiate himself – even to the extent, it was claimed, of pandering his own wife to the future emperor (Phil. *Leg.* 39, 61; Jos. *AJ* 18. 143, 165, 168–204; Tac. *Ann.* 6. 20. 1, 45. 5; Suet. *Cal.* 12. 1–2; Dio 58. 25. 2, 58. 28. 4, 59. 8. 7).

Accession

When Tiberius died in March 37, Caligula had been living in seclusion on Capri for six years and would have been virtually unknown to the Roman world at large. But he had two great advantages. He was the son of Germanicus, a man who, deservedly or not, was adored by the population because of his perceived military skills and his supposedly enlightened political views (it was widely, if naïvely, believed that he favored a restoration of the liberties of the old republic). Germanicus had inherited this dual reputation from his own father Drusus, and the premature deaths of both men meant that early expectations had not suffered from the inevitable disappointments that the passage of time brings. The second, ultimately more important, advantage was that Caligula was the preferred candidate of Macro, who had the praetorian guard behind him. Tiberius' death ushered in an unfortunate sequence of events that was to provide a dangerous precedent for the remainder of Rome's history, whereby the imperial successor was chosen primarily on the basis not of legal procedure or individual qualification but of military support, especially that of the praetorian guard. Unlike other elements of the Roman army, this unit was stationed in the city of Rome, and thus well positioned to influence political events.

On Tiberius' death, Macro sent messages to the military commanders and provincial governors informing them of Caligula's accession. To control developments in Rome he made a very hasty journey to the city. There he reported Tiberius' death and read a letter from Caligula requesting the same honors for the recently departed Tiberius as had been bestowed on Augustus. In requesting this Caligula was no doubt simply going through a show of traditional piety, since there was no prospect of the senate ordering the deification of the unpopular Tiberius; they did not, nor did Caligula pursue the matter. The letter is also said by Josephus to have carried instructions for Caligula's succession. It is unlikely that it contained such a blunt directive, but the consideration that the successor had been approved already by the imperial guard and the commanders of the legions outside Italy would have served to persuade any wavering senators to grant formal political sanction. In the event it appears that the senate were far from reluctant to accept a *fait accompli*. They perhaps thought of Caligula as his father's son, a potential second Germanicus, and they no doubt anticipated that, given his youth and inexperience, they could manipulate him to their will in a way that had been impossible in the case of Augustus or Tiberius. In any event, on March 18, only two days after his predecessor's death, Caligula was proclaimed *imperator* by the senate (Jos. *AJ* 18. 234; Dio 59. 3. 7).[2]

To ease the process of the succession Macro requested that Tiberius' will be annulled, thus removing any lingering hope that Tiberius Gemellus might retain a claim. This is an interesting development. Tiberius could not bequeath the principate, but Macro must have recognized that the will of the princeps did carry by implication considerable political weight. The will was accordingly declared null and void. But this stratagem gave rise to a significant precedent. In the absence of a valid will, Gemellus should have shared in the estate with the other grandchildren. This did not happen – the entire estate went to Caligula – and thus an important principle was established: that in the case of imperial properties the civil laws of inheritance did not apply. The property of the princeps belonged to him not as a private individual but in his capacity as princeps. Later emperors generally omitted to make wills. The treatment of Tiberius' will marks an important step in the evolution of the principate (Phil. *Leg.* 23–7; Suet. *Cal.* 16. 3; Dio 59. 1. 1–3).

Macro had performed well, and he was no doubt largely responsible for the splendid series of staged events that marked Caligula's return to the capital with the body of Tiberius. Mobs of admirers turned out to express adulation for a youth of whom hardly any could have been aware only a few days previously, showering him with greetings and calling him pet names like "baby" and "chick." On arriving in Rome at the end of the month, Caligula went before the senate, where he was granted "power and authority over all things." The legal basis for this measure, in the absence (or annulment) of a will, seems to have been that Caligula became emperor because he was the choice of all the orders of society, through the process of *consensus*. Augustus, when referring to the basis of his own position in the *Res Gestae*, uses the phrase *per consensum universorum potens rerum omnium*. Interestingly, Suetonius employs almost the same phrase to describe Caligula's accession, "with the consent of the senate and the masses," and Dio speaks of senators, equestrians, and ordinary people giving him their support. It is difficult to avoid the conclusion that Suetonius and Dio drew on sources that reflect the official language used at the time. One of Caligula's coins depicts Augustus enthroned, with the legend "with the consent of the senate and equestrian order and the people." In fact, it was a true description of what had happened (*Res Gestae* 34; Phil. *Leg.* 13, 356; Suet. *Cal.* 13, 14. 1; Dio 59. 3. 1).

Caligula

The character of the new regime is no less striking than its legal basis. Suetonius reports that the senate bestowed on Caligula the *ius arbitriumque omnium rerum* ("right and authority over all matters") and granted him in one single measure the powers only gradually acquired by Augustus and Tiberius. This was a remarkable constitutional development. Augustus, in becoming master of the Roman world, had tried to maintain the fiction that he was simply the first citizen, an ordinary magistrate, albeit one with some extraordinary powers. Tiberius had reluctantly assumed what he saw as the burden of office and had tried, with less success, to maintain the same legal propriety. During the course of their reigns both did in fact accumulate powers, but the accumulation was slow and gradual and they tended to refrain from exercising them, by and large preferring to rely on their prestige (*auctoritas*). Caligula appears to have been the first Roman invested at the outset of his reign with total imperial powers by a formal act of the senate.

Now, the first document that has survived setting out the authority of the Roman emperor belongs to December 69, or a few months later, in connection with the accession of Vespasian. The *lex de imperio*, recorded on a bronze plaque, describes the powers conferred by the senate on Vespasian, and the precedents on which they are based. Caligula is not actually cited as a precedent (nor is Nero), for obvious political reasons, but there is little doubt that some of the clauses go back to his time, in particular one sweeping provision that gives the emperor, should he think it appropriate, the right to act as he sees fit. This provision bears an uncanny resemblance to Suetonius' *ius arbitriumque omnium rerum*. Caligula would reputedly later comment to his grandmother Antonia, when she reproached him on some matter, that he had all power over all things at all times. This was a chilling comment, but in fact quite correct. It is not surprising, then, that Philo saw Caligula as a man whose authority was unchecked and whose subjects were in fact his slaves. This authority had been handed to him constitutionally by the senate, presumably on the naïve assumption that they could mold him to their ends. In one sense it might be argued that Caligula is historically important as the first Roman emperor in the proper sense of the word – Augustus and Tiberius being essentially transitional figures who represented a compromise with the old ideas of the republic. In a sense, then, the Roman empire could be said to begin with Caligula in the year 37 (Phil. *Leg.* 119, 190; Suet. *Cal.* 14. 1; Dio 59. 3. 1–2).

What sort of individual was the new emperor, granted such massive powers in so unprecedented a fashion? This question is a complex one, because of the loss of the relevant chapters of Tacitus. The picture that the remaining sources present is of a ruler who was eccentric in a society that did not greatly value eccentricity, a highly strung individual, who suffered seriously from insomnia and nervous tension. But they also describe him as someone whose behavior was so exotic and bizarre that he may have been clinically mad. Modern scholars have debated Caligula's mental state at great length. In the nineteenth century the view developed that he was totally deranged. Modern diagnoses have been more sophisticated, and it has been suggested that he suffered from schizophrenia or the like. The two ancient writers who knew him at first hand, Seneca and Philo, both claim that he was a madman, but neither attributes to him any action that could reasonably be construed as evidence of madness in the clinical sense.

It is, of course, important to remember that Caligula was assassinated, and that he was succeeded by his uncle Claudius, who was highly ambitious and very shrewd. Claudius would have been faced with a dilemma. He was emperor thanks only to his predecessor's murder, so he in a sense had to accept that the act was to some degree justified. But he would not have wanted to set a precedent, which would have been highly dangerous for him. So he had to tread carefully, and to suggest that the institution of the principate was a sound one, to be preserved, but that Caligula had been an unbalanced princeps who had brought destruction on himself. Thus Claudius went out of his way to emphasize the more erratic qualities of Caligula as an individual. Now, Claudius was a historian, and it is very likely that he would have given the lead to other historians in the first generation after Caligula's death, thus clouding the record from the very outset.

At the other end of the spectrum there have been those who have argued for a rational Caligula, someone determined to replace the Augustan principle of government with something much closer to the Hellenistic model, in particular a model derived from the Ptolemaic rulers of Egypt. Those who take this line attribute the distortion of the record to the hostility and irresponsibility of the sources. The issue will probably never be settled unless new ancient material becomes available. The truth may lie somewhere in between. Caligula was an exhibitionist, arrogant, irresponsible, indifferent to and disrespectful of the opinions of others. A totally self-centered individual, with no developed sense of moral responsibility, he had no talent for rule, and no training for it. Consequently, his reign was indeed a disaster; but it was probably the disaster of a self-centered incompetent, rather than that of a madman.

First Months

Whatever unattractive symptoms he may have manifested later, Caligula was certainly on his best behavior for the first few months of his reign. He treated senators with enormous respect, emulating Augustus by promising to work with them toward common goals. What may have reassured them most was the abolition of what had probably been the chief source of resentment under Tiberius, the trials for *maiestas*, treason against the state and, more sinister, against the emperor. He made a public show of burning all the papers relating to earlier attacks against members of his family, and granted an amnesty for those who had been banished into exile. As a grand gesture of reconciliation toward anyone who might have favored his "rival," he adopted Tiberius Gemellus as his son, implicitly marking him out as his successor. He also made certain that he shored up his popularity where it mattered. Tiberius' will had been set aside, but from his personal funds (although the line between the emperor's personal funds and public moneys was difficult to define) Caligula doubled Tiberius' legacy to the praetorian guard, being the first emperor to acknowledge indirectly their role in his succession. He thereby established a precedent for later emperors, including his immediate successor Claudius. Bequests were also paid out to the legions and to the ordinary people. He made a great display of piety toward his dead kin. He went out to the islands where his mother and one of his brothers had died in captivity and brought back their ashes, which were placed alongside those of his father Germanicus within the mausoleum of Augustus. Special honors were voted for his parents, coins were issued to commemorate them, and sacrifices were carried out on their birthdays. On the analogy of July and August the month of September was renamed after Germanicus, though this arrangement did not last long (Phil. *Leg.* 25–8; Suet. *Cal.* 15; Dio 59. 2. 1–3, 3. 5, 4. 3, 6. 1–3, 8. 1).

Caligula combined this public extravagance with a lavish building program, in contrast to the frugal Tiberius, who had discouraged costly public projects. His most noteworthy contribution at the outset of his reign was the completion of a magnificent Temple of Augustus, which though decreed after that emperor's death in AD 14 had remained unfinished twenty-three years later. It was completed within months of Caligula's accession and opened in a grand display of choirs, horse races, and animal slaughter. As a final symbol of the continuity of the Augustan ideal Caligula was granted in September the title of *pater patriae* ("father of the fatherland"), the honor that Augustus ranked among his most prestigious. A gold shield was voted to mark the occasion, to be carried to the Capitol on each anniversary of the event by a college of priests, accompanied by senators and a choir of young people (Suet. *Cal.* 16. 4; Dio 59. 7. 1–4).

Early Tensions

Caligula's first months were euphoric, and presumably also exhausting, since by the early autumn of 37 he had fallen seriously ill. The nature of his illness has been much debated. Many scholars believe that it was some form of nervous breakdown, which may have left him with permanent mental difficulties. It was certainly lengthy and very serious; while crowds slept in the open outside the imperial palace, bulletins were sent out to the anxious provinces. His recovery was greeted with jubilation throughout the empire – Philo reports how Jews in Alexandria marked it with sacrifices. The emperor's return to health, however, was accompanied by a distinct change in the mood of the regime. The period of goodwill was clearly over, for reasons about which we can only speculate: some would argue brain damage from the illness; others would suggest that Caligula was suspicious of the motives of those who had kept the empire operating while he was incapacitated. A number of prominent individuals lost their lives in the months following his recovery. Among them was Gemellus, accused of having anticipated Caligula's death. The execution of the emperor's father-in-law, Junius Silanus, followed, and some time later Caligula eliminated the most powerful man in the court after himself, Macro. He had no doubt been irked by Macro's constant lectures on appropriate conduct, but this can hardly have constituted grounds for this extreme measure. It may well be that Macro was suspected of plotting with Gemellus and Silanus. The presence of these three, all with strong links to the principate, among the victims suggests suspicion, whether well founded or not, of some sort of conspiracy. Certainly henceforth Caligula took the precaution of dividing control of the imperial guard between two men (Phil. *Flacc.* 13–16, *Leg.* 14–73, 356; Suet. *Cal.* 14. 2, 23. 3, 26. 1; Dio 59. 8. 1, 4–5, 10. 6).

The death of Macro left no strong figure in the court in a position to guide and direct Caligula. As he grew increasingly isolated, and increasingly unsure of how far he could trust those around him, he no doubt turned for guidance and comfort to the remaining members of his family, his three sisters, on whom he showered distinctions. They were honored on his coinage, and given the rights and privileges of the Vestal Virgins. Their names were included in various vows and legal formulae used in making proposals to the senate and, perhaps more remarkably, in the vows of allegiance to the emperor: "I shall not consider myself or my children more precious than I consider Gaius and his sisters." This was an unprecedented gesture, and a sign that the principate was still at a very experimental stage (Suet. *Cal.* 15. 3).

Caligula's close ties to his sisters led to charges of incest, an accusation commonly launched against one's enemies in the ancient world. Suetonius claims that he had been caught in the act with his youngest sister Drusilla by his grandmother Antonia, but admits that the story is just hearsay. As is the general rule with claims of sexual impropriety, there is no way to prove or disprove the charges, but it is to be noted that the Jewish writer Philo, who had reason to hate Caligula as a perceived enemy of his people, and who tends to see issues from a highly moralistic position, does not mention incest among the slurs he casts on the emperor. Moreover, Tacitus, when discussing the charges of incest between one of the sisters, Agrippina, and her son Nero, some twenty years later, attributes Agrippina's behavior to her earlier corruption and, as two examples of her incest, cites a supposed affair with her brother-in-law Lepidus, husband of the late Drusilla, and her marriage to her uncle Claudius. It is evident that he did not accuse Caligula of incest in the books that are now missing. The charges, then, should be viewed with caution.

Caligula suffered a devastating blow in 38 when Drusilla, who seems to have been his favorite sister, died. He retired to his country villa and left his hair and beard untrimmed throughout the period of special public mourning voted by the senate. His reaction may seem extreme, but it was in fact within the bounds of Roman tradition. What is more remarkable is that it was decreed that Drusilla was to be deified, with her own personal shrine and her own priesthood. But it must be remembered that the senate had suggested the same honor for Livia, Augustus' wife (the proposal was vetoed by Tiberius), and Livia was later in fact deified under Claudius. Also, Nero granted the same distinction to his wife and his daughter. Thus, although without precedent, Caligula's gesture was not without imitators (Jos. *AJ* 19. 204; Tac. *Ann.* 14. 2. 4; Suet. *Cal.* 24. 1–3, *Claud.* 11. 2; Dio 59. 22. 6).

Crisis

By the beginning of 39 the deaths of suspected plotters and the consecration of his sister must have brought home to the senate that Caligula was not the compliant youth that they had doubtless anticipated. This realization would have been confirmed by a symbolic act. At the beginning of that year Caligula entered into his second consulship, and continued to hold the office in every year until his death. Although he stepped down not long afterwards, just by assuming the office he broke with the precedent of Tiberius and Augustus (at least after 23 BC), both of whom made a point of avoiding the consulship except on special occasions.

To bring home the reality of his independence as a princeps in his own right, early in 39 Caligula entered the senate chamber in person and denounced the members. He berated them for criticizing Tiberius, and blamed them for the deaths that had blighted his predecessor's reign, calling them lackeys of Sejanus and betrayers of his mother and brothers. The evidence underlying these taunts came from the very documents that he had pretended to destroy at the beginning of his reign. What must have caused most consternation was the news that the trials for *maiestas* would be reintroduced. The senators can hardly be said to have responded with courage, giving formal approval to the reintroduction, and adding self-insult to injury by voting special sacrifices to celebrate the emperor's clemency. It seems remarkable that they persisted in believing that they could still control and manipulate Caligula, who seems to have had a fine perception of the effectiveness of collective fear (Suet. *Cal.* 30. 2; Dio 59. 4. 3, 6. 3, 16. 3).

It is to this period of seriously declining relations between emperor and senate that the sources tend to assign much of Caligula's more bizarre behavior. At some point in 39 boats were brought in from all over the Roman world to be linked in pairs to form a pontoon about three miles long, joining Baiae and Puteoli on opposite sides of part of the Bay of Naples. Caligula donned the breastplate of Alexander and, wearing an oak crown and carrying a shield and spear, rode over from Baiae, followed by his troops, spent the night in Puteoli, and then rode back next day, in a chariot pulled by four racehorses. Once at his original destination he gave away money and held a massive and riotous party. This got out of hand: several of the spectators got drunk, fell into the sea, and drowned. Some of the sources say that Caligula went to this trouble to show that he could ride on water, and thus rival the god Neptune, but his intentions may have been more rational: to demonstrate political power through extravagance and conspicuous consumption. History is full of examples of this: witness Louis XIV and the palace at Versailles, or Henry VIII and Francis on the Field of the Cloth of Gold. Caligula's aim may well have been to demonstrate to the senate, in a vivid and concrete way, how much power he could exercise (Jos. *AJ* 19. 5–6; Suet. *Cal.* 19; Dio 59. 17).

Caligula's demand to be worshiped as a god is a familiar theme of his reign, but it must be put into its proper context. It had become established by the precedent of Julius Caesar that on death an emperor was capable of becoming a god, through a decree of the senate. During their lifetimes, emperors were regularly worshiped as gods in the provinces, there is considerable evidence that they were worshiped as gods in Italy, and even in Rome there are indications that informally they were treated almost as gods. It may be that Caligula overstepped this final boundary, but we must be cautious about the evidence, and in particular we should be cautious about conferring too much historical weight on what might have been casual or jocular comments. A somewhat outrageous sense of humor may lie behind stories that he built a house abutting the Temple of Castor and Pollux to have them as his doorkeepers, or that he planned to have a palace on the Capitol so that he could have Jupiter as his neighbor. A cruel humor could also explain the story told about the general Lucius Vitellius, father of one of the usurpers after Nero. After his return from Syria, Vitellius was asked by the emperor if he could see the moon in his presence. Context is very important here. Vitellius was a notorious sycophant – he later carried the shoe of the emperor Claudius' wife Messallina next to his person to prove his devotion to her. Caligula clearly enjoyed his discomfiture: if Vitellius denied the moon's presence he would risk offending the emperor, but if he assented he would be made to look a fool. In the event he was a match for the occasion. He declared that only gods could see gods (Suet. *Cal.* 22. 2, 4, *Vit.* 2. 5; Dio 59. 27. 4–6, 28. 5, 60. 6. 8).

Did Caligula seek to establish his own formal worship in Rome? It is useful to consider the coin evidence. Had he wanted the world to think of himself as a god, he had every opportunity to depict himself as such on his coins. But despite the richly varied and highly imaginative coin series that characterized his reign there is not even the slightest hint that he considered himself anything but mortal. He does not even wear the radiate crown, a symbol of divine associations that Nero used even though that particular emperor is on record as having refused the offer of worship in Rome. The coins surely are concrete evidence that we should be skeptical toward the stories alleging that Caligula claimed divinity. It is possible that he sought only the worship of his *numen*, the power, especially divine power, that may reside in any person, or of his *genius*, the spirit (with its own divine qualities) that every Roman possessed. Such worship would have come very close to acknowledging that a person was divine, but strictly speaking it did not cross that line, and Caligula could have cited precedents from the reign of Augustus.

Caligula's cruel sense of humor may also have been in part responsible for the story that he appointed his horse consul. He was wildly enthusiastic about horse-racing, as were most other Romans. He treated his favorite horse like a true celebrity – it ate from golden dishes and, before important races, it was kept in what was essentially a gated community, with soldiers posted to stop people disturbing its sleep. But despite the well-established popular belief, the sources do not in fact say that he made his horse consul. They say only that he was *planning* to: Dio says that he *promised* it; Suetonius says that there were rumors of just such a plan (and there is a variant that he made the horse priest of his own cult). This story could well have arisen from a deliberate jibe at the senate. It was the practice for the emperor to designate candidates for the consulship. By 39 Caligula had such a low opinion of the senatorial order that he might possibly have commented that the best candidate he could think of was his horse Incitatus, a quip that his enemies would have been eager to exploit and present in the darkest terms (Suet. *Cal.* 55. 3; Dio 59. 14. 7, 28. 6).

Conspiracy

The tension between Caligula and the senate came to a head in September 39, when he removed the two consuls from office and brought a number of charges against various individuals. The sources speak of a climate of fear, and a wave of what we would call McCarthyism, when friendship with a convicted enemy of the emperor could prove to be dangerous. Just how serious the situation was is very difficult for us to determine now, in the absence of concrete evidence. A visible sign of the struggle was the attempt to emasculate the power of provincial legates. The governors of Dalmatia and Lusitania were recalled, although they did not suffer any disgrace. We have already met the most important of the commanders, Lucius Vitellius, the legate of Syria, where he conducted a successful campaign dealing with the Parthians. He was reputedly an object of suspicion and was brought home. Two other commanders were not so lucky. Calvisius Sabinus, governor of Pannonia, was stripped of his command and charged, along with his wife, probably with *maiestas*. They escaped their fate by the traditional device of suicide. Probably the most high-profile of the powerful military victims was Cornelius Lentulus Gaetulicus, the legate of Upper Germany. Gaetulicus had certainly allowed discipline and order among the troops to deteriorate, but his downfall can not be ascribed simply to incompetence, since in October 39 we have a record of celebrations held in Rome to mark the discovery of Gaetulicus' "nefarious plots."[3] It is possible that he was part of a wider conspiracy, perhaps connected with people from within Caligula's own house. In late 39 the emperor traveled north, accompanied by a large entourage, including a unit of the imperial guard and members of his family: his sister Agrippina and probably his other sister Livilla, and Lepidus, husband of the dead Drusilla and reputedly one of Caligula's closest friends. Once the party was well away from the protective custody of Rome, Lepidus was put to death, his throat cut by a tribune of the guard. Perhaps he had been con- spiring with Gaetulicus, but there is no explicit evidence for this, and it may be that there were two separate and unrelated plots (Sen. *Ep.* 4. 7; Tac. *Hist.* 1. 48. 2–3; Suet. *Cal.* 24. 3, 26. 3, 39. 1, *Galb.* 6. 2; Dio 59. 20. 1, 21. 4, 22. 5–9, 23. 8, 27. 4).

The situation had even murkier aspects. Both of Caligula's sisters were implicated, and both were charged with having been lovers of Lepidus. The perceived political crimes of Roman imperial women were often concealed under the cloak of sexual misconduct, and such may have been the case on this occasion. As a special punishment Agrippina was obliged to carry the urn containing her alleged lover's ashes back to Rome, before she was banished, along with her sister, to the Pontian islands. One might wonder why Agrippina should have wanted to conspire against Caligula, since she enjoyed a privileged situation. It is possible that the cause was one of the basic strands that run through Roman history, the obsession with dynasty. Agrippina had an infant son, for whom she no doubt harbored ambitions (they were to be fulfilled, since he became the emperor Nero). By the year 39 Caligula had been married three times. His first wife died while he was still young. He married a second time (the wife's name is uncertain), not long after his recovery from illness, and shortly afterwards divorced this second wife to marry Lollia Paulina, one of wealthiest women in Rome, who carried the bills of sale of her jewels on her person for the benefit of those who could not believe what they were worth. While Lollia could provide much-needed cash, and Caligula's extravagance was no doubt exacting its toll, she was no more successful than his previous two wives in providing him with the most important benefit, an heir. So in 39 Caligula put aside Lollia and married again. This time his bride was Milonia Caesonia, who a month after the marriage gave birth to a daughter. Agrippina may at this stage have been dismayed to discover that Caligula was, contrary to expectations, able to father a viable offspring, and that the prospects of her son had accordingly become much dimmer. She may also have felt that his alienation of the senate placed the prospects of the whole family in jeopardy, and for a combination of those reasons have thrown in her lot with Lepidus (Persius 6. 47; Plin. *NH* 7. 39, 9. 117; Jos. *AJ* 19. 11, 192–3; Juv. *Sat.* 6. 615–17; Suet. *Cal.* 25, 50. 2; Dio 58. 25. 2, 59. 8. 7, 12. 1, 23. 7, 28. 7).

Britain

The removal of Gaetulicus set the stage for one of the most infamous episodes of Caligula's career, his projected invasion of Britain. The sources tell us that he set out on campaign in 39 for purely frivolous reasons, lacking many of the proper preparations, engaged in some farcical maneuvers in Germany, then advanced up to the English Channel. Once there he drew up his troops, went out to sea, came back again, told his troops to advance into the water, collect shells, then take them back for the victory celebrations as spoils of the Ocean. This expedition has been seen as one of reckless madness. In fact it can be justified in terms of realpolitik. In the first place it is important to note the conditions at the time in Britain, where elements friendly to Rome in the south of the island were being gradually subdued by peoples led by the powerful king Cunobelinus and his fiercely nationalistic son Caratacus. This posed a serious threat to Roman Gaul, since the Celts had strong family links on both sides of the Channel.

Claims that inadequate provision was made for the enterprise should be treated with caution. The ancient accounts, when talking about the wisdom of the invasion, say that proper planning did not take place. But in a different context, where the *irrationality* of the emperor is at issue, they essentially contradict themselves, and speak of recruitment on a massive scale, as evidence of megalomania: Dio gives a figure of some 200,000 men. In fact we can confirm that responsible preparations *were* made, again from the material evidence, this time in the form of inscriptions. Caligula died before he could conquer Britain, and it would be left to his successor Claudius to carry out the actual invasion in AD 43. In that later invasion Claudius would use three of the four legions from the Rhine army. They would, of course, have to be at least partially replaced. Two legions were raised to help fill the gap that they left, XV and XXII, and the inscriptions on tombstones, where the military careers of the men who served in these units are often laid out in some detail, shows that these two legions were raised by Caligula. The evidence indicates, then, that the preparations were thorough and responsible (Smallwood 1967: 278; Tac. *Ag.* 13. 2, *Germ.* 37. 5; Suet. *Cal.* 43, *Galb.* 6. 2–3; Dio 59. 22. 2).

What of Caligula's behavior in Germany? The sources claim that he crossed the Rhine at the head of his troops, then ran back in panic, and repeated this procedure at different locations. But the underlying strategy of any projected invasion of Britain must be understood. Such an enterprise would isolate the Roman army from its bases. It would be dangerous enough under the best circumstances, but suicidal if the German frontier were insecure, since a German incursion could cut off the Roman expedition completely. We know that the conspirator Gaetulicus had been a lax commander and that discipline had been allowed to lapse among the Roman legions on the Rhine. He was replaced by the future emperor Galba, a soldier of considerable accomplishment and a strict disciplinarian, who lost no time in whipping the legions into shape. The securing of the Rhine frontier was a crucial preliminary to the British campaign. This strategy would not require a full-scale expedition; indeed, experience would have taught the Romans that a major incursion could in fact lead to disaster. What was needed was a series of raids in the Rhine area to overawe the Germans, to give the impression that the Romans were battle-ready and in an aggressive mood. This could provide an explanation for Caligula's limited forays into German territory (Suet. *Cal.* 45. 1–2, 51. 2–3, *Galb.* 6. 2–3; Dio 59. 21. 3).

What about the incident at the Channel? It is important to note that Caligula left the Channel in March at the latest. The month is important, since he departed before what Romans deemed the safe sailing season. During the winter months sea voyages were not undertaken except in extreme emergencies. It is highly unlikely that Caligula would have risked a crossing with his troops of a dangerous channel during the winter months, and we can therefore probably discount any kind of invasion at that time. We do know that during this general period Adminius, one of the sons of Cunobelinus, defected from Britain to the Romans. The sources do not connect his defection with Caligula's activities on the coast, but the emperor's presence does provide the best context, and Adminius' arrival would have been a godsend to Caligula. He had left Rome amid public expectations that he would invade Britain. The sorry state of the German frontier may well have convinced him that this was not feasible (it would in the event take several campaigning seasons in Germany to render it feasible, in the next reign). It is perhaps not surprising, then, that he exploited Adminius' surrender and exaggerated its significance by presenting it as the conquest of the whole island. The story of the shells can probably be taken more or less at face value. In the Roman literary tradition relating to the anticipated conquest of Britain, one of the persistent themes is that it involved the conquest of Oceanus, the great Ocean that encircled the civilized world. This would be the theme that Caligula would want to stress in his celebrations on his return to Rome, and the shells would have been a perfect device to symbolize the supposed conquest (Suet. *Cal.* 44–7; Dio 59. 21. 3, 25. 1–3; Orosius *con. pag.* 7. 5. 5).

Africa

A similar rationality may be discerned in measures taken in north Africa. The province of Africa was anomalous. It was exposed to military threats, but since it was a prosperous region in which senators had invested heavily and owned large estates, there was clearly a pronounced senatorial interest. The province was one of a very small number that were designated as "public," whose governors were appointed by the senate, but which housed troops: in Africa's case, one legion, under the command of the senatorial governor. This created an anomaly, since military commanders were regularly appointed by the emperor. Under Caligula, the legion was removed from the governor's control and placed under a legate appointed by the emperor. This was a prudent measure and the alternative would have been far more draconian: to remove Africa totally from the jurisdiction of the senate. The arrangement was far from perfect, and there were occasional jurisdictional tensions, which were not solved until Severus created the separate imperial province of Numidia (Tac. *Hist.* 4. 48; Dio 59. 20. 7).

West of the province of Africa lay the Kingdom of Mauretania, stretching some 800 miles to the Atlantic coast. At the time of Caligula's accession it was nominally an independent entity, very closely allied to Rome and ruled by its pro-Roman king, Ptolemy, who had assisted his allies by fighting against the rebellious Tacfarinas during Tiberius' reign. It is difficult to determine the precise sequence of events, but at some point, possibly 40, Ptolemy was summoned to Rome and executed. The circumstances of his death are generally attributed to Caligula's ruthless irresponsibility – explanations vary from his anger at being upstaged by Ptolemy's splendid costume at a theatrical performance to a desire to get his hands on the king's wealth. But the loss of Mauretanian independence was perhaps inevitable: such was the general fate of Rome's client kingdoms, and the area may already have experienced some years of direct Roman rule as early as the late 30s BC. Its incorporation into the larger imperial structure can be understood in strategic terms: the constant rebellions in the region, especially that of Tacfarinas, must have brought home to the Romans how exposed the province of Africa was, and Ptolemy and his predecessors had not shown themselves to be competent in providing protection either for Africa or for the Roman colonies within Mauretania. The change in Mauretania's status can be seen as complementing the reform of the command structure that took place in the province of Africa. That said, we might have expected Ptolemy to be able to enjoy a comfortable and honorable retirement, and it is possible that he had somehow been involved in one of the plots against Caligula. The region was pacified, and it was determined that because of its size it would be divided into two separate provinces, although the implementation of this last arrangement may have occurred after Caligula's death (Sen. *Tranq.* 11. 12; Plin. *NH* 5. 2; Tac. *Ann.* 4. 23. 1, 26. 4; Suet. *Cal.* 35. 1; Dio 59. 25. 1, 60. 9. 5).

The Jews

The one sphere outside Italy where a marked deterioration can be clearly discerned during Caligula's reign is that of Rome's relations with the Jews. The issues were complex, and involved two different Jewish communities: those who lived in the original area of Jewish settlement loosely referred to as Judea and the Jews of the diaspora, especially in the Egyptian city of Alexandria, where the Jewish immigrants lived in awkward proximity to the predominant Greek population. It would be unfair to brand Caligula as antisemitic. He had excellent relations with individual Jewish leaders, most notably Herod Agrippa, and his behavior toward the Jews was probably no more cavalier than it was toward other groups. But the particular national-istic and religious sentiments of the Jews required a deft diplomatic touch, and this he was sorely lacking.

It was in Alexandria where the problems first arose – ironically, since down to the time of Caligula Alexandrian Jews had looked upon the Romans as the defenders of their political and religious rights. The prefect of Egypt,

Avillius Flaccus, a man appointed by Tiberius in 32, had governed with
energy and ability at the beginning of his term but seems to have started to
lose his grip on things by the time of Caligula's accession, omitting, for
instance, to forward to Rome a resolution from Alexandrian Jews honoring
the new emperor; the Jewish writer Philo claimed that Flaccus was under the
influence of extreme Greek nationalists. The growing tension exploded in
38 on the arrival in Alexandria of Herod Agrippa, who paraded through the
city in a showy display of his imperial favor, boasting of the benefits he could
bring to local Jews. This provoked serious disorder, during which synagogues
were burned and demolished. Agrippa himself escaped only by slipping out
of the city. Flaccus seems to have believed that extremists on the Jewish side
had provoked the unrest, and imposed strict controls on the Jews, moving
them into two defined quarters of the city. If anything, he seems to have
aggravated the problems. Tensions increased and led to considerable violence,
even murder, which Flaccus tried to control by the arrest of prominent Jewish
leaders. By October 38 Flaccus had been replaced by the more diplomatic
Gaius Pollio, who managed to maintain a level of calm in the city. Delegates
from both the Greek and the Jewish communities, the latter led by Philo,
were sent to Rome to present their cases, probably meeting the emperor in
the year 40 when he had returned from his northern expedition.

Philo has left us a vivid account of his meeting with Caligula, held in a
mood of near-desperation on the part of the Jewish delegation, since while in
Rome they received news that the Temple at Jerusalem was to be converted
into a center of the imperial cult (see below). The meeting took place in the
imperial residence on the Esquiline hill. The Jewish delegation followed
the emperor as he flitted from room to room checking on the furnishing
and the decorations, the situation aggravated by a string of cryptic jokes
about Jewish customs, and the reputed comment that Jews should be
considered unfortunate lunatics rather than criminals for not believing that
he was a god. In the event, the discussions had no practical impact, since
Caligula was assassinated before he had reached a decision (Phil. *Flacc.* 25–
62, *Leg.* 349–67).

The precise sequence of events in Judea is unclear, but there can be no
doubt that they also took a serious turn for the worse during Caligula's reign.
Tacitus made a famous comment about Judea that "under Tiberius all was
quiet," and while this was a considerable exaggeration, the problems in that
period were mainly of a local character, and settled by the suspension of
Pontius Pilate, prefect of Judea, by Vitellius, governor of Syria, to whom
prefects of Judea were subordinate. On his accession, Caligula sent out a new
official, the little-known Marullus. The appointment was largely irrelevant,

since events took such a serious turn that they required the direct intervention of the new legate of Syria, Publius Petronius. Trouble first broke out in the coastal town of Jamnia, probably in the winter of 39, when Jews tore down an altar to the imperial cult. An enraged Caligula responded by decreeing that the Temple of Jerusalem would be converted into an imperial shrine, along with a huge statue of himself in the guise of Jupiter. Repercussions were inevitable. Riots broke out in Syria, leading to attacks on Jews and the burning of the synagogue. Petronius used his diplomatic skill as best he could, but was met by the adamant refusal of the Jewish leaders to accept what they saw as the desecration of the Temple. Demonstrations throughout Judea, and a deliberate decision to neglect the harvest, convinced Petronius that a disaster was in the offing. He shrewdly intimated to the sculptors in Sidon who were working on the massive statue that they should work slowly, and informed Caligula of how serious the situation had become. The emperor reputedly refused to believe Petronius and suspected him of receiving a bribe, but was in any case dissuaded from going ahead with his plans for the Temple by his good friend Herod Agrippa, who had been so dismayed by the scheme that he fell seriously ill (Phil. *Leg.* 188–338; Jos. *AJ* 18. 261–309, *BJ* 2. 184–203; Tac. *Hist.* 5. 9. 2).

How far Caligula can be held personally responsible for the serious disintegration of good relations is difficult to determine, so confused are our sources of information. Jewish writers like Josephus and Philo were persuaded that he hated the Jews and was planning a massive war against them. This is not convincing. Romans probably found it difficult to distinguish between religious and political fervor. Acts such as the destruction of the altar at Jamnia would have been seen as a challenge to suzerainty, and the fervor of the more extreme zealous Jewish factions certainly aggravated the situation. After Caligula's death Jews in Alexandria, bent on evening scores, drew on previously stored caches of weapons and went on a rampage against the Greeks. This was but one of a long series of bitter clashes following Caligula's death, leading eventually to the final confrontation and the devastating sack of Jerusalem fewer than thirty years later (Jos. *AJ* 19. 278–91).

Final Years

Caligula began his journey back to Rome from his northern expedition in spring 40, and was in the vicinity of the city by May 30; however – perhaps because of fear of assassination – he avoided actually entering until the end of August, when he celebrated his ovation, a lesser form of triumph, for his "victory" over the Britons. Relations with the senate thereafter grew increasingly tense, and the number of executions and treason trials multiplied. It is very difficult to see any pattern in the individual episodes, and whether there was a coordinated conspiracy against him from as early as 40 is difficult to say. Even allowing for exaggeration, the stories from this phase are particularly horrific, of senators being whipped to death, or beheaded, and of individuals being executed in the presence of family members. As before, Caligula exploited the power of collective fear, inciting senators to turn against their fellows. As a body they responded with their traditional servility, voting him festivals and thanksgivings, and, ironically, granting him a bodyguard when he entered the chamber, presumably to protect him from the very men who were voting for the protection (Sen. *Ep.* 29. 6, *Ben.* 2. 12. 1, 21. 5, *Ira* 2. 33. 3–6, 3. 18. 3–19, *Tranq.* 14. 4–10; Jos. *AJ* 19. 32–6; Tac. *Ag.* 4. 1; Suet. *Cal.* 16. 4, 26. 3, 27. 4–28; Dio 59. 25. 5b–9, 26. 1–4; Orosius *con. pag* 7. 5. 10).

Of the three main groups in Roman society, people, senate, and army, Caligula had succeeded in retaining the broad loyalty of only the first. He had begun as an immensely popular figure with the ordinary people, and he seems to have enjoyed the affection of the masses to the end. Some of his measures were decidedly populist, such as the extension of festivals like the Saturnalia. Others have perhaps more serious political and constitutional overtones. He restored to the people an ancient constitutional right that had passed from them to the senate under Tiberius: the process by which magistrates were elected by the popular assemblies. Under Tiberius the elections were transferred to the senate and the assemblies were limited to ratifying the selection already made. Caligula's gesture was, of course, largely symbolic, since the emperor would have had control over the choice of candidates, and could control appointments to the two highest offices, the consulship and praetorship. In the end even this symbolic gesture had to be rescinded, since there seems to have been little appetite among the populace at large for involvement in a process that was essentially empty (Suet. *Cal.* 14. 3, 16. 2–3; Dio 59. 6. 4, 9. 6, 20. 3–4, 28. 10).

Yet on occasion Caligula demonstrated a willingness to suffer unpopularity if circumstances demanded it. Perhaps his most innovative measure was to institute a number of direct taxes previously unknown to the Romans. He placed levies on taverns, slaves, and the hiring of slaves. There was a fixed tax on all edibles sold in the city and a tax of 2.5 per cent on the sum involved in legal actions; there was even a duty on the earnings of prostitutes. Italians had previously been exempt from such direct taxes, thus enjoying an unfair advantage over other parts of the empire. The new measures were resented and Claudius gradually abolished most of them (an indication that the treasury was not in such a financial mess during his reign as is generally assumed). But the final test was that after his murder the people did not seem to look upon Caligula's removal as a blow for liberty. The popular reaction in the theater at the news was distress – Josephus churlishly says that it was just what you might expect, since the audience was made up of women, children, and slaves. Later in the day, however, similar sentiments were again manifested, when an angry crowd gathered in the Forum and demanded that the assassins be arrested (Jos. *AJ* 19. 28, 128–9, 159, 228; Suet. *Cal.* 40; Dio 59. 28. 8).

The level of hostility between Caligula and the senate was no doubt highly exaggerated in the tradition that established itself following his death. One of the recurring themes in the sources is that of the eleventh-hour escape for political figures who incurred the wrath of the emperor and were marked for grim destruction, saved only by the intervention of fate in the guise of the assassin's dagger. Seneca had supposedly faced execution and survived only because it was thought that consumption of the lungs would do the job anyhow. Memmius Regulus, governor of Moesia, Macedonia, and Achaea, Cassius Longinus, proconsul of Asia, and Publius Petronius were all reputedly slated to be put to death but were reprieved at the last minute by Caligula's own demise. In reality, many seemed to have flourished under Caligula, and these accounts sound like hastily concocted stories to explain why some died while others survived and did well. The senators had to face the truth that many of their body accommodated themselves to Caligula, the majority surviving unscathed and possibly even collaborating against the courageous few who took a stand. In fact, the senate as a whole not only passively condoned Caligula's actions but were eager to heap honors on him (Phil. *Leg.* 330–4; Jos. *AJ* 18. 305, 19. 8–10; *BJ* 2. 203; Suet. *Cal.* 57. 1; Dio 59. 19. 7–8, 29. 3–4).

Conspiracy and Death

Caligula could have lost some popular support and alienated the senate and still have survived. But the one element whose support was crucial was the army, and especially that section of the army located in the city of Rome itself, the praetorian guard. As noted earlier, his succession had been the first where the overt use of the imperial guard played an important role in determining events. His reign would also be the first in which the guard played a subsequent role in the ousting of an emperor. Unfortunately, there is little certainty as to how this came about; Caligula's final days are among the best-documented yet least-understood episodes of classical antiquity.

Opposition to him seems to have grown toward the end of 40 and to have become more focused by the beginning of the next year. The main conspirator was supposedly a tribune in the guard, Cassius Chaerea. The imperial guard was not, of course, motivated by sentiment. They were an especially privileged unit of the army, whose existence was dependent on the continued existence of the principate. If an emperor by his conduct placed the institution in jeopardy, the guard was more likely to switch its allegiance than betray the institution. Josephus depicts Cassius Chaerea as a noble idealist, fighting for republican principles, a role that challenges belief. Dio provides more colorful information – that his opposition was personal; that he had an effeminate voice, and that Caligula used to make fun of him when giving the watchword. We are given the unbelievable information that this tribune of the guard went the rounds, recruiting others, even his commanders and a number of prominent senators. This is clearly nonsense. Chaerea was involved, no doubt, but would surely have been used as a tool by some more powerful figure (Jos. *AJ* 19. 17–23, 37–69; Tac. *Ann*. 1. 32. 5, Suet. *Cal*. 56. 1; Dio 59. 29. 1–2).

Late in January 41, during a theatrical performance on the Palatine hill, Caligula made his way to his palace for lunch. In an underground tunnel Cassius Chaerea and another tribune struck him down. We are told that the imperial guard began ransacking the palace and came across Claudius hiding in terror behind a curtain. The guard reputedly decided it would be an amusing gesture to make him emperor, and carried him off to their camp. Now, it is striking that the supposedly terrified Claudius soon recovered his composure. While the senate indulged in an abstract debate on the restoration of the republic, he organized the praetorians behind him, bribed them with a massive handout of cash, and sent the senate clear and explicit instructions that he was in charge. There can be little doubt that the soldiers were aiming not for the end of the imperial system but for a change of emperor, and it is hard not to suspect that, even though he kept himself at arm's length, Claudius was solidly behind what happened. So we should not see the assassination as a blow for liberty to remove a vicious tyrant. It was a fairly conventional attempt by one party to seize power from another. Claudius was certainly looked upon as a usurper – he did not attend a senate meeting for months and, when he did, he adopted the Caligulan precaution of using a bodyguard (Sen. *Const*. 18. 3; Jos. *AJ* 19. 99–271; Suet. *Cal*. 58. 2–3; Dio 59. 29. 7, 60. 1).

Caligula's brief reign was a disaster, but the Romans had only themselves to blame. The army, in the shape of the imperial guard, injected into the imperial system the very worst feature of the final century of the Roman republic: the use of military force to determine political outcomes. The senate certainly did not emerge from Caligula's reign with honor. They may have been under military pressure at the outset; but they have to take the lion's share of the blame for the unprecedented and massive powers bestowed on a totally inexperienced youth. Moreover, they seem to have been willing to respond to each successive humiliation with even more fulsome flattery. Most tragically of all, thirteen years after his death they went through an almost identical process in handing over absolute power to another young man similarly lacking in the experience or the talent for the task: Nero.

Notes

1 Decree from Assos, in Smallwood 1967: 33.
2 Smallwood 1967: 3. 10 (Acts of the Arval Brethren): "because on this day he was acclaimed emperor by the senate."
3 Smallwood 1967: 19. 17 (Acts of the Arval Brethren): "because of the wicked plots of Cn. Lentulus Gaetulicus against Gaius Germanicus."

Further Reading

J. P. V. D. Balsdon, *The Emperor Gaius* (Oxford, 1934; repr. Westport, Conn., 1977)
A. A. Barrett, *Caligula, the Corruption of Power* (New Haven, 1991)
A. Ferrill, *Caligula: Emperor of Rome* (London, 1991)
D. W. Hurley, *An Historical and Historiographical Commentary on Suetonius' Life of C. Caligula* (Atlanta, 1993)
S. Wilkinson, *Caligula* (London and New York, 2005)
P. Wiseman, *Josephus, Flavius, Death of an Emperor* (Exeter, 1991)

IV

Claudius

Donna W. Hurley

When in the early afternoon of January 24, AD 41, the emperor Caligula left the entertainment that he was watching on the Palatine, his uncle, Tiberius Claudius Nero Germanicus, was among his companions. Caligula became separated from his immediate company before he was killed, and in the mayhem that followed, an understandably fearful Claudius took refuge in the palace complex. Caligula's loyal German bodyguards had struck out randomly, and no one seemed safe. By one report, Claudius tried to make himself inconspicuous in a dark and out-of-the-way space, hiding behind a curtain covering a door to a balcony. His presence was betrayed by his feet sticking out. An ordinary member of the praetorian guard, appropriately named Gratus ("Pleasing" or "Welcome"), chanced to find him cowering there and immediately saluted him as *imperator*. Claudius was put into a litter and hurried off to the praetorian camp located just outside the walls of the city. Witnesses feared that an innocent man was being taken away for punishment (Suet. *Claud.* 10. 1–2; Dio 60. 1. 2–3; Jos. *AJ* 19. 212–20).

That is one account. An alternative narrative describes a less spontaneous salutation and abduction. In the immediate aftermath of the assassination, the praetorians met and debated what course of action to adopt. They decided that it was in their interest that a single individual should come to power, and further that such a person should owe his position to them. Their prestige and extra pay derived from the protection that they provided the emperor. Claudius was a suitable candidate, and they deliberately set out to look for him and kidnap him to their headquarters (Jos. *AJ* 19. 162–5).

Both narratives raise the question of leadership. It is scarcely plausible that a random soldier had the temerity to recognize Claudius and name him emperor on the spot. Nor is it likely that the praetorians held a meeting after they knew that Caligula was dead, assessed their interests in the midst of crisis, and only then went looking for him. At least one of the praetorian prefects must have given the order to remove Claudius to the praetorian camp. There were two: Marcus Arrecinus Clemens, whom our sources credit with sympathy for the assassins, and another, whose name is not known. Claudius replaced one (or both) as soon as he became emperor. But it is not surprising that the ancient sources avoid spelling out the roles they played that day. Eagerness to exchange an undependable emperor for a potentially more acceptable one had to be balanced against the consequences of failing to protect the life in their charge (Jos. *AJ* 19. 37–45).

The conspiracy that led to Caligula's assassination was perhaps not so much a single plot as an action taken by an untidy grouping of persons with disparate goals. If senators were involved, they would have shared a fantasy of renewed class power. Caligula's senior freedmen had an interest because they wanted to maintain their privileged positions as they observed their patron's downward spiral. Two senior officers of the guard, the praetorian tribunes Cassius Chaerea and Cornelius Sabinus, and those directly under their command, performed the bloody deed. They allegedly had personal reasons for finding the emperor detestable. Many persons may have been complicit, but even more must have sensed that Caligula's arrogant and erratic behavior would not be tolerated indefinitely and have been unsurprised by the assassination. Claudius himself could not have been blind to the possibilities that would be created if his nephew were eliminated, and in the essay on Caligula in this volume it is suggested that he might even have played an active role (Jos. *AJ* 19. 17–69; Tac. *Ann.* 11. 29; Suet. *Cal.* 56. 1; Dio 59. 25. 8, 29. 1–2).

The senate was already meeting by the time Claudius was on his way to the camp. As soon as its members could collect themselves, they convened under the leadership of the consuls. They were protected by the three cohorts of the *vigiles* as they talked of restoring the republic. When they learned that Claudius was in the praetorian camp, they sent a delegation to persuade him to join them and to submit to their authority. He was, after all, a senator too. Claudius refused. Acceptance would acknowledge his dependence on them; and furthermore, separation from his military protectors could quite possibly prove fatal. Caligula's wife and daughter had already been killed, and Claudius was a family member as well. The Jewish historian Josephus emphasizes the role played by the Judean prince Agrippa (popularly known as Herod Agrippa) as a go-between with the senate. He encouraged Claudius to hold firm. The senate announced a second meeting for early next morning, this one intentionally held on the Capitoline hill, the seat of republican tradition. Only a hundred brave members attended. The possibility of a restored republic was abandoned, and the senators contemplated the alternative of choosing a princeps from among themselves. Marcus Vinicius, married to one of Caligula's sisters, and Valerius Asiaticus, a wealthy Gaul, put themselves forward. But the compromise of a senatorial principate proved beyond reach as well. The *vigiles*, recognizing that they were no match for the professional soldiers holding Claudius, deserted the cause, and the very brief interregnum came to an end.

In the meantime, Claudius had accepted the oath of allegiance from the praetorians and promised them a generous reward for their services and loyalty. Gifts in return for military support were not without precedent: Germanicus, Tiberius, and Caligula had all been generous. But this was the first time that payment was made in direct connection with accession to the principate. When Claudius learned that the senate had acknowledged that they were not in control, he had the praetorians take him to the Palatine hill, the seat of imperial power, and summoned the senate to meet him there. This tale of a reluctant emperor, abducted against his will and helpless before necessity, served two functions in the Claudius story as it came to be told. First, it could be used to refute any suggestion that he himself was involved in the assassination or had purchased the principate. At the same time, the image of a passive and fearful Claudius dragged from behind a curtain conforms to the characterization that hounded him (and continues to this day): the perception that he was undignified, weak, and manipulated by others (Jos. *AJ* 19. 166–84, 229–60, 265–6; Suet. *Claud.* 10. 3–4; Dio 60. 1. 1, 3a–4).

Early Years

Claudius was born Tiberius Claudius Drusus on August 1, 10 BC, in Gaul in the town of Lugdunum (present-day Lyons). Lugdunum was the principal town of Gallia Comata, central and northern Gaul, and the site of an altar where provincial dignitaries gathered annually to renew their allegiance to Rome. His parents were there for ceremonies celebrating the dedication of the altar when Claudius, the last of their three children, was born. He would always be associated with his Gallic birthplace. His father, Nero Claudius Drusus, was the younger son of Augustus' wife, Livia Drusilla, and her first husband. Her other son, Tiberius, would become emperor. Claudius' mother, Antonia the Younger, was a daughter of Marc Antony and Octavia, Augustus' sister. Drusus led the Roman forces that were advancing into the Alps and Germany from 15 BC until he died on campaign in 9. He posthumously received the honorific *cognomen* of Germanicus, and his descendants would carry the name as well. This lineage promised much.

Drusus and Antonia's first-born was Claudius' elder brother Germanicus (his birth name is unattested), born about 15 BC. He was adopted by his uncle Tiberius in AD 4, at which point both he and Tiberius left the Claudian family and joined the Julian, and he became Germanicus Julius Caesar, known to history simply as Germanicus. He held responsible military commands and administrative posts and was in line for succession to the principate when he died young in AD 19. The memory of this popular young prince remained a factor in court politics until the Julio-Claudian line came to an end with the emperor Nero. The middle child was Livilla. She, like all imperial princesses, was born to the task of marrying for the advantage of her family. She would become enmeshed in court intrigue and be put to death in AD 31.

When his brother Germanicus became a Julian, Claudius' birth name changed to Tiberius Claudius Nero Germanicus. He should have followed a career path similar to that of his brother, but the promise of his birth could not be realized, for his physical condition would not allow it (Suet. *Claud.* 2. 1; Sen. *Apoc.* 6. 1). Claudius almost certainly suffered from cerebral palsy, congenital neurological damage. The condition does not necessarily affect brain function, and his adult achievements show him to have been of reasonable intelligence. His affliction was not particularly severe in any case. The right side of his body was weak, and this caused him to walk awkwardly. His head shook, he drooled, and his speech was affected. Stress exacerbated these symptoms, but they were less noticeable when he was at rest or relaxed. He could deliver a speech satisfactorily if it was prepared ahead of time. Spontaneous expression was less successful. But the ancient world did not tolerate physical impairment kindly (Suet. *Claud.* 4. 6, 30; Dio 60. 2.1–2, 12. 3; Sen. *Apoc.* 1. 2, 5. 2–3, 7. 3; Juv. *Sat.* 6. 622–3).

As a child and a young man, Claudius was often kept from public attention. He was not allowed to sit in the imperial box at the games or participate in ceremonies where his appearance would embarrass the family. His coming-of-age ceremony was performed as inconspicuously as possible, and his aborted career advanced only through innocuous and largely honorific priesthoods. According to the wisdom of the time, his unseemly conduct was his fault and could be corrected by imitation of proper behavior, and so he was encouraged to find acceptable mentors. But his education was not neglected, and he remained within the family, judged presentable enough to be used, like a woman, as a pawn in dynastic marriages. He was betrothed twice and married three times in the years before he became emperor (Suet. *Claud.* 2, 4. 1–5).

The first plan was that Claudius should marry a cousin, Aemilia Lepida, the daughter of Lucius Aemilius Paulus and the younger Julia, who was a granddaughter of Augustus. This marriage would keep the prestige of her birth within the larger family. The betrothal was broken off when her parents were charged with adultery and treason in AD 8. Soon afterwards Claudius was given Livia Medullina Camilla, who was connected with important families of the day as well as descended from the legendary Camillus of the fourth century BC. She died on their wedding day. The next choice was Plautia Urgulanilla, whose father had been a military companion of Tiberius and whose grandmother Urgulania was a close friend of Livia. Claudius and she were married by AD 12 and had two children. A boy, Drusus, died in an odd accident perhaps around 24 or 25 when he choked on a piece of fruit that he was juggling. An infant daughter, Claudia, was removed from the household shortly after Claudius had divorced Urgulanilla at about the same time on suspicion of adultery and homicide. This child's paternity was suspect because of her mother's unfaithfulness. Claudius next married Aelia Paetina, who belonged to the family of the powerful praetorian prefect Lucius Aelius Sejanus. The choice bears witness to Sejanus' immense influence during the third decade of the century. A daughter, Antonia, was born to Claudius and Aelia by 29 at the latest. His next wife was Valeria Messallina. Her story and that of his last wife Agrippina will emerge within the narrative of his reign (Suet. *Claud.* 26. 1–2, 27. 1).

The decision that Claudius be relegated permanently to the family's margin was taken in the reign of Augustus. The first emperor's will makes this clear: Claudius received only a modest legacy and was an heir in the "third degree," a level that became active only by default of the first two. It was an empty gesture that promised no money. He fared no better under Tiberius. At one point, perhaps shortly after Augustus' death in AD 14, Claudius hoped for a chance to stand for the quaestorship, the first stage of the *cursus honorum*. Tiberius dismissed his petition and insultingly offered cash and the empty trappings of office instead. The equestrian order, however, of which Claudius was a member by birth, appointed him its representative for its dealings with the imperial family. The senate also tendered respect when it voted a grant for the rebuilding of his house after it had been destroyed by fire, although Tiberius made this recognition meaningless when he paid for the new house himself. Claudius, rebuffed, is said to have retired to amuse himself with the vices of which he would always be accused: wine, dicing, and the company of unsuitable companions. Tiberius' will, like that of Augustus, again made him an heir in only the "third degree" (Suet. *Claud.* 4. 7, 5–6).

Under Caligula, Claudius fared both better and worse. He finally entered the senate, filling his first magisterial office when Caligula made him suffect consul along with himself for July and August of AD 37, the first year of his reign. Caligula was the only surviving son of Germanicus and needed to support his position by means of his family, the only credential that he had. His uncle Claudius was his closest male relative and would accordingly be promoted. Aelia Paetina, whose connection with the disgraced and dead Sejanus was now a serious impediment, was divorced to make room for a union consistent with Claudius' newly more prominent status, and it was probably early in Caligula's reign that he married his third wife, Valeria Messallina. As the great-granddaughter of Octavia through Antonia the Elder, sister to Claudius' mother, Antonia the Younger, she was part of the extended imperial family and thus Claudius' first cousin once removed. Claudius and Messallina had two children: a daughter, Octavia, born in 38 or 39 or, at the latest, early 40, and a son, Tiberius Claudius Caesar Germanicus, born three weeks after Claudius became emperor in January 41. This boy would later be known as Britannicus. Thus the change of regime benefited Claudius in many ways. But on the negative side he was the almost constant butt of Caligula's cruel humor. He was nearly dismissed from his suffect consulship when he was slow erecting statues at Caligula's request. He was forced to be a defendant in serious court procedures, and once, when he greeted Caligula at Lugdunum, as the head of a senatorial delegation, he was thrown into the river. Dinner guests were encouraged to throw food at him. This was Claudius' position when the events of January 41 took place, and he found himself, at the age of fifty, emperor (Suet. *Claud.* 7–9, 26. 2, 27. 1; Dio 59. 6. 5–6).

Accession

Claudius came to the principate a man living in fear. It took him a month to face the senate again after his initial meeting on the day after Caligula's murder, and when he did, he took an armed guard. His position was complicated by an ambivalent relationship with his predecessor. He could neither appear to make use of his nephew's coat-tails nor repudiate him entirely, since his own claim to the principate was precisely the same as Caligula's, that of family alone. Claudius had no military experience and virtually no experience of any kind in matters of state business. On the one hand, in order to separate himself from Caligula, he refused to ratify his predecessor's *acta*, destroyed the papers and poisons that he had left behind, recalled the people he had exiled, and abolished the law of treason. On the other, he did not declare the day when Caligula was killed a day of public rejoicing. He did have his statues removed, but quietly and at night. It seemed best to put the circumstances of his own accession behind him quickly. He declared amnesty for all those who had flirted with the idea of a republic, and the possibility of senatorial complicity in Caligula's death was not pursued. But an emperor could not really afford to condone tyrannicide, and so the praetorians who had put their hands to the deed were executed (Jos. *AJ* 19. 268–70; Suet. *Claud.* 11. 1; Dio 60. 3. 4–4. 5).

As had Caligula before him, Claudius immediately brought his family to center stage, a tactic all the more necessary because, unlike his predecessors, he was not a member of the *gens Iulia*. He remained a Claudian but indicated that he was assuming the role of family head by adding to his name the Julian *cognomen* of "Caesar," which was on its way to becoming an imperial title. He declared that his favorite oath was the one he took in the name of Augustus. He gave long-postponed divine honors to his grandmother Livia and staged memorial games for his parents, for his brother Germanicus, and even for his grandfather Marc Antony. For himself, he chose a low profile. He refused excessive honors or titles and made little of the birth of his son or, later, of his grandson. He forgave those who had wronged him in the period before he became emperor. With the senate he tried to maintain the pretense that he was an ordinary citizen, no more than first among equals. Such a show of modesty might separate him from his predecessor, who had insulted his fellow aristocrats with his arrogant excesses (Suet. *Claud.* 11. 2–12. 1; Dio 60. 5, 12. 5; 60. 30. 6a).

Claudius addressed the difficult and awkward issue of succession at once. Since the principate was technically not a monarchy, hereditary or otherwise, it held no provision for continuity, but a potential successor waiting in the wings offered a degree of protection against court intrigue. Claudius' infant son was an obvious candidate, and he was advertised as such by being displayed before the public and the military. But it would be years before he could step into place, and Claudius was not young. His two daughters would be useful in the interim. He immediately married Antonia, his daughter by Aelia Paetina, to Gnaeus Pompeius Magnus, a young man from an ambitious family. Octavia, his daughter by Messallina, still a small child, was betrothed to Lucius Junius Silanus, a direct descendant of Augustus through the family of Julia the Younger. These two young men, actual and prospective sons-in-law, not only served as potential heirs or regents; their cooption into the family eliminated the possibility that they might become the foci of outside challenges to his position. In time these arrangements would become obsolete and new solutions take their place (Suet. *Claud.* 27. 2; Dio 60. 5. 7).

Conspiracy

The first crisis that Claudius had to deal with came in 42, the year after he became emperor, when an attempt was made to dislodge him through a military coup. In a sense it was unfinished business from the time of his accession when, thanks to the praetorians, his principate was established before military opposition had had time to organize. The challenge came from Lucius Arruntius Camillus Scribonianus, governor of Dalmatia, in command of two legions. His men swore allegiance to the governor, and he sent a letter to Claudius demanding abdication. Allied with him were a number of distinguished senators in Rome, foremost among them Annius Vinicianus, who had been a leader in the senate's negotiations after the assassination of Caligula and who may have been party to the assassination plot itself. But Scribonianus was not joined by other generals in the field, neither by Servius Sulpicius Galba with the legions in Upper Germany nor by Aulus Plautius in Pannonia. Appius Silanus, who had been in command of three legions in Spain, was brought to Rome early in 42 and married to Messallina's mother with the intention of rendering him harmless. The treatment of Appius suggests that Claudius was anticipating a plot. Within days the legions in Dalmatia had a change of heart, the rebellion was over, and Scribonianus either took his own life or was killed. Although brief, the affair was serious; the biographer Suetonius calls it "civil war" (Suet. *Claud.* 13. 2). In its wake, Vinicianus and others were forced to suicide. Other attempts on Claudius' life would come, in 43, 46, and 47, but these were apparently not backed by the military (Suet. *Claud.* 13, 35. 2; *Oth.* 1. 3; Dio 60. 15. 1–4, 18. 4, 27. 5).

Frontiers

In 43 it was Claudius who took the offensive with military action. The role of commander-in-chief would give him the opportunity to gain credence with the army, and this might protect him from ambitious generals in the future. The conquest of Britain was an idea that had been simmering since the first incursions of Julius Caesar in 55 and 54 BC. Augustus contemplated invasion, and Caligula had gone so far as to enroll two new legions and to organize the logistical support that Claudius would find in place. The new legions XV and

XXII were available to help relieve four seasoned legions stationed on the Rhine and in Pannonia and so free the latter to participate in the summer campaign in Britain. As often, Rome found excuse for intervention in internal conflict among local warlords. In charge of the expeditionary force was Aulus Plautius, who was now rewarded for his loyalty during the conspiracy of the preceding year. The troops were initially unwilling to embark on the ships that would take them across the Channel, thought to mark the border of the known world, until they were shamed on board by Claudius' freedman Narcissus, who was on the scene representing his patron. Once across, the force advanced against the less organized enemy quickly, although not without meeting sporadic stubborn resistance. Plautius halted when he reached the Thames, instructed, it was said, to send for the emperor if he ran into difficulty. But Claudius' presence in Britain was clearly prearranged; the weeks necessary for travel made impossible an appearance by unanticipated request. He joined the waiting forces, took nominal command, and led the troops into the local capital of Camulodunum in triumph. Roman victory must already have been essentially achieved, since Claudius would never have dared to venture into an uncertain situation. He could now claim military success, although it had come with little danger or discomfort to himself (Suet. *Claud.* 17. 1–2; Dio 60. 19–21).

Claudius' absence from Rome so shortly after the attempted coup was not without political risk. To protect his rear, he left behind his fellow consul and most trusted ally, Lucius Vitellius, father of the Aulus Vitellius who would be emperor for a short time in 69. His own sizable entourage was chosen with care. With him went his son-in-law, Pompeius Magnus, and his son-in-law to be, Lucius Junius Silanus, who were being given the opportunity for a share of glory. But there were others whom he may have trusted more close at hand than behind his back. These included Marcus Vinicius, Valerius Asiaticus, and Gnaeus Sentius Saturninus, consul in 41, all of whom had been involved in the debate in the senate in the hours after Caligula's assassination. It is possible that Galba may also have been detached from his legions of Upper Germany to join the party (Suet. *Galb.* 7. 1; Dio 60. 21. 2).

Claudius returned to Rome in 44 after an absence of six months, of which only a few weeks had been spent in Britain. He celebrated a triumph, staged an extravagant re-enactment of the storming of Camulodunum, hung the esteemed naval crown above his door, and received from the senate the honorific name Britannicus for himself and his descendants. He awarded triumphal regalia to all those of senatorial rank who had accompanied him. A commemorative arch was built at his embarkation point in Gaul, and another was incorporated into an aqueduct, the Aqua Virgo, in Rome. Games were to mark the anniversary of the victory every year thereafter. Plautius was given an ovation and much lionized when he returned in 47. In 50 Claudius extended the *pomerium*, the boundary of the city that represented the boundary of the empire, and paraded the British chieftain Caratacus through the streets of Rome. He did extract from the conquest all the advantage that he could, but for all that, it was in fact a genuine achievement that would serve as the cornerstone of his reputation (Tac. *Ann.* 12. 36; Suet. *Claud.* 17. 3, 21. 6; Dio 60. 23).

Claudius was hailed as *imperator* by the praetorians on the day he became emperor, and again for the conquest of Britain, but on other occasions too: twenty-seven times in all, a measure of the strong bond that developed between army and emperor. But the intensive effort in Britain curtailed definitive action elsewhere. Revolt was suppressed in Mauretania near the end of Caligula's reign, and Claudius claimed credit, although the victory was not strictly his. Consistent with the modest profile that he tried to project, he settled for triumphal honors, not the genuine triumph that he would accept for Britain. Fighting continued in Mauretania until 44, and the territory was divided into two provinces under imperial control (Suet. *Claud.* 17. 1; Dio 60. 8. 6, 60. 9).

In Germany, there was no attempt to add territory, only the continuing necessity of keeping belligerent tribes decently pacified and out of Gaul. An early success was the recovery of the last of the three standards so disastrously lost by Varus in AD 9, a symbolic victory that brought Claudius another of his salutations. When the Cherusci, bankrupt of leadership, petitioned for a king in 47, Claudius sent them Italicus, a German prince who had been reared in Rome. Italicus did not do well, and it was not a satisfactory intervention. In the same year, the Roman general Gnaeus Domitius Corbulo successfully quieted discord among the Frisii and the Chauci, then withdrew his force west of the Rhine, in a policy consistent with containment rather than conquest. Corbulo himself was soon recalled, and it was assumed that Claudius felt threatened by the popularity of a general in command of a significant force (Tac. *Ann.* 11. 16–20; Dio 60. 8. 7, 30. 4–5).

In the east, Claudius and his advisors adhered to earlier Roman practice. Threats were contained by sporadic shows of force, but more often by the use of buffer states and by the encouragement of internal unrest within hostile nations. Policy toward border territories alternated between the installation of ostensibly friendly kings and their incorporation into the empire as provinces. Rome held Parthia in check in this period by stirring up factional strife and by attempting to control the adjacent state of Armenia, a tactic that avoided conflict until near the end of Claudius' life. It was left to Nero to deal with renewed unrest. Shortly after he became emperor, Claudius gave

Judea to Herod Agrippa, the Jewish prince who had encouraged him to the throne. But when Agrippa died in 44, the territory reverted to Roman control and was annexed to Syria, as was Ituraea in 49. Lycia was annexed in 43. In 46 Thrace lost its independence. Rhodes first lost and then regained autonomy. Claudius supported friendly kings in Commagene and the Bosporus, and the provinces of Achaea and Macedonia were transferred from imperial to senatorial control (Tac. *Ann.* 11. 10; 12. 10, 23; Suet. *Claud.* 25. 3; Dio 60. 8. 1, 17. 3, 24. 4).

Government

Before he became emperor Claudius had been relegated to the sidelines. This turned out not to be totally disadvantageous, since it gave him a long period to observe the operation of government before trying his hand at it. Conservative by nature and with antiquarian interests, he seems to have tried to behave as he thought an emperor should. He honored the charade that Augustus had authored, the concept that princeps and senate could govern together, and his efforts to this end went beyond his initial courtesy in response to the awkward circumstances of his accession and his desire to separate himself from Caligula's excesses. He may honestly have believed that accommodation was possible, that the senate could not only enjoy respect but also share responsibility.[1] It was wishful thinking, of course, plausibly derived from his interest in history and a respect for tradition. At one point he chastised the senate for failing to participate in open discussion, although free discussion was impossible, just as it was impossible for senate and princeps to share real power at a time when initiative was increasingly the monopoly of the court. He sometimes asked the senate's approval on matters that he could execute himself, for example, seeking permission from the consuls to hold markets on his own property. He worked with magistrates as equals or subordinates when he could or when he chose. He courteously rose to his feet when addressing the consuls, and he stood with the crowd at games put on by others. But his efforts did him little good. Distrust lingered, and Claudius would be accused of doing no more than making "a show of citizen-like behavior" (*iactator civilitatis*: Suet. *Claud.* 35. 1). Besides, the senate never forgave him for the manner of his accession (Suet. *Claud.* 12. 2; Dio 60. 6. 1, 12. 3; Smallwood 1967: 367, col. 3, lines 10–23).

Like the emperors who preceded him, Claudius used the consulship to call attention to himself and to reward others. In addition to his suffect consulship under Caligula, he was consul four times during his own reign, and the years when he chose to serve were significant. He was *consul ordinarius* in 42, his first full year as emperor. In 43 he held the office again, thereby enhancing his role as commander-in-chief of the British expedition. Gaius Caecina Largus shared the consulship with him in 42 and Lucius Vitellius in 43, and these two men remained his closest associates from the upper class. He was consul in 47, once more with Vitellius as his colleague; this was the year when he held the Secular Games. His last consulship came in 51, the tenth anniversary of his accession (Suet. *Claud.* 14).

Claudius revived the republican institution of the censorship, an office last filled in 22 BC, when Augustus appointed two prominent men of consular rank to serve the traditional eighteen-month term. But by then the functions of the office had already been ceded to the princeps. Censors were responsible for the economy and for public works; they also had oversight of public morals and, by reason of this, responsibility for the senatorial and equestrian rolls. Claudius did not need the censorship to address any of these issues, but the antiquity and formality of the institution would have appealed to his sense of tradition and respect for Augustan precedent. And so he became censor himself in 47, once again with Vitellius as his partner. They evidently served for the prescribed eighteen months.

As censor, Claudius was for the most part not only fair but generous, and tactful as well. He elevated senators of more humble origin to the ranks of the patricians, a class whose numbers needed to be replenished for ceremonial duties. He asked senators whose status was in doubt to examine their own positions and allowed those who came up short to resign voluntarily. To avoid embarrassment for those he forced to resign, he published their names together with the names of those who left of their own accord. Conversely, he obliged equestrians who had adequate financial resources to assume the rank of senator whether they wished it or not. If they refused, they were removed from the equestrian roll as well. He demoted knights who were disreputable or did not meet financial requirements. He advocated the eligibility of Gallic dignitaries for Roman magisterial office. The senate flattered him as "father of the senate"; he refused the title. But he was often inconsistent, and this opened him to charges of whimsicality. He was lenient with a young knight only because his father vouched for him, and he excused an adulterer with no more than a suggestion that he be circumspect. Errors provoked laughter when he accused wealthy married fathers of poverty, celibacy, and childlessness. His enthusiasm for trivia prompted him to issue twenty edicts on one day. One that dealt with the caulking of wine jars was thought ludicrous. Another suggested a cure for snakebite (Tac. *Ann.* 11. 13, 23–5; Suet. *Claud.* 16, 24. 1; Dio 60. 29. 1–2).

Claudius once again followed Augustan precedent when he staged the Secular Games, a three-day celebration that included races, theatrical performances, and sacrifices. These games were intended to take place every 100 or 110 years, only once in an individual's lifetime. Augustus had proclaimed them in 17 BC in order to advertise a new age of peace and prosperity. Claudius recalculated the date and held them again in AD 47, plausibly in order to commemorate the eight-hundredth anniversary of the founding of Rome. It was a year when he was consul and when he assumed the censorship. The short interval between the two presentations provoked ridicule, for there were indeed those alive who had seen the last celebration. At least one performer participated in both. The formal announcement of the supposedly unique event was greeted by laughter (Plin. *NH* 7. 159; Tac. *Ann.* 11. 11; Suet. *Claud.* 21. 2).

Claudius took great pleasure in producing extravagant shows of great variety. There were numerous chariot races, gladiatorial contests, and beast hunts, in addition to elaborate spectacles like the re-enactment of the storming of the town, intended to celebrate his British victory. Entertainments were one component of the traditional "bread and circuses" aimed at rendering the populace content. But Claudius' enthusiasm for *spectacula* clearly went beyond generosity when he participated along with the rest of the audience by shouting his approval at the proceedings. This conspicuous familiarity made him popular with ordinary citizens, but at the same time caused him to appear less than dignified. He especially liked the most violent exhibitions, the bloodier the better (Suet. *Claud.* 21. 3–6, 34; Dio 60. 13).

It had become expected that an emperor would not only entertain his subjects but also care for them by guaranteeing the grain supply, undertaking public works, and rebuilding the city after fires. In this respect Claudius did his share and more. In order to avoid famine and ensure adequate food supply (the other component of "bread and circuses"), he underwrote the dangerous winter transport of imported grain, offered incentives for the construction of merchant ships, and stationed an armed force in the ports for fire prevention. As a more permanent solution, he enlarged and protected the actual harbors themselves, especially through the massive project of constructing a port at Ostia at the mouth of the Tiber. Work on this began soon after he became emperor and was finished under Nero. Aqueducts were built or repaired to provide a reliable water supply. The draining of Lacus Fucinus, a shallow lake in the mountainous region about fifty miles east of Rome, was an ambitious project intended to control flooding and bring new land under cultivation. Claudius celebrated the completion of the outlet canal with an extravaganza of the sort he liked, a staged naval battle (*naumachia*)

Claudius

between Sicily and Rhodes. Unfortunately, the project was an engineering failure, and the spectacle an anticlimax. He restored the temple of Castor and Pollux that had been altered by Caligula and dedicated the Theater of Pompey rebuilt by Tiberius. He built roads energetically in Italy and the west. He paid in person the firefighters who were attempting to put out one of the fires that frequently ravaged Rome (Tac. *Ann.* 12. 56–7; Suet. *Claud.* 18–21. 1; Dio 60. 6. 8, 11. 1–5).

Again like Augustus, Claudius considered the revival of older religious practices useful for social stability. He personally took responsibility for purifying the city when an ill-omened owl took up residence in the Capitol, and he struck a treaty according to the ancient rites of the *fetiales*, priests responsible for rituals of peace and war. He revived the "augury of safety," an expiatory ceremony that removed the curse of incest. During his censorship he saw to it that the Etruscan diviners (the *haruspices*) were encouraged and maintained. He was sympathetic to foreign rites and practices so long as they had had a long relationship with Rome. He restored the temple of Eryx in Sicily and thought of transferring the Eleusinian mysteries from Athens to Rome. He purged less acceptable practices. Astrologers were banished from Italy in 52, and Druidism was abolished. He was harsh with the Jews when they caused disturbances in Rome but fair about their rights in Alexandria (Tac. *Ann.* 11. 15, 12. 52; Suet. *Claud.* 22, 25. 4–5; Dio 60. 6. 6, 33. 3b).

Claudius seems to have been genuinely interested in seeing justice done, and done efficiently. He was diligent with both criminal and civil proceedings in the praetors' courts that had been inherited from the republic, and he involved himself in the intricacies of jury eligibility and with the terms when the courts sat. A parallel judicial system that was developing at this time allowed him the opportunity for even more personal engagement. Consuls as well as praetors could act as judges because of their magisterial power, and the emperor could hear cases on his own because he possessed permanent *imperium*. These *cognitiones* ("hearings" or "inquiries") heard charges for an open-ended assortment of infractions and so were more flexible than the older praetorian courts that addressed specific breaches of the law. Claudius could use his private court (*intra cubiculum*) to accuse whom he wished, charge him as he chose, and hear the case on his own conditions (Suet. *Claud.* 14, 23. 1; Dio 60. 4. 3–4).

When Claudius presided at public trials, which might be held anywhere, he was on view, and this exposure invited the same disrespect as when he was at the games. During the famine of AD 51, a crowd mobbed him while he was holding court in the Forum and pelted him with pieces of bread. A petitioner once detained him by grabbing hold of his garment, a defendant threw his stylus at him, and another litigant brazenly called him an old man and a fool. His own behavior seems to have provoked this treatment, for he sometimes made arbitrary and overly literal decisions. He persistently decided against any litigant who failed to appear, whatever the reason for his absence, and he declared inanely, reading from a prepared statement, that he was deciding in favor of "those who had spoken the truth." He outrageously called common prostitutes to bear witness against a knight, and once ordered the hands of a forger to be cut off on the spot (Tac. *Ann.* 12. 43; Suet. *Claud.* 15, 18. 2).

Despite, or perhaps as a result of, what seems to have been conscientious diligence in dispensing justice, Claudius was accused of excessive meddling and of abusing his power, especially in cases that he heard in private with only a few advisors present. It was said that he often gave judgment after hearing only one side of a case, and this charge became a signature motif of his character. His private court allowed him to deal with real threats, as when he punished the conspirators of 42, but it also allowed him to manipulate or invent accusations. Appius Silanus was summarily executed as a result of a hasty private judgment in 42. In 47 Valerius Asiaticus was tried privately and forced to suicide. Claudius was said to have killed a total of thirty or thirty-five senators and up to 300 knights. The totals cannot be accounted for, but the names of eighteen senatorial victims are known for certain, and the numbers may not be too far off the mark (Tac. *Ann.* 11. 1–3; Suet. *Claud.* 15. 3, 29. 2; Sen. *Apoc.* 12. 3, 19–22; 14. 1–2).[2]

Claudius occupied himself making law as well as dispensing justice. Laws were generated in several ways, and our sources do not always distinguish between a regulation derived through a *senatus consultum* and an imperial edict. He used both means, issuing prolific edicts but working through the senate as well. The end result was the same, for a proposal by the emperor to the senate invariably received an affirmative vote and eventually became law; ratification by the voting assemblies was at best a formality. As with the dispensing of justice, Claudius seems to have had a sincere desire to do well by his subjects and appears to have initiated fair and efficient legislation in general.

Much of Claudius' legislation was consistent with his desire to maintain the stratification of Roman society, a concern that he addressed during his censorship but also throughout his reign. Rulings reinforced status distinctions between senator, knight, freeborn, freedman, and slave. He set aside a seating area in the circus especially for senators. In order to disgrace knights who had inappropriately appeared on stage when Caligula was emperor, he forced them to perform again. He allowed freedmen to enter the equestrian order if adopted by a knight, but confiscated the property of freedmen who tried to pass for knights and reduced to slavery one who showed disrespect to his patron. He rearranged the sequence of the equestrian military career, a reform that did not last. His freedman Pallas drew up legislation that penalized free women who cohabited with slaves and defined the status of their children. Claudius insisted on clear distinctions between foreigner and citizen and on the primacy of Latin in state business. Foreigners were forbidden the use of Roman family names, and those who usurped citizenship were executed. He took citizenship from a distinguished man of Greek origin because he did not know Latin (Tac. *Ann.* 12. 53; Suet. *Claud.* 24. 1, 25. 1, 3; Dio 60. 7. 1, 4; 60. 17. 4–5).

Some measures were humane. He forbade the arbitrary killing of slaves. Sick slaves, left to die by their masters, became free if they recovered. He arranged for guardians to be appointed for orphans and made more efficient the rules governing trustees for estates. Advocates' fees were limited. Money could not be lent to a minor in anticipation of a father's death. He also demonstrated concern for public order and more efficient government. His adjustments of the court terms and jury eligibility fall into this category. In an attempt to purge the large backlog of cases, especially frivolous ones, he ruled that plaintiffs who did not appear for the hearings that they had initiated would be penalized. He changed the number of praetors and reordered their duties. Charge of the treasury was restored to quaestors, and they were required to produce the gladiatorial games that they had promised as candidates. He rebuked unruliness in the theater, disbanded trade associations, and dealt with Jewish unrest. The initiative of his that no doubt had the greatest impact on governance was the expansion of the authority given to procurators in the provinces. The increased judicial responsibility of these imperial appointees, knights for the most part, who owed loyalty to the emperor alone, came at the expense of senatorial authority (Tac. *Ann.* 11. 6–7, 13, 22; 12. 60; Suet. *Claud.* 23. 2, 24. 2, 25. 2, 4; Dio 60. 10. 4, 24. 1–2, 29. 7. 2).[3]

Under Claudius, the government of Rome was falling increasingly to the emperor and his agents. A deliberate "policy of centralization" has been supposed,[4] but the strengthening of the center was inevitable and derived, in all probability, not from a conscious "policy" but rather from the accretion of individual laws and edicts that addressed immediate issues. For example, Claudius removed from the senate the prerogative of granting permission to senators to be absent from the city, and took it upon himself. The delegation of responsibilities to procurators in the provinces was central to this process. Claudius was emperor for a sufficient period of time to ensure that these individual measures became permanent and so perhaps seem to constitute a policy. Another reason was the ever-increasing quantity of public business and the coterie of imperial freedmen attached to the court who were needed to deal with it. Emperors, as merely *principes* or "first citizens," had few civil servants to assist with affairs that were growing in quantity and complexity, and so they managed the state as though it were an extended household, relying on the most capable of their freedmen. This practice had developed from earlier convention. Wealthy Romans had long trusted freedmen as secretaries or estate managers, and Claudius' predecessors, Augustus, Tiberius, and Caligula, had employed them as well; but it was under Claudius that they attained their greatest prestige. Like the imperial procurators, they owed their loyalty only to him (Tac. *Ann.* 12. 23; Dio 60. 25. 6–7).

Scholarly Interests

Claudius' antiquarian and historical interests are witnessed in his literary output. He did some of his writing while he was princeps, but had already started an annalistic history of Rome when he was young. It had originally opened with the death of Caesar, but his mother Antonia and his grandmother Livia had kept him from pursuing the difficult period of the triumvirate that preceded the firm ascendancy of Augustus. When the history was finished, its forty-one books probably covered the period from 27 BC until the death of Augustus in AD 14. He wrote a defense of Cicero against an attack by Asinius Gallus. A treatise on dicing may have found its inspiration in his own enthusiasm for this pastime. His histories of Carthage and the Etruscans were in Greek, a language that he knew well and revered, despite his insistence on Latin as the language of the empire. He composed a history of alphabets, and, when he was censor, he ordered that three new letters that he had invented be put into use. He wrote an autobiography in eight books. According to Suetonius, its style was presentable, but it included material incompatible with the dignity appropriate to an emperor (Tac. *Ann.* 11. 13; Suet. *Claud.* 33. 2, 41).

Claudius' bookishness found a corollary in his pedantic mode of expression. When he spoke on allowing magisterial careers to prominent Gauls, he reached back to the city's beginnings and gave a rambling discourse on the history of immigration into Rome.[5] When he justified the expansion of the role of his procurators, he expounded on the past history of the judicial role of knights, and when he modified the responsibilities of the quaestors, he recited the history of the quaestorship. He justified tax immunity for the island of Cos on the basis of the famous physicians it had produced. The promotion of freedmen prompted reference to his ancestor Appius Claudius. His encouragement of the *haruspices* and the extension of the *pomerium* also occasioned the explanatory lectures that seem to have been his habit (Tac. *Ann.* 11. 14–15, 22, 24, 12. 61; Suet. *Claud.* 24. 1).

Character

Judged by the public record alone, Claudius seems a relatively sensible and serious-minded, if conservative, monarch. The conquest of Britain, his public works and shows, and the legislative activity directed toward increasing and maintaining order were positive accomplishments. But his contemporaries and near-contemporaries have left a portrait of a man that fits oddly with the more sober and factual account of his reign. It is often difficult to assess character in the ancient world, for it is obscured by layers of interpretation and prejudice, but Claudius clearly gave the persistent and unique impression that he was at once a buffoon and an arbitrarily cruel tyrant. He made the same impression on his contemporaries that his autobiography made on Suetonius: the impression that he behaved in a manner inappropriate for an emperor.

The composite portrait of Claudius is found in varied contexts and is derived from different sources. He is portrayed as a man oddly detached and lacking in the self-censorship that normally saves a person from awkward expression. Suetonius speaks of his "absent-mindedness and blindness" (*Claud.* 39. 1) and writes: "it was thought that he did not know or consider to whom, in what company, when, or where he was speaking" (*Claud.* 40. 1). Anecdotes abound about this unedited view of himself that he showed the world. He reputedly once summoned a dead witness in court, and on other occasions asked the whereabouts of a victim who had been driven to suicide, and even of his wife Messallina, who had been executed. He kept referring to his niece Agrippina as his "daughter," and so worsened the opprobrium of incest when he married her. As has been seen, he was overly familiar when he presided at games. His recalculation of the date for the Secular Games provoked ridicule, and the edicts promulgated when he was censor were fussy and trivial. He was laughed at in court. In his defense, he was evidently somewhat deaf, and this may have caused him to miss some of what went on around him. Heavy drinking would also have added to his detachment, and his limp and speech impairment were probably perceived as evidence of diminished mental capacity (Tac. *Ann.* 11. 2, 38; Suet. *Claud.* 15. 3, 39–40; Dio 60. 33. 6).

Not all of his character traits were so harmless. He was thought timorous and, as a result, suspicious. He had, of course, good reason to be fearful, both at the opening of his principate and in response to the threats that followed, but others seem to have been able to manipulate his timidity to their advantage. Throughout his reign, those who entered his presence were searched. He was prone to self-pity and anger and took offense easily, striking out physically at men who approached him inconveniently. His enjoyment of the bloodiest of the gladiatorial games was consistent with his delight in watching public executions and with a reputation for cruelty that derived from the trail of dead senators and knights that he left behind. He, of course, would have regarded the elimination of his enemies as necessary self-defense. Claudius' character was thus entered beneath the rubrics of stupidity and cruelty, qualities that were illustrated in the anecdotes told about him and specifically identified by Suetonius as *stultitia* and *saevitia* (Suet. *Claud.* 15. 4, *Ner.* 33. 1). His contemporaries thought him a nasty fool (Suet. *Claud.* 34–38. 2, 40. 3; Dio 60. 2. 6–7, 14. 1).

But a second characterization soon joined this first. It was the perception that he was a passive figure, a man under the direction of two groups, his wives and his freedmen. Freedmen were indeed influential assistants, and the most prominent of them were richly rewarded, both by imperial favor and by the opportunities for great wealth that their positions provided. Pallas, in charge of accounts, was awarded the *ornamenta praetoria* and equestrian status for drafting the legislation about the cohabitation of freedwomen and slaves. Narcissus, in charge of correspondence, received the *ornamenta quaestoria* for his loyalty. Claudius' last two wives, Messallina and Agrippina, were, like the freedmen, also influential court insiders. Nevertheless, his total dependence on the two groups is grossly exaggerated, for much of what took place on his watch bears his own mark. His less than commanding physical appearance and his air of detachment may have contributed to the idea that he was no more than a figurehead (Tac. *Ann.* 12. 1, 60; Suet. *Claud.* 25. 5, 28, 29. 1; Dio 60. 8. 4, 14. 1, 33. 3a).

Succession Intrigue

The two women to whom Claudius was married when he was emperor did not dominate their husband so much as they dominated the narrative of his reign. It was the parts they played in the perennial succession problem that put them at the center of the action. The first was Valeria Messallina, whose prestige derived from her trace of blue Julian blood and from the fact that she was the mother of the potential heir, Britannicus. Claudius allowed her participation in his triumph, the use of the ceremonial carriage, and a seat of honor at the games. She was allegedly responsible for the prosecution and death of many innocent men and women. Appius Silanus fell victim because he refused to be seduced by her. Valerius Asiaticus was forced to suicide because she coveted his gardens. Her jealousy was fatal for Julia, the grand-daughter of Tiberius, and for Julia Livilla, the daughter of Germanicus. Her influence on the question of the succession was made clear when Pompeius Magnus, the husband of Claudius' daughter Antonia, was killed in 47 and Antonia was married to Messallina's half-brother, Cornelius Faustus Sulla. Their son, Messallina's nephew, would be Claudius' first and only grandson. All that said, although she can have been no stranger to court intrigue, she was certainly not the sole agent of the destruction of so many people (Tac. *Ann.* 11. 1–3, 13. 32; Suet. *Claud.* 17. 3, 29. 1–2, 37. 2; Dio 60. 14. 2–4, 18. 4, 22. 2, 29. 6–6a).

Messallina was accused of promiscuity as well as of intrigue. She was said to run a brothel staffed by upper-class women and to have been a common prostitute herself. Confected claims of this type cast doubt on the paternity of Britannicus and were useful to those who did not want to see him accede to the principate. Fictions they were, of course, but there is no need to assume that she was a chaste wife, and the concluding chapter of her story shows her capable of using sexual favor for her advantage. In AD 48 Claudius was fifty-seven and, although apparently in reasonably good health, his congenital disability aside, he could be viewed as nearing the end of his life. Messallina was much younger, but, more importantly, Britannicus was only seven. Power and prestige might come from a son as well as from a husband, but it would be difficult, if not impossible, for her to become an influential royal mother if Claudius were to die before his son was safely established in his place. She found a protector in Gaius Silius, consul-elect for 49. In the autumn of 48 she evidently divorced Claudius on her own initiative, and she and Silius married secretly – although not so secretly as they wished. The idea seems to have been that he would serve as regent for the minor Britannicus or become emperor himself, while Messallina's Julian connection would help secure the loyalty of the military for the new family configuration. This radical realignment threw the court into panic as it tried to survive the shipwreck of the power structure. The freedman Narcissus took a gamble and informed Claudius of the marriage. He then directed events so that Claudius remained emperor and he himself stayed afloat. Silius and Messallina lost their lives – as did a large number of others, for the attempted coup had involved more than just the two principals (Tac. *Ann.* 11. 26–38; Suet. *Claud.* 26. 2, 29. 3; Dio 60. 18. 1, 31. 1).

Messallina may have had an additional reason for being impatient and for her timing of this risky course. Agrippina (the Younger) was waiting in the wings with a son of her own. She was a daughter of Claudius' brother, Germanicus, and his wife, a granddaughter of Augustus, the like-named Agrippina (the Elder). In AD 28 Tiberius had married her to a cousin, Gnaeus Domitius Ahenobarbus, descended, like Messallina, from Antonia the Elder. In December 37 they produced a son, Lucius Domitius, who would become the emperor Nero. By 48 Agrippina was free to remarry; Gnaeus Domitius was dead, as was her second, subsequent husband. Lucius Domitius was ten, three years older than Britannicus. By all accounts Agrippina was an energetic and ambitious woman, and Messallina could easily have thought that she was scheming to take her place, as indeed she soon did (Tac. *Ann.* 11. 12).

No sooner was Messallina dead than Claudius married his niece. Despite allegations that she had seduced him, theirs was strictly a political union. This daughter of Germanicus would bring even more family prestige to the principate than had Messallina, and would be more acceptable to the army. The impediment of incest was overcome when Claudius' allies at court persuaded the senate to make it legal for a man to marry his brother's daughter. Agrippina would receive all the honors that Messallina had, and in addition the title of Augusta and a colony named after her, Colonia Agrippinensis, on the site of present-day Cologne. She appeared in public in a golden cloak and sat in state with Claudius to receive homage from Caratacus, the defeated

British warlord (Plin. *NH* 33. 63; Tac. *Ann.* 12. 6, 26–7, 37, 56; Suet. *Claud.* 26. 3; Dio 60. 31. 8, 33. 2. 1–2a, 3, 7, 12).

Like Messallina, Agrippina was accused of engineering the destruction of prominent persons. Statilius Taurus was vulnerable because of his wealth, Lollia Paulina and Domitia Lepida because she thought them her rivals. She had an upper-class woman, Calpurnia, banished on the sole ground that Claudius had praised her. Lucius Junius Silanus, long the fiancé of Claudius' daughter Octavia, was accused of incest and driven to suicide. This left Octavia free to be betrothed to Agrippina's son. Claudius adopted the boy in AD 50, his name was changed to include the Claudian *cognomen* Nero, and a new succession plan was put in effect. Claudius now had two sons, and of these Nero was the elder. The historical tradition has made Agrippina responsible for maneuvering Nero into this position, but the arrangement was in Claudius' interest as well. An extra heir, one several years closer to his majority than Britannicus, provided protection. Nero was awarded adult status early, receiving the *toga virilis* when still only thirteen. Octavia was adopted into another family in order to keep the union between her and Nero possible, and they were married in 53 (Tac. *Ann.* 12. 3–4, 9, 22, 25–6, 58–9; Suet. *Claud.* 27. 2; Dio 60. 32. 1–4, 33. 2–2b).

Yet again, as had been the case with Messallina, Agrippina was said to have grown impatient. Britannicus was following hard on Nero's heels, scheduled to receive the *toga virilis* in 54, and when this took place Nero would no longer be Claudius' only adult son. A rumor circulated that Claudius had begun to regret this last marriage and the prominence that he had given the adopted Nero. He may have planned to make Nero and Britannicus joint heirs, for he commended both to the protection of the senate, presumably in anticipation of his own death. Claudius was now sixty-three, old for a Roman, and he died on October 13, AD 54. He lost consciousness at dinner and was carried out, presumed to be drunk, as he often was. It may be that he suffered a stroke or some other medical catastrophe, but it was inevitable that Agrippina would be thought to have poisoned him, motivated by the impending adulthood of Britannicus and the challenge that this would pose to her and her son (Tac. *Ann.* 64–5; Suet. *Claud.* 43–4. 1; Dio 60. 34. 1).

One story has the poison administered at a banquet of the *Augustales*, the priesthood of Augustus. According to another, Agrippina delivered it by her own hand in a dish of poisoned mushrooms. Stories of Claudius' last hours vary. By one account, he never regained consciousness. By another, the poison was evacuated, and he had to be given an additional dose. In either case, he was dead by morning. Agrippina did not announce his death until noon, an hour that astrologers had declared propitious. The delay provided time to arrange for the praetorian guard to salute Nero as *imperator*, and in the meantime Agrippina kept Britannicus and his sisters out of public view. Claudius was buried with funeral honors that mimicked those of Augustus. The senate quickly declared him divine (Sen. *Apoc.* 2. 2, 12. 1; Tac. *Ann.* 66– 9; Suet. *Claud.* 44. 2–45; Dio 60. 34. 2–3, 35. 2).

A pamphlet soon circulated in the court. The *Apocolocyntosis* ("pumpkini-fication"), probably from the hand of Seneca, lampooned the incongruity of the deceased emperor's divinity on the one hand and his ineptitude and murderous practices on the other (Dio 60. 35. 3). But Claudius had enlarged the empire and had behaved in a way that avoided some of the excesses of Tiberius and Caligula before him, and of Nero, who would follow, and it became desirable to reconcile the contradictions of his legacy. If it could be decided that he was a tool in the hands of his wives and freedmen, his cruelty was mitigated beneath their influence. The unseemly figure that remained was comparatively harmless.

Notes

1　Momigliano (1961), 52.
2　The tally was made by McAlindon (1957).
3　Claudius appears to have been especially busy with legislation of all sorts, although this may be to some degree an accident of the survival of evidence. The laws that came into existence while he was emperor have been arranged in categories by Levick (1990), 115–26, Momigliano (1961), 72, and H. H. Scullard, *From the Gracchi to Nero*, 5th edn (London and New York, 1982), 293–4.
4　Momigliano (1961), 39–73.
5　Claudius' speech about the Gauls is extant in part, engraved on a bronze plaque found near Lyon, his birthplace (Smallwood 1967: 369).

Further Reading

M. Griffin, "Claudius in the Judgement of the Next Half-Century," in V. M. Stroka (ed.), *Die Regierungszeit des Kaisers Claudius (41–54 n. Chr.): Umbruch oder Episode?* (Mainz, 1994), 307–21
D. W. Hurley, *Suetonius: Divus Claudius* (Cambridge, 2001)
B. Levick, *Claudius* (New Haven and London, 1990)
D. McAlindon, "Claudius and the Senators," *American Journal of Philology* 78 (1957), 279–80
A. Momigliano, *Claudius: The Emperor and his Achievement* (Cambridge, Mass., 1961)

V

Nero

Miriam T. Griffin

Nero Claudius Caesar Augustus Germanicus, who reigned for fourteen years, from AD 54 to 68, is one of the best-known, if not the best-known, of the Roman emperors. Born on December 15, 37 to the younger Agrippina, then the wife of Gnaeus Domitius Ahenobarbus, he was adopted in 50 by his stepfather the emperor Claudius, whose daughter Octavia he married three years later. He was now in a stronger dynastic position than the emperor's natural son Britannicus, and when Claudius died in October 54 he was hailed as *imperator* by the praetorian guard and voted the necessary powers by the senate. For the next five years he accepted the guidance of the philosopher Seneca and the praetorian prefect Burrus. His mother Agrippina tried with limited success to exert an influence, but was murdered in 59. As Nero grew more independent, his conduct seemed increasingly wayward to some Romans. He was to divorce the childless Octavia in 62 and marry Poppaea Sabina. She died in 65, having produced a daughter who lived only a few months. After being deserted by some army commanders and then by the praetorian guard, Nero was declared a public enemy by the senate and committed suicide at the age of thirty on June 9, 68. He was the last of the Julio-Claudian dynasty, and his fall from power precipitated a civil war that threatened to destroy the political system of the principate, for it had been designed precisely to prevent such conflict. Nero's failure would in itself have ensured notoriety. But in fact, the reputation he left behind was a mixture of good and bad, prompting reactions of both nostalgia and disgust.

The Reputation of Nero

Though the surviving literary tradition is uniformly hostile, we are told by the Hellenized Jewish historian Josephus that there were favorable accounts written by historians who were grateful to Nero (Jos. *AJ* 20. 154). These may well have been by Greek writers, for Nero had been popular in the eastern provinces of the empire, because he had shared the Greek appreciation of music, athletics, and chariot-racing as aristocratic accomplishments, because he had visited Greece and competed for crowns in the Greek games, and because he had ultimately freed old Greece, the Roman province of Achaea, from direct rule and tribute obligations. For this alone the later Greek writer Pausanias would declare him "a noble soul corrupted by improper education" (Paus. 7. 17. 3), and Plutarch would say that he found mercy in the next world, being reincarnated as "a frog singing in the marshes and lakes" (Plut. *De sera* 567F). As for this world, in the year 69, just after Nero's death, and at ten-year intervals after that, three false Neros appeared in the east, all young and all playing the lyre (Tac. *Hist.* 2. 8–9; Suet. *Ner.* 57; Dio 64. 9. 3, 66. 19. 3b). Though some found these pretenders terrifying, many welcomed them. Dio Chrysostom, a philosopher from Asia Minor, wrote toward the end of the first century, "even now his subjects wish he were still alive, and most men believe that he is" (*Or.* 21. 10). The two later false Neros had support from the king of Parthia, Rome's only remaining imperial rival, for Nero had brokered a rational settlement with the Parthian empire, which brought a long period of comparative stability to the eastern frontier. In fact, the Parthian king asked that Nero be honored in Rome after his death (Suet. *Ner.* 57).

In Rome, too, ordinary people remembered his good looks and his generous entertainments and made unflattering comparisons with the aged and austere appearance – and the stinginess – of his successor Galba (Tac. *Hist.* 1. 4, 7). Even some members of the more affluent and educated classes, the groups which had suffered most from Nero's cruelty and paranoia, remembered his entertainments and the elegant and cultured social scene over which he had presided, a climax of the luxurious lifestyle that was to end with the civil wars and the accession of the parsimonious Vespasian (Tac. *Ann.* 14. 21, 3. 55).

In the longer term, Nero's memory endured, in Rome as in the east, despite the destruction of many of his statues and the erasing of his name from monuments. "For a long time," his biographer writes, "some laid spring and summer flowers on his tomb, and they would set up his overturned statues in the purple-bordered toga on the speaker's platform and then again put up his pronouncements, as if he were alive and about to return to deal destruction to his enemies" (Suet. *Ner.* 57). Dying young and in mysterious circumstances helped to fuel belief in his survival. In the ancient world there were superstitions about those who died before their time, especially if they met a violent death and particularly if they were suicides: there were fears of the ghost that would not rest. Moreover, in Nero's case, few people had seen the corpse, for he killed himself in his freedman's villa outside Rome and was buried by his former mistress and his old nurses in the family tomb of the Domitii, being excluded, as a public enemy, from a public funeral and the mausoleum of the Caesars (Suet. *Ner.* 49. 2–50; Plut. *Galb.* 7. 2). There were also the material remains to keep his memory alive and remind people of Nero: his exciting architecture, his beautiful coins (though some of them were now defaced), the literature that he and his literary associates – Seneca, Lucan Petronius – had produced before they attracted his envy and were killed. "What is worse than Nero? What is better than Nero's baths?", wrote the poet Martial after his death (*Ep.* 7. 34), adding praise of Nero as a learned poet (8. 70). Of the four emperors who followed one another in rapid succession in 69, two, Otho and Vitellius, felt it politic to advertise their connection with Nero, adopting his name, singing his songs, working to finish his palace (Plut. *Otho* 3; Tac. *Hist.* 1. 78; Suet. *Otho* 7, 10, *Vit.* 11; Dio 64. 8. 3; 65. 7. 3). And three centuries after the senate had declared him a public enemy, spectators at the games were still receiving *contorniates* (mementoes) displaying the head of the greatest showman of them all.

Even the existing literary accounts, predominantly hostile as they are, show the excitement generated by Nero's flamboyance. Suetonius, who was born within two years of Nero's death, outdoes himself in this imperial life, producing a long and stirring narrative of Nero's last days and death (*Ner.* 40–9), which forms the principal source of the striking opening chapter of the recent book on Nero by E. Champlin, who also draws on book 63 of the history by Cassius Dio, born a century after Nero's death. Dio's narrative of these years is imperfectly preserved, and yet the magic of Nero's showmanship emerges even from the Byzantine excerpts, and the reader encounters many striking moments, such as the coronation of the Armenian king Tiridates (63. 4–5) in the year 66. Dio describes how the Forum was full of soldiers in shining armor and civilians dressed in white carrying laurel branches. Nero appeared at daybreak, wearing triumphal dress and seated on the speaker's platform. Next Tiridates and his suite passed between lines of heavily armed troops on either side, stood near the platform, and prostrated themselves.

> At this a great roar went up, which so alarmed Tiridates that for some moments he stood speechless, in terror of his life. Then silence was proclaimed,

he recovered courage and, quelling his pride, made himself as subservient as the occasion demanded. "Master", he said, "I am the descendant of Arsaces, brother of the kings Vologaesus and Pacorus, and your slave. And I have come to worship you as I do Mithras: the destiny you spin for me shall be mine, for you are my Fortune and my Fate." Nero replied, "King of Armenia I now declare you, that you may understand that I have power to take away kingdoms and to bestow them." Then when Tiridates had ascended the platform and was sitting at his feet, he took the turban from his head and replaced it with the diadem. [Somewhat abridged.]

This "Golden" Day also featured a celebration in the theater, gilded inside and outside for the occasion, with a purple awning overhead showing Nero driving a chariot with golden stars around him. Nero then performed on the lyre and drove a chariot.

This show was presumably also written up by the best of our extant historical writers, Cornelius Tacitus, an older contemporary of Suetonius, who lived through most of the reign and attests to meeting eye-witnesses (*Ann.* 15. 73). But of the six books (*Annals* 13–18) that were probably assigned to Nero in the *Annals*, a history that covers the entire Julio-Claudian dynasty except for Augustus, we have lost, or Tacitus never completed, about half of book 16 and books 17–18. We can tell, however, that Tacitus highlighted the showmanship and increasing exhibitionism of Nero by turning the set pieces of his narrative into more prolonged and elaborate dramas and tableaux. Whereas the first three books cover eleven years of the reign, the last three will have covered only two and a half or three years, depending on whether Tacitus ended his account with Nero's death on June 9, 68 or with the end of that year.[1] His narrative of Nero's reign proceeds at an increasingly relaxed pace as the imperial crimes and great crises are allotted more and more space: in book 13 the murder of Nero's brother Britannicus in 55 takes under five chapters; in book 14 that of his mother Agrippina in 59 takes eleven; in book 15, the conspiracy of Piso in 65 spreads over twenty-seven (Woodman 1993).

The reasons why Nero's reputation in the short term and the long has been predominantly bad are not far to seek. The first historians who wrote about him were living under the new dynasty of the Flavian emperors, and they endorsed the official view that he had dishonored Augustus and the other respectable Julio-Claudian rulers. The elder Pliny, friend of Vespasian and his son Titus, in his surviving encyclopedia *The Natural History*, vilified Nero as a destroyer of the human race (*NH* 7. 45) and a poison given to the world (*NH* 22. 92); his general history, now lost, was similarly sycophantic toward the new dynasty (*NH pref.* 20). Though Tacitus shows some skepticism about Nero's alleged enormities, he and our other two extant authorities followed the hostile tenor of these first historians. Not without reason. Scrutiny of the proceedings of the senate and the questioning of returned exiles by Tacitus (*Ann.* 15. 73) presumably did little to counteract the attitude of his sources, for many members of the governing class had been exiled and killed, while the letter Seneca had composed for Nero, explaining the death of his mother, virtually confessed to murder by the enumeration of her crimes in justification (Tac. *Ann.* 14. 10–11). Indeed, one of the officers of the praetorian guard reproached Nero to his face with the murder of his mother Agrippina and his wife Octavia (Tac. *Ann.* 15. 67. 2), and it was probably even before the Flavian writers were at work that a historical tragedy, written in imitation of Seneca and called *Octavia*, depicted Nero as a tyrant, responsible for the death of his brother Britannicus as well as those of his mother and his wife.[2] The same officer had included, among his charges, Nero's chariot-racing and acting, for these shocked the sensibilities of the soldiery and many of the governing class, however much they entertained the populace. The further charge of setting fire to Rome (see below p. 122), though probably untrue, was also believed by many then and now (Griffin 1987: 132).

As noted above, Nero was generally popular in the eastern provinces. But not all of Rome's eastern subjects were enthusiastic about him. The Jews, who rebelled against his cruel and extortionate procurator Gessius Florus, lost, as a result, the great Temple in Jerusalem and its treasures, which are shown adorning the Flavian triumph on the Arch of Titus. In the Jewish Sibylline Oracles, written in 79, not long after the destruction, Nero is represented as the exile of Rome, the great king and matricide, who has fled to the Parthians and will cross the Euphrates with tens of thousands to destroy Rome and the whole world (4. 119–24, 1137–9; 5. 137–52, 362–76). The Christians, punished undeservedly for the Great Fire of Rome in 64, similarly inverted the Greek hope that the philhellene emperor would return: in their oracular and apocalyptic outpourings, Nero is the Anti-Christ whose persecution of the Christians heralds the destruction of Rome. This view continued to be celebrated by the Church Fathers (*Sibylline Oracles* 8. 68–72, 139–59; Ter. *Apol.* 5; Lact. *Mort. Pers.* 2; Aug. *De Civ. D.* 20. 19. 3; Jer. *Dial.* 21. 4). The picture of Nero as the incarnation of evil triumphed as Christianity triumphed.

The Golden Age

All three extant historical accounts in fact attest deterioration over time. Suetonius, Tacitus, and Dio believe that Nero had a natural inclination to vice, but that early in the reign he behaved reasonably well out of respect or fear of his mother. Then, in the view of the latter two, he was controlled for a time by his advisors: his tutor in rhetoric, Lucius Annaeus Seneca, and his prefect of the guard, Sextus Afranius Burrus. This tradition of an early period of good government went on to enjoy a long life. Indeed, we find in the later fourth century two historians interpreting in this sense an anecdote attributing to the good emperor Trajan the view that for five years Nero surpassed all *principes* (Aur. Vict. *Caes.* 5. 2–4; *Epit. de Caes.* 5. 2–5). Though these authors speak in terms of Nero's later moral decline, they no longer knew what exactly could be said in favor of the first quinquennium. Therefore they adduced building works and provincial annexations which they clearly did not realize were mostly of later date (Griffin 1987: 84 with n. 8). But the tradition of a five-year watershed had in fact taken shape while Nero was still alive, as is shown by the words of the praetorian tribune mentioned above, which Tacitus claims to give verbatim (*Ann.* 15. 67): "I began to hate you after you murdered your mother and your wife, and became a charioteer, an actor and an arsonist." This was said by Subrius Flavus when accused of participation in the conspiracy of 65 and asked by Nero why he had betrayed his oath of loyalty. The first crime he mentioned, the murder of Agrippina in March 59, took place roughly five years from October 54, when Nero became princeps, and both Tacitus and Cassius Dio show that 59 was an important year by starting a new book at that point.

Poets contemporaneous with those first years celebrate it as a Golden Age and give some idea of the policy of the regime. Thus Calpurnius Siculus writes: "Amid untroubled peace, the Golden Age springs to a second birth; at last kindly Themis [goddess of justice], throwing off the gathered dust of her mourning, returns to the earth; blissful ages attend the youthful prince" (1. 42–5). The poet goes on to celebrate the peaceful accession of Nero, his clemency in jurisdiction, the return of the rule of law, and the freedom of the senate and magistrates.

Vague as this is, it is not difficult to see a set of themes similar to those of Nero's accession speech to the senate in the autumn of 54, of which Tacitus gives us the fullest account (Tac. *Ann.* 13. 4; see also Suet. *Ner.* 10; Dio 61. 3. 1). After mentioning the respectable precedents he hoped to follow (notably, Augustus), the new princeps went on to say that he was above factional prejudices, a promise necessary to reassure those associated with his predecessor Claudius, whose most detested practices he went on to renounce: "He would not adjudicate all matters and allow a few individuals to wield power, by having accusers and defendants heard privately within the palace; corruption and favoritism would be excluded from his house; the palace and affairs of state would be kept separate." Nero was here abjuring, first, the virtual monopoly of jurisdiction and neglect of proper procedure as practiced by Claudius, and second, the excessive and corrupt influence of his wives and the freedmen secretaries of his household on affairs of state. This influence had been felt principally on the emperor's exercise of justice and of patronage, but occasionally on legislation and even military affairs. Nero ended with a formula for a division of responsibility between himself and the senate: "Let the senate keep its ancient functions; let Italy and the public provinces stand at the judgment seat of the consuls; he would look after the armies entrusted to his care."

What he meant by this banal formula can be understood only by scrutiny of what he did in the early years, for Tacitus assures us that Nero kept his promises (*Ann.* 13. 5). With regard to the ending of Claudian habits, he cut down on personal jurisdiction and, more important, ended Claudius' habit of trying political cases of prominent men behind closed doors without access to the senate. Nero disallowed trivial charges of treason altogether, and the first individual to be tried on this charge, in 62, was brought before the senate (Tac. *Ann.* 13. 10; 14. 48–9). As to the influence of his palace minions, Nero immediately dismissed Claudius' powerful financial secretary (*a rationibus*) Pallas, and little is heard of the intervention of such people, except in crises directly concerning the palace, until the year 61 and later (Griffin 1987: 52–5).

The closing formula promised no real division of powers and functions between emperor and senate. That is clear from the narrative of Tacitus, who, having said that Nero fulfilled his vows, shows that no such division took place. In fact the overwhelming military and financial power of the emperor, added to his sweeping constitutional powers, made any idea of truly separate senatorial spheres of authority unreal.[3] Whether emperors expressed the ideal as cooperating with the senate or repudiating a monopoly of power, what made a good princeps was respect for constitutional forms, deference to the senate as a body, and creation of scope for the ambitions of members of the upper orders. Given the fact that the armies were commanded and the provinces governed by members of the senatorial and equestrian orders, the principate as a system of government could be efficient and secure only if it had the consent and cooperation of the senate corporately and of the individual senators and *equites* holding offices. Nero was living up to his promises when he allowed the senate to repeal some of the hated measures of Claudius (Tac. *Ann.* 13. 50), when he was sparing in accepting honors for himself (Tac. *Ann.* 13. 10. 1, 11, 41. 4; Suet. *Ner.* 8), and when he entrusted the war in Armenia to the gifted general Gnaeus Domitius Corbulo, at whom Claudius had balked (*Ann.* 13. 8; cf. 11. 19–20).

It is Tacitus' conception of Nero's government in the early years that has been described above. For, although Tacitus and Cassius Dio agree that, after an initial attempt by Agrippina to run the show (Griffin 1987: 38–40), Seneca and Burrus exercised the dominant influence on government in the initial years of the reign, they differ over the character of the government and over the temporal limits of this ascendancy. According to Dio, Seneca and Burrus made many changes in existing institutions and caused the enactment of new legislation (61. 4. 2). This view is difficult to substantiate, as no examples are provided by Dio himself, or rather by his Byzantine epitomators. While Tacitus' more detailed narrative contains some measures of reform, that author makes it clear that it was not such enactments that constituted what was good about Nero's early years: some he notes as more a matter of appearance than substance (*Ann.* 13. 31. 2), and he shows that the measures to check misconduct of provincial governors (13. 31. 3, 15. 20–2), of which he approves, were accompanied by laxness in punishing such abuses (13. 33, 43, 52). There is also little sign that Seneca regularly attended the senate or that, even on the emperor's advisory *consilium*, Seneca and Burrus were particularly concerned with legislation (Griffin 1987: 50–1, 79–81). As for Suetonius, he is more interested in the character of his subject, and understands the accession promises in moral terms: "He declared that he would govern according to the model of Augustus and he never missed an opportunity to exercise liberality, clemency or affability" (*Ner.* 10). Though Suetonius uses legislation and reform measures to illustrate his point, he clearly regards them as examples of virtuous behavior, on a par with Nero's popular remarks and personal rapport with his subjects. Like Tacitus, and unlike Dio, he finds the key to the initial years of good government in the spirit and manner in which the princeps acted.

As for the length of the initial good period, Dio believes that the active influence of Seneca and Burrus ended with the death of Britannicus in 55, and that even their routine government ended with the death of Agrippina in 59, after which the good period was over (61. 4–5, 7. 5, 11. 1). As we saw, Tacitus also marks 59 as an important point, but he indicates that 62 was the year when Nero began to break his early pledges and carry his crimes outside his immediate family: he takes the first treason trial and the death of Burrus as signs that the good period was at an end (*Ann.* 14. 51. 1, 52. 1, 56. 3, 57. 1). Suetonius maintains that Agrippina was in charge of all public and private business at first (*Ner.* 9, 34. 1), but does not mention the influence of any other advisors. Moreover, since his account is not fundamentally chronological, it is not clear when he thought the style of government changed, though he held that Nero's vices became more pronounced and more openly practiced (*Nero* 26. 1, 27. 1, 38. 1).

Suetonius also differs from Tacitus and Dio in his conception of Nero's role. As is natural in a biographer, he presents his subject as the source of activity throughout the reign, forgetting even what he had said about the role of Agrippina. The only exception is his use of the passive in chapters 16 and 17, where he lists with approval measures that our other sources allow us to date to different periods in his reign, including the punishment of the Christians in 64. Presumably Suetonius was trying to minimize the conflict between these attempts to curtail luxurious eating, entertainments, and superstition, and his portrait of Nero as a man lacking any severity or concern with moral standards. Tacitus and Dio think Nero only gradually liberated himself from the influence of Seneca and Burrus, but they differ in their understanding of precisely how that influence worked. For Dio, when Seneca and Burrus took over from Agrippina the control of government, they encouraged Nero to indulge his pleasures without much interference (61. 4). Tacitus also believed that Seneca and Burrus indulged Nero up to a point in order to counter the baneful influence of his mother, who was keen to continue the Claudian style of government and her role in it, but he shows them involving him in government as an active collaborator and trying to show him that tact, generosity, and clemency could win him admiration. Thus we see the young prince following up the accession speech with speeches on clemency (Tac. *Ann.* 13. 11). As we shall see, a key witness, the philosopher Seneca, backs up the conception of Tacitus.

The Problem of Nero's Youth

Two character traits of Nero stand out from the start: his sense of insecurity and his desire for popularity. They are intimately connected. Seneca and Burrus knew how to turn them in wholesome directions, but, after they were gone, his new advisors, his second wife Poppaea Sabina and the praetorian prefect Ofonius Tigellinus, were to encourage exhibitionism as a means to popularity and repression as an antidote to fear.

Nero's tutor Seneca had known from the start that the prognosis was not good. He did not need a social worker to tell him about the evil effects on a boy of separation from his mother at the age of two, followed by the loss of his father at the age of three (Suet. *Ner.* 6. 3). Seneca also knew well the cruelty and exhibitionism of Nero's paternal ancestors, the Domitii

Ahenobarbi, one of whom attracted the witty remark that "it was not surprising that he had a brazen beard since his 'cheek' was of iron and his heart of lead" (Suet. *Ner.* 2. 2).

However, the chief problem confronting Nero when Claudius died on October 13, 54 was that, by Roman standards, he was far too young to be in a position of power at all. He was less than seventeen when at midday he left the palace and was presented to the praetorian guard by their prefect Burrus as the new princeps. It is true that his mother had seen to it that his transition from boyhood to manhood was accelerated, by having him assume the *toga virilis* at the age of thirteen, but Cicero had referred to his nephew Quintus, when he assumed it at the traditional age of sixteen, as "the boy Cicero, or rather now (smiling indulgently), the young man" (*Att.* 6. 2. 2). Even if Nero had technically not been a child for some years, to some his accession meant entrusting serious matters like the war with Parthia to a boy (*puer*), dominated by his mother and counseled by his tutor (Tac. *Ann.* 13. 1, 6). It is well to remember that the standard age for holding the first magistracy at Rome, the quaestorship, was twenty-five, the age Nero's uncle Caligula had reached when he became the first young and inexperienced princeps. Even imperial princes had not yet held office before the age of twenty. Nero was not even old enough for the preliminary senatorial offices of the vigintivirate or for military service. His own tutor, the philosopher Seneca, believed that rational thinking only came in after boyhood (*Ep.* 118. 13–14; 33. 7), and there is reason to think that he still regarded Nero as a boy after his accession. For, some years before, Seneca had offered in his treatise *On Anger* advice for handling children (*pueri*) of the upper class that is strikingly reminiscent of the description by Tacitus of the way in which Seneca and Burrus managed Nero at the start of his reign: "In guiding the emperor's youth with a unanimity rarely found when power is shared, they exercised equal but contrasting influence. Burrus contributed his military experience and severity of character, Seneca his lessons in eloquence and dignified affability to the joint effort to control the perilous youth of the princeps by measured indulgence, should he refuse real virtue" (*Ann.* 13. 2. 1). Tacitus may well have had in mind Seneca's advice: "And so we must guide the child between the two extremes, using now the curb and now the spur . . . We must give him some relaxation but not allow him to sink into inactivity and laziness" (*Ira* 2. 21. 3–6). It looks as if Seneca was applying methods suitable to children, or at least that Tacitus thought he was.

The nearest parallel to Nero's situation that could be cited was that of the young Octavian, who had joined Lepidus and Antony in the triumvirate at the age of nineteen. But even he had been called *puer* by Antony (*Phil.* 13.

24). In any case, it was a sinister precedent involving seizure of the consulship by force, and a year later, the bloody proscriptions. Augustus himself had prayed that the need would not arise for anyone to become consul when less than twenty years old, as he had done (Dio 55. 9. 2). Seneca was to exploit the parallel to Nero's advantage a year after his accession when, late in 55 or in 56, he addressed to the princeps a fulsome tribute in his treatise *On Clemency*:

> The deified Augustus was a mild prince if one judges him from the beginning of his reign as princeps. But when he was one of a coalition he wielded the sword. When he was at your present age, just past his eighteenth year, he had already buried the dagger in the bosom of his friends ... To compare the mildness of the deified Augustus with yours no one will dare, even if your years of youth be brought into competition with his more than ripe old age ... I do not call weariness of cruelty, clemency. True clemency, Caesar, is that which you display. (1. 9, 11)

By the time Seneca wrote that, Nero had actually murdered his child rival Britannicus, the son of Claudius; the passage reveals not only what fresh fears about the young Nero Seneca now had to allay, but what sinister expectations had been engendered from the start by the only previous example of a ruler under twenty.

There was also a deeper reason why Nero's youth and inexperience would arouse hostility. He afforded the most dramatic proof to date that the principate was cracking the republican mould in which it was supposed to have been cast by Augustus. Whereas the first princeps and his adopted son Tiberius could both have claimed to have proved themselves before attaining power, and even Caligula had at least reached the age for holding public office, Nero's accession made it unambiguously clear that belonging to the royal family was more important than being qualified for office in republican terms, that is, by military experience and service to the state. When Tiberius had proposed that his son Drusus at thirty-four should be given the tribunician power, a way of indicating his ultimate succession, he wrote to the senate: "The promotion was not premature. After eight years of proven service, including the repression of mutinies, the completion of wars, a triumph and two consulships, Drusus knew the work he had to share" (Tac. *Ann.* 3. 56). By contrast, it was the royal womb and the imperial boudoir that had brought Nero to power. Some may have felt that Agrippina, the great-granddaughter of Augustus, was virtually taking office herself, and the first coins of the reign were not reassuring. They showed Nero and Agrippina facing each other and apparently equal (*RIC* 1²: 150, nos 1–2).

Nero put the coins right within a year and had his mother's portrait tucked behind his own (*RIC* 1²: 150, nos 6–7). But he also showed that he was determined to turn the liability of youth into an asset. He made the most of his handsome face (Suet. *Ner.* 51) and youthful body, and the contrast they made with the appearance of the elderly and spastic Claudius: to show them off, he declaimed in public and invited an audience to witness his horse-riding in the Campus Martius (Suet. *Ner.* 10. 2).

He even made a show of his problem, a celebration called the Juvenalia (Youth Games), at which he shaved off his first beard in public to a sacrificial slaughter of animals, and then carried the shavings, deposited in a gold box adorned with priceless pearls, up the Capitoline hill, where it was placed in the temple of Jupiter (Suet. *Ner.* 12. 4). This was in 59, when he was twenty-one and must have had an impressive growth of beard, particularly if the description of it as "tawny" (*subflavus*) means that it had the distinctive bronze color that had given his father's family the *cognomen* Ahenobarbus (Suet. *Ner.* 51; cf. 1. 1). Nero had had to put off the ceremony until he had disposed of his mother, because he wanted to participate personally in the stage performances, and she disapproved of his singing and playing the lyre in public. Even now he only performed in a private theater specially built across the Tiber, but many select guests were induced to perform there as well, and the praetorian prefect himself, the severe Afranius Burrus, was himself on duty, "grieving but applauding," as Tacitus puts it (*Ann.* 14. 14–15).

Contrasting Solutions: Nero vs. Seneca

One point on which the young emperor and his advisors can never have seen eye to eye was Nero's passion for musical and theatrical entertainments in the Greek style, and his own desire to perform in them. Seneca had tried to find a mean between curb and spur here. In the *Apococyntosis*, a spoof on Claudius' deification attributed to Seneca and performed for the court a month or two into the new reign, he had Apollo celebrate Nero:

> Let the normal term of human life be overcome by the man who is like me in looks and grace and my equal in voice and in song. He will guarantee an era of prosperity to the weary and break the silence of the laws . . . like the gleaming Sun, as soon as rosy Dawn has dispelled the shadows and led in the day, as he gazes on the world and begins to whip up his chariot from the starting-barrier: such a Caesar is at hand, such a Nero shall Rome now gaze

upon. His radiant face blazes with gentle brilliance and his shapely neck with flowing hair. (*Apoc.* 4. 30–2)

The admixture of allusion to the promises of the accession speech – the return of proper legal procedure, the ending of Claudian abuses – with this kind of flattery shows how the young emperor had to be cajoled into proper behavior. For Nero's artistic interests were a part of his conception of his work as princeps. He was determined to educate the upper classes in singing and dancing for the festival of the Juvenalia in 59 (Tac. *Ann.* 14. 14; Dio 61. 19. 1) and for the Neronia, his new quinquennial contest in the Greek fashion (*Ann.* 14. 20–1), and to encourage an interest in Greek athletics, for which he included a gymnasium in his new public bath complex in 61 (*Ann.* 14. 47; Suet. *Ner.* 12. 3; Dio 61. 21. 1). He wanted his Roman peers to adopt what he saw as the Greek view of the supreme value of art. Many were prepared to oblige him, but there were enough people as stuffy as Tacitus to cause resentment, especially as he wanted to excel and be a virtuoso. Since the princeps was supposed to be just that, first among his peers, and Nero lacked the obvious achievements to claim that standing, this is one of the ways in which he was determined to stand out magnificently. He was prepared to work hard at his singing, practicing with heavy weights on his chest and submitting himself to enemas and stringent diets. He was determined to perform to an audience. He was persuaded to move slowly on this: first the private performance at the Youth Games; no personal appearance at the first Neronia in 60; then the public stage in 64, but at Naples, a Greek city where the Roman upper classes traditionally assumed Greek dress and generally let down their hair; finally, public performance at Rome in the second Neronia of 65 (*Ann.* 14. 15, 20–1; 15. 33; 16. 4–5). In the end, Nero's susceptibility to flattery and his desire to excel in things that bring applause and a crown (Dio Chrys. *Or.* 71. 9) led him to Greece, where he participated in the six great Greek festivals, which some rescheduling allowed to occur in the one year 66–7: the Greeks alone, he said, had an ear for music and were worthy of his achievements (Suet. *Ner.* 22. 3). He succeeded in being hailed as *periodonikes pantonikes*, "total victor on the grand circuit" (Dio 63. 10. 1).[4]

Seneca had tried to show Nero in *De Clementia* how he could be loved more than Augustus and hence feel secure in his position as emperor. Though the emphasis on the virtue of clemency, interpreted by the philosopher to fit the flexible procedures of imperial and senatorial jurisdiction (Griffin 2003: 175–7), clearly echoed the accession speech, there is no parallel to the constitutional conception of the princeps' power found there, an authority emanating from and shared with the senate. Instead, there is an organic

Nero

conception – the ruler as the *anima* (soul or mind) of the *res publica* (*Clem.*
1. 3. 5–4. 3) – and the role of princeps is likened to that of a king (1. 8. 1, cf.
1. 17. 3; 2. 5. 2): it is the virtue of the ruler that is the only safeguard of
liberty, and the rule of law is guaranteed because the ruler behaves *as if*
he were obliged to obey the laws (1. 1. 4). The reward held out is affection:
"Principes and kings and guardians of the public order, *whatever different
name they bear*, are held more dear even than those bound to us by private
ties."[5] Seneca was drawing here on traditional arguments from treatises on
kingship: he also used them to admonish the princeps, urging him to abstain
from anger and cruelty in the interests of personal security, since that is to
be won only by the subjects' love for their ruler (1. 8. 6–1. 13; 1. 19. 5; 1. 26).

    The policy publicly espoused by Nero, in the accession speech composed
by Seneca, can be summed up as being *civilis*. It meant avoiding outright
autocracy, behaving as an equal toward one's fellow citizens (especially the
upper orders) so far as the emperor's position permitted, and encouraging
freedom of speech and action. But this was a difficult task, and a hypocritical
one, as the conflicting notions of the power of the princeps in Seneca's
two compositions show. *De Clementia* has the more realistic conception,
but that demanded the virtues of a benevolent autocrat – self-control and a

determination not to use all one's power. That Nero ultimately tired of Stoic advice to follow virtue is suggested by the success of the argument first used by Tigellinus in 62, that adherence to that philosophy showed a seditious attitude toward the emperor (Tac. *Ann.* 14. 57; 16. 21–2). This was an exaggeration based on the fact that certain Stoic senators, notably Thrasea Paetus and his associates, showed their disillusionment with the government, namely with the immoral conduct of Nero and with the difficulty of playing one's proper role as a senator, by various acts of abstention from public life. It was a course of action for which Stoicism offered a justification but which Seneca deplored (e.g. *Ep.* 73), fearing that it would lead, as it did, to persecution of the sect. As for real sedition, the only participant in the later Pisonian conspiracy of 65 who was certainly a Stoic was Seneca's nephew Lucan, though Seneca himself was falsely accused and ordered to commit suicide (Tac. *Ann.* 15. 60–4; cf. Dio 62. 24–5).

Being *civilis* was not the only difficulty. The whole system exhibited ideological tensions. Thus Nero, having foresworn the abuses of Claudius' reign, could not be seen to discredit his predecessor openly without undermining his own position, since his claim to power rested on his adoption by his uncle. Not only did he praise Claudius' achievements and qualities as a ruler in his funeral eulogy; he saw to it that he was declared a god by the senate (Tac. *Ann.* 13. 2–3; Suet. *Ner.* 9; Dio 60. 35. 2), and he styled himself *divi Claudi filius*. Agrippina, too, began to build a temple in his honor, though Nero later decided to use the site for part of the Golden House complex (Suet. *Vesp.* 9).

Ultimately, it took a master actor such as Augustus to play the role demanded, and Nero's dramatic talents were of a different kind. He tried to find other ways of achieving the popularity he craved, the popularity that would render his position unchallenged.

Imperial Generosity

The princeps was supposed to be outstandingly generous, to do what Pompey and Caesar had done with their booty in the republic, but on an even grander scale. Personal generosity had always subsidized state expenditure in Rome, for public revenues were limited, and giving largesse bought political credit and power. Now, under the empire, the princeps was expected to help members of the upper class struggling with the expenses of rank; to send relief to cities hit by earthquake or famine; to put up great works of public utility; to make subventions to the public treasury so it could balance its budget. Nero met the challenge. In personal gifts alone he handed out, in the fourteen years of his reign, a sum comparable to Augustus' total gifts to soldiers, people, and the public treasury in his forty years of rule (Tac. *Hist.* 1. 20; *RG* App. 1). He gave a public banquet for which the whole city was the setting of lavish entertainment (Tac. *Ann.* 15. 37). He gave impoverished aristocrats annual pensions (Tac. *Ann.* 13. 34). He built an amphitheater (Plin. *NH* 6. 200; Tac. *Ann.* 13. 31; Suet. *Ner.* 12. 1), an aqueduct (Frontin. *Aq.* 1. 20; 2. 76, 87, cf. *ILS* 218), a grand market (Dio 61. 19. 1), and the magnificent bath complex already mentioned (Tac. *Ann.* 14. 47; Suet. *Ner.* 12. 3; Dio 61. 21. 1). He also subsidized the state treasury annually, and, in case insufficient notice was taken of the fact, he made speeches boasting of his own generosity and reproaching earlier emperors for not balancing the books (Tac. *Ann.* 15. 18).

Not surprisingly, he ran into financial trouble, as he acquired no booty to speak of in war, and incurred heavy military expenses in the struggles with the Parthians in the east, which lasted until the end of 63, and in subduing the rebellion of Boudicca in Britain in 61–2. And then in July 64 came the catastrophic fire in Rome, with its attendant problems of homelessness and starvation (Tac. *Ann.* 15. 39). The fire also inspired Nero with the vision of an enlarged and fireproof Rome, with wide boulevards, detached houses of fire-resistant stone, internal courtyards, porticoes to catch falling debris, and walls that encompassed all the land down to the harbor at Ostia (Tac. *Ann.* 15. 43; Suet. *Ner.* 16). And at the center would be the imperial palace, the Golden House, with a lake, a waterfall, an open zoo, and an architectural novelty: an octagonal dining room in the center of the main residential block on the Oppian hill, featuring a rotating ceiling or lantern that depicted, we are told, the changing seasonal positions of the heavenly bodies, as it went round. Other dining rooms had gadgets for showering the guests with perfumes and flowers. Gilding, perhaps with mosaic tiles, made both the exterior of the house and the interior shine (Mart. *Spect.* 2: Tac. *Ann.* 15. 42; Suet. *Ner.* 31. 1–2). The solar theme, evoking the comparison of Nero with Apollo the lyre-player and charioteer, was perhaps intended to be carried through by installing in the vestibule a colossal bronze statue probably representing the Sun and resembling in its features the emperor himself (Mart. *Spect.* 2. 1–3; Plin. *NH* 34. 45; Suet. *Ner.* 31. 1; Dio 66. 15. 1).[6]

The Golden House was to be a large suburban villa, laid out in the middle of Rome, as though space were no object. Nero said that at last he began to live as a man should (Suet. *Ner.* 31. 2). But this was no private precinct. A newly expanded Sacred Way through the Forum, lined with arcades, would lead up to his front door. A temple of Fortune stood in the grounds and one to Jupiter just south of his entrance hall: there must have been public access for worshippers. The new official mint and Nero's market stood close by. The Golden House was to function as a complex of splendid government buildings laid out in a landscaped park in the center of Rome, which the citizens would also have enjoyed when they sought an audience with the emperor or attended one of his grand social entertainments.[7]

Nero's generosity was often expressed in sweeping gestures. "Let us cancel all the indirect taxes [in Italy and the provinces]," he suggested one day to his *consilium*, when there had been popular agitation about the abuses of the tax collectors. It would be his "magnificent gift to the human race" (Tac. *Ann.* 13. 50). That was in 58, and wiser counsels prevailed. But nine years later he could not be stopped. At the end of his Greek tour he decided to re-enact the dramatic liberation of Greece by Flamininus two and a half centuries earlier, as before in Corinth and, as before, during the Isthmian Games (Plut. *Flam.* 12. 8). But then, a herald had read the brief pronouncement; now, the emperor himself delivered a lengthy address in person, showing off his Greek. The speech, conferring on Greece immunity from taxation and freedom from direct Roman administration, is preserved on a marble pillar in Boeotia, which also records the extravagant honors with which the Greeks rewarded Nero. After all, as he said, "Other rulers have liberated cities; only Nero a province" (Smallwood 1967: 64; Suet. *Ner.* 24. 2).

Imperial Glory

The city of Athens had also honored Nero five or six years earlier, in a spectacular way. Nero never went to see the inscription placed on the architrave of the Parthenon itself, proclaiming him as "greatest of emperors" and anticipating his own decision to prefix to his name the praenomen *imperator*. The neat bronze letters of the inscription were removed after his death, but the inscription has been deciphered from the holes they left.[8] Since the Parthenon was a monument long associated with the Athenian victory over the Persians and later adorned by Alexander with shields dedicated to Athena out of his Persian trophies, it is likely that the Athenians were expecting Nero himself to lead a campaign against the Parthians, the successors of the Persians. Certainly by the time he set out for the Greek tour, and possibly earlier, Nero had such a plan prepared (Griffin 1987: 161, 229).

The Romans of the imperial period followed the tradition of the republic in regarding military achievement as the greatest source of glory. As Tacitus (*Ag.* 39) was to put it, "Good generalship is an *imperial* virtue" (*ducis boni imperatoriam virtutem esse*). Indeed, what was expected of the princeps was clear for all to see from his designation *imperator*, which had strong military connotations (Dio 53. 17. 4), from the laurel wreath the princeps wore, and from the embroidered triumphal toga he sported at festivals. The inscribed list of Augustus' achievements, the *Res Gestae*, proclaimed that it was through his victory in the civil wars that the first emperor had won complete control of political affairs by universal consent (34. 1). The honors recorded for his constitutional settlement maintained the military emphasis, while his victories and annexations bulk large in the body of the document. He lined his new forum with statues of the republican victors in their triumphal robes, "in order to lead the citizens to demand of me, while I live, and the rulers of later times as well, that I attain the standard set by those men" (Suet. *Aug.* 31. 5). Tiberius had a fine military career behind him when he became princeps, and both Gaius Caligula and Claudius, who had no such experience, tried to secure military glory in the conventional way. They both left Rome at the head of armies, and Claudius actually celebrated a triumph and took twenty-seven imperial salutations, six more than Augustus.

Until late in his reign, when he decided to lead an army himself, Nero was content with honoring his generals and taking salutations for their victories: Duvius Avitus in Lower Germany in 57–9; Domitius Corbulo against the Parthians in 57–9; Suetonius Paullinus, who had put down the serious rebellion in Britain in 61 or 62. Though Tacitus recounts the subsequent replacement of the last as governor in terms of a humiliation (*Ann.* 14. 38–9), a lead token showing PAULLINI and symbols of victory probably indicates that Paullinus was honored by a special distribution to the plebs or the soldiers on his return home (Griffin 1976/7). The last of such imperial salutations was taken in 62 for the abortive successes of Caesennius Paetus in Armenia. After that, the emphasis was to be on Nero's personal glory. Indeed, in his last years Nero became reluctant to recognize military success (e.g. *ILS* 986), and began to appoint as military commanders safe men, undistinguished in lineage and in many cases elderly, though not actually incompetent (Griffin 1987: 116–18, 231–2).

By the time he was ready to lead an army, however, Nero had introduced some novel variations on the theme of military glory. In 59, after the murder of his mother Agrippina in the Bay of Naples, he returned to Rome in trepidation. Tacitus depicts his entry as a kind of informal triumph over his dead mother, pointing to

> the tribes on their way to meet him; the senate in festal dress; troops of wives and of children disposed according to their sex and years, while along his route

rose tiers of seats of the type used for viewing a triumph. Then the proud victor over the nation's servility, he made his way to the Capital and paid his grateful vows. (*Ann.* 14. 13)

It is not clear if Nero actually celebrated his escape from the alleged maternal attempt on his life as a kind of triumph or if Tacitus is creating the contrast between Nero's conduct and what a princeps ought to do. The same uncertainty attends Tacitus' claim that Nero tried to justify his racing of chariots as "a royal accomplishment, and practiced by commanders in ancient times" (*Ann.* 14. 14. 1).

There is no ambiguity, however, about what happened six years later in 65, when Nero himself explicitly represented the uncovering of an urban conspiracy as a military victory. The threat to the emperor was real enough: a group of senators, *equites,* and officers of the guard plotted a kind of re-enactment of the murder of Julius Caesar, to take place on April 19, 65: a member of the old republican aristocracy, Gaius Calpurnius Piso, would replace Nero as princeps. For help with detection, Nero rewarded the ex-consul Petronius Turpilianus, the praetor-elect Cocceius Nerva, and his praetorian prefect Tigellinus with triumphal insignia and statues, while even his freedman Epaphroditus was granted military decorations (*ILS* 9505; Tac. *Ann.* 15. 71–4; Suet. *Ner.* 15. 2; Dio 62. 27. 4). Nero himself took his tenth imperial salutation (Griffin 1987: 232, with n. 69). Tacitus was justified in saying that Nero convened the senate "as if he were about to describe his achievements in war." With the year 66 came the visit of Tiridates, already described (pp. 109–10), for which Nero took his eleventh imperial salutation. The achievement this celebrated was not inconsiderable, for Corbulo had brokered an arrangement with the Parthians that was to prove stable: Armenia would be ruled by the Parthian royal house, but the ruler would receive his crown from the Roman emperor in acknowledgement of the suzerainty of Rome (Tac. *Ann.* 15. 24–31). Yet Nero's triumphal dress and the presence of soldiers, and the final placing of a laurel wreath on the knees of Jupiter's statue on the Capitol, where triumphal processions traditionally finished (Suet. *Ner.* 13. 2), made an odd contrast with his theatrical performance on the lyre and in a chariot. The mixture of victor and virtuoso is remarkable.

Then, on his return in 67 from his victories at the Greek games, Nero held what can only be considered the answer to a Roman triumph. He rode in Augustus' triumphal chariot, a portion of the city walls having been specially breached as for victors in the Greek games; he wore triumphal purple but also a Greek cloak; he was accompanied by his claque rather than his soldiers; and he was preceded by a procession featuring the crowns of his victories in the games rather than the names of the cities he had conquered. Finally, to make the point that this was the triumph of an artist, the procession finished up, not at the temple of Jupiter on the Capitoline, but at the temple of Apollo, patron of the arts, on the Palatine (Suet. *Ner.* 25; Dio 63. 20). How much glory Nero claimed for his singing and lyre-playing is shown by the fact that, of all the insults directed at him by the rebel Vindex, Nero most resented the taunt that he was a bad lyre-player (Suet. *Ner.* 41. 1; cf. 40. 2).

"What an artist dies with me!"

Julius Vindex was a Gallic aristocrat, a Roman citizen, and the governor of the unarmed province of Gallia Lugdunensis, and the aim of his revolt in March of 68 was to replace Nero with a more suitable emperor. His criticisms of the reigning princeps went far beyond the aesthetic, for he attacked his murders, robberies, and sexual outrages, as well as his undignified stage performances (Dio 63. 22–3). Meanwhile in Spain, Nero's eventual successor was bemoaning the illustrious men he had put to death (Plut. *Galb.* 5. 2).

The reasons why Nero went back on the promises of his accession speech, brought back treason trials on verbal and other trivial charges, and directed them at members of the high nobility are connected with his lack of pre-accession achievement, a problem augmented by the issue of the succession. Augustus had prepared the ground for a dynastic succession, and his was a potent example. But, as the principate was not an overt monarchy, there could be no law of succession to make clear who was the legal claimant. Intermarriage with foreign royalty being similarly ruled out, the successors of Augustus had married within the Roman aristocracy, which meant that the number of Roman senators with blood ties to the ruling dynasty multiplied alarmingly as time went on. Nero was confronted by the descendants of Augustus and Tiberius, notably the Junii Silani and Rubellius Plautus, as well as by Claudius' son Britannicus and the Plautii who were related to his first wife Plautia Urgulanilla. Nero advertised his own dynastic claim on inscriptions with his full genealogy, beginning "son of the deified Claudius," then continuing (switching to the maternal line, yet cunningly avoiding descent from a female) "grandson of Germanicus, great-grandson of Tiberius, great-great-grandson of Augustus" (Smallwood 1967: 149, 349). This double descent from the past emperors was meant to show how superior his claim was to the claims even of his dynastic rivals.

It was the link with Claudius that held Nero back from divorcing Claudius' daughter Octavia, whom he had married in 53 before his accession, despite the fact that she was unattractive to him and apparently sterile. As Burrus said when Nero wished to divorce her in order to marry Poppaea Sabina, beautiful and of proven fertility, "Well then, give her back her dowry," meaning the throne (Dio 62. 13). Even after the murder of Agrippina in 59, which was motivated by her opposition to Nero's liaison with Poppaea, he did not dare to divorce Octavia until 62 when Poppaea was actually pregnant. But after his infant daughter Claudia Augusta died within four months in 63 (Tac. *Ann.* 15. 23), Nero turned to the methods of dealing with dynastic rivals that his mother had used to achieve his own succession. She had disposed of two of the Junii Silani (Tac. *Ann.* 12. 8, 13. 1); Nero had two more of them condemned for treason in 64 (Tac. *Ann.* 15. 35) and 65 (*Ann.* 16. 8–9), the evidence being their generosity and their habit of giving their freedmen secretaries the same titles as were used for the imperial freedmen (and which no doubt had been traditional in aristocratic homes). Many of their relatives suffered with them.

The Pisonian conspiracy demonstrates that the theoretical constitutional position, whereby the choice of a princeps rested with the senate and people who conferred the requisite powers, was still potent. Suitable candidates without dynastic links could be considered, as Seneca had made explicit in his account of Augustus' lecture to the conspirator Cinna (*Clem.* 1. 9). This lack of a recognized hereditary principle showed itself in the attempt to put Gaius Calpurnius Piso of the old republican nobility on the throne in 65. Nonetheless, it was rumored that Piso tried to strengthen his position against suspected dynastic rivals, such as Lucius Junius Silanus, by marrying Claudius' widowed elder daughter Antonia (Tac. *Ann.* 15. 53. 3–4). Whether or not Nero proposed to Antonia after the death of Poppaea later in that same year (Suet. *Ner.* 35. 4), she was put to death in 66 before he left Rome for the Greek tour (Griffin 1987: 193–4).

It was after the Pisonian conspiracy that Nero began to exhibit a fear of prominent army commanders, summoning to Greece and driving to suicide, in 66 and 67, Domitius Corbulo and the Scribonii brothers, governors of Upper and Lower Germany (Dio 63. 17. 3–6). When Vindex approached a number of provincial governors as prospective replacements for Nero, most of them sent the letters to the princeps (Plut. *Galb.* 4. 2; Suet. *Galb.* 9. 2). The one who did not, and then intercepted orders for his removal, was Servius Sulpicius Galba, an elderly consular of republican nobility with a fine military record, who had been governing the eastern Spanish province of Hispania Tarraconensis for eight years.

In addition to the involvement of senators governing the provinces, it was the widespread resentment of Nero's financial depredations that differentiated this revolt from the earlier conspiracy, which had been provoked by Nero's murders, shamelessness, and licentiousness (Tac. *Ann.* 15. 67; Dio 62. 24. 1–2). The financial burden of Nero's extravagance had been augmented by the expenses of the fire of 64: the reduced weight of the gold and silver coinage and the reduced percentage of silver in the denarius show clearly the extent of the strain in 64–5. Seneca had asked to withdraw from Rome at this point, wishing to dissociate himself from the acts of sacrilege performed by Nero's agents, who were collecting treasures from the temples in Greece for the Golden House (Tac. *Ann.* 15. 45, cf. 16. 23; Dio 63. 11). Vindex was moved by heavier taxes and forced levies in Gaul and Britain; in Spain, Galba sympathized with those pursued by Nero's agents (Plut. *Galb.* 4. 1); in Africa, Nero is said to have put to death six landowners who owned one-half of the land of the province between them; Judea suffered at the hands of the rapacious procurator Gessius Florus, and Egypt through the exactions of the prefect Caecina (Smallwood 1967: 391. 1, 4; Dio 63. 22. 1a; Plin. *NH* 18. 35; Jos. *BJ* 2. 293; Dio 63. 11).

Unlike the British revolt of 61 and the Jewish rising of 66, however, this rebellion gave the verdict of the Roman governing classes on their emperor. As Galba said, "It was not Vindex with his unarmed province or I with one legion that freed the people from Nero's yoke, but his own monstrousness and extravagance" (Tac. *Hist.* 1. 5). Nonetheless, Nero's fall, if explicable, was not inevitable. Tacitus tells us that he was driven from his throne "by messages and rumors, rather than by force of arms" (*Hist.* 1. 89). For, whatever hesitation was shown by the governor of Upper Germany, Verginius Rufus, neither he nor his colleague Fonteius Capito failed Nero in the end, and the seven legions belonging to them defeated the rebels under Vindex at Vesontio in May 68. Had Nero himself appeared before the German troops or his forces in northern Italy, they might not have demanded Verginius as emperor, a demand that the governor in any case refused. The British legion XIV Gemina was loyal to Nero even after his death (Tac. *Hist.* 2. 11; cf. 2. 27. 2). In Rome the praetorian guard, "long accustomed to swear allegiance to the Caesars, had been brought to desert Nero more by deceit and incitement than by its own inclination," in the words of Tacitus (*Hist.* 1. 5. 1): their prefect Nymphidius Sabinus told them that Nero had already left for Alexandria (Plut. *Galb.* 14. 2). Only when Nero had in fact left the city did the guard acclaim Galba in the praetorian camp (Suet. *Ner.* 48. 2); and only then did the senate, which had declared Galba a public enemy, condemn Nero and proclaim Galba emperor. Had Nero been more resolute in the face of the crisis, the guard would probably not have followed the lead of a prefect who had betrayed praetorian officers in the Pisonian conspiracy (Tac. *Ann.* 15. 72).

A hunted outlaw hiding in the villa of his freedman Phaon on the outskirts of Rome, Nero managed to commit suicide with the help of another freedman, Epaphroditus. His last concern was that his body should not be mutilated, and Galba's freedman was to spare him that aesthetic humiliation (Suet. *Ner.* 49). It was while he was ordering his grave to be decorated with any bits of marble that could be found that he uttered his famous lament, "What an artist dies with me!" (*Qualis artifex pereo*). As Dio implies, he was thinking primarily of his skill as a lyre-player (cf. Suet. *Ner.* 20. 1), for, as the end approached, he had hoped to escape and earn his bread as a wandering minstrel (63. 29. 2; cf. 63. 27. 2). Had he only been allowed to be a professional musician rather than an emperor, how much better it would have been for Nero and for Rome!

Notes

1 See *Ann.* 15. 72, where Tacitus looks forward to further mention of the prefect of the praetorian guard Nymphidius Sabinus, "who will play a part in the Roman disasters." This should point to the *coups d'état* that followed Nero's death and thus show that the *Annals* continued to the point where Tacitus' earlier work, the *Histories*, had finished. But the remark might only indicate Nymphidius' desertion of Nero for Galba, which ensured Galba's triumph and the start of the civil conflicts. The assumption of eighteen books for the *Annals*, as opposed to the notion of sixteen books, fits with the idea of triadic organization of the work, of which the chief advocate is Syme (1958), app. 35.

2 P. Kragelund, *Prophecy, Populism, and Propaganda in the "Octavia"* (Copenhagen, 1982); cf. R. Ferri, *Octavia* (Cambridge, 2003).

3 The precious metal coinage of the first ten years of the reign might appear to show Nero's abdication of authority and the senate's acquisition of power, for it differs from all other imperial issues of gold and silver in carrying the formula EX SC (*ex senatus consulto* = "in accordance with a decree of the senate"). The related formula SC had appeared on the low-value coinage from the time of Augustus. Does this mean that the imperial senate had up to now been responsible for token coinage, but now was given control over the minting of gold and silver? Though the matter is controversial, other explanations are available. Thus the presence of SC on the bronze probably was meant to distinguish it from local bronze coinages in the provinces, there being no need for it on the gold and silver (A. Wallace-Hadrill, "Image and Authority in the Coinage of Augustus," *Journal of Roman Studies* 76 (1986), 66–87, esp. 80–2). The Neronian EX SC may simply have been intended to emphasize the senatorial sanction for the emperor's honors and powers inscribed on the coins – a mark of respect, consistent with the meaning of the accession speech suggested here. See K. Kraft, "S(enatus) C(onsulto)," *Jahrbuch für Numismatik und Geldgeschichte* 12 (1962), 7–49, repr. in W.

Schmitthenner (ed.), *Augustus* (*Wege der Forschung* 128; Darmstadt, 1969), 336–403; Griffin (1987), 57–9; Wallace-Hadrill, "Image and Authority," 81, n. 93; Griffin (1992), 514.

4   See N. M. Kennel, "ΝΕΡΩ ΠΕΡΙΟΔΟΝΙΚΗΣ," *American Journal of Philology* 109 (1988), 239–51.

5   *Ideo principes regesque et quocumque alio nomine sunt tutores status publici non est mirum amari ultra privatas etiam necessitudines.*

6   See M. Bergmann, *Die Strahlen der Herrscher. Theomorphes Herrscherbild und politische Symbolik im Hellenismus und in der römischen Kaiserzeit* (Mainz, 1998); R. R. R. Smith, "Nero and the Sun-god: Divine Accessories and Political Symbols in Roman Imperial Images," *Journal of Roman Archaeology* 13 (2000), 532–42.

7   Griffin (1987), 138–41; R. H. Darwall-Smith, *Emperors and Architecture: A Study of Flavian Rome* (Brussels, 1996); Champlin (2003), 200–6.

8   K. K. Carroll, *The Parthenon Inscription* (Durham, NC, 1982).

Further Reading

E. Champlin, *Nero* (Cambridge, Mass., and London, 2003)

M. T. Griffin, *Nero, the End of a Dynasty*, 2nd edn (London, 1987)

M. T. Griffin, *Seneca, a Philosopher in Politics*, 2nd edn (Oxford, 1992)

M. T. Griffin, "Nero's Recall of Suetonius Paullinus," *Scripta Classica Israelica* 3 (1976/7), 138–52

M. T. Griffin, "Clementia after Caesar: from Politics to Philosophy," in F. Cairns and E. Fantham (eds), *Caesar against Liberty? Perspectives on his Autocracy* (Cambridge, 2003), 157–182

D. Shotter, *Nero* (London, 2005)

A. J. Woodman, "Amateur Dramatics at the Court of Nero: *Annals* 15. 36–7," in T. J. Luce and A. J. Woodman (eds), *Tacitus and the Tacitean Tradition* (Princeton, 1993), 104–28

VI

Vespasian

Barbara Levick

Rise to Power

Under the Roman republic, office and status, readily accessible to the well-born, were also conventionally to be won by merit, especially courage in the field (*virtus*). From Caesar onwards, emperors found it convenient to keep up the convention. The worthy men they advanced were useful and unthreatening. The target of conspiracies in 65 and 66, Nero chose such a man to deal with the revolt in Judea that broke out in the latter year.

Titus Flavius Vespasianus, born in AD 9, came from Reate, a town in the Sabine territory north of Rome, as his vowels betrayed. His forebears were soldiers, tax collectors, and bankers, men of equestrian rank or below; but his mother's brother had entered the senate and reached the praetorship. This helped Vespasian, and his elder brother Sabinus, although Vespasian is said to have been reluctant to embark on a senatorial career, perhaps not surprisingly at the end of Tiberius' reign. Vespasian was aedile, on his second attempt, under Caligula, and allegedly discharged his duties so unsatisfactorily that the emperor had mud left uncleaned on the streets tipped into his toga (Suet. *Vesp.* 5. 3; Dio 59. 12. 3). Stories of demeaning behavior and humiliation accompanied him to the end, remembered by anyone who resented the rise of such a person. And it is possible that his further progress to the praetorship was due to his liaison with Antonia the Younger's freedwoman, Antonia Caenis, just as his ensuing appointment to command Legio II Augusta, at Argentorate (Strasbourg), was reputed to be on the recommendation of one of Claudius' most influential freedmen advisors, Narcissus. But Vespasian enjoyed support from high senatorial circles as well: Claudius' friends the Plautii, Petronii, and Vitellii. To Vitellius, emperor in 69, Vespasian was a "client."

Claudius used Legio II in his invasion of Britain (43–7), and Vespasian distinguished himself on the west wing, taking the Isle of Wight, storming a number of hill forts, and establishing the Roman presence at Isca Dumnoniorum (Exeter) and perhaps also at Alchester, in Oxfordshire. Such service earned triumphal regalia and led to the consulship, though only in 51 and for the last two months of the year. Vespasian as praetor-designate had proposed increasing the penalties imposed on Marcus Lepidus by Caligula and was the protégé of Narcissus: he would not have been favored by Agrippina, Claudius' last wife. In about 62 he governed Africa, where hostile reports still dogged him, in pointed contrast with the popularity of the administration of Aulus Vitellius: he was pelted with turnips at Hadrumetum (Sousse), perhaps during a grain shortage (Suet. *Vesp.* 4. 3). The hostile Agrippina was long dead by 67, and in 66 Nero's currently most successful general Domitius Corbulo was forced to suicide. But Vespasian's experience made him a good choice to tackle the strongpoints of Judea. He was even allowed to employ his elder son Titus, born in 39, as a legate of one of his three legions. Meanwhile his brother Sabinus, who had also fought in Britain, was holding the prefecture of the city in Rome. In 67–8 Vespasian conducted campaigns that carried him within striking distance of Jerusalem.

When Nero fell in June 68, Vespasian suspended operations. He recognized Galba as emperor, but would have been well informed from Rome of the precariousness of the new regime. He was poised from the start of the Year of the Four Emperors (AD 69) either to continue campaigning, or to participate in the struggle for power with his legions and equivalent auxiliary forces (and probably with the three legions of his neighbor Gaius Licinius Mucianus, governor of Syria, and the two of Tiberius Julius Alexander, prefect of Egypt). Titus had been sent to Rome to greet Galba, but turned back in January when he heard of his death, and helped to bring about good relations between Vespasian and Mucianus. These two men had not got on in the past, a pattern observable also in friction between other governors of Syria and the men who had received special and prestigious commands in the east (Germanicus and Gnaeus Piso were the prime example, early in Tiberius' reign); but they knew that they needed to unite in the face of a strong central power, together drawing in all the resources of the east.

Otho, who put himself at the head of the praetorian guard and assassinated Galba, lasted only until April, when he was defeated in northern Italy by an invasion force acting for Aulus Vitellius, leader of the Rhine armies. His victory, followed up by a march on Rome, left in its wake a plethora of defeated and discontented provincials, senators, and, more dangerously, soldiers, especially Otho's praetorians and the legions of Moesia. These are said to have been the first to declare for Vespasian, but the official bid did not come until July 1, 69. That was made on the initiative of Alexander in Egypt, and was followed two days later by a "spontaneous" salutation from the troops in Judea. The bid was neatly launched.

Vespasian went to Egypt and remained there, controlling much of the grain supply to Rome, and with some idea of advancing to Africa to complete the stranglehold. Mucianus, in charge of an expeditionary force, marched through Asia Minor and the Balkans, annihilating a group of invading tribes from over the Danube as they went. But before Mucianus could invade Italy, a legionary commander from the Moesian garrison, Antonius Primus, cut in and defeated the followers of Vitellius in a second battle in northern Italy. Primus entered Rome at the end of December, soon followed by Mucianus, though not before Vespasian's brother had been killed when negotiations for the surrender of Vitellius broke down. The inevitable power struggle between Mucianus, who had Vespasian's commission, and Primus, was won by the former, and Primus retired to his birthplace in Narbonensis (Provence). Mucianus killed Vitellius' son and other possible rivals, and saw senate and people offering their allegiance to Vespasian as readily as they had done to his three predecessors. Days away in Alexandria (longer in the winter), Vespasian had kept his hands clean.

A New Emperor

By the end of December 69, Vespasian was in possession of all the formal powers that his predecessors had enjoyed. All the same, the advantages of having emerged as the victor when the Roman world was worn out with fighting were counterbalanced by disadvantages, some unavoidable for any emperor in that position. He had to face the inevitable resentment and fear of those who had been on the losing side. Then there were the inevitable economic and moral results of a civil war. And there were other problems peculiar to Vespasian.

Up to and including the accession of Nero, the succession of "Julio-Claudian" emperors had a certain appearance of legitimacy. Some, Tiberius in particular and Nero to a limited extent, had had powers conferred on them before the death of their predecessors. That was not true of Caligula and Claudius, but there was also the hereditary factor: Caligula was the grandson of Tiberius, Claudius at least the uncle of Caligula and the brother of the lost hero Germanicus. That line broke in 68, but Galba had aristocratic republican birth and ties of friendship with the imperial house to supplement his reputation as a military man; Otho's family was new in the triumviral period, but he was a friend and twin spirit of Nero; Vitellius, whose forebears were allegedly slaves, nonetheless came of a family that had risen to the consulship and military command at the end of Augustus' reign, while his father shared the censorship with Claudius and held the consulship three times. Over this period a decline in the significance of family can be seen; with Vespasian it was precipitous. The victors lacked personal authority and prestige (*auctoritas*). Moreover, Vespasian took up arms against Vitellius, having initially acknowledged him, on the pretext that he had something to fear from the new emperor, and the struggle for Italy had been bloody. Even among commoners there were survivors who might have seemed to have a better title than Vespasian: the generals Gaius Suetonius Paullinus and Tiberius Plautius Silvanus Aelianus. They just happened not to be in charge of armies when the moment came. Vespasian consoled Silvanus with overdue triumphal regalia.

Before he returned to Rome in the autumn of 70, Vespasian did what he could to consolidate his position and secure his authority. First, he made up for his lack of ancestry and reputation by experiencing a vision in the shrine of the great deity Serapis in Alexandria and performing "miracles" that involved the healing of the disabled (Suet. *Vesp.* 7). All very well, but such effects were more likely to impress Alexandrians than Roman aristocrats, or even Roman plebeians. Second, he ratcheted up his formal powers to the highest level and sought *auctoritas* through a series of consulships, held every year except 73 and 78. Some scholars hold that the famous *lex de imperio Vespasiani*, part of an enactment in his favor preserved on bronze, embodies the original measure that the senate passed in December 70; others that it represents a special enactment of a few months later, designed to fill gaps left by the original law, and to guarantee Vespasian the right to perform any act that he deemed to be in the interests of the commonwealth – that is, it allowed him to do by right precisely what the Julio-Claudian emperors had done through *auctoritas*. His ostensible model was Augustus the founder, but Claudius the despised populist was the immediate precedent; significantly, Vespasian completed his ruinous temple.

Some senators had been giving Vespasian's representatives at Rome a hard time. The new regime was headed in his absence by his nineteen-year-old son Domitian, who had escaped from the Capitol when Sabinus had been captured and became praetor with the powers that a consul enjoyed; real power was in the hands of Mucianus, a man of ability and experience but compromised by past public failings and private scandal. Now men who had suffered for their principles under Nero's regime, or who had seen their friends and relations punished, were looking for a chance to prosecute those who had accused the victims. Beyond that, some hoped to bring about a return to a form of government that had prevailed when Nero was under the tutelage of Seneca and Burrus in the first years of his reign: the senate consulted on many issues, able to express its opinions freely, and likely to have its advice taken. Perhaps something even better was hoped for: that the senate should become the deciding body in government. One who belonged to both groups and was evidently ready to fight for the fullest rights for the senate was Gaius Helvidius Priscus, the son-in-law of Thrasea Paetus; opportunely he held the praetorship in 70.

A series of confrontations exposed the issues. The senatorial cause lost every time. Only minor concessions were granted. But what also emerges is the sense of proportion, even humor, that the emperor showed in meeting these gambits. With one exception, his response was limited, and in spite of his determination to keep the control and initiative that his Julio-Claudian predecessors had enjoyed he earned the praise of Tacitus: he was the only emperor who improved in office. The coinage, with its comfortable, well-worn themes, promised what Vespasian delivered. In the long run, though, his restraint, praiseworthy in itself in view of the power he wielded, depended on the personality of the princeps. Senators could not be sure that his successors would follow his example.

After the original powers were conferred came the question of who should convey the senate's congratulations to the new emperor. The consul-designate proposed an embassy chosen by lot; Helvidius wanted Neronian miscreants excluded and the members chosen by magistrates, then voted on by the senate. The issues were two: whether the senate was willing to take decisions on important matters; and who Vespasian's official friends were to be. Eprius Marcellus, the notorious accuser of Thrasea Paetus and others forced to suicide for disloyalty to Nero, frightened the senate off giving any opinion on that. Then came an urgent religious question, the restoration of the incinerated Capitol. The praetor Helvidius Priscus proposed that the restoration should be undertaken at the charge of the Roman state, that is, of its treasury, the *aerarium*; however, this had long been short of funds, partly because of the extent to which public monies were controlled by the princeps. So Helvidius proposed that Vespasian should "assist." The proposal was neglected, but Vespasian answered, when he returned to Rome in the autumn of 70, by carrying the first load of debris away from the site. The initiative lay with him. The proposal for a curb on public expenditure espoused by Helvidius, which might have redrawn the boundaries between imperial and public funding, was stopped by a tribunician veto. The emperor was to control finances (Tac. *Hist.* 4. 6–9).

An attempt to indict or expel accusers was encouraged by a small success against a minor figure. But access to the imperial archives was denied by Domitian. And Marcellus knew that his services in keeping the senate in order were indispensable, and said so – a new emperor was looking round to see whom he could trust for reliable information and support. Two offenders were returned to exile and the senate found itself performing another gratifyingly traditional judicial function, that of disciplining a city that had shown insufficient respect to one of its members by manhandling him. The ringleaders were punished and the people of Siena rebuked. Vespasian's further response was adroit: Marcellus spent three years as governor of the province of Asia, which would have needed steadying after the wars. Normally, the two senior ex-consuls drew lots for Africa and Asia, to hold the positions for a year. Marcellus' continuation, if not his good luck, was due to Vespasian, who thereby rewarded loyalty at the expense of other eager candidates, but also removed an objectionable person from the sight of his peers. Marcellus returned to a second consulship in 74.

As to membership of the senate in general, Vespasian and Titus held the invidious position of censors in 73–4, following the example of Claudius and wielding the right to inscribe men of merit, as it seemed to them, or to remove the disreputable or poverty-stricken (unless they chose to subsidize them). Gaps left by the casualties of Neronian war gave scope for filling ranks. The country towns of Italy would have been the places to look first, but money and ambition were to be found elsewhere, and Vespasian's supporters came largely from the east. The men he chose were approved, on the whole, by Tacitus, who nevertheless observes that some of them had more money than merit. They included men who had been serving in the eastern legions, such as Tiberius Julius Polemaeanus of Sardes, tribune of the Third Legion in Syria, who was to rise to the consulship in 92, and Gaius Caristanius Fronto of the colony of Pisidian Antioch, another soldier, whose consulship came even earlier, in 90. The merits of some deposed royals, such as Tiberius Claudius Antiochus Epiphanes Philopappus, of the royal house of Commagene, consul in 109, are uncertain, but in this case wealth perpetuated his memory: his monument still rises opposite the Acropolis in Athens. There is nothing to be said for the view that Vespasian leveled Italy and the provinces; there was simply beginning to be more money outside Italy; towns developed, most famously in Britain under Agricola, and multiplied. But even Spain was given only *ius Italicum*, which gave citizenship to city magistrates at the end of their year of office.

Another privilege associated with adlecting men into the senate, promoting or ejecting them, was that of making them patricians; this Vespasian and Titus exercised largely in favor of military men, such as Gnaeus Julius Agricola, Sextus Julius Frontinus, and Marcus Ulpius Traianus, father of the emperor Trajan; Vespasian himself had been plebeian until he became emperor and membership of the patriciate must have been granted him in December 69.

Toward Helvidius Priscus, Vespasian was unrelenting, although one source, Dio, perhaps influenced by the language of Mucianus, portrays Helvidius carrying on an aggressive feud against the emperor and challenging Vespasian to act against him. Certainly in praetorian edicts Helvidius referred to Vespasian as if he were a private person. On one occasion Helvidius was removed from the senate by tribunes of the plebeians, and if that took place while he was still in office, it was an evocative and symbolic conflict between magistrates who had often clashed in the past and occasionally did so under the principate: the tribunes represented the popular interest; the praetors, curule magistrates, represented the prerogatives of the senate. There is also a story that Vespasian requested Helvidius not to attend, and that Helvidius refused, insisting that it was his duty to attend – and to speak. We do not know when or why Helvidius was sent into exile, but his expulsion probably coincided with the exile of street philosophers, including radical Cynics, and astrologers. Scholars have connected it with a phrase attributed to Vespasian as he rushed out of the senate on one occasion: "Either my sons [or "son"] will succeed me or no one will!" (Dio 66. 12). That means, provided that the remark is part of the quarrel with Helvidius, that the crisis developed over the succession.

There were personal objections to accepting Titus as the heir; but a principle was at stake. The senate had last had a real say in the choice of emperor – frustrated, it is true – in 41. Men such as Helvidius believed that the senate had the right to choose the successor, or at least to have its advice heard. This does not seem to have been the case with Titus: they were presented with a motion that conferred tribunician power in June 71, after the joint triumph with which Pliny prudently concluded his *History*.

Helvidius did not survive his exile: an order arrived for his execution, allegedly carried out before a second order rescinding the first could arrive. If we do not believe this story, perhaps Vespasian pretended to change his mind to save his reputation or, possibly, that of Titus (see below). The death of Helvidius, heir of the Stoic hero Thrasea Paetus, lowered Vespasian's stock. But the second half of the reign was comparatively tranquil.

Economic and Financial Problems

We have already noted the difficulties of the Roman state treasury, the *aerarium*. These were in part attributable to the siphoning off of incomes into finances under the control of the emperor, consisting largely of his funds as governor of provinces that held substantial military forces; the ruler's private purse, augmented by what he inherited from his predecessors, had varied sources. The poverty of the *aerarium* was of little consequence outside Rome and Italy, but Vespasian, after Nero's expenditures, followed by eighteen months of unrest, fighting, plundering, devastation, and provincial revolt, confronted problems in the imperial funds. He is reported as complaining of a deficit of four thousand million sestertii, about five times one estimate of the annual tax revenue of the empire (the original manuscript of Suetonius reads an incredible forty thousand: Suet. *Vesp.* 16. 3).

Whatever the figure, Vespasian faced problems. His reaction was speedy and evidently drastic. He raised a new tax in Egypt while he was still there in 70 which led to his being execrated by the Alexandrian mob as a "fish-fingermonger." At Rome one notorious novelty was the tax on urine from public lavatories that fullers used in their work. Most famous is the tax that Jews had to pay for the upkeep of Capitoline Jove, previously their offering to the Temple. We are told that Vespasian multiplied tax rates, but there is no evidence for specific increases.

Census operations promised greater efficiency in determining what exactly was liable to tax or belonged to imperial provinces or the emperor's estates. When Domitian went to Gaul in 70 it was allegedly to conduct a census. There was more occasion for it after the disorder of the civil wars and the opportunities for illegal encroachment on state property encouraged by the inattention or absence of officials. Vespasian and Titus held the censorship in 73–4; thus they were able to take account of each man's property and to recover true boundary lines. Either then or in 70, Vespasian had the north African boundary known as the Fossa Regia properly marked out. Royal land was restored to the "Roman people" in Cyrenaica. On a smaller scale, the boundaries of the colony of Arausio (Orange) in Narbonese Gaul were demarcated afresh. In Italy, too, Vespasian was attentive to territory owned not only by himself but by cities and shrines, which would thus be put in control of their rightful rents and taxes. In Italian colonies land left over from allocation (*subseciva*) was sold for the benefit of the imperial treasury, arousing such strong protests from those exploiting it that Domitian brought the scheme to an end (*ILS* 5955; Suet. *Dom.* 9. 3).

There were other ways of raising revenue. One was to take over "free" states such as the cities of Achaea liberated by Nero and so acquire the tax revenues that would consequently become due. The cost of defense would then fall to the Roman government; but many "free" cities with or without immunity from taxation were far from military zones and required only policing. Then there were "client" kingdoms, notably in the east of Asia Minor, several of which Vespasian reduced to provincial status. The best-known case is that of Commagene. Antiochus IV had held it since the reign of Caligula, receiving it back after a period of provincialization under Tiberius. His substantial tax revenue, perhaps five million sestertii each year, now entered the imperial coffers, for despite loyal service, the kingdom was taken over in 72 on the pretext that Antiochus had been in contact with the Parthians (Jos. *BJ.* 7. 7. 1; Suet. *Vesp.* 8. 4). There were strategic considerations and effects (see below), but a redeployment of troops was sufficient to assure the security of Commagene, so there was little additional cost.

A more risky method of increasing revenue was military conquest. The effort, expensive in itself, might not succeed, and, if it did, the product might still not justify the cost. On the face of it, the two areas within which Vespasian ordered expansion, Britain and the Black Forest between Rhine and Danube, both came within this last category. Even in the mid-second century, when Roman power in Britain was at its greatest, bounded by the Antonine Wall, the historian Appian pronounced that the areas under Roman control did not balance the expense of the occupation (*Rom. Hist. praef.* 5). Other considerations, discussed below, determined the Flavian advances in Germany and Britain. Judea was different: the Romans had been committed to crushing the rebellious province long before Nero's death. This was achieved in part when Titus captured Jerusalem in August 70 and destroyed the Temple, and completed when Masada fell in 73. The booty was awesomely large, both in metal and in men. The latter could be used in the arena or sold to private owners. As a result of the "liberation" of gold onto the market by Titus, interest rates fell markedly in neighboring provinces. In the mid-70s Vespasian's Temple of Pax and the Colosseum were to be funded from the war booty. Building operations at Rome absorbed funds but also distributed them among contractors and workers: "my little plebeians," in Vespasian's phrase.

Leaving expansion aside, there was also economy. Vespasian was known for personal frugality, and the same characteristic marked his administration. Since the army accounted for the main burden of expenditure, he was anxious not to increase the army list. One legion, XVI, had been disbanded, but was reconstituted to appear in the east at Satala, Cappadocia. Before and during the civil wars two additional legions had been recruited; they survived, but

no more were added. The numbers of praetorian guardsmen had risen
markedly when Vitellius favored his legionaries by recruiting them into the
Italian garrison. It is claimed that Vespasian reduced the number of cohorts
from sixteen to the original nine.

With the exception of a few war zones – Judea, the Rhine, areas south of
the Danube where tribes had come over, northern Italy, Rome itself, and
a limited area in north Africa – damage within the Roman empire during
the civil conflict had been limited. Cremona had been sacked while it was
holding a fair even as the civil war raged. Now Vespasian gave confidence to
men with money to use. They returned to their normal occupations, farm-
ing and trade. There was more money to be made, and taxes would be
forthcoming. Rome, "rising again," as the coins had it, was a sign for the
empire. Even so, Domitian was to complain that the provinces were hardly
able to support the costs of empire.

Vespasian was unable to continue the denarius at the level set by Nero,
and the content of precious metal was reduced, to be raised in 82 by Domitian
and reduced once again in 85, fluctuations apparently not reflected in the
provincial coinage. A long-standing shortage of coin was particularly marked
in Italy, where people were used to living well and had been ready (as Pliny
the Elder complains) to expend precious metal on eastern luxuries such as
pepper, silk, and spices and were not always ready (as the emperor Tiberius
had complained) to exploit their estates for the greatest profit.

Of the crops that were grown in Italy, viticulture seems to have been doing
best in the Flavian period, and held a place that the emperor Domitian was
to find inappropriate. Grain was what the Roman people needed, and it had
to be imported from abroad, especially from Africa and Egypt, which entailed
dependence on shippers and the weather. Grain shortages had often led to
riots at Rome, while the effect of wine was obviously undesirable. Towards
the end of his reign, Domitian thought that he had found a simple solution
to all these problems: he banned the planting of new vines in Italy and
ordered the destruction of half of those in the provinces. There could be no
means of enforcing this regulation, and at least one deputation was sent from
the province of Asia to beg for its revocation. Domitian relented.

Mutiny and Rebellion

Even as the senate swallowed the humiliations of December 69 and January
70, rebellion was blazing up in the north, and it seemed that the empire
might still break up. Druids heard of the burning of the Capitol and predicted just that. To understand how things had come to this point we need to

look back to March 68, to the first rebellion in Gaul, that of Vindex against Nero. Vindex was an Aquitanian Gaul, but also a Roman senator, governor of Lugdunensis. It was private difficulties and possible disgrace that drove him to revolt. His influence as a nobleman and the Gauls' hatred of their burdens won him (it is said) an army of 20,000; how many rankers knew what they were fighting for is unknown. Vindex was crushed and killed by the Rhine legions under Lucius Verginius Rufus. When Galba (allegedly Vindex's only open supporter among the governors of the west) came to power, the legions knew that they would win no favors from him. So they backed Aulus Vitellius in his attack on Rome; Gauls and Germans closely linked with the Rhine fortresses and their surrounding townships shared their grievances. Besides the disgruntled Vitellianists there were the Batavians, who had been recruited by Vespasian against them, but who had long suffered the consequences of recruitment into the Roman auxiliaries and service away from home. Whether the rising should be regarded as "nation-alistic" is a matter of dispute. Only the Jews in antiquity were a nation; Gauls and Germans thought in smaller units. They were united in defending their own various interests, political and economic, in a time of crisis, and they used Roman political vocabulary to express their unity. Nobles from the Treveri and Lingones took command, representing themselves as "Roman" leaders who would care for the interests of their kinsmen and allies better than any central authority; they dressed as Roman commanders, or claimed descent from a son sired in the area by Julius Caesar.

The rebellion did not last long in Gaul. Severance from the rest of the empire meant loss of trade profits. The Remi, between the Rhine and the Channel, began the return. On the Rhine, however, resistance was obstinate. Mucianus set out for the north, accompanied by Vespasian's son Domitian, the only member of the dynasty who had not yet won military glory. But a careless if brilliant general, Quintus Petilius Cerialis, defeated the rebels before Mucianus and Domitian arrived, and the prince returned home. In the end of the story as told in Tacitus' *Histories*, the Batavian leader Julius Civilis reached a *modus vivendi* that allowed him to go free on the east bank. The Romans did not wish to continue a struggle that alienated more provincials and would carry them into perennially hostile territory. It was time for reconstruction.

Pushing Forward the Frontiers

That did not mean that Vespasian intended to follow Augustus' advice to Tiberius, that he should confine the empire to its existing boundaries. He had good political and strategic reasons for advancing them, even in Britain and Germany, and by force rather than diplomacy.

Augustus' attempt to subdue the tribes between the Rhine and Elbe had failed in AD 9 and, after retaliatory raids, which Germanicus tried between 14 and 16 to turn into reconquest, the strategy of allowing the tribes to destroy each other and of imposing friendly rulers when possible was tried until Rome was strong enough once again to tackle a weakened people and continue her inexorable advance to the Ocean. The balance of power between the German tribes shifted too. Arminius' tribe, the Cherusci, lost pre-eminence, and the Chatti began to occupy more of Rome's attention. Between the sources of the Rhine and Danube a re-entrant angle exposed the provinces to attack. Vespasian entrusted the task of bringing this area, the *Decumates Agri* (the Black Forest and adjoining territory), under Roman control to Gnaeus Pinarius Clemens, who achieved it without fuss in two years of campaigning. Roads were built, and at the center a town was founded as a focus of administration and cult, Aquae Flaviae (now Wiesbaden). It was a minimal substitute for the Augustan conquest and it was not necessarily to be regarded as a final step. Indeed, Domitian, after successful action against the Chatti in 83, expanded the area of Roman control in the Wetterau and established a permanent boundary there (the *limes*) as well as along the eastern edge of the *Decumates Agri*. The strategy of letting one German tribe turn on another was continued: Tacitus gloats over the massacre of "sixty thousand" Bructeri (Tac. *Ag.* 33).

In Britain Vespasian's achievement was more spectacular, and that was the point. Augustus had declined the option of conquest that Julius Caesar left his successors, on the grounds that Rome was making as much from customs dues as occupation would bring. Tiberius followed suit, but Claudius had to display his military qualifications. Since Vespasian's first campaign in Britain, Roman control had advanced to a line running north-east from what would later be Exeter to Lincoln, along the Fosse Way, although in the west, tribes in Wales had repulsed attempts on their territory. In 60, as Suetonius Paullinus was intent on Anglesey, East Anglian tribes rose under Boudicca against extortionate taxation and brutality. Her defeat was followed by a decade of quiet reconstruction. Just as the Romans were about to extend their control northward under a general experienced in mountain warfare, Vettius Bolanus, they found that they had to suspend aggressive action for the duration of the civil wars. The governor kept his province quiet and the dependent ruler Tiberius Claudius Cogidubnus evidently worked in the interest of Vespasian: he stayed in his kingdom in Hampshire and Sussex into the Flavian era.

This was the province in which Vespasian had won his first distinction. Since the revolt nothing had been achieved; it was said that Nero once thought of giving up Claudius' conquest. Now Vespasian would take up his patron's enterprise, recover imperial glory for the Roman people, and uncover resources to help pay for the advance. Lead from Flintshire (and under Domitian from Yorkshire too) is stamped with the imperial name.

The first governor charged with the offensive was the dashing Petilius Cerialis, the commander who had recovered the Rhine. He was also a man to be trusted with three legions in any province, for he was a kinsman by marriage (another was Nero's general in Syria, Caesennius Paetus, who had been forced to submission by the Parthians at Rhandeia, but was now given a second chance). The achievements of Agricola's predecessors naturally were not trumpeted by Agricola's biographer, but Bolanus had made himself felt in the north. There was a change there that demanded firm handling: the deposition of Cartimandua, ruler of the Brigantes, who had obligingly handed Caratacus over to the Romans under Claudius. The Brigantes were a formidable confederation that stretched from one side of Britain to the other and from southern Yorkshire to the north of the later Hadrian's Wall. Now they were no longer friendly. The operations of Cerialis were followed up by those in Wales under another loyal general of distinction, Sextus Julius Frontinus, who survived into Trajan's reign and held three consulships. Then in 77 (or, though less likely, in 78) came Agricola, who subdued north Wales and conquered Anglesey at last, and continued the push beyond the Brigantes into Scotland. He won Vespasian, Titus, and then Domitian salutations as *imperator*. A hard-fought (mainly by auxiliaries) battle at "Mons Graupius," in which he defeated the rebel leader Calgacus in 93, won Agricola at least temporary control of the north (he had already looked out toward Ireland, but decided against an invasion). That was the end of his seven-year governorship. There were pressing concerns in central Europe, notably the encroachments of the Chatti on the Rhine and problems on the Danube in 85. These concerns made it unwise to stretch Roman resources in Britain any further (for other considerations, see below). Inchtuthil, a fortress under construction at the gateway to the highland glens, was evacuated. Agricola's successors were not front-rank generals. Trajan would later continue the withdrawal, bringing the troops back to the line of Hadrian's Wall.

The Danube frontier was permeable, as incursions under Nero and in 69 had shown. The first governor sent to secure Moesia after Mucianus had repelled those invaders, Fonteius Agrippa, had been slaughtered. Vespasian did not attempt massive retaliation, but sent Rubrius Gallus to restore morale and reinforce the garrison of the Moesian provinces, turning the Danube once and for all into the real focus of attention in the north. Whereas at the end of Nero's reign there were seven legions on the Rhine and six in the Balkans, by Nerva's time a quarter-century later there were six on the Rhine and ten in the Balkans. Vespasian's solution proved adequate until the mid-80s, when Domitian had to intervene in person. He used both money and intimidation, but a Roman force under Cornelius Fuscus, Domitian's prefect of the praetorian guard, was massacred in 88 by the Dacians and the reign ended in stalemate. It was left to Trajan to reduce the king of Dacia to apparent obedience, and then to defeat and provincialize the kingdom.

In the east, too, Vespasian had no immediate plans for expansion, but made sure that the option was open. The obvious threat came from Rome's old antagonists, the Parthians. They had offered help when he was making his bid for power, but he was too clever to accept it. There was skirmishing with the Parthians during Vespasian's reign, but nothing came of it. His annexations of client kingdoms such as Commagene and probably Emesa, and his reluctance to return Judea to the son of Claudius' favorite, Agrippa I – preferring to assign it instead to a praetorian governor with one legion – bear witness to his firm policy. This is further illustrated (the measures were not simultaneous) by his creation of the vast province of Cappadocia–Galatia, and the installation of legions in Commagene and Cappadocia, which, except during Nero's Parthian wars, had been under an equestrian procurator since Tiberius provincialized them. Flavian stress on protecting the Black Sea, Cappadocia, and the Caucasus passes may also have been connected with the arrival in the Caucasus of tribes from the north. Domitian installed a centurion near Baku to watch over Roman friends in the Caucasus. At one point the Parthian king is alleged to have asked Vespasian for help against opponents in the east, the Hyrcanians. That was refused (Dio 65. 15. 3).

Vespasian's Sons

It was considered an advantage in Vespasian that, unlike any of his predecessors except Claudius, who ended up being outmaneuvered by his wife Agrippina, he had sons of his own body to succeed him; this factor may have been one of those that induced the homosexual Mucianus to give way to his claims. His elder son, Titus, though only an ex-quaestor, had been a legate in Vespasian's army. His military success continued with the capture of Jerusalem and the burning of the Temple, which friendly sources were unwilling to ascribe to him.

Titus was intelligent, personable, and brave, if Josephus' accounts of his daring exploits in the Jewish War are to be believed. On his way back to Vespasian he had stopped in Cyprus to consult the oracle at Paphos. These were dangerous times; ambition may have been the motive. But there were points against Titus, apart from the low status of his late mother, who was allegedly of servile origin. He had an oriental mistress, Berenice, the sister, consort, and allegedly lover of Agrippa II of Chalcis. The ambition of Berenice and Agrippa was clear enough: they hoped to recover the kingdom of Judea that their father Agrippa I had been given by Claudius. Romans would see her as a poor man's Cleopatra VII, intent on transferring power from Italy to the east.

Titus returned to Rome in June 71 to a triumph shared with his father, to further consulships and the censorship, but most significantly to two offices that made Vespasian's intentions perfectly transparent. After his consulship in 71 he took the tribunician authority, the token of supremacy which his father had held since the senate granted it to him in December 69 – but which he counted himself as holding since 1 July, the day of his declaration. So much for the authority of the senate. Now Titus was counting the term of his tenure too, and his total was only two years behind his father. He was his father's colleague and would succeed him. More important from a practical point of view was the proconsular power that Titus must have shared to some extent and degree with his father. By the time Tiberius came to take over from Augustus he was ruling the empire as an equal colleague. The same may have been true of Titus, who was thus consort as well as heir, but we do not know when or how far his authority was extended from control over the eastern provinces; probably in 71, when he was awarded the tribunician authority, and over the whole empire.

But Vespasian took another step, an unprecedented one, for the prefecture of the praetorian guard was an equestrian post. Some of its past holders, from Sejanus to Nymphidius Sabinus, had proved dangerous to their masters. Now Titus, back in Rome, was appointed to the role. As commander of the guard, Titus was able to have executions carried out. Brutality was another failing imputed to him: suspects were denounced in the theater or praetorian barracks and summarily executed, claims Suetonius. It must have been an officer of the guard who killed Helvidius. The order could have come from Titus, not from Vespasian. It could even have been forged. So people may have thought, given the prince's gift for imitating handwriting (Suet. *Tit.* 3).

Vespasian's younger son, Domitian, having been at Rome during the final struggle with the Vitellian forces, was brought on to front the new regime. This was a brief hour of glory, as he tried to conciliate bitter enemies. Domitian did not succeed in taking part in the crushing of the revolt on the Rhine and at the end of his praetorship he sank into obscurity, to return to office from time to time, usually as a suffect consul. Moreover, among the shower of honors obtained for the family at the beginning of the reign was the title of *princeps juventutis,* "Youth Leader," for each of the two young men. Titus did not hold the title for long, but Domitian kept it until the end of the reign. That meant that he belonged in the next generation of the dynasty, and would be looked upon for the moment not as Titus' colleague in power but as his successor. In spite of the accumulated consulships, Domitian does not seem to have held the proconsular power in any form until he became emperor in September 81.

Unease about the young men cannot have been assuaged after the death of Helvidius in 74. Discomfort with the political situation is shown in Tacitus' *Dialogus,* set in that year. Evidence for the end of Vespasian's reign is poor, but there was at least one other act of violence in which Titus was involved. Of Vespasian's old allies, Mucianus slipped from favor after his months of glory during the assault on Italy and the beginning of 70. He probably did not live beyond the middle of the reign. Eprius Marcellus, his agreeable ally Vibius Crispus, and Aulus Caecina, who had defected from commanding Vitellius' troops in northern Italy, all survived. Only Crispus, however, lived on into the reigns of Titus and Domitian. It was discovered toward the end of Vespasian's life that Marcellus and Caecina were plotting against the emperor. Marcellus was arrested and brought before the senate (he cut his throat), while Caecina was killed as he left a banquet attended by Titus, who found proof of the plan in his clothing: the text of a speech, written in his own hand, to be delivered to the praetorian guard. The story is implausible. The two "plotters" were advanced in years and expendable; the most likely explanation of what happened is that the unscrupulous Titus decided that he was unwilling to be burdened with their advice and the obligations that the dynasty owed them.

In 79 Vespasian suffered increasingly severe intestinal problems. He died on the night of June 23–4, at the spa of Aquae Cutiliae, near his home town. Without imperatoriai salutation Titus was acknowledged as emperor in the senate on the following day, taking the name Augustus, receiving the supreme pontificate and, by September 7, the title *pater patriae,* "father of the fatherland."

Imperial Cult

Near his end, Vespasian reportedly exclaimed: "Oh dear! I think I'm becoming a god!" (Suet. *Vesp.* 23. 4). Sometimes taken for a heartwarming specimen of imperial humor, this saying represents a satirical attack on him, modeled on purported last words of the emperor Claudius. Vespasian was deified, though some scholars have claimed that Titus hesitated for some weeks: coins mentioning deification appear only after a delay. The only emperors previously to have been granted the status of an official deity of the state religion, with all the servicing and cost that this entailed, were Augustus and Claudius (Vespasian, in another anecdote of the time, is said to have offered to let his body be thrown into the Tiber, if only he were given the price of the funeral). But, as Pliny the Younger (*Pan.* 11. 1) remarked, it was the need of the heir that brought about deification. The plebeian Flavians needed prestige from whatever source they could get it. In the event Vespasian was one of the few rulers whose flamens continued to serve after his death, and to the customary temple Domitian added another, to the entire Flavian gens.

Cities, individuals, and provinces had seen their rulers as more than human in the west since Augustus' time, and in the east since the time of Alexander and his successors. Several parties benefited: the emperor or whichever kinsman was offered the tribute; the initiators of the cult, who drew attention to their homage; the individual who proposed and perhaps paid for the buildings, ceremonies, and games that made up the cult; and the people who benefited from new facilities.

Given the anecdotes that are reported about Vespasian's down-to-earth attitude to his own status, it is surprising how far the cults are claimed to have developed under Vespasian; yet the needs of the dynasty were pressing, and he had allowed himself to be represented in Alexandria as a miracle worker. It is the geographical spread of the cult under Vespasian, rather than any intensification, that is most remarkable. A document discovered at Narbo (Narbonne), attributed to the reign of Vespasian or of Domitian, sets up rules for the conduct of the high priest (*ILS* 6964; McCrum and Woodhead 1961: 128). Newly established cults of the Flavian period have been detected in other provinces: Baetica, Africa, Mauretania, Lesser Armenia. Doubts subsist. The date of the Narbo document remains uncertain, and it is hardly credible that one of the wealthiest public provinces had voluntarily gone until the Flavian era without the advantages of united representation for its ruling elite, public honors for its leaders, and something worthwhile to offer the emperors that the cult gave it. If structures that support cults appear first only under Vespasian, that does not mean that they did not exist beforehand.

At Rome on his death a temple was constructed in Vespasian's honor, soon to become the Temple of Vespasian and Titus. It was left to Domitian, in his need for personal adulation, to prescribe the use of "Lord and God" to his equestrian agents as an address for himself. Domitian also developed the interest of the Flavians in Jupiter, as against the patronage of Apollo to which Augustus had looked. It began with the restoration of the Capitol and was continued with Domitian's establishment of his quinquennial Capitoline Games. In particular, Domitian regarded himself as under the protection of Jupiter's daughter Minerva, if not as her child. Minerva herself had been born from Jupiter's head, and, as she was a virgin, there would have been something prodigious about Domitian's birth as well; certainly it would have dispensed with Domitian's embarrassing mother. Intellectuality was Minerva's hallmark, and Domitian's as well.

Cultural Life

Vespasian, though not exceptionally well educated, had a way with words (he wrote his own war memoirs) and respected education; Titus for a time was allegedly the schoolfellow of Britannicus, and both Titus and Domitian wrote poetry. Vespasian founded chairs of rhetoric at Athens and Rome and granted teachers, doctors, and physiotherapists privileges in the cities in which they resided. He also subsidized individual writers. The accession into high society of men from the country towns of Italy and from the provinces had an effect on manners, according to Tacitus. A reaction against clever brevity in literature would go along with this, as would a return to favor in poetry of grand old forms, namely epic, with Virgil as the model. Valerius Flaccus began his *Argonautica*, embellished with flattering addresses to members of the dynasty, but had not finished it when he died, in the early 90s; Silius Italicus (*c*.25–101) wrote a *Punica* (and restored Virgil's tomb at Naples), Statius (*c*.45–96) produced a *Thebaid*. The same author's *Silvae* was adulatory and, as with Martial (*c*.40–104), whose writing career spanned four reigns, there is sharp controversy about such apparently adulatory treatment of Domitian. In exculpation, boldness in dealing with the subject of tyrants, as in the *Thebaid*, proffered a challenge to the ruler to prove that he was not one; praise provided a standard for him to maintain. Martial's sharp epigrams certainly would have been met with the controlling Domitian's approval, given their attacks on contemporary *mores*.

Correspondingly in oratory the pointed style gave way to something more expansive; Cicero's was in vogue, Seneca's out, like his politics, as can be seen from Quintilian (*c*.35–90s), one of Vespasian's first professors and tutor to Domitian's heirs. Setting his Ciceronian *Dialogus* in 74 Tacitus, unlike

Vespasian

Quintilian, makes the imperial political system responsible for the perceived decline in oratory. Eloquence continued nonetheless to be cultivated with assiduity, as can be seen from Tacitus' interest, and from the *Letters* of Pliny the Younger, where the writers' performances are celebrated, but great causes were lacking. Men were taking rather to poetry and plays; they too could be dangerous.

Architecture also saw an assertion of classical styles, in spite of the boldness of the Colosseum, sculpture a resurgence of Atticism, portraiture of realism, (as Vespasian's own busts attest), painting of illusionistic art, skillfully rendered and technically effective. But there is danger of over-schematization. The Fourth, intricate, style at Pompeii, exemplified in the house of the Vettii, was one of several available contemporaneously, and itself went back to Claudius' time.

In religion, for all Silius Italicus' emphasis on tradition, there was a renaissance of Egyptian gods outside Egypt; perhaps the two most important long-term developments in Vespasian's reign, though not intended by him, were the precipitation of Christianity into an empire-wide religion distinct from Judaism, and the growth of rabbinic Judaism in the Diaspora, both due to the destruction of the Temple in Jerusalem.

The Reigns of Titus and Domitian

Men were naturally apprehensive of the accession of Titus (the emperor Hadrian mentioned a story that he poisoned his father). Extravagance, the fate of opponents, and Titus' liaison with Berenice were justifiable sources of fear. But they proved unjustified. Titus was aware of his unpopularity and of the need to please. In his short reign of just over two years, from June 79 until September 81, he proved affable, generous, and sensitive to public opinion; skeptics wondered how long it would have lasted. As it was, he punished informers and promised to ignore defamation; there were no political executions, and it was probably Titus who originated the oath undertaking that an emperor would not put any of his peers to death (Domitian refused it). Berenice was immediately sent away and the ceremonial opening of the Colosseum, which he adorned with an inscription claiming the building for himself, attended by spectacularly generous displays, won over the people. Soon he needed to offer relief work. The reign was marred after only two months by catastrophe: the eruption of Vesuvius, destroying Pompeii, Herculaneum, and Stabiae.

When Titus died, mourning was intense: the "love and darling of the human race" was lost. Besides, the young man of thirty who succeeded him, despite having been at the center of government for over ten years, was known to have been studiously kept out of real power since his extraordinary praetorship of 70, and that raised suspicions about his ability and good will. Rumors of poisoning circulated, probably unfounded. Titus died, apparently of fever, like his father in their native territory, aged forty-two.

Domitian hastened to his brother's deathbed and with equal haste back to Rome to claim his rights. The senate did not delay. September 13 was the date when Domitian was empowered, as Vespasian had been, at one stroke, and with any additions that had been accorded later. He never troubled to celebrate it as far as the records show. He told his peers that he had given his father and brother the power; the senate had given it back to him. Forgery of Vespasian's will was also mentioned – not, perhaps, in the senate.

For a young man with no military experience, little contact with the troops, and no benefactions to win over the people of Rome, Domitian had a major task in front of him. It might be wondered what danger he was in, but the Flavian family was prolific, and that was where Domitian saw threats. Vespasian's brother Sabinus, dead in 69, had a grandson, and he was married to Titus' daughter (Flavia) Julia. Domitian himself had been offered his niece, a union legal since Claudius had married Agrippina the Younger. Dynastically the marriage would have strengthened Domitian's claims to power, but he had refused. That may have been because he remembered the earlier such marriages when men had wed the emperor's daughter. The relation of son-in-law put the groom firmly in the younger generation, and Domitian may have felt all along that he should have been his brother's partner in power. We do not know when this refusal took place, but quite early in Vespasian's reign Domitian married the daughter of Nero's great general Gnaeus Domitius Corbulo. Perhaps he hoped to gather Corbulo's friends round him. Julia, given to Flavius Sabinus, helped make him a rival for the principate. During Domitian's first, conciliatory, years, Sabinus was courted with the consulship of 82, the first regular consulship that Domitian had to offer. He was, indeed, Domitian's putative heir, as the emperor's only known child, a little boy, died in infancy.

After this we enter a grey area, where reconstruction is particularly uncertain. Suetonius relates that when Sabinus was declared elected consul, the herald made a verbal slip and declared him emperor (Suet. *Dom.* 10. 4). Most scholars associate this with a second consulship. Because Sabinus was executed, and a conspiracy is recorded for 87, they suppose that after the mistake Sabinus was arrested before he could take office. But there was also trouble in 83, and the mistake may have been thrown up against Sabinus after he had completed his term. The date matters, because it gives an indication of how long Domitian's "good period" lasted. The years 83–4 were particularly significant in other ways. To secure power, winning over the army was Domitian's main aim (neither Vespasian nor Titus had had to leave Italy after their triumph of 71). Domitian campaigned as emperor, but at first stayed at Rome and took his salutations as *imperator* from the victories of Agricola. In 83 he went to Germany and won a success against the infiltrating Chatti. In the same year Agricola's final victory over the Britons gave Domitian another salutation and enabled him to withdraw the governor from his post, which he had held for an exceptional length of time. Domitian now possessed a military success of his own, and from 85 onwards he made other expeditions, on the Danube. There were defeats at the hands of the Dacians, but it is evident that he won the hearts of the soldiers – not least, no doubt, by increasing their pay by one-third. When he was assassinated, the troops – evidently Suetonius means the praetorian guard – became restive. It was during the same period of 83–4 that he sent his wife Domitia Longina away and thought of marrying Julia (that does not necessarily mean that her husband was dead, but it would be easier if he were). He was dissuaded from this course (incestuous marriage; insult to the prestigious former husband, if he was still alive, and to Domitia Longina and her friends). The man who gave this advice was Lucius Julius Ursus, prefect of the guard (Dio 67. 3. 1–2). He was removed from office in 83–4 and "promoted" to senatorial rank and the consulship.

These events seem to be interconnected, and the importance of 83–4 is brought out by a development of 85: Domitian, like his kinsmen, took up the invidious censorship, and this time it turned out to be not for eighteen months but for life. Membership of the senate and advancement of its members were now permanently and overtly under his control. That did not mean that some men who might have been expected to stand out against him were hindered in their careers. Notable among these was Helvidius Priscus, son of the martyr who died under Vespasian. It looks as though he was consul in about 87; Quintus Junius Arulenus Rusticus, a defiant tribune in 66, held the office in 92. One might even suspect that in his earlier years as emperor Domitian was following up political relations that he had formed under Vespasian and Titus, that is, favoring men with whom he had sided when he was out of power.

This attitude did not last. The reign entered its final phase in 93, when the politicians whose championship of the senate's rights was bolstered by their philosophical tenets were brought before the senate by their opponents and charged with infringing the majesty of the emperor. The most notable victims then were Arulenus Rusticus and Herennius Senecio. The younger Helvidius fell because of his biography of Thrasea Paetus. Tacitus in the *Agricola* graphically presents the guilty anguish of the senate as they condemned these men (Tac. *Agr.* 2 and 45). Attempts have been made to exonerate Domitian, but at the very least he allowed the proceedings. And there was a series of events leading up to these events which cannot be ignored. Domitian was unmistakably determined to control the lives of his peers, and infringements of ancient rules were mercilessly punished: Vestals alleged to have broken their vows of chastity were buried alive and their lovers beaten to death. Again, Domitian was rapacious, confiscating even from provincials. The wealthy Athenian Hipparchus, acquitted under Vespasian, did not survive. The rapacity has led to charges of profligacy with money for army pay, buildings, and the Capitoline games, but they are not convincing. One need not be short of money to want more.

After 83 the first conspiracy came in 87, then, early in 89, came the revolt of Antonius Saturninus on the Rhine. Saturninus looks like a man caught up in the mutiny of his own troops. But the deaths of military men followed, notably Sallustius Lucullus, a former governor of Britain, and the governor of Asia, who was scandalously succeeded for the moment by an equestrian procurator. In 95 another relative died, Flavius Clemens, the brother of

Sabinus, under a charge of "atheism," which might be disrespect for the imperial cult or perhaps a commitment to Judaism.

Domitian, without an heir to succeed him, and to avenge him if he fell victim to assassination, had adopted the children of his cousin Clemens. It did not save him. The inner circle of courtiers, including a prefect of the praetorian guard, Domitian's freedman chamberlain Stephanus, saw that he would fall and that their own futures were bleak, and decided to take the initiative. There were probably senatorial participants, but they remained concealed; his wife's alleged involvement is uncertain. On September 18, 96, Domitian was assassinated and the compliant old senator Marcus Cocceius Nerva, a survivor from Nero's time, put in his place.

Conclusion

Suetonius' verdict on the dynasty is one of qualified approval: they took the empire in hand and gave it renewed strength. They could not come up to their successors, his and Tacitus' contemporaries. Personal failings, and Domitian's desire for an unattainable control, brought about the end of the dynasty and nominally the return of "Liberty." But Domitian had the virtues of his failings: his government was keen and observant, and Suetonius reports that governors of provinces were particularly competent. The same governmental virtue was practiced to a more moderate degree by the conscientious Vespasian and Titus. In a period of recovery their care for all aspects of government, including even Vespasian's stinginess, when the money saved was spent on public works, was particularly valuable.

Their even more basic and valuable service was to show that the empire could survive the downfall of the family whose century-old tenure of power had guaranteed peace and whatever prosperity the ancient economy and technology could proffer. Their very tenacity in holding on to power increased confidence, and Vespasian's private economy and public munificence (a combination of which Cicero had said long ago was what the Roman people loved) made both him and Titus loved by the people; Suetonius says that they bore Domitian's assassination with indifference (Suet. *Dom.* 23. 1). The senate was glad of his fall, but Domitian's contribution to the Flavian achievement was a particular one: he reduced the senate to a cautious and alert talking shop that gratified provincials' ambitions and supplied conscientious administrators. It would cause emperors no more trouble.

Their low origin also served the Flavians. Vespasian allowed no pretence about his birth. Pragmatic and down-to-earth – Domitian was the exception

Barbara Levick

ᴗᴇnted a new, workmanlike and duteous, image of the principate,
ᴗᴇ that came to perfection in the reigns of the traveler Hadrian, Antoninus
Pius, and the Stoic philosopher Marcus Aurelius.

Further Reading

P. A. Brunt, "The *Lex de Imperio Vespasiani*," *Journal of Roman Studies* 67 (1977), 95–116

M. T. Griffin, *Cambridge Ancient History*, vol. 11, 2nd edn (Cambridge, 2000), 1–84

B. W. Jones, *The Emperor Domitian* (London, 1992)

B. W. Jones, *The Emperor Titus* (London and New York, 1982)

B. Levick, *Vespasian* (London, 1999)

J. Nicols, *Vespasian and the Partes Flavianae, Historia* Einzelschrift 28 (Munich, 1978)

P. Southern, *Domitian: The Tragic Tyrant* (London, 1997)

VII

Hadrian

Mary T. Boatwright

From Domitian to Hadrian: Nerva and Trajan

When the senators proclaimed Marcus Cocceius Nerva emperor following the assassination of Domitian they ushered in a new and happier era of Roman history. Nerva did not live long enough to make a major impact, except through one important act. He nominated as his successor a man chosen on the basis not of family connection but of proven competence, Marcus Ulpius Traianus. Trajan had pursued a successful career as a soldier before his accession in 98. As emperor his military achievements were considerable, most notably the conquest of Dacia (roughly, today's Romania and Moldova), which he incorporated into a Roman province, and the annexation of much of the Parthian empire, which took Roman dominion to the shores of the Persian Gulf. On the domestic front his approach was humane and progressive. Under him Rome saw an ambitious building program, the most notable product of which was the Forum of Trajan, and a revision of the tax system and the grain supply. He died in 117, widely respected and admired.

Hadrian

To write a biography of Trajan's successor, Hadrian, is to introduce the Roman world at its peak in lieu of thoroughly depicting the man who ruled it from August 11, 117 to July 10, 138. In large part this is due to the nature of our information, which falls into three types. We have copious yet scattered documentary sources, including a detailed honorific inscription raised in Athens to Hadrian in 112 (Smallwood 1966: 109), coins and medallions, and Hadrian's public responses and laws recorded on inscriptions and papyri.[1] These are supplemented by less obviously factual material: a few of his poems, jokes and quotable sayings, numerous images of him and his intimate circle,[2] and the literature written by others during and after his long life and rule.[3] For ancient historical analyses of the emperor and his effects we now have only a few, short pieces. These, sections of the *Historia Augusta*, Cassius Dio, and fourth-century abbreviated histories, have various deficiencies. Their generally poor chronology is reflected below in the broadly topical arrangement of this biography.[4] Nevertheless, their concurrence on Hadrian's restiveness, multiple interests, changeability, and contrary impulses seems validated by Hadrianic material found from Britain to Egypt, north Africa to Dacia. The glimpses into Hadrian the sources provide – his competitiveness, firm direction, administrative talents, and aesthetic pursuits – reveal a man who successfully held together intense contrasts for many years.

This "little Greek," as he was derisively termed for his impassioned Greek studies and sensibilities, was also an exemplary military and administrative Roman leader. He was deliberately sociable with all ranks and types, and strikingly respectful toward his older female relatives. But he often seems a loner more at ease with his hunting dogs and horses, and his young lover Antinoos, than in protracted, sincere interactions with others, including his wife Sabina. Despite his many abilities and all of Rome's resources, Hadrian was a perfectionist who could never be satisfied. He was often disagreeable, and ultimately unhappy. Yet the scholarly and human curiosity that underlay his restlessness, even his meddlesomeness, meant that he touched most of the Roman world he inhabited from 76 to 138. Given the charismatic foundation of the Roman empire, Hadrian's extensive personal interactions and structural changes greatly strengthened imperial rule, establishing him as one of Rome's most significant emperors.

Life before Accession

Publius Aelius Hadrianus was more than qualified when, at the age of 41, he became emperor of Rome. His most important training had come in multiple stints as a commander in the Roman army, and as Roman governor of unsettled provinces. In 94 or 95, when only eighteen or nineteen, he was tribune of Legio II Adiutrix, then stationed in Aquincum in Pannonia (near Budapest, Hungary). The next year (96–7) saw him in a second military tribunate, now for Legio V Macedonica stationed in Oescus, Moesia (Gigen, Bulgaria). In 97–8 he was tribune again, this time of Legio XXII Primigenia in Moguntiacum (Mainz, Germany). It was very rare for a man to serve three times as military tribune. The three positions gave Hadrian singular knowledge of Rome's difficult northern frontier, from the lower reaches of the Rhine to those of the Danube. Domitian's involvement in Germany in 85 and in Dacia in 85–6 and 88 had unsettled these areas, and Aquincum and Oescus would see much action during Trajan's Dacian Wars of 101–6. The tribunates also kept Hadrian out of Rome during the anxious years of Domitian's assassination (96) and Nerva's brief rule (96–8). They located Hadrian near Trajan, his distant relative and former tutor (see below), when Trajan twice was governor on the northern frontier. Hadrian was chosen to carry Legio XXII's congratulations to Trajan when Nerva adopted him in 97, and for a similar mission in 98 when Nerva's death brought Trajan to imperial power. But the repeated military service was also important in introducing Hadrian personally to many of Rome's soldiers and officers. As emperor he was said never to have needed prompting for anyone's name, and he could recognize all soldiers he had honorably discharged (see *HA Hadr.* 10. 8; Dio 69. 9. 2). He probably developed at this time his tough habits of riding bareheaded with the troops and otherwise sharing their meager meals and disciplined life.

Hadrian's military merits led Trajan to choose the younger man as companion and then legionary commander during the First and Second Dacian Wars (101–2, 105–6). During these conflicts, which resulted in Rome's acquisition of a new province, Dacia, stretching from the Carpathian basin to the Black Sea, Hadrian twice won military prizes from Trajan, undoubtedly for real distinctions in battle. Toward the wars' end he was entrusted with the governorship of Lower Pannonia (?106–8), one of the two provinces into which Pannonia had just been divided. Stationed again at Aquincum, he may be responsible for the "governor's palace" built around this time on an island in the Danube; its baths and opulent appointments reflect the impression of peace Rome wanted to strike here after the death of the enemy king Decebalus and the decimation of the Dacians. Hadrian's military strengths were called upon again less than a decade later. With other chosen men he may have accompanied Trajan to the initial stages of Trajan's Parthian War in 113. In 115 he and Trajan miraculously escaped the earthquake that devastated Syrian Antioch (Antakya, Turkey), at the time teeming with soldiers and military preparations for an eastern operation. Two years later Hadrian had risen further: as the Parthian War ended and Trajan, now ill, started toward Rome, the emperor chose Hadrian to step in as governor of Syria in 117. Supervision of this province, like that of Lower Pannonia ten years before, demanded unquestionable loyalty, a steady hand, and strict organization.

But by this time Hadrian had also served politically in Rome in numerous circumstances. Such service was key to his future success as an emperor. It opened a man's eyes to the many mundane tasks fundamental to Rome's elaborate functioning, and the collegiality essential to most posts set an important precedent for ruling in the principate. Perhaps by the age of sixteen Hadrian was one of the board of ten men who presided over minor lawsuits (*decemviri stlitibus iudicandis*). Some two years later (?94) he served as *praefectus feriarum Latinarum*, the prefect left in nominal charge of the city of Rome when curule magistrates went to the Alban Mount to celebrate the age-old festival of the Latin League. As *sevir turmae equitum Romanorum* in 94 Hadrian led a squadron of Roman knights past the emperor Domitian in an annual equestrian review. With hindsight we can hazard that Hadrian's stint as a minor judge piqued his legal bent, while also impressing upon him the need to make Roman law more organized: as we shall see, sources like to point out his interest, as emperor, in Rome's law. The other two positions were archaic and prestigious, held by highly placed youths of senatorial rank. They coincide with Hadrian's later archaizing interests in Latium and Rome's earliest cults and practices. Further, good relations with the equestrians, the second echelon of Rome, were also a hallmark of Hadrian's rule.

After these initial steps (which were followed by his military tribuneships), Hadrian smoothly moved upward in Rome's *cursus honorum*. He was plebeian tribune in 102, praetor (perhaps in 105), and then *consul suffectus* in 108, a position he reached ten years before the norm. He was designated to serve as consul again in 118. Along the way he entered two prestigious religious societies, assuming the life-long religious positions of *septemvir epulonum* and *sodalis Augustalis*. He also held special posts, such as the *ab actis senatus* that put him in charge of the official reports of proceedings of the senate (?101/2); a quaestorship specially connected to the emperor Trajan in 101; and the charge of being Trajan's speech-writer. The first position ties in with Hadrian's attention to detail, and possibly also with his later historical interests. Hadrian's service as *quaestor imperatoris Traiani* and as Trajan's speech-writer indicate that emperor's approval of the rising young man, but such imperial encouragement of talent was not extraordinary in this period. The literary sources stress that Hadrian was never clearly designated as Trajan's heir. The bluff soldier Trajan may have been put off by Hadrian's more artistic pursuits, which must already have been apparent (see below).

Yet Hadrian and Trajan had similar origins and some special ties. Like Trajan, Hadrian came from a wealthy senatorial family with property in

Italica, Baetica (today Itálica, Spain); indeed, we do not know whether Hadrian was born in Italica or Rome. Trajan was a distant cousin, whose father had reached the consulship and the coveted governorship of Asia. Although Hadrian's own father, Publius Aelius Hadrianus Afer, had risen no higher than the praetorship, his family had enjoyed senatorial standing for some generations and presumably had land in Rome and in its ancestral Hadria, on Italy's Adriatic coast. Hadrian's mother, Domitia Paulina, had land in Gades (Cádiz). Perhaps in the late 80s Hadrian's sister, also named Domitia Paulina, married Lucius Julius Servianus (*consul suffectus* in 90). When Hadrian's father had died in 85 or 86, the ten-year-old boy became the ward of Trajan, then embarking on his own career, and of Publius Acilius Attianus, who would later serve both Trajan and Hadrian as praetorian prefect. Perhaps in this early period Hadrian developed his strong and affectionate relationships with the women of Trajan's family: Trajan's wife Plotina (born before 70, perhaps married to Trajan by 84 or 86) and sister Marciana, and Marciana's daughter Matidia the Elder (born before 68). Hadrian's ties to the family became even closer when, probably in AD 100, he married Sabina, the daughter of Matidia the Elder and thus the great-niece of Trajan. She was probably then around fifteen, the usual age of marriage for elite Roman women. These ties may have facilitated Hadrian's entry into political life in 94, and perhaps sparked the imperial favor of 101. Without individual talent and resolve, however, Hadrian could not have attained continued success.

So far we have evidence of a dedicated, accomplished elite Roman who embraced Rome's traditional means to eminence. As for almost all others in his position, there is almost no information about Hadrian's personal life as a youth. What little we know is inferred from his activities and interests as emperor. We assume that as a youth he developed his fascination with hunting and with Greek culture, for which he gained the nickname *Graeculus*, or "little Greek." By the time he was Trajan's speech-writer the erudite young man may already have employed his archaizing tastes to dignify the words of the plain-spoken emperor. And Hadrian's well-known interests in poetry, painting, sculpture, and architecture (Dio 69. 3. 2, 4. 2–6; *HA Hadr.* 16. 8–10; *Epit. de Caes.* 14. 2) must also have begun early. Most emperors wrote poetry and prose, and all were supposed to be skilled at oratory and rhetoric, but Hadrian is one of the very few known to have personally engaged in arts usually practiced by persons of lower-class status.

The inscription raised to Hadrian in 112 in Athens, on the occasion of his holding the eponymous archonship there, may evoke Hadrian's life before his elevation to imperial rule. It gives us more details of Hadrian's political career than we have for most other Romans. But it is the circumstances of the inscription that call our attention here. Identifying a statue of Hadrian that Athens' *areopagus*, council of 600, and *demos* installed in the Theater of Dionysus, the bilingual inscription presents Hadrian's lengthy *cursus honorum* in Latin, and its short dedication to "their own archon" in Greek. Although various emperors, members of the imperial family, and senators had sporadically assumed local magistracies and priesthoods, most held such posts *in absentia* and relatively few had thus honored Athens. But Hadrian was almost certainly in Athens during his archonship of 112. As emperor, Hadrian would amply demonstrate his love of Athens, visiting the city three times, reaching the highest level of initiation in the Eleusinian mysteries, and frequently providing the Athenians with buildings, festivals, reconstructions, and administrative aid. Indeed, in a letter to the city of 132, Hadrian stated: "You know that I take advantage of every excuse for doing good to the city as a whole and to individual Athenians" (Smallwood 1966: 445, 10–11). The bilingual division of the inscription for Hadrian of 112, together with his statue's location, illuminates Hadrian's simultaneous dedication to Roman and Greek traditions: Roman political and military ideals, and Greek history and aesthetics.

Finally, a cluster of events prior to Hadrian's accession is worth noting for their bearing on his decisions as emperor: the Parthian War of 115–17 and the contemporaneous Second Jewish Revolt. By 116 Trajan had pushed deeply into Parthia. In the north, Roman troops had crossed the upper reaches of the Tigris, and in the south they had reached Babylon, from where commanders planned to venture to the Persian Gulf. But the territorial gains, organized as the provinces of Armenia, Mesopotamia, and Assyria, could not be secured. Uprisings in the newly won territory necessitated redeployment of Rome's advance troops and the abandonment of further offensive warfare. Moreover, in 115 news came that the Jews were in rebellion in Egypt, Cyrene, and Cyprus. It was unclear whether the various insurgencies were coordinated or would spread further in the Diaspora or consume Judea itself. Cassius Dio luridly describes the death and destruction attributed to Jewish rebels (Dio 68. 32). The desperately violent Jewish uprising contributed to the cancellation of further missions and abandonment of the new provinces. This withdrawal was later invidiously attributed to Hadrian rather than to Trajan, the *optimus princeps*: Roman ideology preferred military expansion and audacity to consolidation and vigilance (e.g. *HA Hadr.* 9. 1–2; Eutropius 8. 6. 1). Whoever made the decisions, Hadrian apparently saw at first hand how overextension could weaken Rome, spreading troops too thinly over recently acquired territory and diverting attention from internal discontent. Well-known features of his rule were Rome's non-expansion, and his own constant awareness and drilling of Rome's army. We might also hazard the guess that the Second Jewish Revolt, which continued into 117 in Alexandria and a few other spots, may have contributed to his erratic and ultimately lethal treatment of the Jews (see below).

Hadrian's Accession and First Two Years

But in 117 few would have envisaged Hadrian as the next emperor, despite his appointment as governor of Syria for that year and his designation as consul for 118. Many talented, hard-working men from northern Italy, Spain, southern France, Greece, and other parts of the empire were already in, or entering, the senatorial and equestrian ranks. The childless Trajan, despite increasing illness during the Parthian War, had not publicly adopted anyone (in contrast to Nerva's celebrated adoption of him in 96), perhaps to encourage all to meritorious service and to lessen envy. But as Trajan returned to Rome with Plotina and the rest of the imperial entourage, his health worsened. His adoption of Hadrian was announced just before his death in Selinus, Cilicia (Selinti, Turkey). Many suspected the deathbed adoption as a forgery Plotina concocted for her favorite, Hadrian. But such qualms did not prevent official acceptance of the adoption. Hadrian's troops at Antioch saluted him as emperor on August 11, 117 (*HA Hadr.* 4. 6). Childless, as Trajan had been, Hadrian would be more methodical about transferring imperial power to a successor at the end of his own life; such foresight contributed to the likelihood of political stability being maintained during the inherently volatile days surrounding an emperor's death.

Despite rumors about his adoption, the 41-year-old Hadrian exhibited numerous qualifications for his new role. He brought to it extensive military, political, and religious experience. He spoke and wrote compellingly, thanks to an excellent education he constantly honed by memorization and composition (see *HA Hadr.* 3. 1). Long acquainted with Rome and central Italy, he also knew at first hand Rome's northern border from Germany to Moesia, south-western Spain, Athens, Antioch, other parts of Syria, and Parthia. His journeys to these locales had introduced him to many cities strung along Rome's roadways, coasts, and rivers, and to long stretches of farmland, forest, and uncultivated waste. Years in the army and administration had familiarized him with most of Rome's governing elite, and as emperor he would be markedly generous with senators – whom he often personally visited and would invite into his carriage – and with equestrians. His genuine friendship with Plotina and other women of Trajan's household promised continuity in

Hadrian

the imperial court. He had also developed, and cherished, an easy affability with the common man. He inspired loyalty and restraint among his staff, who included the erudite freedman Phlegon of Tralles, one of many known to have worked closely with Hadrian.

Further, the new emperor was elegant and strong, favored with a tall and vigorous physique, flashing eyes, and a fine head of hair. His well-trimmed beard, defying the prevailing Roman fashion, may have disguised a scar or been aimed at demonstrating his enthusiasm for Greek philosophy and culture; it now also reflects Hadrian's quest for distinctiveness. He was rumored to have indulged in wine and young boys as a youth so as to ingratiate himself with Trajan, who was notably fond of both. But by 117 Hadrian was nobody's man but his own. His way combined rigorous discipline, keen inquisitiveness about natural phenomena, history, and the arts, and dedication to excellence. It also coupled strict adherence to some traditions, such as military preparedness and familial piety, to a distinctive appraisal of merit.

As emperor, Hadrian turned first to Rome's army, the empire's foundation, and to the organization of the provinces. A change of emperor was often marked by provincial and military instability, and the Second Jewish Revolt was not yet completely suppressed. Unrest in Dacia had been reported in 116 and was still troubling the new province. Disturbances were also reported in Mauretania and Britain. Hadrian first removed the new governor of Judea, Lusius Quietus, from that province, perhaps because of Quietus' brutal suppression of the Jewish insurgency in Mesopotamia; it may be this imperial decision that earned Hadrian his early acclaim as a deliverer of the Jews (e.g. *Or. Sib.* 5. 46ff.). Sensible postings of qualified individuals to Egypt and other locales aimed both at quelling unrest and at putting in key spots men loyal to the new regime. But Dacia and the Danubian regions were too insecure and important to entrust to others. Hadrian went there himself about a month after his imperial acclamation in Antioch.

By winter 117–18 he was on the lower Danube in an area he knew well from his service as military tribune in 96–7 and then during the Dacian Wars. He made a decision similar to the one that had just ended the Parthian War: to retreat from territorial gains. When established in 106, Trajan's new province of Dacia had extended all the way to the Dniester river and the Black Sea. Rome fought for this vast north-eastern territory even while annexing Arabia Petraea ("rocky Arabia": southern Jordan and north-west Saudi Arabia) in 105–6. Arabia's annexation helped precipitate war with the neighboring Parthians a decade later, when Trajan's deployment of troops east began to undermine Rome's control of Dacia. Hadrian now abandoned as untenable Trajan's gains above the lower Danube, sparking critical comparison of him with the gloriously martial Trajan. Restricting Rome's new province Dacia within the Carpathian mountains, Hadrian negotiated with various Transdanubian groups. By 118 he had settled matters on Rome's north-eastern frontier. He could then devote attention to "the affair of the four consulars," a manifestation of internal discontent among Rome's most highly placed citizens that would forever taint his reputation.

As with other failed imperial conspiracies, we now have little understanding of motivations and events. While Hadrian was still in the north, four eminent senators were implicated in a plot against him: Lusius Quietus, Gaius Avidius Nigrinus, Aulus Cornelius Palma, and Lucius Publilius Celsus. Since the first two had served during the Parthian War and in Dacia, it has been conjectured that the conspiracy arose in response to Hadrian's renunciation of Roman territory. Action against the four was swift: the senate met and condemned them, and they were cut down at or while traveling to their homes outside Rome. Attianus, the praetorian prefect and Hadrian's former tutor, was directly responsible, and Hadrian protested that he had not wanted the executions. When he arrived in Rome in 118 he announced a cessation of treason trials, and throughout his rule he went out of his way to attend to senators and the senate. Nonetheless, the killing of so many eminent men with the complicity of the senate marred Hadrian's accession.

The new emperor's absence from Rome allowed rumors and suspicion to spread. After settling matters in Dacia, Hadrian did not come directly to Rome. Rather, he went west to Pannonia, the site of his first governorship, where he hunted, inspected the troops, and performed administrative tasks, such as granting different types of city status to various new and emergent communities. The tombstone of one of his personal horse guards, a physically powerful sharpshooter originally from Batavia (at the Rhine delta), illustrates Hadrian's encouragement of merit, and the splendid relationship he enjoyed with his troops. It reads in part:

> I am the man once well known on the Pannonian shore, brave and foremost among a thousand Batavian men: with Hadrian as my judge I was able to swim the vast waters of the deep Danube in full armor . . . While an arrow from my bow was hanging and descending in the air . . . I shot another . . . and split it in two. No Roman or barbarian could ever best me . . . It remains to be seen whether anyone else will rival my deeds. (Smallwood 1966: 336; see Dio 69. 9. 6)

An aggressively competitive atmosphere is palpable in another incident from this time. Among the visitors to Hadrian's traveling court in Pannonia was the 17-year-old Herodes Atticus, with an ambitiously prepared speech. The youth, who was to go on to fame as a sophist and political man, was so flummoxed in the presence of the emperor that he choked on his words; in despair he almost threw himself in the Danube (Philostr. *VS* 2. 14. 565). Such tales, which flesh out the chronology of Hadrian's voyages, contextualize the biography of this emperor and his ceaseless push for excellence.

Early in July 118 Hadrian finally entered the capital city as the new *princeps*. His presence in Rome in the next three years established his authority and brought him before the public eye. Among other spectacular gestures he gave soldiers a double donative, and the Roman people a twofold largesse. He declined the customary contributions made by Italian communities at an emperor's accession, reduced those from the provinces, and remitted taxes, publicly burning tax records in Trajan's Forum. He requested the senate to grant divine honors to Trajan, and then honored his predecessor with a posthumous triumph for the Parthian victories. In the capital he began an impressive building program that included the Pantheon and the vast Temple of Venus and Roma: such public structures provided jobs, beautified the city, and advertised piety and confidence in the *pax Augusta*. Other urban changes, like the restoration of Rome's sacred boundary (*pomerium*), linked with raising the ground level of the Campus Martius, similarly had practical and symbolic meanings: the terracing worked to control flooding, and Hadrian's careful attention to the pomerial line evinced his devotion to Rome's earliest traditions. The Pantheon, an Augustan shrine Hadrian had rebuilt on a unique design, was rededicated with its original inscription documenting as donor Augustus' right-hand man Agrippa. It remains a striking example of Hadrian's assiduous emulation of Augustus, the first *princeps*, but its exceptional architecture bears Hadrian's idiosyncratic stamp.

Hadrian's Journeys

Also like Augustus, Hadrian made lengthy trips to the provinces. But Hadrian traveled much more than his exemplar, spending more than half of his 21-year rule away from Italy. He visited almost every Roman province, in trips noted in the literary sources and substantiated by inscriptions, coins, and other documentary sources. As befitted Rome's beneficial ideology, which held that the emperor and others at the top were to demonstrate and justify eminence by benefactions, Hadrian was frequently generous to communities and individuals as he traveled. In return, or sometimes in anticipation of boons, cities and wealthy individuals commemorated the emperor's presence or made a big showing of their worthiness to receive him. Hadrian's trip to Rome in 117–18 carried the new emperor from Syria through Cilicia, Cappadocia, Galatia, and Bithynia (and probably Thrace), then through Moesia, Dacia, and Pannonia. He did not stay long in Rome after his arrival in 118, making further journeys around the provinces in 121–5 and again in 128–32 (or, less likely, 128–34). The itineraries below exhibit the extent of his personal acquaintance with the Roman world; we then detail a few of their events as a way to illuminate Hadrian himself.

In 121 Hadrian set out for a four-year trip that began north-west of Italy and finished in the east, touching at most provinces north of the Mediterranean. Moving through Gallia Narbonensis and Gallia Lugdunensis (southern France), he went to visit Roman troops in Upper and Lower Germany, and in Raetia and Noricum. By summer 122 he had turned his attention to Britannia (where he presumably began his famous wall, which would ultimately stretch for 80 Roman miles [117 kilometers]). Returning via Gaul to the milder south, he wintered in 122–3 in Tarraco (Tarragona, Spain). But within a few months he had already crossed the Mediterranean to Syria, through which he traveled to the Euphrates. Still in the easternmost reaches of Rome's empire, Hadrian turned north to the southern shore of the Black Sea, to Trapezus, Cappadocia (Trabezon, Turkey). By winter 123–4 he had gone west again, to Bithynian Nicomedia and Nicaea (Izmit and Iznik, Turkey). Descent into Asia in spring 124 brought him to cities renowned for their intellectual life, brilliant sophists, stunning architecture and arts, and fabled history: Ilion/Troy (now Hisarlik, Turkey), Smyrna (Izmir), and Ephesus (Efes), among others. By autumn he had turned west. Athens, which he reached via Rhodes in October 124, was to be his base until late spring or early summer 125. He used the city as a starting point for travel to the Peloponnese; Delphi, Phocis, and the Copaic Lake in central Greece; and Euboea (Evia), among other spots. He returned to Rome via Sicily, and by September 125 he was in his newly built villa at Tibur (Tivoli, Italy). He was to remain in and around Rome for some three years.

What is often called Hadrian's "second trip" is known with less precision. In contrast to the first, this included provinces south of the Mediterranean. In summer 128 Hadrian briefly visited Africa and Mauretania, returning to Rome by early autumn. But soon he left the capital again. In 128–9 he wintered in Athens, with at least one side trip to Sparta. By early spring he was in Asia, traveling first to Ephesus (March–April), then further south to Miletus. An inland route took him through cities along the Meander river valley, including Tralles (Aydin, Turkey). Then, turning south-east through Pisidia and Cilicia, he arrived at Syrian Antioch in autumn 129. It was now over ten years since he had stayed in the capital of Syria; to judge from the many buildings and festivals he supported there (see below), he was interested in reconstruction after the terrible earthquake of 115, which he had experienced personally. By the beginning of 130 Hadrian had moved farther south-east, to Palmyra (Tadmor, Syria) and, fleetingly, to Trajan's new province of Arabia, where he stopped in Gerasa (Jerash, Jordan). A jog west took him to Judea, where he visited Gaza and perhaps Jerusalem. He then went to Egypt via Pelusium at the Nile's easternmost mouth. Hadrian and his entourage spent most of 130 in Egypt, primarily in the sophisticated center of Alexandria but also elsewhere, such as up the Nile at Thebes (Luxor). He left Egypt in early 131, coasting along Judea, Syria, and the southern coast of modern Turkey (ancient Cilicia, Pamphylia, and Lycia). By the latter half of 131 he was back in south-east Europe in Thrace, Moesia, Dacia, and Macedonia. He wintered again in Athens in 131–2, returning to Rome probably in 132. After this we lack details about any trips, and presume that he spent the rest of his life in Rome and in his villas at Tibur and Baiae, perhaps with brief breaks elsewhere in central Italy.

Roman emperors had customarily traveled primarily for military purposes, to and from foreign campaigns, and sometimes to sites of internal insurrections. Some of Hadrian's trips clearly had these objectives, confirming the sources' stress on his abiding interest in the army. We have already discussed his journey to Dacia in 117; in 123 he went to the Euphrates to allay a Parthian threat by personal intervention (*HA Hadr.* 12. 8). These two trips must also have included inspection of Roman troops and borders, known aims of Hadrian in Upper and Lower Germany, Raetia, and Noricum (in 121); in Britannia (122); in Africa (128); and probably also in Trajan's new province of Arabia (130). An unusual document illuminates Hadrian's handling of his frontier troops. At Lambaesis, Africa (Tazzoult-Lambèse, Algeria) on July 1, 128 Hadrian addressed Legio III Augusta, which had just been moved here to a new camp from elsewhere in the province (Smallwood 1966: 328). The series of short orations to individual cohorts, inscribed later for public exhibition in the camp, shows Hadrian's keen and personalized attention to his soldiers. He carefully notes various units' distinction at drills and maneuvers, comparing their exertions to those of other groups and generally praising exercises as discipline. Despite criticizing one cavalryman, he individually commends officers as well as the troops themselves, reinforcing loyalty and morale. Such contact with the troops was essential to Rome's military power and longevity.

But even such practical, conventional trips offered other opportunities for Hadrian. In his day Rome's troops were stationed on distant borders that could be reached only by lengthy travel though peaceful territory and cities: on his way to Lambaesis, for example, he stopped in Sicily. Further, other trips, such as those to Tarraco, Egypt, Asia, and especially Athens, had no overt military justification. The journeys were expensive for communities and individuals accommodating them, despite Hadrian's shunning of imperial trappings as he traveled. Yet an imperial visit conferred much prestige on a community. This, deeply appreciated in the competitive system of Rome, accounts for the extensive documentation of his travels. Just as importantly, imperial visits offered individuals and communities direct access to the emperor, a significant advantage given the real obstacles to communication and travel in the Roman world. In the emperor's presence regional disputes could be settled, financial problems cleared up, and political debacles resolved; local projects, imperative or unessential, could gain backing. These, and many other material and structural benefits, are attested as occurring during Hadrian's voyages.

Further, many particulars of Hadrian's activity and personality are detailed in accounts of his trips, allowing us to appreciate him as a person, not merely as a "good" Roman emperor. His insatiable curiosity about nature and history emerges in his ascent of Mount Etna to see its rainbow in 125, his night-time hike up Mount Casius (near Syrian Antioch) so that he could see the sunrise, and his trip in 130 up the Nile to Thebes, to hear the Colossus of Memnon sing at dawn. His passion for hunting and the wild is corroborated in many different ways, from his poem to his steed Borysthenes at the splendid creature's tomb in Apta (Apt, France) (Smallwood 1966: 520) to another poem composed in honor of a dangerous but ultimately successful hunt with Antinoos on the Libyan coast in 130 (Athen. 15. 677 d–f; *P. Oxy.* 1085). Hadrian coupled this zeal to practical liberality in the mountainous interior of north-eastern Turkey, where he founded at least two cities at the sites of successful hunts in 124 (Hadrianoutherae and Hadrianoi, near Balihesir and Orhaneli, Turkey).

Hadrian's particular and somewhat idiosyncratic assessment of merit, clear in the inscriptions relating to his dealings with his soldiers, is reaffirmed in letters he wrote to Ephesus to promote the election to the city council of the sea-captains Lucius Erastus and Philokyrios.[5] His backing of these two, who had transported him safely to and from the coastal city, challenged Roman traditions that those in political positions should have landed, rather than commercial, wealth. The generosity that supreme power can give may be seen in Hadrian's discreet pardon of a mad slave who had ineffectually attacked him in Tarraco (*HA Hadr.* 12. 3). His appreciation of the arts is well known, but his admiration of finesse and erudition comes through all the more in a story concerning municipal rivalries: Hadrian was so impressed by the rhetorical brilliance of the sophist Polemo that in one day he transferred to Smyrna, which Polemo was representing, all the money he had earmarked for Ephesus (Philostr. *VS* 1. 25. 2). On the other hand, his occasional intellectual arrogance is also evident in various vignettes. For example, the learned sophist Favorinus conceded a grammatical dispute to Hadrian despite being in the right, later declaring he should always think more erudite the man who commanded thirty legions (*HA Hadr.* 15. 10–13). Less charming is the story of Hadrian's visit to Alexandria's "Mouseion," an intellectual academy and library, where he belittled the leading professors in debate (*HA Hadr.* 20. 2).

Hadrian's affections and passions are also highlighted in various stories set in the provinces. Chief among these is the account of Antinoos' death and its consequences (Dio 69. 11. 2–4; *HA Hadr.* 14. 5–6; Aur. Vict. *Caes.* 14. 7–9). Hadrian's grief at the death of his lover is the more poignant for its exotic setting on the Nile, where traditions about the resurrected god Osiris encouraged recognition of Antinoos as a hero/god after the youth drowned in October 130. Hadrian's unrestrained anguish is exemplified in his foundation of a city in Antinoos' name at the site of his drowning, and his disregard of others' opinions about his personal life surfaces in the comparison of this "overreaction" to his moderation after his sister's death. That the city thrived as an admirable amalgamation of Greek, Roman, and Egyptian elements accentuates Hadrian's organizational and conceptual brilliance. His donation to Plotina's home town, Nemausus (Nîmes, France), of a basilica or temple in her name, like the temple raised in Rome to his mother-in-law Matidia after her death and deification, strikingly commemorates his affection toward the elder women of the imperial court (*HA Hadr.* 12. 1–2; Dio 69. 10. 3^1–3a). More, his recorded correspondence with Plotina about favors to the Epicurean school at Athens in 121 shows that intellectual bonds were important in their friendship (Smallwood 1966: 442). His contrasting apathy, even coldness, toward his wife Sabina, reported in the context of the trip to Britain in 122 (*HA Hadr.* 11. 2), may seem less cruel in the setting of the arduous journeys that minimized their time alone together. Yet he seems possessive of his wife, dismissing Septicius Clarus, the praetorian prefect, and Suetonius, the biographer and writer who was then in charge of Hadrian's official correspondence (*ab epistulis*), because they had treated Sabina more informally than befitted the imperial court. Hadrian emerges as a man who could never forget the duties of his position.

The numerous provincial locales for these and other scenes highlight the range of Hadrian's interests and activities. Although he might be seen as fickle and inconstant – a criticism frequently encountered in the literary sources (e.g. *HA Hadr.* 14. 8–11, 15. 10–16. 11; Dio 69. 3. 1, 5. 1, 11. 3) – he can also be seen as admirably flexible. Rome's best emperors, attentive to the wide diversity of the lands and peoples under their control, were reluctant to establish rigid rules that would be universally binding. More, Hadrian's persistent restlessness implies a decentralized vision of Rome and its empire. His recurrent travels and inquisitiveness intensified his impact on the many constituent parts of the Roman world. But focus on his journeys should not obscure structural changes associated with Hadrian.

Law

Hadrian involved himself in Roman law and administration, in keeping with Augustan precedence; among the various personifications publicized on his coinage is IUSTITIA (Justice), a beautiful woman. He was personally responsive to petitions and requests, with more rescripts in the *Digest* than are attributed to earlier emperors.[6] His rescripts and other legal pronouncements range widely. They include matters from allowing inheritance from deceased soldiers who died intestate (an interpretation in a "more humane sense" of a "rather stern rule laid down by my predecessors" [Smallwood 1966: 333]; soldiers could not legally marry until the rule of Septimius Severus) to the appropriate penalties for rustling cattle. One scholar concludes that Hadrian's legal rulings reveal impatience with corruption, with wasting time, and with shirking public duties; at the same time, however, they disclose Hadrian's deeply generous impulses and his conviction of his own legal acumen.[7] Hadrian's rescripts emphasize the emperor as the originator of law, as do his other legal measures.

He was responsible for the codification of the legal procedures and types of proceedings that praetors would allow in office, the so-called *edictum perpetuum*. Previously, individual praetors could choose or modify the rules and procedures they would follow in jurisdiction, although by the early empire the various praetorian edicts were more or less standardized. Hadrian asked the eminent jurist Publius Salvius Julianus to compose a revised version of this "praetorian edict," and in 131 the senate ratified the document. Specific motivation and effects are hard to discern. From what we can tell, the Hadrianic Perpetual Edict was not notably systematic, but at the least it meant that henceforth the procedures of civil law at Rome could be changed only by the *princeps* or a decree of the senate.

In other ways Hadrian encouraged assumption of jurisdiction by appointees ultimately responsible to the emperor. He established a new position, the board of four consular men, appointed by the emperor; these were to decide non-criminal cases in Italy, divided administratively into four regions for this purpose. Roman citizens in Italy previously had to come to the senate in Rome itself to have appeals heard or for cases of more than local significance. Although Hadrian's innovation acknowledges the burdens of the earlier system, it apparently likened Italy to a province, and the senate may have thought it insulting. It was dropped by Antoninus Pius, and little is known of the board and its functions. Hadrian also declared that in court cases the unanimous opinion of authorized jurists could count "as if it were law" (Gaius, *Institutes* 1. 7). Plainly signaling that others as well as the *princeps* could make law, this proclamation recognized the expertise of jurists; indeed, as Gaius goes on to state, in cases of disagreement a judge could follow the opinion he thought best suited to the case. Jurists, men learned in the law, had become increasingly influential in the Rome of the late republic and early empire. Many advised emperors, and often even men with lesser legal expertise had been consulted (for instance, Pliny the Younger by Trajan, *Ep.* 4. 22). Hadrian's specification of unanimity, however, actually worked against the power of individual jurists. From this time on legal opinions were couched as imperial rescripts issued by the emperor.

Another alleged change, however, indicates Hadrian's high estimation of jurists. A laconic statement locates Hadrian as judge together with the great jurisconsults Salvius Julianus, Publius Juventius Celsus, and Lucius Neratius Priscus (*HA Hadr.* 18. 1). This has suggested to some that Hadrian re-established the *consilium principis*, an unofficial body of friends who served as the emperor's sounding board, as a kind of standing organ of state whose permanent salaried members included leading jurists. Although this assumption is probably overstated, Hadrian did make a point of turning to legal experts in matters of law and administration. This tendency seems tied less to a focus on legal innovation than to the desire, attested in many other ways, to involve as many senators and equestrians as possible in Rome's administration.

The delicate interplay of this emperor and his legal advisors is reflected in Cassius Dio's description of Hadrian's performance as judge (69. 7. 1): "He conducted all the most important matters in conjunction with the senate, and he heard cases about the most significant issues, sometimes in the palace, sometimes in the Forum or the Pantheon, or in many other places, from a raised platform so that the proceedings would be public. And he would join the consuls when they tried cases." All who have entered the Pantheon, perhaps Hadrian's most remarkable extant building, can vividly imagine how its centralized space and diffused natural light would have concentrated attention on the emperor elevated in his judicial role, albeit in a crowd of advisors and friends.

Administration, Society, and Economy

Yet no one person could shoulder alone all the responsibilities of the Roman world. Some information suggests that Hadrian moved toward a more articulated imperial service in which more positions were opened up. An administrative reform has been traced in the fiscal sphere as one bureau, the *a rationibus*, began to coordinate the activities of three lower ones. There may also have been reorganization of the offices of *a libellis* and *ab epistulis*, charged with responding respectively to correspondence to the emperor about administrative concerns and about questions of private law. Moreover, second-century inscriptions attesting officials at Rome and in various municipalities indicate that in Hadrian's rule lower administrative positions in imperial service were arranged more regularly and hierarchically than had been the case previously. To judge again from the rather erratic epigraphic record, Hadrian was also responsible for increased social promotion of provincials from Egypt and north Africa to the equestrian order. But such variations do not look like a systematic overhaul of administration. Rather, they were almost certainly the result of ad hoc responses to immediate concerns.

During Hadrian's rule the composition of the senate changed slightly. Consonant with his reputation as a philhellene, Hadrian is thought to be the first emperor whose rule saw senators with origins in Achaea appointed as governors in the Latin west. At the same time, numerous men from Africa and Numidia were enrolled as senators. The expansion of Rome's governing base to the provinces was a process that began in the late republic and intensified over the centuries. But it was never deliberate imperial policy. Throughout imperial history few or no senators came from some provinces (among them Lower Moesia, Mauretania Tingitana, Britain, and Egypt), and Italy always predominates in the number of identified senators.[8] Hadrian did not overturn the traditional bias toward a Roman ruling elite from Rome and Italy. Nonetheless, his championing of Greco-Roman culture and aesthetics may have signaled one way for "outsiders" to move to prominence in Hadrianic Rome.

More difficult to document in detail are the widespread, subtle differences Hadrian made in the lives of the middle echelons of Roman society: the municipal elites and the free men who constituted the backbone of the Roman army. In the Roman senate Hadrian proclaimed attentiveness to the local political traditions of Rome's municipalities, which he felt were worth preserving (Aul. Gell. *NA* 16. 13. 1–9). He strove always to speak with the common man and to know his troops personally (e.g. *HA Hadr.* 20. 1; cf. Dio 69. 6. 3). His constant trips, frequent troop inspections, and omnivorous curiosity brought him to many regions and people. Although he could not attend to every city in the Roman empire – probably encompassing 60 million inhabitants in his day, some 12 million of them in cities – he is documented as leaving a personal mark on many communities in Africa, Mauretania Caesariensis, Cyrenaica, Syria, Asia, Bithynia-Pontus, Achaea, and Italy, effecting more than 210 interventions in over 130 local communities.

The general terms used in the ancient sources for such work – *beneficia*, *euergesia*, and other words connoting benefaction – cover a variety of different activities and structures. Over forty interventions can be categorized as city foundations or official recognition. These include entirely new cities (Antinoopolis; Mursa in Upper Pannonia [Osijek, Croatia]), reconstructions of devastated cities (as Cyrene, Cyrenaica [near Banghazi, Libya], pillaged in the Second Jewish Revolt, and Syrian Antioch, demolished in the earthquake of 115), and the much more frequent grant of a Roman city status to a pre-existing community (as colonial rights to his home town Italica, or municipal status to Aelium Choba, Mauretania [near Bejaia, Algeria]). He demonstrated encouragement of civic life by personally assuming local positions: besides his archonship of Athens in 112, as emperor Hadrian served at least thirteen cities nominally as city magistrate or civic priest, sometimes for repeated periods. He is also associated with a more general innovation, that of "greater Latin rights," or *Latium maius*, which conferred Roman citizenship on men who chose to serve in their own town councils. By example and inducements Hadrian fostered local pride and promoted individuals' assumption of municipal positions.

Besides donating numerous civic buildings, discussed generally below, Hadrian favored cities by conferring territory (as when he gave two islands and a nearby port in the Peloponnese to Sparta) or by endowing or supporting grain supplies (as to Athens, Ephesus, and Tralles). At times he confirmed earlier tax exemptions (as for Asian Aphrodisias [Geyre, Turkey] and Delphi). These boons, like patronage or imperial recognition of periodic games that brought fame, competitors, and spectators to a city (as the Demostheneia in Oenoanda [Fethiye, Turkey]), conferred on the recipients immediate economic advantages. This was true also for the more than twenty engineering projects he undertook, ranging from drainage schemes (as at Lake Copais in Achaea and the Fucine Lake in Italy) and aqueducts (e.g. Argos, Achaea; Sarmizegetusa, Dacia), to roadwork and harbors in central and southern Italy and elsewhere.

Such civic generosity was not sustainable without general peace. Although Trajan's success in the Dacian Wars brought 500,000 pounds of gold and a million pounds of silver into Rome's treasury, Trajanic public building had been largely restricted to Rome itself, and to roads and harbors serving military needs. Even while remitting taxes at the start of his rule Hadrian detailed economic difficulties (*HA Hadr.* 6. 5); these were undoubtedly due to the ineffective Parthian War. Hadrian's withdrawal in Dacia and the abandonment of the Parthian War lowered state expenditures. The money could then be earmarked for reconstruction and embellishment projects. Hadrian's example apparently encouraged other wealthy individuals to contribute materially to their cities. Many of the Roman cities still so impressive today, from Ostia to Ephesus, are largely the creation of the second century.

Hadrian's municipal interests must relate to his concern for Rome's army. We saw above his interest in personally viewing individual soldiers and exercises: such discipline and leadership ensured the military cohesiveness and preparedness that were approvingly cited by later authors (Dio 69. 9. 4; *Epit. de Caes.* 14. 11). Hadrian seems to have added a fourth prefecture (or lower command) to the army hierarchy, a move that increased the number of positions for equestrians even as it made for closer supervision. During his rule local recruitment for military service became common, often drawing on new municipalities that had sprung up alongside army camps (as in Aquincum). Such recruitment may have been an inevitable consequence of greater attention to peace within fixed borders. These have been traced not only in Hadrian's Wall in Britain, but also in wooden palisades between the upper Rhine and Danube in south-western Germany, and in the *fossatum Africae*, a ditch and mud-brick barrier found south of Mons Aurasius (Aurès Mountains, Algeria and Tunisia). His disparaged abandonment of Rome's traditional expansion largely freed the rank-and-file from warfare.[9] Despite Hadrian's apparent lack of interest in founding cities or otherwise obviously promoting urbanization in Rome's more distant provinces, his preference for stationing Rome's troops in frontier camps brought significant economic and social changes to at least Britain, Upper and Lower Germany, and the Danubian regions.[10]

Religion

But the Roman world was certainly not untroubled under Hadrian's tutelage. In his first two years firm and decisive action had quickly resolved disturbances in the Danubian region, Britain, and Mauretania; as the Second Jewish Revolt came to an end Hadrian was even hailed as Judea's restorer. But Hadrian himself precipitated a convulsive insurrection, the Third Jewish Revolt. This, also known as the Bar Kokhba War, lasted from 132 to 135, butchering 580,000 insurgents, destroying almost a thousand villages, killing innumerable Roman troops, decimating Judea, and hastening the spread of the Diaspora. Ancient authors attribute the violence to Hadrian's decisions to found at Jerusalem a Roman colony, Colonia Aelia Capitolina, and to construct a temple to Jupiter Optimus Maximus over the site of the Jewish Temple (Dio 69. 12. 1). Hadrian aggravated these affronts by universally prohibiting circumcision (*HA Hadr.* 14. 2) and by banning Jews from Jerusalem. As further insult, it seems, one of the city gates of the new Roman colony was embellished with the statue of a boar. This was an insignia of Legio X Fretensis, which had been stationed at Jerusalem since the First

Jewish Revolt (66–70/73), but its power as a symbol of uncleanness to the Jews was patent. Although it now seems clear that Hadrian caused the revolt, at the time its instigation may not have been so apparent. Hadrian's contemporary Pausanias neutrally notes, "When the Jews who live beyond Syria rebelled, [Hadrian] subdued them," after praising Hadrian as "the one who has gone furthest to honor religion . . . the sovereign who has done most for the happiness of his subjects [and who] never willingly went to war" (Paus. 1. 5. 5).

It is hard to reconcile Hadrian's insensitivity toward the Jews with the ample evidence for his open support of many different rituals and shrines. Hadrian was noted for conscientiously fulfilling his duties as pontifex maximus, the head of Roman public religion. He was initiated into the first grade, then later into the highest grade of the Eleusinian mysteries in Athens (in 123 and 128). He is repeatedly said to have made use of astrology, divination, and incantations. From the beginning of his rule come stories of his amicable disputations with rabbis. In some twenty-five cities, he sponsored, or was otherwise identified with, games and festivals. These ranged from ones associated with "mystic" Dionysiac religions (as in Ancyra [Ankara, Turkey]) to the venerable Nemean Games (Paus. 6. 16. 4). In the provinces and in Rome itself many of the buildings he restored, constructed *ex novo*, or embellished were religious structures, some forty in all.[11]

Deities thus honored again range widely. We find the Olympian gods, with Zeus (Olympios) especially frequent in the Greek east (for instance, the Olympieion in Athens; the towering Temple of Zeus at Smyrna; the Temple of the Nymphs at Antioch, to which Hadrian added a statue of Zeus), as well as archaic Italic gods like Diana of Nemi, Juno Gabina of Gabii, and the Bona Dea at Rome. Many of Hadrian's buildings and festivals involved imperial cult (*HA Hadr.* 13. 6). This was particularly noticeable in Rome, where Hadrian raised a temple to his deified mother-in-law, Matidia the Elder, another Temple to the Deified Trajan and Plotina, and the completely rebuilt Pantheon. In other shrines, however, we can see a more subtle connection of emperor and imperial family to a more time-honored religion. For example, Hadrian approved the addition of a large statue of himself to the venerable Temple of Hermes in Trapezus. In Megara, Achaea, where he completely rebuilt in white marble an archaic Temple of Apollo associated with the Lesser Pythian Games, Hadrian is attested with the epithet *Pythios* (like Pythian Apollo).

Still other holy places that bear Hadrian's mark, such as the tombs of heroes that he rebuilt or otherwise ornamented (including those of Ajax and Hector in Troy, and of Pompey in Pelusium), indicate an even more eclectic understanding of sacredness and religiosity. This impression is supported by Hadrian's encouragement of a cult for Antinoos after his young lover drowned in the Nile in 130. Antinoos' death was variously claimed as an accident, a suicide, or a ritual offering as surrogate for Hadrian himself. All agree, however, that Antinoos was officially declared a hero-god, and worshiped especially in the Greek East. The many busts and statues of Antinoos, of which over eighty have now been identified, suggest at the least that the cult was understood as meeting with Hadrian's favor. And even the scant information concerning Hadrian and Christians indicates general tolerance: Hadrian seems at most to have continued the policy established by Trajan, that Roman authorities were not to try to seek out Christians, nor were they to accept anonymous denunciations (see Pliny the Younger, *Ep.* 10. 96–7).

This background makes even more puzzling Hadrian's harsh measures against the Jews. One is reduced to speculation, rendered all the more unsatisfactory by the absence of any obvious provocation by the Jews. Perhaps Hadrian, eventually finding these people antithetical to the Greco-Roman ideals he embraced (see *HA Hadr.* 22. 10), attempted in anger to eradicate their collective memory and distinctiveness. That he ultimately regretted the war is clear enough from his report to the senate at its end, when the terrible losses of Roman troops caused him to suppress the customary imperial greeting, "I and the legions are in health" (Dio 69. 14. 3).

Hadrian's Aesthetics and Further Marks of Personality

One remarkable facet of Hadrian was his abiding interest in arts and literature, which he fostered in many ways. He was always involved in literature, writing poetry and prose himself, searching out historical sites, debating points of grammar and style with scholars, and reconfirming privileges for philosophers, rhetors, and grammarians. More unusually, he himself designed buildings and painted. The former pastime has been thought instrumental in the unusual design of the Pantheon and the audaciously domed structures at Hadrian's villa at Tibur. But other architecture sponsored by Hadrian is just as striking, albeit for different reasons. The huge Temple of Venus and Roma, placed at the edge of Rome's traditional heart, the Roman Forum, eclectically combined a classical exterior with Hellenistic decoration. The Library of Hadrian in Athens evoked in its design the Flavian Temple of Peace in Rome as well as gymnasia in the Hellenistic east, perhaps underscoring that imperial Rome was fundamental to the intellectual renaissance of Athens and the Greek east. At times the novelty of Hadrian's architectural work lay in a strict adherence to archaic precedent, as with Megara's Temple of Apollo (noted above). At other times it depended upon unusual combinations, as the addition of an expansive Roman terrace to Athens' massive Temple of Olympian Zeus, whose archaic architectural sculpture Hadrian's workmen faithfully reproduced.

Hadrian's vast resources ensured the achievement of immense projects: for example, the Temple of Zeus he completed at Cyzicus (Kapu-Dagh, Turkey) was deemed one of the Seven Wonders of the World. But he was also attracted to the delicate, recondite, and small-scale. He dedicated a new statue of Alcibiades in Parian marble at the virtually forgotten tomb of the unreliable but brilliant Athenian in the interior of Asia; he wrote a new epigram for the tomb of the Theban military genius Epaminondas at Mantinea (Paus. 8. 11. 8). Many of the mosaics remaining from his Tibur villa are *emblemata*, detailed pictures made from tiny glass cubes that caught the light and could be used only for wall decoration. The variety and elegance of Hadrian's coins, and one way in which "Hadrianic" taste was spread throughout the Roman world, are striking. The finesse of Hadrianic sculpture, which often juxtaposes a highly polished and smooth surface to chiaroscuro obtained by deep drilling, now seems also to reflect Hadrian's assimilation of opposites, and his perfectionism.

Even with his undeniable talents and limitless means, Hadrian was a man who pushed himself relentlessly. His demanding nature affected those around him, for he seems often to have been frustrated with others as well as with himself. His legal proclamations and responses repeatedly urge individuals and communities to make their own decisions justly, and to rule themselves. He publicly criticized Sabina for moroseness, and said that he would have divorced her had he been a private citizen. His one-upmanship must often have been hard to take, and rumors held that his competitiveness could turn lethal, as when he quarreled over architectural design with Apollodorus of Damascus, Trajan's architect and engineer (Dio 69. 4. 1–5). The vast number of Hadrian's "friends" and acquaintances, and the constant, overwhelming press of imperial business, may have paradoxically isolated him. He seems to have fully trusted only one person, Antinoos. But Hadrian's heartfelt grief at Antinoos' death, and the relative surfeit of Antinoos' images, can mask the lovers' disparity. Antinoos was nineteen when he died in 130, and Hadrian fifty-four. We know nothing about the young man other than his beauty, his mysterious death, and Hadrian's love of him. Yet even this little reveals the complexity of Hadrian, allowing us to see him as a human with raw emotions he otherwise subordinated to his imperial calling and duties.

The End of Hadrian's Life, and His Death

The absence of detail after Hadrian's return from Athens in 132 incidentally underscores the importance of his travels for the history of his principate. He remained in Italy, perhaps in growing seclusion. At least part of his time was spent at his amazing villa at Tibur, which is said to have evoked various parts of the Roman world, and even the underworld, in its many pavilions, suites and groves (*HA Hadr.* 26. 5; Aur. Vict. *Caes.* 14. 6). We cannot date the advent of his fatal illness, which increasingly narrowed the small blood vessels supplying blood and oxygen to the heart. The attendant fatigue and shortness of breath must have been especially chafing for a man habitually so active, and Hadrian bitterly lamented the weakness that rendered him incapable even of suicide. He was also isolated by the deaths of acquaintances and relatives in his last two years. Rumors held that Hadrian's discussions about individuals who might be qualified to serve as the next emperor resulted in the deaths of the most eminent candidates (*HA Hadr.* 23. 2–9; Dio 69. 17–20). Hadrian's ninety-year old brother-in-law, Servianus, was forced to commit suicide on a charge of conspiracy, together with his grandson Gnaeus Pedanius Fuscus. Sabina died in 137. Lucius Ceionius Commodus, whom Hadrian adopted as Lucius Aelius Caesar to ensure the succession, died on January 1, 138. Hadrian then adopted the older and more experienced Titus Aurelius Fulvus Antoninus, and had him adopt the two younger men who would later rule as Marcus Aurelius and Lucius Verus. These arrangements helped the imperial power pass smoothly to Antoninus when death finally came. After repeated attempts at suicide, Hadrian died naturally in his villa at Baiae on July 10, 138. He was sixty-two years old.

The biography claims that Hadrian died hated by all, and that only with difficulty did Antoninus gain the senate's acquiescence in Hadrian's deification (*HA Hadr.* 27. 1–2). The first comment reflects Hadrian's personality; the second, his merited eminence in the Roman world. Hadrian's unremitting dedication to excellence made him a difficult person, and his perfectionism must have played a part in his toxic decisions about the Jews. But he just as surely advanced Rome, by attending to its traditional strengths: Rome's army and law; the empire's municipalities and provinces; and Roman openness to innovation in religion and culture. Rome's resultant vigor was to carry it safe through the benign but inactive rule of Antoninus Pius, and beyond.

Notes

1 See e.g. N. Lewis, "Hadriani sententiae," *Greek, Roman and Byzantine Studies* 32 (1991), 267–80 for Hadrian's *sententiae*, apparently impromptu responses to petitioners that were collected for use as a school exercise for translation into Greek. Other translated writings by Hadrian can be found in Sherk (1988) and Oliver (1989).

2 See e.g. M. Wegner, *Hadrian, Plotina, Marciana, Matidia, Sabina* (Berlin, 1956); H. Meyer, *Antinoos: die archäologischen Denkmäler unter Einbeziehung des numismatischen und epigraphischen Materials sowie der literarischen Nachrichten* (Munich, 1991).

3 The younger Pliny (who died before Hadrian became emperor), Plutarch, Arrian (a personal friend), Appian, Pausanias, Fronto, Aulus Gellius, and Philostratus, for example, are indispensable for Hadrian's cultural milieu, but furnish only indirect information about Hadrian himself.

4 Hadrian's is now the first of the imperial biographies collected in the late fourth-century *Historia Augusta* (*HA Hadr.*); Dio's compendious third-century account of all Roman history now treats Hadrian in a heavily excerpted section; and the fourth-century summaries tend toward brief tropes.

5 Oliver (1989), 82 A–B.

6 Trajan, for example, abstained from such written responses to private petitions (termed *libelli*) so as to avoid setting legal precedents (*HA Macr.* 13. 1).

7 W. Williams, "Individuality in the Imperial Constitutions: Hadrian and the Antonines," *Journal of Roman Studies* 66 (1976), 67–83, esp. 70–4.

8 The proportion of provincials in the senate rose to nearly 50 per cent by the mid-second century, and was to remain at that level until the early third century, when it rose again: M. Hammond, "Composition of the Senate, AD 68–235," *Journal of Roman Studies* 47 (1957), 74–81, esp. 77.

9 In some cases troops are known to have aided Hadrian's provincial building (for instance, the aqueduct at Caesarea, Judea, about halfway between Tel Aviv and Haifa, Israel).

10 His interest in general rural welfare may also be traced in laws that encouraged the cultivation of marginal land in Africa (Smallwood 1966: 463–4).

11 These comprised more than half the buildings known to be built or reconstructed by him. Of course most temples had multiple uses, including ones we might term secular (storing money or laws), and all public temples and cults had to be ratified by the Roman senate.

Mary T. Boatwright

Further Reading

P. J. Alexander, "Letters and Speeches of the Emperor Hadrian," *Harvard Studies in Classical Philology* 49 (1938), 141–77
A. R. Birley, *Hadrian: The Restless Emperor* (London and New York, 1997)
M. T. Boatwright, *Hadrian and the City of Rome* (Princeton, 1987)
M. T. Boatwright, *Hadrian and the Cities of the Roman Empire* (Princeton, 2000)
E. Speller, *Following Hadrian: A Second-Century Journey through the Roman Empire* (London and New York, 2002)
M. Yourcenar, *Memoirs of Hadrian* (New York, 1954)

VIII

Marcus Aurelius

Anthony R. Birley

Family Background

Marcus Aurelius was born on April 26, 121, in the family mansion on the Caelian hill at Rome. For the first seventeen years of his life he had the same names as his father and grandfather, Marcus Annius Verus. The grandfather was consul for the second time in that year and prefect of the city of Rome; five years later he was to hold the consulship again, a sign of his exceptional status under Hadrian. A third consulship, as *ordinarius*, for a non-member of the imperial family was a great rarity; previous holders had all been the closest allies of their respective emperors.[1] The origin of the Annii was in southern Spain, the Caesarian *colonia* Ucubi (modern Espejo) in Baetica. Verus, the grandfather, like Trajan and Hadrian part of the "colonial elite," was the husband of Rupilia Faustina, a descendant of several great republican houses – the Pompeii, Licinii Crassi, Calpurnii Pisones, and Scribonii Libones. The marriages of Verus' children enhanced the family's standing further. One daughter-in-law, the mother of the future emperor Marcus, was Domitia Lucilla, a great heiress, granddaughter of the immensely wealthy Domitius Tullus. Marcus is said by Dio to have been favored by Hadrian as his successor, among other reasons, "because of his kinship." He supposedly had as ancestor a legendary king, "Malemnius, son of Dasummus, founder of Lupiae" in southern Italy. Perhaps it was through his mother that Marcus was indirectly related to Hadrian, himself presumed to have been related to the Dasumii of Corduba: Lucilla's grandmother, Marcus' great-grandmother, seems to have been a Dasumia.[2]

Hadrianic Succession

The man whom the childless Hadrian had initially perhaps regarded as his heir was Pedanius Fuscus, son-in-law of Hadrian's sister Domitia Paulina and her husband Julius Servianus; he shared the consulship with Fuscus in 118. But Fuscus and his wife Julia Paulina thereafter disappear from the record; they evidently died young, leaving a son, also called Pedanius Fuscus, to be brought up by his grandparents. By the 130s, however, Hadrian had become captivated by the young Marcus (who at that point still bore his grandfather's name, Marcus Annius Verus), whom he nicknamed "Verissimus," "truest," playing on his *cognomen* Verus. After his father's early death, the boy had been adopted and brought up by his grandfather. Marcus early on "took a passionate interest in philosophy" and as an eleven-year-old "began his studies wearing the *pallium* [the philosopher's traditional rough Greek cloak] and sleeping on the ground, although he reluctantly, at his mother's insistence, lay on a little couch strewn with skins" (*HA Marc.* 2. 6). He later recalled that he had been inspired to this regime and to his first acquaintance with philosophy by a teacher named Diognetus (*Med.* 1. 6), called his "painting-master" in the *Historia Augusta* (*Marc.* 4. 9), who also taught him among other things to disbelieve in "miracle-mongers, wizards and the like." Marcus had a great many teachers. Before beginning regular lessons, as a small boy he had a "governor" (*educator* or *tropheus*), whose name is not preserved, but whom he remembered affectionately for teaching him to work hard, have few wants, mind his own business, and ignore slander, and not to be a fan of charioteers or gladiators (*Med.* 1. 5). The earliest tutors named by the *Historia Augusta* biographer were three elementary teachers, followed by grammarians, two for Latin and one for Greek. The latter, Alexander of Cotiaeum, advised Marcus not to be pedantic or critical about other people's grammatical mistakes (*Med.* 1. 10) – apart from Diognetus, Alexander was the only early teacher recalled in the *Meditations*.

"In his fifteenth year" Marcus took the *toga virilis*, probably in March 136, shortly before his fifteenth birthday, and "was at once betrothed, at Hadrian's wish, to the daughter of Lucius Commodus." Lucius Ceionius Commodus, a neo-patrician, was one of the *consules ordinarii* of that year. Hadrian's health was now failing and he clearly felt obliged to nominate a successor by adopting a son. There was general surprise and considerable indignation among the elite when the name was announced: the consul Commodus, now renamed Lucius Aelius Caesar, designated to a second consulship for 137, and despatched with proconsular *imperium* to govern both Pannonian provinces, obviously to gain experience. Most contemporaries were baffled by Hadrian's choice. The *Historia Augusta* biographer, typically enough, alleged that Aelius Caesar's "sole recommendation was his beauty."[3] One modern scholar even tried to prove – but with flawed evidence – that Aelius was Hadrian's bastard son. The truth is probably simpler: Hadrian wanted Marcus eventually to succeed him, but the boy was still too young. An intermediate successor was needed, hence the previously arranged betrothal of Marcus and Aelius Caesar's daughter. As Aelius was in poor health – he was "coughing blood" – he was presumably not expected to survive Hadrian for long. The man's own son was at the most only six or seven; but his fifteen-year-old son-in-law Marcus would be ready to take power within a few years.

Such seems to have been the calculation. Hadrian either had not foreseen or did not care how his grandnephew Pedanius Fuscus, now aged twenty-four or twenty-five, would react. Clearly feeling that he had been robbed of his birthright, Fuscus attempted a coup and was put to death. His grandfather, old Servianus, was forced to take his own life. Then Aelius Caesar returned to Rome, after less than a year in Pannonia, and was due to speak in the senate on January 1, 138. But he fell ill the night before and died from "a haemorrhage." Hadrian forbade public mourning but waited for another three weeks, until his sixty-second birthday, January 24, before announcing a new heir. Now seriously ill, he summoned a group of senior senators to his residence. Dio reports a short speech, no doubt on the lines on which Hadrian addressed them. After praising the adoptive principle, he explained that since heaven had taken his first choice,

> I have found an emperor for you in his place . . . a man who is noble, mild, tractable and prudent, neither young enough to act rashly nor old enough to be neglectful, brought up according to the laws, with experience of authority practiced in our traditional manner, not ignorant of any matters involving the exercise of imperial power, but well able to deal with them all.

Then he revealed the name: Aurelius Antoninus.

Accession of Antoninus Pius

Hadrian knew, he added, that Antoninus had no ambition to hold the imperial power, but was confident that he would in the end accept, however unwillingly. Antoninus asked for time to consider, but after four weeks consented and was formally adopted on February 25, with the style Imperator

Caesar Titus Aelius Aurelius Caesar Antoninus. Following Hadrian's wishes, Antoninus was in turn obliged to adopt both his wife's nephew Marcus and Aelius Caesar's son Lucius; and Lucius was betrothed to Antoninus' daughter Faustina. Marcus now became Marcus Aurelius Verus Caesar; his adoptive brother became Lucius Aurelius Commodus, without the title Caesar – which Antoninus never granted him. A two-tier succession system, surely already planned in 136 with Aelius Caesar and Marcus, was now explicitly in place. The model was Augustus' arrangement in summer AD 4, when he adopted Tiberius, who was himself required to adopt Germanicus, evidently with the possible intention that the latter should somehow rule jointly, after Tiberius' death, with Tiberius' own son Drusus.

The adoption of Antoninus "caused pain to many, especially to Catilius Severus, the prefect of the city, who had designs on the imperial power himself"; he was removed from office. Linked with Catilius elsewhere in the *vita Hadriani* are Ummidius Quadratus and Marcius Turbo, the long-serving prefect of the guard: all three were "assailed harshly" by Hadrian. Catilius was connected with Marcus' family, probably having married Marcus' widowed great-grandmother some thirty years earlier – he is no doubt the unnamed *propappos* (great-grandfather) who had recommended that Marcus should not go to school but be tutored at home (*Med.* 1. 4) – and Marcus had even borne his names in early boyhood. Ummidius may have been married to another aunt of Marcus; his son was in due course to marry Marcus' sister. Both Catilius and Ummidius possessed far greater experience of provinces and armies than Antoninus, who had had no military service at all and had only once governed a province – for one year, as proconsul of Asia. It may be inferred that each man, one of them perhaps with the support of Marcius Turbo, had seen himself as a better qualified "place-holder" to keep the throne warm for Hadrian's favorite Marcus.

Sources

Antoninus was only ten years younger than Hadrian, but in the event was to reign for as long as Tiberius, nearly twenty-three years, after which Marcus ruled for more than eighteen. Yet to construct a narrative of the years 138–80 is far from easy. Nothing survives that remotely resembles Tacitus' *Annals*. For Marcus' reign Dio's *History* is available only in the eleventh-century *Epitome* by Xiphilinus and in a few other Byzantine excerpts from book 71. Book 70, on Antoninus' reign, was already missing when Xiphilinus was at work. Hence one must rely heavily on the *Historia Augusta*: its brief *Pius* is, fortunately, almost free of fiction, and most of the *Marcus* is also factually reliable. The source for the early *vitae* was probably the lost *vitae Caesarum* of Marius Maximus, written in the early third century on the lines of Suetonius' *Caesars*, but evidently much more extensive. As part of his attempt at originality, however, the author of the *Historia Augusta* produced a separate *vita* of Lucius Verus, evidently hived off from Maximus' lengthy *vita* of Marcus, and, even worse, created largely fictional *vitae* of two minor figures, Aelius Caesar and the usurper Avidius Cassius. Chopping up his source got the author in a muddle: the *Marcus* goes to pieces from Verus' death in 169 onwards. The author first tried to cut his losses and finish his account by inserting a long passage of Eutropius, the fourth-century chronicler, then decided that more was needed after all. Further items on the 170s were added, followed by some fiction. The result is that such major events as the invasions of Italy and Greece were not mentioned at all.

All the same, to compensate for the lack of narrative history, inscriptions, papyri, and coins are very abundant for the age of the Antonines. Particularly important for the chronology are the record of Ostia, *Fasti Ostienses*, and the ever-increasing number of military diplomas. Further, there are numerous contemporary writings. Of Latin works one must single out Fronto's *Letters*, not least those to Marcus and Verus, with their replies, Aulus Gellius' *Attic Nights*, and Apuleius' *Apology*, *Florida*, and *Metamorphosis*. The Greek writings are much fuller. Of Aelius Aristides' copious *œuvre*, his *Oration in Praise of Rome*, delivered in 143 or 144, has probably contributed most to the perception of the Antonine era as a golden age. Pausanias' *Guide to Greece*, Lucian's numerous essays, and Galen's vast corpus of medical treatises all contain a considerable amount of historical material; there is a great deal more in a work from the early third century, Philostratus' *Lives of the Sophists*. The first Christian apologists were writing at this time and there is also the *Ecclesiastical History* by Eusebius of Caesarea, written in the early fourth century but citing many second-century sources verbatim. Further, there are copious rescripts of Antoninus and Marcus in the law codes – and, of course, Marcus' own private notebook, the so-called *Meditations*. The Column of Marcus, although not exactly providing a continuous pictorial narrative in chronological order, supplies, along with other historical reliefs, remarkable insights into the nature of his wars.

The Reign of Antoninus Pius

After Hadrian's death on July 10, 138, Antoninus' succession went through smoothly, the only difficulty being his insistence, against the senate's wishes, on having Hadrian deified. His loyalty (*pietas*) to the memory of the man who had adopted him was no doubt the real reason for his acquiring the additional name Pius – by which he will be referred to in what follows. As one of his first actions Pius set aside the betrothals arranged by Hadrian, of his daughter Faustina to the young Lucius – both of whom were then aged only about seven or eight – and of Marcus to Lucius' sister Ceionia Fabia. Pius had first asked Marcus if he was willing to accept this; the new betrothal to his cousin Faustina meant waiting for seven years.

In 139 Marcus entered the senate as quaestor and was appointed *princeps iuventutis*; it made a good impression, Dio says, that in this capacity "he entered the Forum with the rest [of the *equites*], although he was a Caesar." Many years later Marcus told himself: "See that you do not turn into a Caesar, do not be dipped in the purple dye" (*Med.* 6. 30). He now had to move into the imperial residence on the Palatine. His dislike of this is a recurrent theme in the *Meditations*. But his adoptive father "was able to rid me of all my pride and make me realise that one can live in a palace without needing bodyguards, embroidered clothing, torches, statues and such pomp, but can live very nearly as a private citizen, without thereby losing any dignity or being less active in the state duties required of a princeps" (*Med.* 1. 17. 3). The next year, now eighteen, he was consul with Pius; they held the office together again in 145, when the long-planned marriage to Faustina took place. The *Fasti Ostienses* reveal that their first child, a daughter, Domitia Faustina, was born on November 30, 147, and that on the next day Marcus was granted tribunician power and *imperium*, while his wife became Augusta. This daughter, who was to die in 151, was the first of numerous children. Short-lived twin boys followed in 149 and further daughters in 150 and 151; these two girls, Lucilla and Annia Faustina, survived to adulthood and marriage, as did two more daughters born in 159 (Fadilla) and 160 (Cornificia). Meanwhile two further sons had died shortly after birth, in 152 and 157.

Marcus' Intellectual Background

By the time of his adoption Marcus had begun the study of oratory and now acquired a law tutor as well, the jurist Lucius Volusius Maecianus (who wrote a handbook for his pupil, partly preserved, on the Roman coinage system). He had three Greek tutors in oratory: one of these – Herodes Atticus, the Athenian "millionaire" – was probably too grand to give more than occasional instruction; another was Caninius Celer, who had been Hadrian's chief secretary (*ab epistulis*). His only tutor in Latin oratory was Marcus

Cornelius Fronto, a native of Cirta in Numidia, regarded as a formidable speaker – indeed, as a second Cicero. Apart from a few fragments of his speeches, only some of Fronto's letters survive. They hardly support the comparison with Cicero, but they do offer precious insight into Marcus' life over the next quarter of a century. Marcus had already acquired, from his intended father-in-law Aelius Caesar, his first philosophy tutor, Apollonius of Chalcedon, a Stoic, whose lectures he continued to attend after his entry into the imperial family. In due course "he also attended lectures by Sextus of Chaeronea [Plutarch's nephew], Junius Rusticus, Claudius Maximus, and Cinna Catulus, all Stoics." Marcus "especially revered and followed" Rusticus (*HA Marc.* 2. 7–3. 5), whose father of the same name, the Stoic "martyr," had been executed by Domitian in 93 while the son was still in infancy. Marcus later thanked the gods that he "had got to know Apollonius, Rusticus and Maximus" (*Med.* 1. 17. 4). Another philosophic mentor was the Peripatetic Claudius Severus, whose son later married Marcus' daughter Annia Faustina.

Marcus paid tribute to all his philosophy teachers and mentors, along with members of his family, in book 1 of the *Meditations*, probably written later than the other eleven books. His expression of gratitude to the memory of Pius (1. 16) is far and away the longest, far too long to quote in full here. He had earlier composed a brief tribute, telling himself to do "everything as a pupil of Antoninus." He recalled his

> constancy, equability, piety, serenity of expression, sweet nature, contempt for empty fame, determination to understand issues and never to dismiss a question until he had scrutinised it thoroughly. He never found fault with his critics, was never in a hurry, refused to listen to slander . . . His wants were modest, for lodging, dress, food or servants . . . , he was always loyal to his friends, he revered the gods but was not superstitious. May you be as much at peace with your conscience as he was when your last hour comes. (*Med.* 6. 30. 2)

The full version in book 1 expands this appreciation and adds among other points Antoninus' high appreciation of true philosophers and his readiness to acknowledge without jealousy the excellence of those with special gifts in public speaking, law, ethics, or any other subject (the contrast with the jealous polymath Hadrian is obvious); it notes also that he was loyal to traditional Roman political practice – without parading the fact. Marcus reveals here that Antoninus was a sufferer from violent headaches (probably migraines), but that when they were gone he returned to work with his usual energy; and that he had very few secrets, and these concerned only affairs of state.

Fronto and his painting-master Diognetus are the only non-philosophers among the teachers and mentors included in book 1, and Fronto is thanked, not for his lessons in rhetoric, but for having taught Marcus "to be aware of the envy and duplicity and dissimulation that are habitual to a tyrant; and that as a rule those among us who are called patricians are in a way lacking in natural affection" (1. 11). The content of many of the early letters between Fronto and Marcus concerns literature and exercises that Marcus had been set. Some give an insight into the imperial house's family life: visiting the ancient town of Anagnia to look at the monuments and temples, being mistaken for sheep-stealers and chased away by shepherds when out riding in the hills, hunting for boar or helping with the vintage. By the mid-140s Marcus had tired of rhetoric and had turned to philosophy, to Fronto's regret. But tutor and pupil remained close friends.

Military Campaigns in the Reign of Antoninus Pius

The apparent stability and peacefulness of Pius' reign are a little misleading. Apart from the dearth of narrative sources, the impression may be largely due to his refusal to leave Italy at all and the firm hand with which he guided the empire. There was indeed some military activity, summed up by the *Historia Augusta* in a few sentences:

> Through his legates he waged a number of wars: he conquered the Britons through his legate Lollius Urbicus, another wall, of turf, being set up when the barbarians had been driven back, and compelled the Moors to sue for peace; and he crushed the Germans and Dacians and many peoples, including the Jews, who were rebelling, through governors and legates. In Achaea too, and Egypt, he put down rebellions and frequently curbed the Alani when they began disturbances. (*Ant. Pius* 5. 4–5)

The war in Britain lasted up to three years. Urbicus was already active in the north of the province in 139 and Pius had taken his second imperatorial acclamation (the only one of the reign) by August 1, 142.[4] Hadrian's Wall, only just completed, was given up, southern Scotland reoccupied and the new Antonine Wall built where Agricola had noted a possible *in ipsa Britannia terminus* (*Agr.* 23), between the Firths of Forth and Clyde. Pausanias also refers to a British conflict: the emperor never voluntarily waged war, but "confiscated a large part of the territory of the Brigantes in Britain because they invaded the Genunian district, of which the inhabitants were subject to

Rome" (8. 43). No "Genunian" district is known in Britain: Pausanias clearly confused two episodes, Urbicus' war and some otherwise unrecorded fighting in Raetia between the Brigantii and their neighbors the Genauni. Neither the *Historia Augusta* nor Pausanias explains the motives for reoccupying southern Scotland. The reversal of policy is remarkable. J. P. Gillam offered two explanations: "In a sense Hadrian's Wall had been a strategical failure, because the potential enemies to north and north-west were out of its reach . . . Tactically the Wall had been so complete a success that it was decided to move the system, with modifications, bodily northwards."[5] Equally, one may suspect political motives: perhaps Pius was offering a "sop" to the *viri militares*, disgusted by Hadrian's retrenchment. Besides, like Claudius a century earlier, an emperor with no military experience needed military prestige. A *casus belli* was perhaps provided by an uprising, for example in south-west Scotland, where the siege of the hill fort at Burnswark might be datable to this time. At all events, most of the now obsolete installations of Hadrian's Wall were dismantled, and garrisons moved forward. The new barrier, being of turf and only half the length of Hadrian's Wall, was much cheaper. But it also had outposts to the north: Camelon, Ardoch, Strageath, and, at the confluence of the Almond with the Tay, Bertha, all previously occupied in the Flavian period.

The British success was praised by Fronto, probably in his speech of thanks for his consulship in 142. A fragment is quoted by a panegyrist praising Constantius I for his recovery of Britain 150 years later: "Fronto . . . , when praising the emperor Antoninus for completing the British war – although he, staying in the city palace itself, had delegated the command of it – averred that he deserved the glory of its whole launching and course, as if presiding at the helm of a warship" (*Pan. Lat. vet.* 8 (5). 14. 2). There is even an allusion to the Wall in the *Roman Oration* of Aelius Aristides, delivered a year or two later. After elaborating on the pre-eminence of Rome in all aspects, he turns to Rome's "unexampled work of perfection," the army, "sent to the frontiers of the empire." As for fortifications,

> to place walls around the city itself as if you were hiding her or fleeing from your subjects you considered ignoble. Nevertheless you did not forget walls, but these you placed around the empire, not the city . . . Beyond the outermost ring of the civilised world, you drew a second line . . . Here you built walls to defend you . . . An encamped army like a rampart encloses the world in a ring . . . as far as from Ethiopia to the Phasis and from the Euphrates to the great outermost island toward the west. All this one can call a ring and circuit of walls. They have not been built with asphalt and baked brick, nor do they

stand there gleaming with stucco. Yet these ordinary works too exist, yes, in very great number, and, as Homer says of the palace wall, "fitted close and accurately with stones, and boundless in size, and gleaming more brilliantly than bronze." (*Or.* 26K. 72, 78, 80–3)

Ironically, "gleaming with stucco . . . fitted close and accurately with stones . . . gleaming more brilliantly than bronze" were descriptions that applied not to Pius' new wall of turf, but to the recently abandoned stone-built Hadrian's Wall, which may well have been rendered with white stucco.

Aristides claimed that war was now a thing of the past, in spite of "a few wretches like the Libyans and Getae or ill-doers like the dwellers on the Red Sea" – allusions to campaigns in Mauretania, Dacia, and Egypt, also referred to in the *Historia Augusta*. Only the war in Mauretania is better attested by inscriptions, which register the transfer of troops there from other parts of the empire in the first half of the 140s. There was further trouble in Dacia in the late 150s. Nothing is known about the rebellions in Achaea and Judea (now renamed Syria Palaestina). As for the Alani of the Caucasus, well beyond the frontiers, Pius exerted a firm hand here as with other client states, of which the *Historia Augusta* gives examples.

Conspiracy

All the sources convey a positive picture of Antoninus; so it is a surprise that the *Historia Augusta* names two men who conspired against him, Atilius Titianus and Priscianus (*Ant. Pius* 7. 3–4; cf. *Epit. de Caes.* 15. 6). The former must be Titus Atilius Rufus Titianus, consul *ordinarius* in 127, whose name is erased from the *Fasti Ostienses* for that year; the *Fasti* also, under September 15, 145, give some detail on the other man: "Judgment was passed on Cornelius Priscianus in open session in the senate, because he disturbed the province of Spain in hostile fashion," perhaps while governor of Hispania Tarraconensis. The *Historia Augusta* notes: "After being accused of attempted usurpation, he committed suicide and the emperor did not allow an investigation into his conspiracy" (*Ant. Pius* 7. 4).

Celebration

An opportunity for general celebration was the 900th anniversary in 148 of the founding of Rome. The coinage had been preparing for this long in advance, with allusions to the city's legendary origins. These reminders of the distant past fitted the aspirations of the age – archaizing in Latin literature, as Fronto and Aulus Gellius show – and of Pius himself, who was appropriately enough compared to Numa, Rome's second king, supposedly responsible for much of the state's religious ritual. The correspondence between Marcus and Fronto from these years mainly concerns family news, not least about illness. One passage in a letter of Fronto reminds us that images of the imperial family were omnipresent:

> You know that in all the banks, shops, taverns, eaves, colonnades and windows, everywhere, portraits of you are exposed to public view, badly painted for the most part and modeled or carved in a plain, not to say worthless, style. All the same, your likeness, however unlike you, never meets my eyes without making me part my lips in a smile and dream of you. (*Ad M. Caes.* 4. 11)

Further Military Campaigns

By the 150s Lucius had entered the senate and in 154, in his early twenties, he was allowed to hold the consulship. But he was still very much kept in the background. On official journeys Marcus traveled in the same vehicle as Antoninus, while Lucius followed in a second carriage with the praetorian prefect. In the late 150s the prefect, Gavius Maximus, who had held office from the start of the reign, was replaced (*HA Ant. Pius* 8. 7). He had probably largely guided military decisions throughout. It may be no coincidence that there was a surprising change of policy at this time. The Antonine Wall, constructed only at the beginning of the 140s, was abandoned *c.*158,[6] and Hadrian's Wall was being rebuilt in that year (*RIB* 1389). The governor was Gnaeus Julius Verus, previously legate of Lower Germany. He is attested by several inscriptions in Britain, including a dedication at Newcastle by the *vexil[l]atio leg. II Aug. et leg. VI Vic. et leg. XX V.V. con[t]ributi ex[ercitibus] Ger[manicis] duobus sub Iulio Vero leg. Aug. pr. pr.* The interpretation is uncertain: men *from* the British legions about to go *to* Germany; men previously sent *to* Germany returning; the British legions being reinforced by men *from* the German armies? (*RIB* 1322 + *add.*). Whatever the circumstances, it is a paradox that, just when the outer *limes* in Britain was being abandoned, one was being created in Upper Germany, where the line created by Hadrian's palisade was pushed forward.

The replacement of Gavius Maximus probably meant yet more responsibility for Marcus. There were several new military threats. In Dacia, Marcus

Statius Priscus, a man promoted to senatorial rank early in the reign, won a victory and was rewarded by being made consul *ordinarius* in 159. In the east a legionary legate in the Syrian army, Lucius Neratius Proculus, took reinforcements into the province "because of the Parthian war." Pius, now 75, was in failing health. "While delirious with fever, he spoke of nothing except the commonwealth and the kings with whom he was angry." He died at his estate at Lorium on March 7, 161, having given his final watchword to the officer of the guard: "Equanimity."

Accession of Marcus

In 161 Marcus and Lucius held the consulship together, probably in anticipation of their adoptive father's passing. Marcus had been in effect deputy emperor for more than thirteen years, as holder of *imperium* and tribunician power: to be emperor he lacked only the name Augustus and the position of pontifex maximus. But at the first meeting of the senate he refused to accept the position unless equal powers were conferred on Lucius. Clearly Marcus' sense of duty led him to implement Hadrian's intention that the two should rule jointly. Pius had set aside the betrothal between Lucius and Faustina, and Lucius had "remained a private citizen for twenty-three years" in the imperial household. Now he was granted tribunician power and *imperium*. He and Marcus both became Augustus and altered their other names. In memory of his adoptive father Marcus replaced his name Verus with Antoninus, and Lucius took the name Verus in place of Commodus. The two thus reigned as "Marcus Aurelius Antoninus" and "Lucius Aurelius Verus." The change of names led to confusion in several sources.

The new emperors behaved *civiliter*, like fellow citizens, which went down well with the plebeians, and freedom of speech was allowed; a writer of comedies named Marullus was unscathed after open criticism (*HA Marc.* 8. 1). Fronto was delighted that his former pupils were now co-emperors. He told Marcus, who had been rereading Fronto's panegyric of Pius, delivered in 142, that the praise of Marcus which he had then included was fully justified: the outstanding natural ability had now become "perfected excellence . . . The hope has become reality" (*Ad Ant. Imp.* 4. 2. 3). To Lucius he expressed his gratitude that the brothers, in spite of their high position, still showed him warm feelings (*Ad Verum Imp.* 1. 2–3).

By the summer there were grounds for general celebration. Faustina, who had already borne nine children, was pregnant again when Marcus became emperor. She gave birth on August 31 to twin boys, who were named Titus

Aurelius Fulvus Antoninus, after Pius, and Lucius Aurelius Commodus, after Lucius. The imperial coinage, which had been proclaiming the unity between the two emperors, *concordia Augustorum*, now advertised "the happiness of the age," *felicitas temporum*. Lucius, apparently still unmarried at thirty, was now betrothed to Lucilla, who was just eleven; she was the eldest of Marcus' four other surviving children, all girls.

Meanwhile, however, not all was well with city and empire. Marcus had initially "given himself wholly to philosophy and to seeking the affection of his fellow-citizens," and continued to attend lectures, notably those by Sextus of Chaeronea. This did not last long. He soon asked Fronto for some reading matter, perhaps "some poet, for I need distraction . . . by reading something that will uplift and diffuse my pressing anxieties." Trouble had begun with a severe spring flood: the Tiber destroyed many buildings, drowned many animals, and left serious famine in its wake. The brothers "dealt with all these matters personally," relieving Italian communities hit by food shortages.

Eastern Problems

Most serious was an outright war in the east. Antoninus' death emboldened Vologaeses III of Parthia to march into Armenia and replace its king with his own nominee, Pacorus. The nearest Roman commander, Marcus Sedatius Severianus, governor of Cappadocia, moved east with one legion, but was trapped at Elegeia. Realizing that resistance was futile, he committed suicide and the legion was "wiped out" (it might have been Legio IX Hispana, last attested at York under Trajan and in the early second century at Nijmegen, but perhaps then transferred first to Judea by Hadrian, and thereafter to Cappadocia, when the Alans were threatening). Before long the Parthians invaded Syria as well: the governor Lucius Attidius Cornelianus was defeated and put to flight. There were serious problems on other frontiers too. War "threatened in Britain," in spite of the evacuation of the Antonine Wall. The province had just been given to Statius Priscus; but now it was decided to move him to Cappadocia to replace the fallen Severianus. Calpurnius Agricola was transferred to Britain, as Priscus' successor, from Upper Germany, itself under threat from the Chatti beyond the *limes*; that province was entrusted to Marcus' close friend Aufidius Victorinus, Fronto's son-in-law (*HA Marc.* 8. 7–8). In his *Strategica* dedicated to Marcus and Lucius in 162, Polyaenus refers to "the Britons being defeated" (6, *pr.*), presumably by Calpurnius Agricola.

As for the Parthians, by winter 161–2, with the people of Syria reported to be rebellious, it was decided that one emperor must direct the counter-attack in person. Neither had been given military experience under Pius, but it was agreed that Lucius, being "physically robust and younger than Marcus, was better suited to military activity" (Dio 71. 1. 3). The *Historia Augusta* suggests other motives: Marcus sent Lucius "so that he would not transgress in the city before the eyes of all, or so that he might learn thrift by foreign travel, or so that he might return reformed by the fear which war inspires, or so that he might realise that he was an emperor" (*Verus* 5. 8). Lucius finally set off in summer 162, with a massive entourage, accompanied as far as Capua by Marcus. Progress was slow: Lucius hunted and feasted at country estates, then fell ill at Canusium, where Marcus rushed south to see him. Three days of fasting and a bloodletting evidently cured him and he embarked from Brundisium. His journey though Greece, accompanied by musicians, was uncomfortably reminiscent of Nero's, whose birthday (and allegedly some other tastes) Lucius shared. At Athens he stayed with Herodes Atticus and, unlike Nero, but following the precedents of Augustus and Hadrian, was initiated in the Eleusinian mysteries. Then he took ship to Asia and proceeded to Antioch by the coast of Pamphylia and Cilicia, dallying on the way in pleasure-resorts, the biographer claims.

Meanwhile Statius Priscus had taken command in Cappadocia and campaigned vigorously. He took the Armenian capital Artaxata by storm in 163 (*HA Marc.* 9. 1; cf. *Verus* 7. 1) and founded a new one, which he garrisoned (Dio 71. 3. 1[1]). Lucius assumed the title Armeniacus (which Marcus at first declined) and he and Marcus were acclaimed Imperator II. According to Lucian, in one of the instant histories produced just after the war, readers were told how "Priscus the general merely shouted out and twenty-seven of the enemy dropped dead" (*How to write history* 20).

Lucius had senior advisors with him, *comites Augusti* of consular rank. Measures taken by one of them, Marcus Pontius Laelianus, "a man of weight and old-style discipline," to bring the Syrian army back into condition, are described by Fronto (*Ad Verum Imp.* 2. 1. 19). A cousin of Marcus, Marcus Annius Libo, was initially made governor of Syria, evidently to keep an eye on Lucius; but he died before long and was replaced by another *comes Augusti*, Julius Verus, the former governor of Britain. Lucius' own participation in the war was indeed largely as a figurehead. He spent much of his time at Daphne, the pleasure resort near Antioch, and acquired a mistress, the beautiful and gifted Panthea, subject of two admiring essays by Lucian. It is not surprising that in 164 Lucilla, Lucius' intended bride, just fourteen years old, was dispatched by Marcus to Ephesus, where the marriage was celebrated: Lucilla was given the title Augusta.

In that year there was evidently a lull in the fighting. A Roman nominee, Sohaemus, was crowned by Lucius as king of Armenia, registered on the coinage with the legend *rex Armeniis datus*; and Marcus now accepted the title Armeniacus. In 165 there was a major Roman push into Mesopotamia. First, in the north the pro-Roman Mannus was restored to the throne of Osrhoene. Then the Parthians were pursued eastwards to Nisibis, which was captured, and their general Chosrhoes escaped only by swimming the Tigris. A force under a young senator of Syrian origin, Gaius Avidius Cassius, advanced down the Euphrates, winning a victory at Dura and then assaulting the twin cities on the Tigris, the Greek Seleuceia on the right bank and the Parthian capital opposite, Ctesiphon. Laureled dispatches were sent to Rome: Lucius was awarded the title *Parthicus maximus*, while he and Marcus took a further salutation as *imperator*. Although Cassius seems to have had the lion's share of the glory, other young generals also played a part, notably Marcus Claudius Fronto, Quintus Antistius Adventus, and Publius Martius Verus.

The war was now virtually over. Lucius commissioned Fronto to produce a suitably laudatory account, which he began enthusiastically but never completed – it is assumed that he died not long after Lucius returned to Rome. Lucius was evidently reluctant to leave Syria, which had felt like his own kingdom. In 166 there was a final campaign, with Avidius Cassius taking Rome's arms beyond the Tigris into Media, leading to the conferring of the title Medicus on the emperors and a fourth imperatorial acclamation.

Among numerous other measures taken by Marcus during these years, one must single out the institution of the Italian *iuridici*. Unlike the four consular legates established by Hadrian and abolished by Antoninus, who were in effect governors of four Italian provinces, the holders of the new office were only ex-praetors and their duties were confined to the administration of justice. During these years Marcus and Faustina had had another son, born in 162, named Annius Verus, but in 165 one of the twins died.

The triumph was celebrated, jointly by Marcus and Lucius, on October 12, 166. Both now accepted the title *pater patriae*, and, at Lucius' request, the surviving twin, Commodus, and his little brother Annius Verus were made Caesars. An unfortunate by-product of the return to Rome of the troops who had fought in the east, notably elements of the praetorian guard, was that they brought "plague" with them. Whatever the nature of the epidemic, it was to have disastrous effects and spread rapidly over much of the west.

The superstitious later blamed Avidius Cassius and his men: the plague was Apollo's vengeance for their sacking of his temple at Seleuceia on the Tigris.

Marcomannic War

"While the Parthian war was being waged the Marcomannic war broke out . . . held in check by the skill of the men on the spot." So records the *Historia Augusta* (*HA Marc.* 12. 13). Further, Marcus had ordered the raising of two new legions, later named Legio II and III Italica: the levy, in northern Italy, was conducted in 165 by Julius Verus and Claudius Fronto. Writing at this time, Appian, in the preface to his *History*, recalls seeing "envoys from poor and unprofitable peoples at Rome, offering themselves as subjects; but the emperor would not accept men who would be no use to him." The *Historia Augusta* shows that this was becoming a real problem: "peoples which had fled under pressure from the remoter barbarians were threatening war unless they were taken into the empire" (*HA Marc.* 14. 1). Some of the invaders had their women with them, and later Marcus was to settle "large numbers" in the northern provinces and some even in Italy, near Ravenna – but these seized the town and had to be expelled, after which no more were accepted. It seems likely that the long migration of the Goths, which was to take them from the Baltic to the Black Sea, had begun, creating a snowball movement. In 166 or 167 the first wave, including one of these "remoter" peoples, the Langobardi, broke into Pannonia. They were checked by a mixed force of auxiliary cavalry and infantry. Soon afterwards a delegation of eleven peoples, led by Ballomarius, king of the Marcomanni, arrived and sued for peace, which the legate of Upper Pannonia granted (Dio 71. 3. 1a).

The fighting in the Danube area which began thus and lasted, with an intermission in 175–6, until Marcus' death in 180, was to be known as the Marcomannic War. But the *Historia Augusta* said that it should really be called the "war of many nations," and elsewhere notes that "all the peoples from beyond Rhine and Danube conspired against Rome." The Dacian gold mines were evidently attacked in May 167 or soon after. Marcus no doubt intended that he and Lucius should take immediate personal charge of counter-measures, but the increasing virulence of the plague made it impossible for them to leave Rome: "the dead were carted away on carts and wagons . . . thousands died, including many prominent persons." There was a hysterical atmosphere in the city, supposedly "from the terror of the war with the Marcomanni" and no doubt exacerbated by the plague. Priests were summoned, special religious rites were performed, and the city was purified

(*Marc.* 13. 1ff.). The great doctor Galen, at Rome in 166, left for his home city Pergamum to avoid infection. It may have been as a result of the public panic and the religious rituals that anti-Christian agitation broke out, leading to the conviction and martyrdom of Justin. The magistrate who sentenced him and his companions was the prefect of the city, Marcus' revered mentor Junius Rusticus.

By now the Marcomanni and others "were throwing everything into confusion, threatening war unless they were allowed into the empire." The "German expedition" was finally launched by Marcus and Lucius in 168: their arrival at Aquileia evidently caused "most of the kings, with their peoples, to withdraw." Then, "after the Alps had been crossed, they proceeded further and settled everything pertaining to the protection of Italy and Illyricum" (*Marc.* 14. 6). The "protection of Italy and Illyricum" surely refers to the special command held by Antistius Adventus over the *praetentura Italiae et Alpium*, to protect the passes through the Julian Alps from Pannonia into Italy. Marcus and Lucius took up winter quarters at Aquileia, evidently planning a spring offensive. But in January 169 the prevalence of plague in the camp – leaving large numbers of dead, including the guard prefect Furius Victorinus – led Galen to recommend returning to Rome, which Lucius was anyway urging. But after two days' journey Lucius suffered a seizure in his carriage, and soon afterwards he died. Marcus had him deified as *divus Verus*. The heavy losses had caused a financial crisis, to which Marcus responded by auctioning palace treasures. High casualties meant a recruitment crisis: as an emergency measure, gladiators and "brigands" were conscripted. Before the end of the year he had to return to the north, where the situation was worsening. But first, "although the official mourning had not ended, he gave his daughter Lucilla in marriage to Claudius Pompeianus, son of a Roman knight from Antioch, who was of an advanced age and not of sufficiently noble birth."

Another blow to Marcus was the death of his younger son Annius Verus Caesar in mid-September: he was mourned for only five days, for the war urgently demanded Marcus' presence. His base for the winter of 169–70 was evidently Sirmium, where he was accompanied by Faustina and their youngest child, a three-year-old girl, Vibia Aurelia Sabina. His delayed Roman offensive across the Danube opened in spring 170, but the two eastern German peoples, Marcomanni and Quadi, seem to have made a pre-emptive strike. Outflanking Marcus' forces, they broke through the Julian Alps and actually besieged Aquileia, although they failed to capture it. It was the first foreign invasion of Italy for nearly 300 years. The invasion is referred to briefly in a fragment of Dio and the siege of Aquileia is mentioned in a somewhat improbable anecdote in Lucian's essay on the "pseudo-prophet" Alexander of Abonutichus (Dio 71. 3. 1–2; Luc. *Alex.* 48). Much later Ammianus Marcellinus, in a passage about the Quadi of the late fourth century, recalled how they and the Marcomanni had burst through the Julian Alps to besiege Aquileia and sack Opitergium, with Marcus barely able to resist (29. 6. 1).

Drastic steps, led by Pompeianus, with the able assistance of Publius Helvius Pertinax (the future emperor), were needed to repel the invaders, clear the northern provinces, and restore army supplies along the Danube. The last of these tasks was given to an equestrian officer from Poetovio in Pannonia, Marcus Valerius Maximianus. In 171 another invasion from the north followed, this time by the Costoboci from beyond Dacia, who struck through the Balkans, tore through the provinces of Moesia, Macedonia, and Achaea, reaching Attica before their attack spent itself. An equestrian procurator, Julius Julianus, was given a task force to clear these provinces – and shortly afterwards had to take his men to the far west, where Baetica had been invaded by the Moors, while Marcus' friend Aufidius Victorinus, now governor of Hispania Tarraconensis, took over Baetica as well.

The governor of Upper Moesia, Claudius Fronto, had to take over first part, then the whole of Dacia, but lost his life, "fighting to the last in defense of the commonwealth." In 172, as the Marcomanni sought to escape back home, they were caught by Marcus at the Danube crossing, laden with booty, which was "returned to the provincials." Marcus had established his new headquarters at Carnuntum. The long-postponed offensive could now begin, but the truncated state of Dio's text, as well as the confused nature of the *Historia Augusta* biography of Marcus at this point, make it hard to follow the course of events. Clearly the German peoples, mainly the Marcomanni and Quadi, were defeated first, and Marcus took the title Germanicus. The famous "Rain Miracle," a storm that supposedly rescued Roman troops, took place in enemy territory. It is depicted prominently on the Column of Marcus, but neither the exact date nor its location is certain. The headings between books 1 and 2 of the *Meditations*, "Among the Quadi, on the Granua [the river Gran or Hron, a northern tributary of the Danube]," and between 2 and 3, "This at Carnuntum," indicate that books 2 and 3 were written in 172 and 173.

In 174 Marcus moved his headquarters back to Sirmium on the River Sava, from which he launched the second phase of the war, against the Sarmatian Jazyges, named in one of the later books: "A spider takes pride in catching a fly, and one man in catching a hare, another a little fish in a net, another wild boars, another bears and another Sarmatians – aren't they brigands, if you test their principles?" (*Med.* 10. 10). Otherwise one has to search hard even for indirect reflection of the circumstances under which Marcus wrote.

The *Historia Augusta* asserts that Marcus' plan was to annex the territory of the most dangerous peoples beyond the middle Danube, as the provinces of Marcomannia and Sarmatia. Dio appeared anxious to deny that Marcus had such intentions, and modern scholars also find it hard to believe that the philosopher emperor could have been an expansionist (Dio 71. 20. 1–2). However this may be, in early summer 175 he was obliged by an unexpected turn of events to bring his campaigning to an abrupt close. News arrived that Avidius Cassius, the hero of the Parthian war, who had been governing Syria since 166, had been proclaimed emperor in the east. The likeliest explanation is that he was misled by a false report of Marcus' death. But once this step had been taken, he could not back down. Cassius was recognized in Syria, his native province, in Egypt and in some other parts of the east, but Martius Verus, governor of Cappadocia, remained loyal to Marcus.

Marcus summoned his only surviving son, Commodus, now aged thirteen, to the front, where the *toga virilis* was conferred on him. Faustina came too, and was given the title of "mother of the camp," *mater castrorum*. Marcus himself assumed the title Sarmaticus, and the Sarmatians were given a peace treaty; now they and the eastern Germans had to supply large numbers of young men to serve in Rome's armies – a massive number, 5,500 out of 8,000 Sarmatians, were sent to Britain, either to keep them as far away from home as possible or because there was again trouble in Britain. Then, with his wife and son and a large expeditionary force, Marcus set off for the east. Well before he reached the affected area the usurper was dead, killed by one of his own men after "a dream of empire" lasting for three months. It was still thought desirable for Marcus to tour the eastern provinces, not least Syria and Egypt. On the journey through the Taurus mountains, Faustina died, at a place called Halala in Cilicia. She and Marcus had been married for thirty years and she had borne at least fourteen children, of which Commodus and five daughters survived her. On the return journey Marcus and Commodus were initiated into the Eleusinian mysteries. They reached Rome at the end of 176. Marcus had been away for seven years. He now had Commodus raised to the rank of Augustus so that there were once more two co-emperors. Commodus held the consulship in 177 and a little later was found a bride, Bruttia Crispina.

Marcus was to be back at Rome for less than two years. During this stay he initiated a decree of the senate on gladiators. No doubt as a result of these

Commodus

men being conscripted into the army during the emergency of 169–70, the costs of putting on public shows had soared: the shortage of trained men meant that promoters had pushed up fees. An appeal from the council of the Gallic provinces allowed a concession: they could purchase criminals condemned to death from the imperial procurator, at a low price, for use as gladiators. It may well be that this measure helped to provoke the violent persecution of the Christians at Lyon and Vienne, so vividly described in the letter of these churches to their fellow Christians in the east, quoted verbatim by Eusebius; for all Christians who refused to apostasize were automatically sentenced to death, and could thus be used as cheap substitutes for gladiators.

Meanwhile, warfare on the Danube had resumed. Victories were won by the Quintilii brothers, for which Marcus accepted a ninth acclamation, "but they could not end the war." On 3 August 178 Marcus had to leave for the front again, taking Commodus with him, on the "second German expedition." In 179 the prefect of the guard Taruttienus Paternus won a victory, for which Marcus took his tenth and last acclamation. The Jazyges were granted some concessions and Marcus received delegations from various other peoples. Twenty thousand men were now stationed in the lands of the Quadi and Marcomanni, where they wintered in forts with bath-houses and all amenities. An inscription from Trenčín in Slovakia, of which the ancient name was Leugaricio, records that Valerius Maximianus was wintering there, 120 kilometres beyond the Danube, with a detachment of over 800 men. The *Historia Augusta* insists that the plan was still, or again, to annex new two provinces, Marcomannia and Sarmatia; Herodian too seems convinced that Marcus had such a plan, and a medallion of Marcus and Commodus calls them *propagatores imperii*, "extenders of the empire."

Marcus' Ideals

In his private notebook, Marcus gave thanks that he had been able "to learn about Thrasea, Helvidius, Cato, Dion and Brutus, and the concept of a state based on equity and freedom of speech, and of a monarchy which cherishes above the liberty of the subject" (*Med.* 1. 14). The reconciliation of *libertas et principatus* proclaimed by Tacitus in 98 (*Agr.* 3. 1) may have taken time to mature, but this and other passages in the *Meditations* show that it really had reached the summit. Marcus' attitude was, indeed, far loftier than that of Tacitus: "My city and fatherland as Antoninus is Rome, as a human being it is the cosmos" (6. 44). But he was a realist: "Do not hope for Plato's ideal state, be content to take a very small step forward and reflect that even this is no trivial achievement" (9. 29). Further, he did not have an inflated idea of his own worth: "If anyone can prove and convince me that an idea or action of mine is wrong, I will gladly amend it – I seek the truth, which never harmed anyone" (6. 21); "If you can see your course, take it gladly, and do not turn aside; if not, suspend judgement and use the best men to advise you" (10. 12; cf. 8. 16). This memorandum to himself is confirmed by the *Historia Augusta* biographer: "Before taking action, he always consulted with the leading men, not only on matters of war but on civilian affairs too, indeed he used to say: 'It is fairer that I should follow the advice of so many and such good friends than that they should follow the wishes of a single man'" (*HA Marc.* 22. 4).

Death

Of course, when Tacitus wrote, Nerva had just adopted as his successor a man totally unrelated to him. But there was never a so-called "adoptive principle": Trajan was succeeded by his nearest male kinsman, and Hadrian, as has been seen, was connected to Marcus' family by some kind of kinship. Hence, as the first emperor since Vespasian to have a male heir, Marcus clearly felt unable to dispense with hereditary succession. He fell ill in the late winter, not long before the new campaigning season was due to begin, and died on March 17, 180, either at Vienna or Sirmium. His eighteen-year-old son, already Augustus, was the unchallenged successor. Marcus' five sons-in-law, in particular Claudius Pompeianus, Lucilla's husband, were wise and trusted counselors, as was Aufidius Victorinus, his close friend. He obviously hoped that they would guide Commodus; but the young man turned out quite otherwise.

Dio's judgment was that Marcus "did not have the good fortune that he deserved, for he was not physically strong, and for almost the whole of his reign was involved in a series of troubles. But I for my part admired him all the more for this very reason, that amid unusual and extraordinary difficulties he both survived himself and preserved the empire." In spite of external afflictions – wars, rebellion, plague – to Dio, Marcus' reign had been a golden age; what followed, that of Commodus, one of iron and rust (71. 36. 3–4). Over 200 years after Marcus' death, Ammianus Marcellinus hailed the patriotism that had inspired Rome's resistance to external threat in those days: "After calamitous losses things were restored anew, . . . with unanimous ardor highest and lowest hastened, as if to a calm and peaceful haven, to an honorable death in the service of the commonwealth" (31. 5. 14).

Notes

1   Under Augustus, Marcus Agrippa (27 bc); Claudius, Lucius Vitellius (ad 47); Nerva, Lucius Verginius Rufus (97); Trajan, Sextus Julius Frontinus (100) and Lucius Licinius Sura (107). Only one other man achieved this: Lucius Julius Ursus Servianus, Hadrian's brother-in-law, in 134; not long after this the old man was forced to suicide (see below). Verus was still alive and influential in 138.

2   A daughter of Verus, Annia Galeria Faustina, was married to Titus Aurelius Fulvus Boionius Arrius Antoninus – the future emperor Antoninus Pius – consul in 120, and another member of the "colonial elite": the Aurelii Fulvi came from Nemausus (Nîmes) in Gallia Narbonensis. His paternal grandfather and his father, both called Titus Aurelius Fulvus, had had distinguished careers under the Flavians, while his maternal grandfather, Gnaeus Arrius Antoninus, had been consul twice, in 69 and 97.

3   The *Historia Augusta* (followed by many modern writers) mistakenly calls Aelius Caesar "Aelius Verus." But he was never called Verus, and his son took the name only when becoming emperor in 161 (see below).

4   *RMD* 264, 394. These diplomas of August 1, 142 also show that Fronto's consulship was in that year, not 143 as previously supposed.

5   J. P. Gillam, "Roman and Native ad 122–197," in I. A. Richmond (ed.), *Roman and Native in North Britain* (Edinburgh, 1961), 60–89, esp. 66–7.

6   See esp. N. Hodgson, "Were There Two Antonine Occupations of Scotland?," *Britannia* 26 (1995), 24–49.

Further Reading

A. Birley, *Marcus Aurelius: A Biography*, 2nd edn (London, 1987; repr. 1993)

A. Birley, "Hadrian to the Antonines," *Cambridge Ancient History*, vol. 11, 2nd edn (Cambridge, UK, 2000), 132–94

E. Champlin, *Fronto and Antonine Rome* (Cambridge, Mass., and London, 1980)

R. B. Rutherford, *The Meditations of Marcus Aurelius: A Study* (Oxford, 1989)

R. B. Rutherford, *A Selection from the Letters of Marcus and Fronto* (Oxford, 1989)

G. R. Stanton, "Marcus Aurelius, Emperor and Philosopher," *Historia* 18 (1969), 570–87

G. R. Stanton, "Marcus Aurelius, Lucius Verus, and Commodus: 1962–1972," *Aufstieg und Niedergang der Römischen Welt* 2; 2 (1975), 478–549

IX

Septimius Severus

David Potter

We are fortunate in having an account of the character of Severus from the pen of a man who knew him. Cassius Dio tells us that Severus was a person of intense activity, possessed of a powerful moral stance that was often at odds with those ordinarily found within the senatorial class. In general terms, he worked hard every day, and disliked large parties, holding banquets only when he had to. He rose each day to conduct public business before sunrise, at which point he would take a walk, discussing the affairs of empire, and then hold court, making sure that the advocates for both sides had time to make their case, and allowing those in council to speak freely. At noon he would end his hearing of legal proceedings to take as long a ride as his strength would permit, exercise, and bathe. After a large lunch, which he would take either alone or with his sons, he would nap. Waking up, he would commit himself to his other duties and then go for a walk, speaking in both Greek and Latin until the approach of evening. He would then take a second bath and dine with his closest associates. He was avid for knowledge and, although given to massive public expenditures, especially on buildings, chary of expenditure on his own pleasures, and frugal in his tastes. He believed deeply that the world was governed by the decrees of fate, was devoted to his wife and disappointed in his sons. He had few close friends (Dio 76. 16; see also *HA Sev.* 18. 4–5, 19. 8–9).

Although Severus is one of the best-documented emperors in Roman history – we have, for example, the benefit of a description of him from someone who sat, occasionally at least, in council with him, of a papyrus that reveals his personal disposition of legal cases over the course of several days in Egypt, of the remains of many building projects that he must have personally approved, of praise from his personal physician, and of several direct quotations that reveal his conduct in council – he remains very difficult to know.[1] And so he seems also to have been to some Romans of his time. Dio admired his work ethic, that much is clear; but he also feared the man, and placed his reign in the era of rust and iron that he says followed upon the golden age of Marcus Aurelius (Dio 71. 36. 4). While proud that Severus respected his work as an historian – he even dreamed, years after Severus' death, that the emperor commanded him to write about the affairs of his sons – he could be deeply critical of decisions that Severus made, and says several times that he thought the man was a liar (Dio 75. 7. 3–4; 76. 5. 2; 78. 10. 2). Later historians have been no less puzzled. Edward Gibbon described him as the "principal author of the decline and fall of the Roman empire," and Michael Rostovtzeff held that he "militarized the principate," handing its flourishing civic life over to the peasant soldiers of the army.[2] His most significant modern biographer concludes that he "must remain an enigma" (Birley 1988: 200).

Despite all the evidence that we have, Severus defies ready classification as either a "good" or a "bad" emperor. He could be cruel, of that there was no doubt. He could be deceitful, of that too there could be no doubt. He had a powerful sense of personal morality that was, it seems, out of touch with that of his upper-class contemporaries in Rome: when he decided to enforce the existing laws on adultery – laws that dated back to the regime of Augustus – he found that there were so many cases he had to abandon the effort (Dio 76. 16. 4). He spent an enormous amount of money on public building projects, but was so sparing in his personal style that the treasury he left upon his death was in far better shape than the one that he had inherited when he seized the throne in 193 (Dio 76. 16. 3). If his record is judged simply upon its immediate, short-term results, there is little that can be said to have been obviously foolish: the frontiers were stable, the armies had not suffered notable catastrophes, the cities prospered, and he had done his very best to ensure that his sons would not turn out disastrously. If he made a mistake in leaving his eldest son, Caracalla, in a position where he could achieve supremacy, it was because he could not bring himself to kill him (Dio 76. 14. 3). That was no worse an error than the one that Marcus made when he ensured that Commodus would succeed him. Dio is entitled to think that the occupation of northern Mesopotamia was a terrible error, but it was not self-evidently one when Severus decided to incorporate the region within the empire, and there were other emperors whose judgment in matters strategic may be regarded as far better founded than that of Dio – emperors like Diocletian and Constantine – who felt that the region was crucial. Severus' big problem was not that he was foolish or evil. His problem is that he seems never to have felt at home with the governing class of the empire, and that his discomfort translated into behavior that undermined the subtle balance of power between different interest groups that had been the basis of Antonine government. The problem is perhaps best summed up in the final advice that he is said to have uttered to his sons: pay attention to the soldiers and ignore the rest (Dio 76. 15. 2).

Early Years

Severus' background was radically different from that of the emperors of the Antonine age. While Trajan, Hadrian, Pius, and Marcus were all from families of Italian extraction, with deep connections within the senatorial aristocracy and homelands of long-standing Latin connections, Severus' background was Punic. Also, while he was part of a family that had entered the senate under Hadrian, he was from the cadet branch of the family that had remained in north Africa. His grandfather, also named Lucius Septimius Severus, had spent some time in Italy toward the end of the reign of Domitian (he is praised by the poet Statius) before returning home to become a local dignitary in Lepcis, holding, among other offices, that of *sufes*, a title that is a clear hold-over from a Punic past that was also, to some degree, a Punic present (Birley 1988: 23). Although Dio portrays Severus speaking to his advisors in Greek and Latin, we are told by another witness that Severus always spoke Latin with enough of a Punic accent, meaning that he may have pronounced his own name Sheptimiush Sheverush – in contrast to his more skilled grandfather, who is said to have spoken Latin without an accent (Birley 1988: 35). Severus' father, Publius Septimius Geta, seems not to have followed his own father into local office; perhaps he was saving his money to support the careers of two sons, both of whom had aspirations to senatorial dignity. Whatever else he may have been, Publius Septimius Geta must have been very rich. His wealth would have been derived from his large estates around Lepcis, and his ability to ship the surplus – presumably grain and olive oil – off to Rome.

Far from being the son of a famous general, as Trajan had been, or the nephew of an emperor, raised to the purple, as had been Hadrian, or a distinguished member of the senate (Pius), or a youth raised to be king (Marcus), Lucius Septimius Severus was the son of a very wealthy man who had never undertaken a public career. His claim to high status came not from birth, but rather from the fortune that his father had accumulated. If it will often seem that he did not fit in with the "old" Roman nobility, the reason was quite simply that he came from outside the charmed circle (Potter 2004: 99–102). He would have been far from the only one making this move in the second half of the second century, but the Severans were unusual in that they were of Punic rather than Greek or Italian extraction. The Semitic regions of the empire as a whole provided very few senators.

Although Severus' grandfather Lucius and father Publius avoided imperial service, the same was not true of the two sons of Lucius' brother, Gaius Claudius Septimius Afer. They both began senatorial careers that led to the consulship. Given the success of Septimius Afer's sons, it was perhaps to be expected that both Septimius, who was born on April 8, 146, and his brother would try their luck in the senate, and it would have been no surprise that both were granted the "broad stripe," the *latus clavus*, that signified that the emperor supported a man's aspiration to join the senate, or that both received positions among the *vigintiviri*, whose various offices were the first testing ground for a man who would be admitted to the senate when awarded the quaestorship at the age of twenty-five. The future emperor began his official career in Rome at the age of eighteen, and would have held one of the twenty offices assigned the *vigintiviri* in 164; the exercise of patronage may have been sufficient to excuse him the more onerous duty of a military tribunate that would ordinarily have followed (*HA Sev.* 2. 2). Five years later he became quaestor, and in 170 was assigned to assist the governor of Baetica. During the intervening years he likely learned how to act as an advocate in the courts, quite possibly with instruction from Cornelius Fronto, the leading Latin orator of the time who was himself from north Africa (Birley 1988: 37–52).

Severus would have received his assignment as quaestor in the summer of 170, but before he could take up his post two things happened. His father died, requiring him to return home to sort out family affairs; and Baetica was invaded by tribesmen from north Africa. In light of the emergency, Marcus reassigned Baetica to an official with military competence, and sent Severus to Sardinia. Two years later the young man served as *legatus*, or assistant, to Gaius Severus as governor of Africa. It was in this year that he claimed to have consulted an astrologer who gave him a horoscope predicting a "great" – meaning, as both men understood it, "imperial" – future for him (*HA Sev.* 2. 9). That future would, however, have to wait. For the present Severus married a local woman named Paccia Marciana, and was appointed to the position of tribune of the plebs by Marcus for 175 (*HA Sev.* 3. 3). Two years later he became praetor, with the governorship of southern Spain to follow in 178. In 180 he moved on to Syria, and his first military command, as *legatus* of the fourth legion. His career was, to date, thoroughly respectable, but gave little sign that he would ever be in a position to realize the promise of the prophecy he had received years before.

The Reign of Commodus

Marcus Aurelius died on March 17, 180, as he was finally bringing an end to the long wars with the tribes north of the Danube that had broken out more than a decade earlier. His son, Commodus, then eighteen years old, and designated as his co-emperor in 177, continued now to rule as sole emperor. He would prove to be dreadful at the job.

Not only was Commodus too young, with far too little experience of the world, to be able to rule in his own right, but he succeeded to a government staffed by men much older than himself who were used to specific kinds of relationship with an emperor. It was perhaps no bad thing for Severus to have been away from Rome as the sole reign of Commodus began. He was distant from the decision-making process on the Danube when the new young emperor took the advice of favorites who realized that he had not the temperament suitable to life on the frontier and extended meetings with experienced senior staff officers, preferring drinking parties with close friends. So too, while action continued under these generals for the next couple of years, Severus missed the triumph that Commodus celebrated six months after his father's death, and would not have seen his ruler exchanging kisses with his *cubicularius*, Saoterus, in the triumphal chariot as he entered Rome (*HA Com.* 3. 6). But he could not remain immune from the growing tensions within the palace. In 182, Commodus' much older sister, Lucilla, the widow of Lucius Verus and estranged wife of Claudius Pompeianus, organized a plot to kill her brother. The ostensible reason was her jealousy of Bruttia Crispina, whom Commodus had married in 175. The plot proved a miserable failure when the designated assassin shouted "see the dagger the senate sends you" as he drew his weapon, thereby alerting the guards (*HA Com.* 4. 1; Dio 72. 4. 4). The attempted assassination brought chaos to the government when one of the praetorian prefects took advantage of the confusion to arrange the murder of Saoterus, and then fell victim to a carefully crafted plot by his colleague Tigidius Perennis (*HA Com.* 4. 5). There were other plots, one indirectly implicating one of Marcus' more able commanders, Pertinax – then governing Syria – who went into temporary retirement only to be recalled in 185 to govern Britain. Severus himself, who had commanded a legion in Syria while Pertinax was governor, seems to have thought it wise not to return to Rome as these events played themselves out, and had spent time in Athens; then, in that same year, 185, he was given the province of Gallia Lugdunensis to govern. It was at this point that Paccia Marciana died.

At this distance in time it is hard to know what to make of the story that Severus certainly would have publicized later about his decision to remarry. His new wife was Julia Domna, a member of the family that had formerly ruled the city of Emesa. According to the biography in the *Historia Augusta*, a work informed, like Dio's history, by heavy doses of Severan propaganda, Severus learned that Julia had a horoscope that predicted that she would marry a king, and thus sought her hand in marriage (*HA Sev.* 3. 9 with caveats in Rubin 1980: 178–9). Less spectacular is Dio's story that their wedding feast was prepared in the temple of Venus by Faustina, one of the three surviving daughters of Marcus Aurelius (Dio 74. 3. 1). This story is nonetheless significant, for it suggests that Severus was indeed coming up in the world; he seems to have been a loyal subordinate of Pertinax, and now that Pertinax's star was again on the rise, his own connections improved. It did not hurt that he had earned a good reputation in his new post (*HA Sev.* 4. 1), something that may have helped him escape a charge of consulting astrologers (almost certainly true, given what we know of his habits) while governor of Sicily in 189 (*HA Sev.* 4. 3). A year later, he was included in the vast consular college that Cleander designated for the year 190. While there was no particular glory in being one of twenty-five consuls, the appointment gave him access to far more important commands than those for which he had previously been eligible; it also suggests that the new power set in the palace saw him as a man they could trust. In 191, the year after Cleander was ousted from power by yet another conspiracy carefully arranged to take best advantage of Commodus' insecurities, Severus was appointed to govern Upper Pannonia, a genuinely important post with several legions under his command. It was evidently Aemilius Laetus, the praetorian prefect, also from Africa, who suggested the appointment. The governorship of Upper Pannonia also enabled him to miss one of the most bizarre spectacles in Roman history.

Commodus liked gladiators. He liked them so much that he wanted to be one himself. He also liked Hercules, so much that he wanted to be like him. He also rather liked himself, and so had Rome renamed *colonia Commodiana* in his own honor. The renaming of Rome took place in 190, the same year that Commodus added the name Hercules to his own, after displaying his skill as a beast hunter in the amphitheater at Lanuvium.[3] At the *ludi Romani* in 192, Commodus appeared in the Colosseum as both a beast hunter and a gladiator in a series of performances that were intended to evoke the twelve labors of Hercules. The events of the *ludi Romani* may well have been the last straw as far as the people who were running the government for him were concerned. On New Year's Eve, 192, Marcia fed Commodus poisoned beef. When it looked as if he might survive, she summoned a professional wrestler named Narcissus, who was then resident in the palace, to strangle him (Potter 2004: 93).

Revolutions

It should perhaps not be surprising that the conspirators, two of whom had links with the family of Pompeianus, should look to Pertinax for support. It was in the early morning hours of January 1 that Laetus arrived at Pertinax's house and invited him to come to the praetorian camp to be proclaimed emperor in return for a promised gift of twelve million sestertii (twelve thousand per man), significantly less than its members had received from Marcus after his accession. Pertinax did as he was asked, and when the senate assembled for the ceremonies that would open the new year, it followed the lead of the guard by proclaiming him emperor.

Pertinax proved a disastrous choice, not because he was a bad man, but rather because the contrast between his style and that of his predecessor was too great. In so far as Commodus had a mode of government it involved the devolution of virtually all day-to-day authority into the hands of his subordinates. Pertinax, whose own life was not entirely scandal-free – he dealt with his own unhappy marriage by carrying on an affair with Marcus' daughter Cornificia (*HA Pert.* 14. 9) – had a radically different style. His tastes were simple, he insisted on showing a great deal of deference to the senate, and he disliked what he considered pandering to the praetorian guard, which seems to have been fond of his predecessor. It did not help that his relationship with Laetus deteriorated very fast, largely through Pertinax's inability to pay the agreed donative, and Laetus supported an abortive effort to make one of the consuls for the year, Quintus Pompeius Sosius Falco, emperor. Pertinax put a stop to this when he denounced the plot in the senate, but made a fatal error in executing some guardsmen who had been implicated, while allowing Falco to retire to his estates. The guard did not take well the punishment of their colleagues while the principal went free because Pertinax had sworn never to execute a senator (*HA Pert.* 10. 1–4; Dio 74. 8).

On March 28, 200 members of the guard set out for the palace in close formation. Pertinax, who had dismissed his personal guards for the day, met them when they entered the palace and was killed. According to Dio "he had failed to understand . . . that one cannot with safety reform every-thing at once" (74. 10. 3). This was the perspective of another senator. A better observation might have been that he had failed because he did not realize that in times of uncertainty the wise emperor put his faith in the soldiers first.

The praetorian camp became a very busy place as news spread that the emperor had been murdered. When news of the uprising had reached him, Pertinax had sent his father-in-law, Flavius Sulpicianus, then prefect of the city, to the camp to discover what was going on. Sulpicianus now tried to negotiate his own promotion to the imperial office with the guard, but as he did so another senior senator, Didius Julianus, showed up outside the camp with a band of supporters seeking entrance so that he could make his own bid. Urging the soldiers not to choose an emperor who might avenge Pertinax, and advertising his affection for Commodus, Julianus was admitted to the camp and negotiated successfully for the throne (*HA Jul.* 3. 2. 6–7, a superior account to that in Dio 74. 11. 2–5). Before the sun had fallen Sulpicianus was dead, and, having promised a donative of 25,000 sestertii a man to win the guard's support, Julianus went to the senate house to secure recognition of his claim. The senate duly passed a *senatus consultum* granting him the title of *imperator*, the tribunician power, and proconsular authority *ius proconsulare* (*HA Jul.* 3. 3; the passage of the *senatus consultum* is also attested in Dio 74. 13. 1, who was present at the meeting).

Septimius Severus appears to have been aware that Pertinax was in trouble, though the extent of his preparations to intervene are now difficult to discern. According to accounts that may be heavily based upon Severus' autobiography, he began to explore the possibility of taking the throne through conversations with small groups of officers, testing out the will of the men as soon as he heard that Pertinax was dead (Herodian 2. 9. 7). There is no reason to believe his version of the chronology: he was proclaimed emperor on April 9 (*HA Sev.* 5. 1; *P. Dura* 54. ii. 3), just about the earliest possible day after he could have received news of the events at Rome on March 28, and a version of the story that seems to derive from his own pen suggests that he had ensured the support of his army before his proclamation (something that would not have happened overnight).

Having tested the will of the troops, Severus had also to test that of his colleagues in surrounding provinces (something else that could not have happened overnight, given the distances separating them in a day when significant communication was conducted by horse-borne messengers). In all of this, Septimius derived an advantage from the fact that his elder brother, Publius Septimius Geta, was governor of Lower Moesia. He may also have had some personal connection with the governor of Dacia, Quintus Aurelius Polus Terentianus, who was a member of the same priestly college to which Severus had been admitted a few years before. The odd men out were the governors of Lower Pannonia and Upper Moesia, but they too appear to have signed on with some alacrity. (Herodian 2. 9. 12, 10. 1; Birley 1988: 97). A series of coins minted at Severus' behest later in the year commemorates fifteen of the sixteen legions encamped in the Danubian provinces. The process must have taken several weeks, and must have begun before April 9.

Severus was not alone in seeing opportunity in the demise of Pertinax. Clodius Albinus, the governor of Britain, was proclaimed emperor even as Severus marched on Rome, as was Pescennius Niger, the governor of Syria, and though Severus later suggested that their proclamations were prior to his own, the facts of geography speak against his claim. Both men may even have known of Severus' revolt at about the same time that they learned of Pertinax's murder, and their actions may reasonably be seen as responses to the Severan coup; the fact that Albinus moved as fast as he could to secure the loyalty of the legions that formed the garrisons of the Rhine provinces suggests that he was looking to stabilize his position against Severus, while Niger seems to have set out for the Hellespont as fast as he was able. No one could have expected that Julianus would be able to mount any sort of effective defense against the Danubian legions. Letters from Severus were delivered to many quarters, troops occupying key points deserted, and Julianus lost heart (*HA Jul.* 8. 5; Dio 73. 17. 3). On June 1 he summoned a meeting of the senate to ask that Severus be named co-ruler with himself, but it was too late. The praetorians had received letters promising that they would suffer no harm if they surrendered the murderers of Pertinax. They did so, and announced the fact to the consul Silius Messalla, who convened a meeting of the senate on his own authority to pass three motions: one sentencing Julianus to death; the second naming Severus emperor; the third conferring divine honors on Pertinax (Dio 74. 17. 3–4; Herodian 2. 12. 6–7). A soldier was sent to the palace where he found Julianus, abandoned by his supporters, and killed him (*HA Jul.* 8. 7).

Severus' advance had demonstrated a thorough command of the political structure of the city, and he took immediate steps to ensure that he would remain in control. The praetorians were summoned, without arms, to a meeting outside of the city and dismissed (Dio 74. 1; *HA Sev.* 6. 11; Herodian 2. 13. 1–12). A new guard was created from the soldiers who had marched from the Balkans, and Julianus' prefects, who had changed sides at an opportune moment, were retained in office (*HA Sev.* 6. 6). There was, however, a new prefect of the watch, appointed by Severus, who distinguished himself by rounding up the children of Niger. His name was Fulvius Plautianus, a tangential relative of Severus himself (*HA Sev.* 6. 10; *HA Pesc. Nig.* 5. 2).

Severus' entry into Rome shows that he fully appreciated the role of spectacle in authorizing the power of an emperor. According to Dio, who was there,

> the whole city had been decked out with garlands of flowers and laurel and adorned with richly colored stuffs, and it was ablaze with torches and burning incense; the citizens wearing white robes and with radiant countenances, uttered many shouts of good omen; the soldiers, too, stood out conspicuous in their armor as they moved about like participants in some holiday procession; and finally we [senators] were walking about in state. (Dio 75. 1. 4, trans. Cary)

The procession, with the distinct elements of the power structure of Rome marked out by their dress, gave visual confirmation of the social order. It was supplemented a few days later by another spectacle: the formal funeral of Pertinax, culminating with the release of an eagle from a box atop the funeral pyre, which signified his soul's ascent to join the gods (Dio 74. 4. 2–5; *HA Sev.* 7. 8–9). As Pertinax moved into the next realm, Severus enhanced his claim to legitimacy by adopting himself into the dead man's family (Herodian 2. 10. 1). It all had to be done fast, for the war with Niger had already begun.

Niger's effort was doomed to fail. Severus could muster the sixteen legions of the Danube against a mere six in the eastern provinces. Thus, even though his forces crossed the Dardanelles and defeated a portion of Severus' army before Severus completed arrangements in Rome, Niger would be unable to exploit his success. An army group, assembled from the Pannonian legions, drove his forces back into western Turkey.[4] A fleet arrived from Italy to transport a sufficient force to pursue Niger while still leaving enough troops behind to initiate a long and bloody siege of Byzantium, which had welcomed Niger and remained loyal to his cause. This siege would last for three years.

Despite later traditions about the sloth of Niger, and the equally unmilitary qualities of his men (owing much, if not all, to the pen of Severus), the eastern army fought hard and well; its retreat, the most difficult of all military operations, was conducted with skill, and the final battle at Issus in May 194 was hard fought even though the ultimate outcome of the war could scarcely have been in doubt (Rubin 1980: 92–6; Birley 1988: 113 n. 13). Long before the battle, Severus had been able to exploit his control of the children of provincial governors who had remained at Rome and the rivalries between cities throughout the region. The governor of Arabia changed sides, presumably taking with him the legion under his command; a second legion, stationed in Palestine, also deserted, and various cities rose up in revolt (Potter 2004: 104–7).

No sooner had he defeated Niger than Severus launched an invasion of northern Mesopotamia to "punish" the Parthians for supporting his rival. The result was the reduction of the kingdom of Osrhoene to the status of a province in the spring of 195 (Millar 1993: 125–6), an act that was followed shortly afterwards by the proclamation of Caracalla as Caesar, and the adoption of his family into that of Marcus Aurelius. The proclamation of Caracalla was as good as a declaration of war on Albinus, who was now accused of conspiring to assassinate Severus, and on December 15 the senate declared Albinus a public enemy.

The war with Albinus was as much a foregone conclusion as had been the war with Niger, for even though Albinus had a larger army, combining the three legions of Britain with the six in the Rhineland, Severus still had a significant advantage in numbers. He also had the advantage of excellent advance preparation. Despite the fact that Albinus had a relatively rapid path to Italy – Vitellius had made the march in the winter of 69 within three months of proclaiming himself emperor – he was unable to launch any sort of effective offensive even as Severus returned from the east. We can only now surmise that significant forces had been moved into northern Italy before the final breakdown in the relationship, and there is some evidence that Severus had organized something of a fifth column in the Gallic provinces. Dio tells of a schoolmaster named Numerianus who imitated a senator and led a privately raised band of soldiers to disrupt Albinus' operations, capturing some seventy million sestertii in the course of the war (Dio 75. 5. 1). It is unlikely that he was alone, and Severus may well have been able to exploit connections that he had made as governor of Lugdenensis, which lay on Albinus' route south, to foment dissension. The final battle, which was fought near Lyons in the late summer of 196, proved to be another bloody affair, but one from which Severus emerged triumphant.

In the wake of his victory over Albinus, Severus again marched east, with only a brief sojourn in Rome, to launch yet another invasion of Parthia. He sacked Ctesiphon and withdrew by way of northern Iraq, where he notably failed to capture the city of Hatra. It is not entirely clear what he hoped to accomplish by taking Hatra – a significant place, with strong links to the indigenous tribes of the area – but Severus seems to have had no plans for any sort of lasting occupation of the region, long recognized as deeply impractical. The whole point of the operation may simply have been to overawe Rome's eastern neighbors, and if that is the case, even the failure before Hatra does not appear to have had an overtly negative impact (see Millar 1993: 127–41 on the eastern arrangements in general). As the history of the next twenty years would show, the Parthians wanted nothing to do with the Romans if they could avoid it.

Severus and the Cities of the Empire

The activities of the able Numerianus were but one aspect of the linkage between local and imperial politics that was manifest in the years of the civil wars. The schoolmaster saw in the disruption a way of enhancing his status, even though he later refused senatorial rank and contented himself with a quiet life in retirement with an imperial pension; his conduct on both a small and large scale was scarcely exceptional. On the other side of the empire a brigand named Claudius came upon Severus, riding with what must have been a small party somewhere in Syria, saluted the emperor and kissed him before riding off into the desert. No Roman official ever saw him again, and we can but imagine how the tale of his encounter reverberated in the tents of his people (Dio 76. 2. 4). Elsewhere the effects of contact with the imperial government were more obvious, though in all cases it appears that the initiative came largely from provincials who had become acclimatized to exploiting the central administration for their own ends in the previous two centuries of imperial rule.

It is in the context of long experience and a massive sense of despair that we can interpret the extraordinary resistance of Byzantium to the armies of Severus. Members of the upper class must have been conscious that their action in receiving the armies of Niger was an irrevocable step in light of the state of their defenses. It would have been much wiser to have shut their gates and wait to see who was winning – unless, of course, there were past bonds of obligation, unknown to us now, that linked them with Niger. Very different, though, was the case elsewhere, where local rivalries that had been fought out for years through embassies asking favors turned now to open warfare as cities mimicked the behavior of the Roman authorities. The first instance appears in the case of Nicomedia and Nicaea, ancient rivals for supremacy in Bithynia.[5] Immediately after learning the Severan victory at Cyzicus in 194, Nicomedia had sent an embassy to Severus proclaiming its adherence to his cause. The consequence, so Herodian tells us, was that "the people of Nicaea, by contrast, because of their rivalry with Nicomedia, joined the other side, by opening their gates to Niger's army and taking in any fugitives that came their way, as well as the garrison that Niger sent for Bithynia. The two cities were like army camps and provided the bases from which the forces clashed" (Herodian 3. 2. 9, trans. Whittaker).

The further consequence of the devotion of Nicaea to the cause of Niger was that Nicomedia's position as metropolis of Bithynia was confirmed. It may be a mark of the attention that people were paying to the progress of the war that further defections, those of Tyre and Laodicea, took place as Niger was preparing his position south of the Taurus. What is significant is that the leading citizens of these places were willing to take extreme risks to further the position of their cities. The individual civic hierarchies of the empire could not see themselves in isolation from the power of the central government, and regional politics of necessity took their direction from those of the imperial administration. The nexus of relationships could not be made clearer than they are by Herodian, when he writes: "While these events [the retreat of Niger] were taking place in Cappadocia, there was an outbreak of civil war, the Laodicians in Syria through hatred of Antioch, the Tyrians in Phoenicia through enmity with Beirut. Learning of Niger's defeat, they ventured to tear down his honors and proclaim Severus" (Herodian 3. 3. 3, trans. Whittaker).

Laodicea and Antioch were the leading cities in the valley of the Orontes, and both were Seleucid foundations. In this case the rivalry stemmed from causes similar to those that divided the two great cities of Bithynia, though Antioch had always been the more important place as a primary seat of the Seleucid kings. The penalties inflicted on Antioch were remarkable: it was reduced from the rank of a city to that of a village and attached to Laodicea, which was awarded the status of a *colonia*. Antioch's Olympic games were transferred to Antioch in Cilicia, where they would henceforth be held in association with games commemorating Severus' victory.[6]

The situation in Phoenicia was somewhat different. Tyre was one of the most ancient cities of the region, while Beirut owed its prominence to its foundation as a veteran colony by Augustus in 15 BC (Millar 1990: 10–18). In culture and background the two places could not have been more different. Tyre preserved the memory of the ancient Phoenician kings, minting coins with Phoenician legends, celebrating ancient Phoenician divinities, and claiming primacy among the cities of Phoenicia. It was thoroughly bicultural, mixing elements of its Phoenician past with the Greek needed to make its uniqueness comprehensible on the imperial stage. This seamless mingling of traditions may be taken as characteristic of Phoenician culture, and was opposed to the inherent Romanness of Beirut, where Roman gods appear on coins and public inscriptions, as the city flaunted the title of *colonia*. No wonder there was tension between the two places; but they were able to coexist so long as there was unity in the imperial administration. And there was more to the civil war than that. After Severus had proved victorious, we are told, he punished the supporters of Niger in all the cities of the east (Dio 74. 8. 4). He had his own supporters in these places as well, and in each place we may imagine desperate efforts to exploit division for personal advantage. It is impossible to see the civil war as an isolated event involving only the armies of Rome.

It is arguable that, as a man who himself united the culture of his homeland with that of the capital, Severus was particularly conscious of the empire-wide impact of his conduct. He appears to have been determined to leave his mark upon the provinces. The old province of Syria was itself divided into two new provinces, Syria Coele ("hollow Syria"), encompassing the regions whose urban culture had been fundamentally reshaped by the Seleucid kingdom, and Syria Phoenice, "Phoenician Syria," encompassing those regions that retained a more strongly Semitic urban character. His own wife, Julia Domna, was, of course, another product of this region, and her homeland of Emesa defected from Niger, as did Heliopolis, which was rewarded with the title of *colonia* and the *ius Italicum*. Tyre was similarly made a *colonia* as a reward for what it had done (Millar 1990: 35–8; 1993: 121–4). In Palmyra, also awarded the title of *colonia*, there was a somewhat different development as the family of a local dignitary named Odaenathus began to achieve a position of dominance. The local oracle of Zeus Belus at Apamea, which had achieved some significance under Trajan, found its position ever further enhanced through predictions to Severus that were widely enough publicized to gain the attention of Dio (Potter 1994: 170).

Later in his reign, after the second Parthian War, Severus delayed his return to Rome with a tour that took him through Egypt to his homeland in Africa, where again his interest in the Semitic contribution to Roman history was on display. In any program of urban renewal, it is not always possible to know where the true initiative for a project lies. The people of Lepcis obviously had a strong interest in celebrating the family of their most famous citizen, and that, at least, may account for the statues that have been found (probably reflecting a larger program) celebrating members of his family, including Paccia Marciana, his parents, and his grandfather. So too local initiative seems to lie behind the erection of a shrine to Liber Pater in the forum; but the inclusion of Lepcis in the broader Semitic world is reflected in a single surviving dedication to Severus' younger son, Geta, by the *colonia* of Tyre as metropolis of Phoenicia. It must once have been accompanied by statues of other family members (Birley 1988: 149 with n. 6). Likewise, local initiative seems to lie behind the redecoration of the large arch over a major crossroads in the city to celebrate the victory over Parthia. Severus responded by granting Lepcis the *ius Italicum*, constructing a new forum, along with a basilica, reconstructing the colonnaded street that ran from the harbor to the main bath-house (a Hadrianic structure), and providing the city with a thoroughly modernized athletic facility, linking the amphitheater with a state-of-the-art circus.[7] Finally, it is just possible that the enormous temple at Lepcis that was once thought to be a temple to the Severan house is in fact the gigantic temple of Bacchus and Hercules, about whose cost Dio would later complain. Bacchus and Hercules in this context are none other than Shdrp' and Mlks'htrt, Shadrapa and Melquart, the ancient patrons of Lepcis, who were commonly identified with these two Greco-Roman divinities (Birley 1988: 5). The main point to all of this, however, is that the construction does not seek to recreate Rome in Lepcis, but rather to create a specifically new, modern, urban landscape that incorporates the Semitic past with the Roman present, and asserts an equality of the traditions.

Severus' integration of the Semitic portions of the empire into the center of government is a profound movement beyond the cultural activities of the previous two centuries, whereby the traditions of the east had only been accepted in so far as they could be Hellenized. In the Severan dispensation these traditions are not so much "Hellenized" or "Romanized," if those words are to be understood as implying a transformation in the meaning of an indigenous tradition, as they are equalized. Severus' work in Syria and Mesopotamia resulted in the most significant alteration of the shape of the eastern frontier since the time of Augustus, and, in general, his actions offer a novel assertion of the cultural unity of the empire.

Severus and Roman Tradition

Severus' reading of Roman history was arguably eccentric. When he was in Egypt, he sacrificed at Pompey's tomb, fearing, it seems, that Pompey's spirit would be angry with him, because a Severus had murdered him (Dio 75. 13. 1, with Birley 1988: 136). In Rome itself, after the defeat of Albinus, he had given a speech to the senate in which he criticized Pompey and Caesar for their mercy, which had proved to be their undoing, while praising the "rigor" and ferocity of Marius, Sulla, and Augustus as their salvation (Dio 75. 8. 1). The word that Dio uses for "rigor" – *austeria*, a moral quality – looks very much like an effort to catch the sense of a Latin word such as *rigor* or *disciplina*, for the qualities of *severitas* and *disciplina/rigor* seem to have been ones in which Severus himself took pride. The Rome of his time, he seems to have felt, was insufficiently devoted to moral rectitude, and it is likely to have been for this reason that he attempted to enforce, with notable lack of success, the penalties for adultery under the *Lex Julia de adulteriis*. Why should the senate, he went on to ask, object to his adoption of his line into that of the Antonines, and his restoration of the *memoria* of Commodus, when they shared in the very vices for which they condemned that emperor (Dio 75. 8. 2)? By recalling the dark years of civil war in the first century BC, Severus not only defended his own behavior, but asserted his adherence to a vision of Roman history in which the monarchy emerged from the successive careers of military strongmen, it was a view more akin to that of Tacitus than to that of the later second century, which sought to establish a clean break between republic and monarchy with the battle of Actium (Dio 53. 17. 1).

Severus' decision, in 197, to adopt himself into the Antonine line was the logical extension of the decision that he had made as soon as he seized the throne to have himself depicted with a heavy beard in the style of Marcus and Commodus. Pertinax had made the same decision, as had both Albinus and Niger. Perhaps all these men really did have thick beards; but, if they did, their tonsorial choices were surely a reflection of their feeling that important people looked that way, a mark of respect for the style adopted by emperors after Trajan. In Severus' case the further result was to stress continuity with a past that was considered glorious – Dio was surely not alone in considering the reign of Marcus a sort of golden age. Severus' point was that he was continuing this age. The glory of the past would also figure in other significant public aspects of Severus' time in Rome, with the caveat that it was important that the Roman aristocracy and Roman people, who had expressed a strong preference for Niger in 193, should live up to the tradition of their ancestors. One of those traditions, in his view, was respect for the traditions of other peoples. He was thus appalled that the exhibition of female athletes – whose performances had gained currency in the east during the previous century and had figured prominently in games that were returned to Antioch when that city had been restored to metropolitan status in 198 – elicited a shameful response from the audience when he sponsored an exhibition of their talents in 200 (Dio 75. 16. 1 with Potter 2006: 404–8). The result was that he banned a scheduled display of female gladiators.

Severus had more success with a much more traditional performance in 204: the celebration of the Secular Games. These games, celebrated on the Augustan/Domitianic reckoning, marked the 900th anniversary of the foundation of the city, with several months of ceremonies that summed up

Severus' tendency to emphasize the integration of his career into the traditions of the Roman state. Most striking is the fact that, while the traditional prayer formulae of the Augustan age were uttered by Caracalla, the divinities who presided over the affair seem to have been Hercules and Bacchus (Birley 1988: 159). The insertion of the chief divinities of Lepcis into these ceremonies, whose rituals bound the emperor with his people through mutual exchanges of gifts, is to some degree paralleled by the way in which Severus inserted himself into the palace. For even as he resided in the traditional home of the emperors on the Palatine, he had "the stars under which he was born" painted on the ceilings of the rooms where he held court, with the exception of that portion of the sky which revealed the precise hour (Dio 76. 11. 1). That information, which would also have provided the educated viewer with the opportunity to predict the moment of his death, was reserved for the ceiling of his bedchamber alone.

Severus' interest in astrology, and his emphasis on the role of Fate in determining his success, was further emphasized through the construction of a remarkable fountain on the south-east corner of the Palatine, the Septizodium, which combined elements borrowed from the grand Nymphaea and other spectacular facades of the Greek east with traditional elements from the Roman theater. Facing the triumphal route of the via Appia, the Septizodium displayed groups of statues that summed up the essence of Severus' image. These included references to the role of Fate with the seven planetary gods, his family – including, most likely, members of his extended adoptive family in the form of the emperors from Nerva to Commodus – and images evocative of the eastern campaign.[8] Not far away from this monument rose a vast new set of baths, with which Severus made his mark on the urban landscape in a region that was particularly linked to the pleasures of the Roman people: the Septizodium stood next to the end of the Circus Maximus and within sight of the Colosseum. Although the arch that he had constructed in the Forum at the foot of the Capitoline hill and close by the Curia Julia may have symbolized his aspiration to be seen in the context of earlier emperors in the Forum, these new buildings celebrated the link between his dynasty and the Roman people.

The stress on Fate that appears in the decoration of the Septizodium had by now become a significant aspect of Severan discourse on the civil wars. There is every reason to think that contemporary narratives of the war with Niger were embellished with references to various miracles intended to recall the days of Marcus, most notably the famous "Rain Miracle" that was said to have saved some portion of the northern armies from imminent catastrophe, turning the tide decisively against their foes (Rubin 1980: 66–74). In the

Arch of Severus, Rome

wake of the eastern campaign pictures seem to have been widely distributed showing vast storms bringing chaos to the forces of the eastern armies in spectacular mountainous terrains that defy ready identification with known locations of the major battles. Severus himself had also circulated a memoir in which he gave details of the signs that predicted his rise to power (along, evidently, with a highly tendentious narrative of the events that they had predicted) and advertised those signs on other public monuments; he even seems to have attributed his check before the walls of Hatra to the intervention of the local Sun God (Dio 75. 12. 4). An altar found at Lyons that dates to roughly 198 shows the emperor in the company of the planetary gods upon whose signs he had relied.

Severus' use of the imaginary and the language of Fate, while seemingly reflective of his deeply held personal beliefs, was scarcely eccentric. After all, Marcus had first advertised a weather miracle, claiming that his prayers had brought down a thunderbolt to destroy a siege weapon employed by the northern tribes; he had respected the claims of Alexander of Abonuteichos to be the prophet of a divinity when he had two lions cast into the Danube, and had circulated a procedure to ward off the plague that had been obtained from the oracle of Apollo at Claros.[9] The language of Fate seems to have resonated deeply throughout the dominant classes of the empire. Dio himself seems to have believed as strongly as did Severus, and had attracted the emperor's favor with a book on the signs that had predicted the events of the civil war,[10] a classic illustration of the reciprocal lines of communication between emperor and subject.

Portents did not, however, cease after Severus had established himself securely in power. A comet appeared in the skies in 200 that was thought to portend nothing but good (Dio 75. 16. 5); rather different was the implication of an eruption of Vesuvius that Dio observed from his house in Capua. This indicated that some change in the regime was imminent.

Dynastic Politics

At some point in his reign Commodus had ordered that provincial governors leave their families at Rome. One of the signs of the strength of Severus' organization in Rome in the wake of Pertinax's assassination was the fact that Julia and their children were spirited out of town before Julianus could react (Herodian 3. 2. 4). Niger had clearly made no such effective arrangements, for his family was taken into custody when Severus entered the city. The agent of their arrest was Gaius Fulvius Plautianus, a tangential relative of the new emperor, who had allegedly been, in the period of their mutual youth, his lover (*HA Sev.* 6. 10; Herodian 3. 11. 2–3).

We know little of Plautianus' life in the years before 193. What is clear, however, is that he became fabulously rich – after his death it was necessary to appoint a special procurator to oversee the disposition of his property – and his daughter married Caracalla. Dio compared him to Sejanus (58. 14. 3), but the role that he seems to have filled in these years was not so much that of Sejanus as it was that of Lucius Verus, or, perhaps more accurately, Marcus Agrippa. Severus' own reading of Roman history appears to have been deep enough to enable him to appreciate the parallel, and a subtle variation upon the Augustan formula for the Secular Games, where the 110 *matronae* who traditionally offer sacrifice for Juno on the Capitoline are replaced by 109 *matronae* and Julia Domna, the *mater castrorum*, suggests that he gave some thought to ways in which Augustan formulae might be adapted to his needs. Like Augustus, Severus also seems to have seen the ultimate succession in terms of a pair of heirs – Caracalla and Geta – who needed time to grow into their prospective *statio*.

That the role of Agrippa was to be Augustus' heir apparent until an heir or heirs from the family could emerge may help explain the depth of Caracalla's hatred for Plautianus. Caracalla aspired to his father's position as sole ruler – he hated his younger brother as much as he hated Plautianus – and in 205 had finally arrived at an age where he might have an opportunity to eliminate the competition. On the evening of January 22, Caracalla produced three centurions of the guard who told Severus that they had been suborned, with seven others, to murder him. The emperor summoned Plautianus to a meeting at the palace with himself and Caracalla, who had secreted the centurions in the room. When Plautianus began to defend himself against the charge, Caracalla hit him, and would have killed him had Severus not prevented him; in any case, the act was consummated immediately afterwards by the centurions, who burst from their cover. When Severus summoned the senate on the following day to explain what had happened, he did so in such a way that men such as Dio understood that Plautianus had been the victim of a conspiracy rather than a conspirator himself (Dio 76. 4. 1–5. 3; cf. Herodian 3. 12. 1–12).

The murder of Plautianus, which Severus may have accepted as the action of Fate, left Caracalla and Geta as the heirs apparent. Severus would never give up his design that the pair would succeed as co-Augusti, and seems to have spent the rest of his reign trying to create sufficient understanding between them to make this possible. So it was that when he departed Rome in 208 to take personal command of campaigns in northern Britain, he took his sons with him (Dio 76. 11. 1). The three years of campaigning, during which time Severus weakened so much that he had to be transported with the army in a litter, did little to improve the relationship between the siblings (Dio 76. 13. 3). These years also seem to have done little to alter the situation on the frontier, for, although Roman armies reached the northern extremities of modern Scotland, and the old wall of Antoninus Pius was reoccupied, there could be no long-term change. Scotland was simply too underdeveloped to support the mechanisms of Roman imperial government.

Dio says that Severus knew when he departed Rome for Britain that he would not return alive (Dio 76. 11. 2). As his health worsened, he made no effort to return, evidence, perhaps, that what Dio says is correct. If Severus knew his own fate so well, it is deeply unlikely that he had not also cast the horoscopes of his sons. Despite intense provocation, and his own criticism of Marcus for not pushing Commodus out of the line of succession, Severus refused to do anything about Caracalla, perhaps because he knew that the time of his son's death was not yet upon him, and he could not himself alter the laws of Fate; the best that he could hope to do was create a situation in which Caracalla's fierce temper would be controlled. In his will he designed a government in which Caracalla and Geta would share power, and in which they would be surrounded by men whose judgment he trusted. If he could not change Fate, at least he could try to make sure that the empire would be in good hands when he was no longer there to see to it himself. On February 4, 211, Septimius Severus died, at York.

The Severan Dynasty

Severus seems to have relied throughout his reign upon a number of close advisors, many of them apparently of considerable ability, continuing the sort of cabinet style of government that can be detected behind the emperors from Trajan to Marcus Aurelius. He intended that style of administration to continue once he was gone, putting his trust in such counselors as Fabius Cilo; the great jurist, Papinian; Maecius Laetus, Papinian's colleague as praetorian prefect in the years after the fall of Plautianus; and Julius Asper, who held the post of prefect of the city in 211. The fact that these men failed to keep the peace between the brothers after Severus' death – Caracalla murdered Geta in their mother's arms on December 25, 211 – is perhaps less significant than the fact that they had built up a network of subordinates who were no less capable and managed to bring some order to the government of the state even during the utterly erratic sole reign of Caracalla. In fact, the fall of Caracalla appears to have been due to the fact that the praetorian prefects controlled the paper flow – Macrinus was allegedly inspired to arrange Caracalla's assassination by the discovery, through information that came to him in the normal flow of business before it went to the emperor, that charges of treason were being leveled against him. Although Macrinus failed as emperor, and the reign of Elagabalus was marked by eccentric conduct on the emperor's part, the ability of the palace officials who had arranged Macrinus' downfall was sufficient to ensure that the day-to-day affairs of a state in which the emperor seems to have shown little interest were competently arranged. It was only in the later reign of

Severus Alexander that the collective nature of the administration showed serious strain. While the officials around the throne were capable enough – despite obvious tensions with the rank and file of the army – they were inadequately prepared to handle the new threat that emerged when Ardashir of Persia established his aggressive new regime to replace the Arsacids in that realm.

The most lasting accomplishments of the Severan regime were in the area of law, for the age of Severus and his successors was the golden age of jurisprudence. Papinian and Ulpian were truly superior legal thinkers, and their work set the standard for later Roman jurists.[11] Concomitant with the rise of the jurists to positions of genuine importance in the administration of the empire was a shift away from government by the traditional senatorial class. The jurists were themselves of equestrian background, and the bulk of Severus' closest advisors were, like Severus himself, from groups outside the Italian aristocracy. It is perhaps a sign of the importance of these changes that very few Italians were ever again to be in a position where they could claim the throne. It might have been the emphasis on technical ability, which was evidently a feature of success for those seeking advancement within the central government, with less respect shown to the claims of birth and cultural achievement in the arts, that led men like Dio and Philostratus to regard the age of Severus and his successors as inferior to what they saw as the golden age of the Antonines. Looked at from a less particular perspective, the Severan period continued trends that had been evident since the time of Trajan, which included encouragement of the spread of Greco-Roman culture throughout the territory of the empire, the overall enhancement of urban culture, and the increasing recruitment of provincials in the governing class. The weakness of the Severan dispensation was perhaps an inevitable corollary of its success. The creation of a style of government that did not depend upon the ability of the ruler – Severus' successors were all very poor chief executives – reinforced an inherently conservative view of the role of that government. Serious deficiencies in the training and tactical doctrine of the army went unremarked and unfixed even as Rome's neighbors, at long last, developed the competence to deal with the imperial army. Basic structural problems, most notably the fact that the financial system could not generate the reserves that would be needed in the face of new military challenges, were not addressed, for Severus seems to have thought that if he could build up some savings in the treasury through parsimonious living habits, that would suffice. He did not draw the obvious conclusion from the state of the treasury at the death of Commodus that the thrift of one emperor could rapidly be undone by the excess of a successor, indicating that some reform in the basic system of imperial finance was necessary.

Severus was effective within the framework of government that he had inherited. He was certainly no radical in the Rostovtzeffian sense that he aimed at creating a military monarchy, nor can he reasonably be awarded the title of the principal author of the decline and fall of the Roman empire. That title, as far as the third century goes, must be awarded to the most unconventional and creative figure of the age, a ruler whose importance became obvious only in the decade after Severus' death. This ruler was Ardashir of Persia.

Notes

1   Oliver (1989), 226–38, 227b; M. Peachin, "Jurists and the Law in the Early Roman Empire," in L. De Blois (ed.) *Administration, Prosopography and Appointment Policies in the Roman Empire* (Amsterdam, 2001), 109–20.

2   E. Gibbon, *The Decline and Fall of the Roman Empire*, ed. D. Womersley (London, 1994), 148; M. Rostovtzeff, *The Social and Economic History of the Roman Empire* (Oxford, 1957), 402.

3   For details see O. Hekster, *Commodus: Emperor at the Crossroads* (Amsterdam, 2002).

4   J. Hasebroek, *Untersuchungen zur Geschichte des Kaisers Septimius Severus* (Heidelberg, 1921), 42–3, 54–7.

5   L. Robert, "La titulature de Nicée et de Nicomédie: la gloire et la haine," *Harvard Studies in Classical Philology* 81 (1977), 1–39.

6   G. Downey, "Malalas on the History of Antioch under Severus and Caracalla," *Transactions and Proceedings of the American Philological Association* 68 (1937), 141–56.

7   J. Humphrey, *Roman Circuses: Arenas for Chariot Racing* (Berkeley, 1986), 25–55.

8   S. S. Lusnia, "Urban Planning and Sculptural Display in Severan Rome: Reconstructing the Septizodium and its Rome in Dynastic Politics," *American Journal of Archaeology* 108 (2004), 517–44, esp. 525, 533–4.

9   C. P. Jones, "Ten Dedications 'To the Gods and Goddesses' and the Antonine Plague," *Journal of Roman Archaeology* 18 (2005), 293–302.

10 A. M. Gowing, *The Triumviral Narratives of Appian and Cassius Dio* (Ann Arbor, Mich., 1992), 20.

11 B. W. Frier, "Early Classical Private Law," in A. K. Bowman, E. Champlin, and A. Lintott (eds), *The Cambridge Ancient* History, vol. 10, 2nd edn (Cambridge, 1996), 959–78.

Further Reading

A. R. Birley, *Septimius Severus* (New Haven, 1988)

F. Millar, "The Roman *coloniae* of the Near East: A Study of Cultural Relations," in
H. Solin and M. Kajeva (eds), *Roman Eastern Policy and Other Studies in Roman
History: Proceedings of a Colloquium at Tvärminne 2–3 October 1987* (Helsinki,
1990), 7–58

F. Millar, *The Roman Near East* (Cambridge, Mass., 1993)

D. S. Potter, *Prophets and Emperors: Human and Divine Authority from Augustus to
Theodosius* (Cambridge, Mass., 1994)

D. S. Potter, *The Roman Empire at Bay* AD *180–395* (London, 2004)

D. S. Potter, *A Companion to the Roman Empire* (Oxford, 2006)

Z. Rubin, *Civil War Propaganda and Historiography* (Brussels, 1980)

X

Diocletian

Simon Corcoran

Early Life

The future emperor Diocletian was born on December 22. This detail is almost all that is certainly known about his early life. Everything else regarding his first forty years is generally obscure, deriving from thin and disputed evidence. Later estimates of his age at death suggest his year of birth was in the mid-240s, shortly before Rome reached her momentous yet troubled one-thousandth birthday in 248. His birthplace was in Dalmatia, almost certainly Salona (his choice of retirement home). His original name was probably Gaius Valerius Diocles. There were different traditions regarding his background. Thus he was either the freed slave of a senator, Anulinus, or else his father was a scribe, or clerk, which makes his father the more plausible freedman (Eutropius 9. 19. 2). That the son of a former slave could rise to become emperor had already been demonstrated by the meteoric career of Pertinax, who rose to equestrian, then senatorial rank before his ephemeral reign as successor to Commodus in 193. In the changing circumstances of the mid-third century, Diocletian's career was probably largely military, served under Claudius II, Aurelian, and Probus (268–82). He may have been prefect of the First Cohort of Galatians, then military tribune of Legio VII Gemina (based at Leon in Spain), then prefect of a cohort of Dardanians. Legend also placed him in Gaul, with his imperial fate foretold by a Druid prophetess (the story later given musical treatment in Purcell's "semi-opera" *Dioclesian* [1690]). At some point during his service he married Prisca, of whom virtually nothing is known, except that she bore him their only child, Valeria. By the time he accompanied the emperor Carus on his Mesopotamian campaign in 282–3, he had risen to be commander of the *protectores*, the corps of staff officers around the emperor forming his personal bodyguard.

Diocletian's Accession

Carus looked to be a fortunate emperor. He had two sons, whom he was able to elevate to share power with him, and he also enjoyed initial success in Mesopotamia. But he and his were extinguished in murky circumstances. In 283, Carus himself was killed by lightning (so the story goes). Numerian, Carus' younger son, returned slowly across Asia Minor with his army, traveling in a litter, its curtains closely drawn to protect his eyes, which were suffering from infection. He had not been seen in public for a while. But when the army descended from the freezing Anatolian plateau and reached the milder climate of Nicomedia in November 284, a smell of decay was detected emanating from the litter and the emperor's corpse was discovered. Before the assembled army, Diocles was acclaimed emperor (November 20), and as his first act he declared himself innocent of any crime, instead blaming Numerian's father-in-law, the praetorian prefect Aper, whom, with sudden and unaccustomed violence, he struck down with his own sword. Was this a guilty Diocletian shifting the blame, or was he simply deflecting inevitable if groundless suspicions from himself? Aper seems an unlikely assassin of his son-in-law. Perhaps he had concealed a natural death, while assessing support for his own proclamation as emperor or else trying to contact Carinus, Numerian's elder brother, although the latter was too far away to be of any help. Whatever the truth or the guilt regarding Numerian's demise, Diocletian's decisiveness trumped Aper's indecision.

The new emperor quickly assumed a more Latinate and grand name, as Gaius Valerius Diocletianus. There was still, however, another legitimate emperor elsewhere. Carinus had been left behind by Carus to deal with the Rhine frontier, and had then moved to Italy. Carinus is depicted in the sources as a conventional tyrant, and had a troubled reign. A major fire devastated the Roman Forum in 283, and he had already had to deal with at least one pretender. He left Italy to confront Diocletian advancing across the Balkans, and their two armies clashed at the River Margus (not far from the Danube near Viminacium). Yet even as Carinus' troops appeared to be gaining the upper hand, a disgruntled officer assassinated him, leaving Diocletian in undisputed control. Conciliation was the order of the day as Diocletian took over Carinus' *comitatus*, keeping on his praetorian prefect,

Aristobulus. Indeed, he retrospectively shared the consulship of 285 with Aristobulus, himself taking the place of the dead Carinus. Aristobulus remained in favor, becoming later both proconsul of Africa and urban prefect. A general amnesty was also granted.

Maximian and the Dyarchy

Diocletian now advanced into northern Italy, but may not have traveled down the peninsula to take formal possession of Rome itself.[1] From a strategic point of view, Rome was an unnecessary distraction. Instead, he made the most important decision of his reign. Realizing that the empire was too large for one ruler to manage simultaneous crises, in the summer of 285 he appointed Maximian, a comrade-in-arms and fellow Danubian, as his *Caesar*, probably at Milan, creating what modern scholars style "the dyarchy." This choice was to prove felicitous. Although Maximian is often regarded as typical of the crude Balkan soldiery and portrayed as a conventional tyrant, greedy, lustful, and cruel, there was one key virtue in which he excelled – unswerving loyalty to Diocletian. On this point, imperial propaganda was not short of the truth, well mirrored in the invective of Lactantius, whose pamphlet *On the Deaths of the Persecutors* (*Mort. Pers.*), written *c.*315, is a crucial contemporary source, filled with the accurate detail of an eye-witness in Diocletian's Nicomedia, yet brilliantly spun to invert the official line.[2]

The imperial brotherhood of Diocletian and Maximian was the axis that brought almost two decades of stability to the empire, and allowed Diocletian the space to plan, execute, and even rethink a whole raft of reforms, and so to lay the characteristic foundations of the late Roman state. The two "brothers" marked their bond by each adding the other's *nomen* to his own (thus Diocletian became Gaius Aurelius Valerius Diocletianus). Then in 287 each adopted a divine protector, choosing Jupiter and Hercules respectively and assuming the titles *Iovius* (from Jupiter/Jove) and *Herculius*. This appears symbolic of their relationship. Diocletian devised policies and issued commands like the king of gods, while Maximian carried them out as his labors without complaint.

Maximian was immediately sent off to Gaul to suppress the Bagaudae, usually seen as rural insurgents, although their leaders claimed imperial titles. This Maximian did with efficiency, and on April 1, 286 he was rewarded by elevation to the full rank of *Augustus*. Unfortunately, Carausius, one of Maximian's key lieutenants, having successfully completed his allotted task of dealing with Saxon pirates, was accused (probably correctly) of keeping for himself recovered plunder. To forestall retribution he proclaimed himself emperor, using his naval force to take control of Britain and northern Gaul. Against him Maximian proved to be remarkably ineffective. In any case, he was distracted by the German tribes, in particular having to abandon the elaborate inauguration ceremonies for his first consulship at Trier on January 1, 287 to deal with an invasion from across the Rhine. Here he was more successful, and in the following year he accepted the submission of an important Frankish king, Gennobaudes, and his followers, who were granted deserted lands near Trier.

Leaving affairs in the west to Maximian, Diocletian returned eastward. He campaigned against the Sarmatians on the Danube in the autumn of 285 and then retired for the winter to Nicomedia, which quickly became his favored residence and the site of frenetic construction work. In the spring of 286, having approved Maximian's promotion to *Augustus*, he traveled through Syria to Palestine, staying at Tiberias and Paneas, where he held audiences with senior rabbis. The following year Diocletian was still dealing with affairs on the eastern front, negotiating with the Persians and installing Tiridates III as ruler of Armenia. About this time he also dedicated a new market at Tyre in honor of "his brother Herculius," a fitting gesture since the city's tutelary deity was Melqart/Hercules. In 288 he returned west, invading Germany from Raetia in a coordinated pincer movement with Maximian. The following year saw him back on the Danube frontier before wintering in Sirmium. Leaving there in the spring of 290, he crossed into Asia and reached Antioch in May, ready for a campaign against the Saraceni in the Syrian desert. By the summer he was back in Sirmium, but decided to descend into Italy for the winter in order to confer with Maximian. The two met with some pomp in Milan during December 290 and January 291, attended by a great throng, including many senators, who toiled up from Rome. Then Maximian returned to Trier and Diocletian to Sirmium.

The First Tetrarchy

It was becoming clear to Diocletian that one colleague was not enough, and perhaps this issue was already on the agenda at the Milan conference. Maximian was able to hold his own on the Rhine frontier, but that left Carausius in control of Britain and the Channel coast of Gaul. Carausius' coinage proclaimed him the colleague of the two *Augusti*, but Diocletian had no intention of recognizing him. He himself had now spent seven years wildly see-sawing between the Danube and Syrian frontiers, successful but overstretched, while trying to keep a brotherly watch over Maximian as well. It would only take one additional crisis or threat to overwhelm them.

This was the moment, therefore, when Diocletian decided that the imperial college needed expansion. He had no son or close male relative, while Maximian's son, Maxentius, was only ten. But both emperors had marriageable daughters. So, just as Augustus had used his daughter Julia, Diocletian used marriage as the means of adlecting into the imperial college suitable candidates, while maintaining dynastic coherence. The men he chose were each of predictable Illyrian origin and proven military ability: Constantius and Galerius Maximianus (usually referred to by the latter name in the ancient sources, but less confusingly as Galerius by modern writers). Constantius married Maximian's daughter Theodora, while Galerius married Diocletian's daughter Valeria. On March 1, 293 the two men were elevated to the rank of *Caesar* (they lacked the full style of *Imperator* and *Augustus*), Constantius being invested by Maximian at Milan and Galerius by Diocletian at Sirmium. Thus the tetrarchy (a modern, not ancient term) or "rule of four" was born, a hierarchical imperial college with the *Caesars* as juniors and assistants to their *Augusti*, but also with their future succession fixed in advance. The exact respective timings of marriage and elevation are unclear. While it is no longer thought that Constantius was Maximian's praetorian prefect, he still seems to have held an important command and been married to his daughter by 289 (*Pan. Lat.* 10 (2). 11. 4; Barnes 1982: 125, 1996: 546–7). The reason this matters is that Diocletian is often credited with crafting a deliberately meritocratic college that was consciously anti-dynastic in the choices made in 293 and again in 305. There is a different flavor to making the new *Caesars* into sons-in-law as opposed to appointing existing sons-in-law as the new *Caesars*. Similarly, the choices of 305 appear very different, depending on whether or not the adult sons of the existing tetrarchs were the originally intended successors. Historically, emperors had chosen sons as heirs whenever practicable, and only lack of sons forced the adoption of outsiders. This can be seen in the case of both Augustus and the Antonines. Therefore Diocletian's policy can be interpreted as pragmatic, using the relatives that chance had given, rather than consciously anti-dynastic.

The Campaigns of the Tetrarchs

The expanded imperial college quickly proved its worth. Constantius went straight to Gaul and captured Boulogne from Carausius, whose failure led to his assassination and replacement by his finance minister, Allectus. After considerable preparations, in 296 Constantius then mounted the unavoidable seaborne invasion of Britain, supported by the praetorian prefect Asclepiodotus. Allectus' forces were easily routed, and quick action by the *Caesar* saved London from being sacked by Frankish mercenaries. Constantius' victory is famously commemorated on a medallion depicting him on horseback, greeted by a kneeling London, with the legend "restorer of the eternal light." In the meantime, Maximian made a rare imperial visit to a troubled Spain in 296, before crossing the straits of Gibraltar and making a progress along the coast of Mauretania. He defeated a dangerous tribal confederation, the Quinquegentiani, and finally reached Carthage in 298, from where he returned in triumph to Rome in 299. He then settled quietly in Milan, while Constantius from his seat at Trier was kept busy on the Rhine frontier.

Diocletian, meanwhile, based himself at Sirmium to deal with the Danube frontier, and immediately sent the newly appointed Galerius east to deal with a revolt in the Thebaid. Galerius then moved to Syria, since Narses, the new king of Persia, was showing himself dangerously ambitious. In 296 Narses invaded Armenia. Diocletian took time gathering troops, before setting out for the east. An impatient Galerius, however, did not wait for his *Augustus'* arrival, but advanced prematurely into Mesopotamia in the spring of 297 and was defeated by Narses south of Carrhae. When Diocletian met Galerius near Antioch, he made the *Caesar* run for a mile beside his chariot wearing full purple. This is usually interpreted as a deliberate act of humiliation by the enraged *Augustus*. But, although all the tetrarchs were capable soldiers, Galerius in particular was renowned for his physical prowess and stamina, and this display may have been symbolic of his determination to win back his laurels. Having gathered even more troops from the Balkans, in the autumn of 297 Galerius finally set out from Satala into Armenia, while Diocletian kept guard in Syria. When his army approached that of Narses, the *Caesar* personally went on reconnaissance of the Persian positions with only a couple of followers. He then attacked suddenly and routed the Persian forces. Narses fled in haste, leaving behind his extensive harem and luxurious baggage train. The booty from this victory became legendary. Galerius then proceeded down the Tigris, finally entering Ctesiphon in January 298. When the Persian envoy Apharban came to sue for peace, Galerius angrily reminded him of the cruel treatment of the defeated Valerian in 260, whose skin was stuffed after his death. The terms were to be stiff, but not ruinous. Diocletian, now overflowing with congratulations for his *Caesar*, met Galerius at Nisibis in the spring of 299 to thrash out the details and sent Sicorius Probus, the *magister memoriae* (literally, "master of memory"), to present them to Narses. When the king attempted to bargain, Probus said he had no power to revise the terms. Anxious to secure the return of his family, Narses accepted them. Thus a great swathe of northern Mesopotamia became Roman, with Nisibis as its gateway, and even five satrapies beyond the Tigris became client states. This was the greatest of all the tetrarchic victories and secured peace with Rome's powerful and troublesome neighbor for forty years (for the current chronology, see Barnes 1996: 543–4).

Even as Galerius moved into Armenia, news arrived that a usurper, Domitius Domitianus, had seized much of Egypt. Diocletian may have waited for some initial signs of success from Galerius before daring to leave Syria, but he then moved to reoccupy the rebel areas, completing this before Galerius had entered Ctesiphon. Only the volatile city of Alexandria remained defiantly under siege, finally surrendering in March 298. Legend has it that Diocletian swore to let the blood run in the city till it reached his horse's knees, only for the horse to stumble and kneel in the blood. Diocletian, ever superstitious, immediately stopped the killing. As part of his settlement of affairs in Egypt, he then traveled south to Elephantine and negotiated a revised southern border with the Nobatae. From 299 he took up residence in Antioch, the likely place from which he issued the famous Prices Edict of 301 (see below). He spent the winter of 301–2 in a forgiven Alexandria, where he established a free grain distribution. He then turned westward to Nicomedia at the end of 302. Meanwhile, after his Persian victory, Galerius was sent to the Danube frontier, which, like the Rhine, needed active supervision.

While neither Rhine nor Danube was entirely quiescent, nonetheless the great series of military victories (the essential aim of the expanded imperial college) had increased the empire's strength, confidence, and peace. The heading to the Prices Edict of 301 showed that since 285 the emperors had won six German victories, four Sarmatian, two Persian, and one each for Britain, the Carpi, Armenia, Media, and Adiabene (Barnes 1982: 255). This justified Diocletian's claim in the edict's preamble that, courtesy of soldiers' sweat, "the world was seated in the lap of a most profound calm."

Administration and Reform

It is time to turn from the chronological progress of key political and military affairs to Diocletian's government of the empire and the reforms he carried out. The first half of the third century was a time of difficulty and disruption marked by war, plague, inflation, economic collapse, and the decline of cities, although it is not clear that these are part of a single overarching crisis engulfing all parts of the empire. The structures of the Augustan principate, still functioning in most essentials under the Severans, were swept away in interlocking cycles of invasion from without and usurpation from within. Suddenly aggressive and capable external enemies, new tribal formations on the Rhine and Danube as well as revived and ambitious Persian kings in the east, posed a direct threat, while rendering a faltering emperor liable to overthrow, as the army promiscuously raised usurpers in the hope of military effectiveness and rich donatives. The nadir came in the wake of Valerian's humiliating capture and death at the hands of the Persian king Shapur I, Narses' triumphant father, in 260, when the empire split into three, with the "legitimate" ruler Gallienus controlling only a central core. After 268, however, the Illyrian "soldier emperors," generally of humble origins and from the least wealthy and cultured provinces (like Diocletian and his colleagues), reunited the empire and started to recover military dominance, although at the cost of abandoning some exposed territory (principally Dacia).

Becoming emperor against this background, Diocletian initiated reforms that set the pattern for the late Roman state. Some of his success was a matter of longevity. Because he retained power for twenty years, he had the opportunity to plan and experiment, implement and modify. The detailed chronology, however, is seldom certain. Diocletian must have built on the efforts of his less well-attested predecessors, but we should not discount his personal qualities, which combined prescient caution with flashes of boldness, and a readiness to consult both gods and advisors. Of course, he did not see himself as a radical reformer, but rather as a conservator and restorer.

The Imperial Office

Given that a key feature of the third-century crisis was the insecurity of the emperor, it is hardly surprising that there was significant change in the office. Diocletian's major innovation was to attempt realistic collegiate government. There had been joint emperors since the reign of Marcus Aurelius and Lucius Verus (161–9), but co-rulers were often under-age ciphers. It had become clear, however, that the simultaneous management of events on far separated fronts was impractical. Diocletian's initial response was to appoint a colleague to look after the west, before he decided that more bodies were required. The pattern of the First Tetrarchy, with two *Augusti* and two *Caesars*, seems too consciously crafted to have been simply an emergency measure. It created more princes to deal with multiple crises, while fixing in advance the vexed question of the succession. Abdication, however, does not seem to have been originally envisaged, let alone a policy of cyclical retirement and replacement within the imperial college. And when the abdication did happen, it appeared to the population unexpected and inexplicable.

Within the college of four, Diocletian retained seniority. Although each tetrarch had sufficient authority to act in his own sphere, and a pronouncement issued by one was headed by the names of all, Diocletian could intervene anywhere: for instance, he responded from eastern locations to petitioners and officials in Africa (Corcoran 2000: 116, 271–2). Enactments – such as that instituting the persecution of the Christians, and conceivably the Prices Edict (see below) – could simply be sent to his colleagues for them to enforce, since extensive consultation between geographically distant rulers was hardly practicable. Conversely, compliance was difficult to monitor, and on one occasion Constantius is said to have deceived Diocletian's messengers (Euseb. *Const.* I. 14). Diocletian, however, must have wielded sufficient prestige throughout the period to keep the college harmonious and cooperative during years of reform, despite the potential for conflict. If the high-handedness of some measures late in his reign is a sign of Galerius' growing influence, it is perhaps no surprise that it was after Diocletian's retirement that collegiate rule finally faltered and failed.

The ancient sources generally attribute to Diocletian a major change in imperial manners (e.g. Eutropius 9. 26; Aur. Vict. *Caes.* 39. 2–4; Amm. 15. 5. 18). The affected *civilitas* of Augustus, his pseudo-republican theater of "first among equals," was now abandoned in favor of glitter and ceremonial. The emperor was set apart, clad in purple, wearing a diadem, even his shoes studded with gems. Subjects now had to prostrate themselves before him, with the more fortunate permitted to kiss the hem of the imperial robe (*adoratio, proskynesis*). The emperor was *dominus noster* (our master). Specific attribution of these innovations to Diocletian, however, is difficult to establish. The *consilium*, a relatively informal, even *ad hoc*, body of advisors chosen by the emperor, still existed under both Diocletian and Constantine, although we may guess that it was starting to manifest the style of its successor, the protocol-bound consistory. Eunuch chamberlains are first attested as prominent at Diocletian's court, which might be a response to the capture of the Persian king's entourage in 297. Grand ceremonial, however, seems already the order of the day at the imperial conference at Milan in 290–1, judging

1558 - ROMA - Diocleziano - Museo Capitolino - Sala degli Imperatori   Ripr. Int. - Anderson

Diocletian

by Mamertinus' description (*Pan. Lat.* 11 [3]). It was probably the length of Diocletian's reign that allowed existing trends to crystallize and become normal. The refusal, however, of Maximian's son Maxentius to perform *proskynesis* before either his father, or his father-in-law Galerius, may be a sign of tension over a relatively new practice, although Maxentius is not said to have refused this to Diocletian (Lact. *Mort. Pers.* 18. 9).

Despite these changes, the tetrarchs spent much time on the road, in relentless motion, so that they remained highly visible and even approachable. Diocletian was very open to receiving petitions, as witness the thousands of rescripts (responses to petitions) that he issued, even to those of low status (Corcoran 2000: 96–114). The formal entry (*adventus*) of an emperor into a city was a much repeated ceremony. People would flock from miles around to see the imperial train pass by, as happened when Diocletian and Maximian crossed northern Italy in the winter of 290–1, and afterwards in Milan, when they were seen around the city, although only the more privileged got close to them within the palace. When Diocletian visited Tyre it was deemed acceptable for a rabbi to cross a cemetery (usually an act of pollution) in his haste to appear before the emperor. Of course, the space within a palace was always more tightly controlled, as indicated by Lactantius' account (*Mort. Pers.* 17. 4–9) of the last months of Diocletian's rule, when much had to be deduced from the emperor's emergence or non-emergence from the palace on periodic anniversaries. The idea, however, that imperial business was something conducted secretly and away from public scrutiny went right back to the beginning of the principate (Tac. *Ann.* 1. 6. 3).

A final development is in imperial iconography. On coins the curly-bearded Greek style of the past 150 years gives way to a severe, trimmed, military look, while collegiality is reflected in less individualized depictions, best illustrated by the famous porphyry group of the hugging tetrarchs in Venice.

Rome

The position of Rome changed dramatically. Troubled third-century emperors had spent time there when they could, taking formal possession as an act of legitimacy. But Diocletian did not do this in 285, and it was only for his *vicennalia* (twentieth year celebrations) in 303 that he finally visited the imperial capital. Even Maximian, often resident in Italy, may not have visited Rome until 299. Whatever Rome's symbolic importance, its strategic position was weak and it ceased to be the capital in practice, though remaining the locus for scattered ceremonial visits. During this period only Maximian's son, Maxentius, already resident as a senator before his proclamation in 306, made Rome his principal base. Indeed, it was precisely Galerius' lack of acquaintance with Rome's size that led to his misconceived expedition against Maxentius there in 307. Yet this proved Rome's marginality. Maxentius was Gallienus in reverse. In the 260s the latter had ruled Rome, while usurpers reigned elsewhere. In contrast, Maxentius controlled Rome as a usurper, with little practical consequence for the rest of the empire.

Rome nevertheless retained a primacy of honor and the lavish privileges of the formal capital, its population still treated to bread and circuses. It was the home of the wealthy senate and the principal base for the praetorian guard. There was constant imperially sponsored building work, especially to restore the Forum area destroyed under Carinus, including an imposing set of columns behind the Rostra, bearing statues of the tetrarchs and Jupiter. The current senate house (Curia Julia) is the building restored to its tetrarchic form. When he returned in triumph from Carthage in 299, Maximian matched the baths he had had built there in his own name by providing for Rome its largest ever bath complex, the Baths of Diocletian.

The Tetrarchic Capitals

In practice, the seat of government was where the emperor was, and the peripatetic tetrarchs traveled with a *comitatus* that contained all the necessary apparatus of rule. Constantine characterized the officials of the *comitatus* as acquainted with the "dust and toil of the camp" (*Cod. Theod.* 6. 36. 1). But while many sites served as temporary seats of the roving government, a number of cities in strategic locations near critical frontiers or on major lines of communication became more regular imperial residences. They took on the form of alternative capitals, furnished with monumental buildings: a circus/palace complex, grandiose baths, even imperial mausolea. The principal "tetrarchic capitals" were: in Gaul, Trier (capital of Constantius); in Italy, Milan (seat of Maximian) and Aquileia; in the Balkans, Sirmium on the Sava, not far from the vital Danube frontier, but also Thessalonica (Galerius' choice); and in the east, Nicomedia (Diocletian's favorite), Antioch (nearest to the Persian front), and Caesarea (popular with the *Caesar* Maximinus from 305). Even in Rome, home of the original palace–circus complex (Palatine–Circus Maximus), Maxentius built himself a tetrarchic imitation a short way beyond the walls along the Via Appia. Lactantius (*Mort. Pers.* 7. 9–10) gives a vivid picture of Diocletian's frenzied and capricious building activity in Nicomedia, with buildings constantly erected, then pulled down to be redesigned. Unfortunately, the modern city (İzmit) has virtually no trace of Diocletian's presence. Apart from Rome, only Trier and Thessalonica, along with Diocletian's retirement palace at Split, have sufficient monumental remains to give a flavor of how a tetrarchic capital looked.

The Central Administration and the Provinces

The multiplication of emperors, and even of capitals, entailed a multiplication of the imperial *comitatus*, the core of the administration and army, each a replica staffed in a similar manner. The chief officials at court were now almost exclusively of equestrian rank. Most senior were the praetorian prefects, one at the side of each *Augustus* (but not the *Caesars*), and they alone held the high rank of *vir eminentissimus*, acting together as a college, in the manner of the emperors they served. Although not yet entirely stripped of military duties (thus Asclepiodotus played a key part in the reconquest of Britain), they were now principally civilian officials, with wide powers, even inappelable jurisdiction, much concerned with provisioning the armies. The remaining officials were ranked *viri perfectissimi*, including the chief financial officers for the *summa res* (treasury) and *privata* (privy purse), and the masters of the *scrinia* (*magistri scriniorum*), the secretarial bureaux concerned with the emperor's correspondence and judicial functions. The civil service at lower levels was no longer dominated by the *familia Caesaris* (the emperor's household of slaves and freedmen), whose role became more limited. Instead, the long-standing practice of second-ing soldiers as administrators set the tone for the military appearance of the staff, whose service came to be called *militia*. A new tendency also began to emerge for officials serving the emperor to adopt his *nomen*. Thus many are found bearing the name 'Valerius' (as carried by Diocletian, Galerius, and Maximian), although this did not become universal practice until the time of Constantine, when his *nomen* 'Flavius' became the sign essentially distinguishing state officials from civilians for several centuries to come.

The provinces themselves were, in Lactantius' well-turned phrase, "sliced and diced" (*in frusta concisae*: *Mort. Pers.* 7. 4). This was not new, but Diocletian was in a position to undertake more extensive reorganization than his predecessors, although it was carried out in phases. One sweeping act, however, was the creation of the dioceses, probably not long after 293. These were twelve large administrative units into which the provinces were grouped, each headed by a *vicarius* or vicar (literally, "deputy") of the praetorian prefects, representing an intermediate level of jurisdiction between governor and prefect or emperor. Like the new vicars, provincial governors (*praesides*) were now mostly of equestrian rank, no longer exercising military but only civil duties. In theory, by concentrating the efforts of governors on matters of law and tax in smaller provinces and creating the additional tier of diocesan administration, greater efficiency and control should have been achieved. This also affected the financial hierarchies of the treasury and privy purse, which mirrored the new provincial and diocesan structure. At every level, both central and provincial, there were clearly many more administrators, and as their numbers grew, so did a tendency toward the minute regulation of seniority and remunerations. It is no wonder that Diocletian is sometimes credited with the mind of a petty bureaucrat, especially as it is difficult to assess how far more government meant more effective government. Lactantius (*Mort. Pers.* 7. 3–4) criticizes this apparatus as unwelcomingly ubiquitous, with too many administrators feeding off too few taxpayers. After the chaos of the mid-third century, however, it did ensure a greater degree of stability and predictability.

The Army

In a similar manner, Lactantius (*Mort. Pers.* 7. 2) accused Diocletian of "multiplying the armies, since each of the four [tetrarchs] strove to have a far larger number of troops than previous emperors had had when they were governing the state alone." On the other hand, Zosimus (2. 34) praises Diocletian for keeping forces stationed along strengthened frontier defenses, in contrast to Constantine's withdrawal of troops to distant inland cities. Both these views are at least in part true. There was certainly a marked increase in the overall size of the army, as fighting units became smaller, while increasing in number. These units ceased to be under the control of provincial governors, but were placed under *duces* (generals with equestrian rank), who often commanded troops spread over several provinces. There was some growth in the mobile field armies which formed part of each emperor's *comitatus* – for instance the new legions of *Ioviani* and *Herculiani* – but there was no distinction, as there was later, between high-grade "palatine" troops and low-grade "frontier" troops (*limitanei*). We should probably still think of forces being brought together from the regular legions and *auxilia* for particular campaigns, as in the widespread gathering of forces for the Persian War. Four rulers, each with troops at his disposal, meant that multiple military operations could be carried out, although cooperative actions could also be effective (as in the case of Diocletian and Maximian in 288). At the same time there was considerable work on frontier defenses, as attested, for instance, by a series of inscriptions from repaired forts along the lower Danube, and by the *Strata Diocletiana*, an important road with associated forts running south from Callinicum on the Euphrates via Palmyra to Damascus and beyond.[3]

Senators

Senators, the key players of the Augustan principate, are largely absent from all this reorganization. Indeed, it is under Diocletian that they reach their nadir in terms of office-holding, a fact sometimes attributed by modern scholars to the rough Illyrian soldier's dislike of the traditional elite. Ancient sources, by contrast, suggest that Gallienus banned senators from the army. Yet this appears to be less one or another emperor's act of jealousy or prejudice than a gradual process. Even as the army became more important politically, the incremental advance of equestrian military officers and governors, together with the increased social and geographical distance of the emperors from the Senate in Rome, rendered senators decreasingly likely to hold the legionary commands and military governorships previously the prerogative of their rank. So, by the time of Diocletian, senators had already been eclipsed, a process that could hardly be reversed, given his own long-term absence from Rome and even Italy. The senatorial life was now one of general *otium* (leisure), punctuated by brief moments of *negotium* (public business). Offices held were mostly the traditional magistracies and other administrative posts in Rome, or else governorships (usually as *corrector*) of the newly created Italian provinces (*regiones*). Senators were rarely governors outside Italy, the principal exceptions being the prestigious (but geographically diminished) proconsulships of Asia and Africa. Prestige also attached to being one of the consuls *ordinarii* (after whom the year was named), but over 70 per cent of these in the period 285–305 were members of the imperial college or their praetorian prefects (who were thereby promoted into the senate). The last detailed list of suffect consuls comes from 289, and although they continued to be appointed, they disappear from view. The most powerful senatorial post now was that of the *praefectus urbi* (city prefect), in charge of the city of Rome and its environs; the position was enhanced by the absence of the emperor and, like the praetorian prefecture, came to entail an inappelable jurisdiction. Although Maximian is said to have targeted several senators because of their wealth, the fact that even he seldom visited Rome will have meant that senators were largely free of the pressures of active office or court intrigue. One reason why Maxentius became so unpopular in Rome during 306–12 may well have been simply the unaccustomed reminder to the senate of how uncomfortable for them an emperor in residence could be.

The Cities

The cities were perhaps the crucial subdivision within the empire, adorned during the prosperous years of the principate with magnificent monuments erected by the competitive beneficence of local elites. The third-century crisis saw this activity reduce to a trickle. The richest locals had now been absorbed into the imperial aristocracy, and, as burdens pressed down on those left behind, local office-holding grew less attractive and the search for exemptions and immunities became incessant. This was a constant theme in petitions presented to Diocletian, who found himself refusing benefits to people claiming exemption on the grounds of their occupation (for instance, as philosopher, water-organist, hunter, or accountant) or because of age or illness, not necessarily their own! (Corcoran 2000: 101–5). Others, however, were more successful. Even so, for those appointed to local office or the local curia, their rank, which Diocletian upheld, put them into the favored class of *honestiores* (the "better sort"), entitled to more lenient treatment than the *humiliores* (the "lower classes") under the otherwise grim criminal justice system. Two inscribed letters show Galerius optimistically fostering the increase in the number of new cities, with grants of civic status to Tymandus (in Pisidia) and Heraclea Sintica (in Macedonia).[4] Diocletian encouraged development in Syria and Palestine, including the building of granaries and reservoirs. Yet Diocletian's own reforms had tended to undermine the desirability of local office-holding, turning councilors into unpaid tax collectors with personal liability for shortfalls, supposed to act only as directed. The civic duties (*munera*) demanded of the population were piled up, coupled with a tendency to hereditary compulsion at all levels. At Aphrodisias in Caria, the last imperial letters in Greek to be inscribed in public, confirming proud civic privileges, were issued by Valerian and Gallienus (AD 257). Under Diocletian the inscribed texts are weighty imperial edicts in Latin put up by the local governor, who now comes to control management of the urban fabric (Corcoran 2000: 296). Of course, even earlier a profligate city could be put under official oversight to restore financial prudence (this being Pliny the Younger's purpose in Bithynia), but now the provincial governor occupied the vacuum left by the attenuated local elite, while also stifling any independence of maneuver that might have allowed a revival. Cities are told, for instance, that they cannot fund festivals before carrying out necessary repairs on their defensive walls (*Cod. Just.* 11. 42. 1). This is a requirement, not simply sensible advice. Perhaps the grimmest evidence of Diocletian's attitude toward the cities was provided in 303, when the city council of Antioch used its own initiative to raise forces and defeat an attempted usurpation in its port of Seleucia. This was met not with the grateful emperor's approbation, but with the execution of the entire council for their presumptuous interference (Liban. *Or.* I. 3). This claustrophobic surveillance of local government, however, was not necessarily effective. The Panopolis papyri witness that even the imminent arrival of Diocletian in September 298 could not force unwilling locals to carry out tasks as the harassed *strategos* repeatedly begged them to do (Rees 2004: 35–6).

Finance and the Economy

The empire's finances were in chaos at Diocletian's accession. The coinage was debased, the old denarius being reduced to base metal in a silver wash. Thus worthless money taxes mattered less than those raised in kind, which, however, were levied in irregular and extraordinary ways rather than in a predictable system. Diocletian applied the new diocesan structure to the financial hierarchies. Almost every diocese had a mint, usually conveniently sited near important frontiers or arteries of communication. A network of state factories was established, producing arms, clothing, purple-dyed cloth, and linen for both types of _militia_, and store-houses were constructed to hold purchased or requisitioned goods such as grain. The five-year census cycle was revitalized so that the whole empire could be assessed on a more systematic basis, now including the last of the previously exempt areas (principally Italy). When the various taxes in kind or money were to be levied, it would be on an assessment designed to give a theoretically fair estimate of wealth in land and the size of the (rural) population. Urban areas and populations were generally exempt (although some other taxes did fall upon them). This new Diocletianic system is generally referred to as _iugatio vel capitatio_. Various types of land were reduced to notional units called _iuga_, and individuals (including slaves) similarly to notional units called _capita_. These were then added up to give a total for a city or village. Although details and terminology differed between regions, the system was broadly consistent. It also brought officials of the central government into contact with the minutiae of local conditions: _censitores_ in Syria fixed village boundaries, while in the diocese of Asiana (western Anatolia and the Aegean islands) inscriptions were erected to record the valuations of various estates regarding their land, livestock, and people (Corcoran 2000: 175–6, 346–7). Lactantius (_Mort. Pers._ 23. 1–9) describes the census of 306 in typically unforgiving fashion, with waves of officials resorting to torture of the taxable population in order to maximize the value of census returns. Yet this critical description of the Diocletianic state projecting its will directly down to the lowest level is mirrored positively in optimistic official texts, as in the edict of Aristius Optatus, prefect of Egypt, enacting the census of 296/7 (_P. Cairo Isid._ 1; Rees 2004: 158). Ironically, this census in Egypt may have been a catalyst for the revolt of Domitius Domitianus. Yet Diocletian was aware of the potential for abuses by officials, and suppressed one unruly corps (the _frumentarii_), while trying to weed out false claims by officials of the privy purse (the _Caesariani_) against people's property.

Diocletian sought to stabilize the currency, with a sweeping coinage reform in the mid-290s which also saw the ending of the last separate coinage in the empire (that of the Alexandrian tetradrachm). In addition to a more plentiful gold coin (the *aureus*, struck at 60 to the pound, valued at 1,000 denarii), a new true silver coin (the *argenteus*) was introduced, with the low-value copper coins still freely minted, representing vestiges of the old denarius. Lack of precious metals, however, led the government to pay out even donatives in base metal (at least to ordinary soldiers), as shown in the Panopolis Papyri of AD 300 (Rees 2004: 155), while itself making compulsory purchases of gold (Corcoran 2000: 143–4 no. 50, 176 no. 8). This manipulation was not successful. So in 301 (another census year), Diocletian, perhaps urged on by the energetic Galerius, embarked on an ambitious plan to stabilize the currency. While the coinage was retariffed in a series of decrees, Diocletian also promulgated the most famous of all his pronouncements, the monumental Prices Edict (Rees 2004: 139–46). This set a ceiling on prices for several hundred categories of goods and services. The ambition of this measure is quite staggering, as is the fact that some governors were sufficiently supportive of it to cause at least forty copies to be inscribed on stone across their provinces. The sustained rhetoric of the edict, while portraying accurately the hard-won peace in the empire, sees the debilitating inflation as caused by the greed of men as uncivilized as the recently subdued barbarian hordes (parodied in Lactantius' view of a greedy Diocletian as the cause of the empire's economic woes: *Mort. Pers.* 7. 5–7). This economic analysis was certainly flawed, although the emperor's perception of the problem was anyway distorted, unduly influenced by the temporary price fluctuations wherever his massive and disruptive *comitatus* appeared. The aim of price control, however, was not entirely misconceived and was probably intended to operate in the immediate interest of soldiers on fixed money wages and of the administration, which often paid cash when levying goods and services. The market, by contrast, did not prove amenable to such management. While some infringers were executed, goods disappeared and inflation continued. This bold measure was a failure, as Lactantius was pleased to point out. It was repealed, or else simply allowed to lapse, leaving the mighty inscribed copies as witnesses to imperial overstretch.

Legal Policy

Caracalla had granted Roman citizenship to most of the free population of the empire in a sweeping edict of AD 212 (the *Constitutio Antoniniana*).

Yet while this made millions of new citizens, it did not make them into Latin-speakers or users of an unfamiliar Roman law in their daily lives. Thus the jurist Modestinus wrote in Greek explaining excuses for avoiding burdensome duties as guardians. By midcentury, however, Beirut boasted an established law school (to whose students Diocletian later granted immunities: *Cod. Just.* 10. 50. 1), and Latin was being learnt in the east, not for its literary qualities (if you have Homer, who needs Virgil?) but for the access it provided to legal and administrative careers. The Illyrian emperors no longer came from those elites for whom Greek literary culture was a prerequisite, and, when Diocletian settled in Nicomedia, a Latin court became more or less permanently anchored in a Greek cultural environment. This seems to have had several related effects, inasmuch as it brought out the Roman chauvinist in Diocletian. First, he tried to foster Latin as the administrative language. Thus he summoned Lactantius from Africa to be professor of Latin rhetoric at Nicomedia, although student recruitment proved difficult. Second, as he traveled around the provinces, receiving and replying to countless petitions, many of them regarding legal disputes (a routine part of the emperor's task), he would have become aware of the extent to which large parts of the theoretically Roman population were barely cognizant of Roman legal norms. Not that Diocletian was a lawyer, but he knew how to listen to good advice, for instance from the key official who dealt with such cases, the master of petitions (*magister libellorum*), who was usually an experienced jurist.

Three identifiable and capable jurists served in this post between 285 and 295, writing replies (rescripts) in the names of the emperors. The first, from 285 to 290, is an anonymous official, emblematic of the Roman chauvinism of Diocletian's government. Thus non-Roman practices are strictly disapproved: bigamy, disherison, marriage by abduction, incest. Next in 290–91 is the more rhetorical Arcadius Charisius, perhaps less happy writing pithy rescripts than the lengthy elaborate edicts, like the Prices Edict, which he produced later as *magister memoriae*. Finally, in 293–5, comes Aurelius Hermogenianus, who expounds and explains with rational clarity. The rescripts produced by these men, however, even though posted up in public and often copied, could achieve only haphazard circulation. Since there had always been a demand for copies of imperial rescripts, which represented the professional effort of experienced jurists, it was perhaps only logical that such texts should be collected and published in systematic works. First, in 292, a man called Gregorius (perhaps the master of petitions 285–90) produced the Gregorian Code, consisting of imperial rescripts issued by emperors from Hadrian down to 291. This was published in fifteen books, which were no longer in separate rolls, but bound together in a single large *codex* (hence Code) like a modern book. This move from roll to codex was one of the most epoch-making changes during the third century. Next, in 295, Hermogenianus published the Hermogenian Code, a one-book codex containing a mass of rescripts from the years 293 and 294, texts originally issued in the names of the tetrarchs but written by himself as master of petitions. Shortly afterwards he was promoted to be Diocletian's praetorian prefect. What was the status of these two codes? Were Hermogenianus and Gregorius acting principally as jurists taking advantage of material (rescripts), which they had already written, to produce works under their own names, or were they state officials collecting imperial texts for a government publication? Perhaps semi-official is the best answer. Knowing his men, Diocletian was content to let those best qualified use imperial materials to fulfill a useful project, without claiming any credit for himself (as Lactantius says was otherwise his habit), in contrast with the later imperial codes of Theodosius II and Justinian. Yet innovative juristic writing comes to an end with Charisius and Hermogenianus. The Diocletianic codes are thus liminal, marking the final change from juristic to imperial control in the interpretation of law. Henceforth governors, advocates, and even the litigious citizen could have in each hand a volume of up-to-date and authoritative legal interpretation to mine or consult.

Religious Policy

As regards religion, Diocletian was conservative and sought security in the traditional. The chief Roman god became his own tutelary deity, with Jupiter's son Hercules chosen for Maximian, reflecting their real-life relationship. At the same time, this not only invoked divine support for the emperors, but made explicit their trust in these gods. This was widely advertised on the coinage (where the two figures were joined by Mars and Apollo/Sol), and, although not normalized as part of the otherwise extensive imperial titulature, the adjectives *Iovius /Herculius* recur regularly as matching designations of military units, provinces, and buildings.

As noted earlier, an emphasis on traditional Roman manners is prominent among Diocletian's legal rulings, which associated ancient Roman virtue with divine favor. This is well expressed in his fulminating edict of 295 on incestuous marriages, which are characterized as both impious and un-Roman. Religious novelty is also seen as seductively subversive. In reply to a query from the proconsul of Africa in 302, Diocletian wrote back from Alexandria enjoining strong punishments against the Manichees, seen at once as unwarranted innovators and Persian surrogates (Rees 2004: 174–5). Diocletian's *Caesar* Galerius seems to have shared his ultra-Roman outlook, which only makes more pointed Lactantius' portrayal of him as the real barbarian (Lact. *Mort. Pers.* 34. 1 vs. 9. 2).

Since the "peace of Gallienus" ended a previous bout of persecution in 260, Christians had enjoyed long years of quiet advancement, becoming an increasingly accepted presence even in the army and at court. Despite his good fortune, Diocletian seems to have remained an over-anxious peerer into the future, and tried to avoid anything that might bring divine displeasure. The presence of Christians in the army had not prevented the great victory over Persia. Yet loyal Christian soldiers, such as the much traveled Aurelius Gaius (known from his epitaph: *AE* 1981. 777, Barnes 1996: 542–3), were purged from the army in 299. Next, apparently failed sacrifices and an arson attack on the palace finally roused the emperor against the Christians, egged on as he was by his *Caesar*, by pagan intellectuals at his court, such as Porphyry and Sossianus Hierocles, who had already assailed Christianity in their writings, and even by an oracle from Apollo at Didyma. Suspicion at court led to the execution of two Christian eunuch chamberlains, while the imperial women, who may have been sympathetic to Christianity, were forced to offer sacrifice. Finally, on February 23, 303 the prominent Christian church opposite the palace in Nicomedia was demolished by soldiers, and the next day an edict was promulgated under which churches were to be pulled down, Christian scriptures surrendered for destruction, Christians of rank stripped of their status, and even those who were imperial freedmen re-enslaved. The edict was being enforced in Palestine by March and in Africa by May. There followed later in 303 the arrest of clergy, to be freed if they apostatized by offering sacrifice – although many were freed after coerced or notional compliance under the *vicennalia* amnesty (November 303). Finally, in 304, came a further measure requiring universal sacrifice, although this may have been more the initiative of Galerius, as Diocletian was ailing, and it seems to have been implemented only in the east.

The persecution outlasted Diocletian and Maximian's abdication in 305, but in the west it abated before formal termination by Constantine and then Maxentius in 306. Even Galerius, perhaps distracted by the disintegrating tetrarchy, seems to have lost direction, so that it was only the fervor of the new *Caesar* Maximinus that repeatedly revived the persecution in the east, even beyond Galerius' toleration edict of April 311. Only when defeated and near death did Maximinus finally concede toleration, thus marking the end of the Great Persecution in summer 313.

The Christian church survived this sustained attempt to destroy its essential features (buildings, clergy, scriptures) and to discourage any supporters of rank or aspiration. What the persecutors most desired for their targets (and the persecuted most feared) was not death, but apostasy. Enforcement, however, was patchy, depending largely on the eagerness of magistrates or would-be martyrs. Even within the imperial college Constantius complied in rather muted fashion. It is also notable that the popular outcries against Christians which had often lain behind earlier episodes of persecution had faded away as Christianity became normalized. Top-down persecution, without widespread popular agitation, lacked reach and staying power. Ironically, the most long-lasting effects of persecution were bitter schisms between Christians over treatment of the lapsed, such as the Donatist dispute in Africa, where Constantine in his turn found attempts at persecution futile. The whole saga of the persecutions initiated by Diocletian and Galerius well illustrates the ambitions of late antique government, but also its limits.

The Abdication

The last act of Diocletian's reign involves the most innovative but least successful of his political experiments: the abdication. There was no precedent for this in the history of the principate. Lactantius compares it to the succession of Trajan to Nerva, but Nerva remained emperor till he died, despite having Trajan forced upon him as *Caesar*. Perhaps the closest parallel is Sulla's laying down of his dictatorship in 80 BC, an act that was later viewed by some as noble self-abnegation, but also (by Julius Caesar) as political folly, given that his settlement had started to unravel even before he died. As already noted, it is unlikely that Diocletian originally envisaged abdication as an integral aspect of the tetrarchy, although the line of succession was made clear. While Lactantius ascribes the abdication to Galerius' putting pressure on Diocletian and Maximian just weeks before the event, the idea seems to have arisen earlier. In November 303 Diocletian visited Rome for probably the first time to mark his twentieth-year celebrations (*vicennalia*) and the victory over Persia, in company with Maximian. A lavish triumphal procession was staged, magnificent games were put on, and the *Augusti* scattered gold and silver coins to the crowd in the circus. There was a general amnesty, even for Christian priests. Diocletian, however, seems to have found the Roman populace rather more free-speaking that he was accustomed to, and left the city earlier than expected in mid-December. Before this, however, he had extracted from Maximian an oath, sworn in the temple of Capitoline

Jupiter, to join him in abdication. The succession, although probably not its exact timetable, was settled. The new *Caesars* would in due course be the only two adult sons of the existing tetrarchs: Constantius' son, Constantine, and Maximian's son, Maxentius.[5]

After leaving Rome, Diocletian reached Ravenna to celebrate his ninth consulship on January 1, 304, but as he traveled north in atrocious winter weather his health deteriorated. Despite this, he spent the summer inspecting the Danube frontier, finally returning to his beloved Nicomedia to dedicate a new circus for the closing of his *vicennalia* on November 20. Then on December 13 he collapsed; all winter he lay near death, not being seen in public until March 1, 305, when he emerged from the palace looking thin and drawn. On that day far away in Trier, an oblivious Constantius was handing out medallions celebrating the *Caesars'* thirteenth year. Meanwhile Galerius undertook a daring political maneuver. Whatever his involvement in the earlier succession talks, he certainly did not like the outcome. Ever since the Persian victory, commemorated on his arch at Thessalonica, his pride and confidence had grown. His role in Diocletian's government became more important, and it may have been his energy that drove or at least facilitated such ambitious policies as the Prices Edict and the Great Persecution. Even so, had he and Maxentius, who was his son-in-law, not hated one another, history might have been very different. As it was, he foresaw himself sidelined in a college containing Constantius, Constantine, and Maxentius. So he decided to create a college more to his liking. Here Lactantius is probably correct in depicting Galerius first bullying a fearful Maximian before arriving in Nicomedia in March to confront the convalescent Diocletian and overturn what had appeared settled. Thus, on May 1, 305 at Nicomedia, Diocletian took off his purple robe and placed it over the shoulders of the new *Caesar*, Galerius' nephew Maximinus, as Galerius himself was acclaimed *Augustus*. On the same day in Milan, Maximian likewise invested as *Caesar* Severus, one of Galerius' military buddies. It was Constantius, technically the new senior *Augustus*, who was now isolated.

Retirement and Death

Diocletian retired to the great palace at Split on the Adriatic, near Salona, his birthplace. It is not clear if this was purpose-built for an ex-emperor (and with how much notice), or if it was adapted from other purposes. It included a small temple to Diocletian's special deity, Jupiter, as well as a grand mausoleum (today the cathedral). From here Diocletian must have observed with bitterness the unraveling of the neatly regulated succession enabled by the abdication. At first the new order looked impressive. Galerius issued a major series of edicts reining in abuses by financial officials (Corcoran 2007), while the Baths of Diocletian in Rome were dedicated, probably by Severus, in the names of all four tetrarchs as well as the two retired *Augusti* (*ILS* 646; Rees 2004: 147). But the unwelcome proclamation of Constantine on the death of the ailing Constantius in 306 upset Galerius' plans, and control over the imperial college slipped ever further from his grasp amid war, usurpation, and intrigue. And so, in 308, Galerius decided to invoke the prestige of the man he had hurried into retirement, and Diocletian held the consulship for the tenth time, consenting to attend a conference at Carnuntum (on the Danube) in November to try to re-establish order. Here Maximian, who had greedily grasped the purple again, tried to persuade Diocletian to recreate their successful partnership. But Diocletian refused, knowing that there was no turning back the clock, and famously extolled to an uncomprehending Maximian the joys of growing one's own vegetables (*Epit. de Caes.* 39. 6). So Maximian reluctantly retired for a second time, although his restless plotting led him to a violent end in 310.

Despite his efforts at Carnuntum, Galerius was unable to impose control, and, stricken by cancer, he died in agony and disappointment in May 311, having failed in his sincere attempt to maintain the tetrarchic system by playing Tiberius to Diocletian's Augustus. Thus Diocletian, having been near death in 304, was now the only surviving member of the First Tetrarchy. Worse was to follow. While still living, he was aware of his statues and inscriptions being erased in *damnatio memoriae* associated with the disgraced Maximian, and then was unable to help his daughter Valeria, Galerius' widow, as she was subjected to unwanted and threatening marriage plans from two of the remaining *Augusti*, Licinius and Maximinus. The latter contemptuously dismissed the retired *Augustus'* pleas that his daughter be sent back to him. The cabbages may have lost their attraction.

In the end, it seems that a sick and bitter Diocletian starved himself to death. The date is uncertain. Just as we know the day of Diocletian's birth, but not the year, so with his death. December 3 is the day recorded. Lactantius places his death between those of Galerius and Maximinus, so the year must be 311 or 312. Since Diocletian is the only member of the First Tetrarchy not to appear on Maxentius' *divus* coinage, and since the latter clearly felt he needed all the help he could get from his recently deceased and deified relatives, Diocletian was presumably still alive in October 312 at the time of Maxentius' overthrow. This also matches one source which reports that, when Constantine and Licinius issued an invitation to the nuptials of the latter to Constantine's sister (scheduled for February 313), Diocletian declined it on the grounds of ill-health and this rendered his continued existence obnoxious and suspect to them (*Epit. de Caes.* 39. 7). Thus it was probably on December 3, 312, that Diocletian finally expired in his palace at Split, not far from where he was born. And there, in the mausoleum adorned with purple hangings, he was interred. Eutropius (9. 28) records that he was unique in dying a private individual but being enrolled among the gods. This is true in the sense that all deceased but not damned emperors, even in the Christian empire, could be called *divus*; but formal recognition of his divinization by contemporaries seems unlikely, given that no emperor issued a consecration coinage for him.[6]

One final indignity Diocletian avoided. After defeating Maximinus in the summer of 313, Licinius did not repeat the mistake of 305, leaving spare imperial claimants alive, but killed them all: the sons of Galerius and Severus and the family of Maximinus (an example also followed by Constantine's sons in 337). But when he finally caught up with Valeria and her mother, Prisca, it was surely revenge for her spurning of him that motivated his execution of them as well. Thus Diocletian's daughter and wife were put to death at Thessalonica (where Licinius himself would later perish) in the summer of 314, a miserable end for the family of such a long-lasting and successful ruler.

Assessment

The period after Diocletian's abdication was one of disaster for the style of cooperative collegiate rule that he had tried to maintain, as well as for himself and his family. He failed, as later did Constantine, to solve the succession conundrum. But while he did not create a reliable model for long-term collegiate rule, he did show it was possible, and his achievement in making it work for two decades under his skillful management was fundamental in fostering sustained military success and enabling substantial administrative and other reforms to be enacted and embedded.

The character of the man remains elusive, given the uneven evidence. The grim soldier, the petty bureaucrat, the Roman chauvinist, the superstitious persecutor: all seem at once true, but less than fair. Lactantius probably gives us our best view of Diocletian as ruler, if we can peer below the mud of his invective. He perceives the "fraternal" relationship of Diocletian and Maximian as pernicious, yet cannot deny the essential success of the regime up to 303, made possible by the crucial ties between the two (Lact. *Mort. Pers.* 8. 1–2, 9. 11). Similarly, Lactantius' image of a timid Diocletian, ready to blame failure on others, but keep all successes to himself (Lact. *Mort. Pers.* 11. 5), may be significantly true (rulers routinely seek scapegoats for failure), while obscuring with satire the reflection of a ruler ready both to take counsel and to delegate. Whether it is in his choice of his imperial colleagues or officials such as Hermogenianus, or in his ready creation of new chains of command, his cautious and consultative style worked. Later fourth-century writers are not uncritical (for instance, Eutropius 9. 26), but are generally appreciative of Diocletian's collegiate manner (Aur. Vict. *Caes.* 39. 8, 39. 29; Julian *Caes.* 315A–B) and his combination of measured boldness and crafty caution.

There is, of course, an element of overreach. Some enactments were optimistically ambitious in trying to regulate prices or beliefs – perhaps a sign of Galerius' influence on his aging *Augustus* – and expose a mismatch between self-righteous rhetoric and the limitations of enforcement. This certainly set the tone for all his successors, who only intensified the rhetoric, as also the gorgeous ceremonial of the late antique court. Yet it was perhaps only by attempting so much in so many areas that Diocletian achieved such a significant degree of success in at least some of them. It is a sign of the essential soundness of his reforms that Constantine built in many cases on what he had started. It is not for nothing that scholars talk of the "new empire" of Diocletian and Constantine.

Notes

1 An early visit to Rome is possible, but uncertain. See Barnes (1982), 50 and (1996), 537.

2 Compare *Pan. Lat.* X (10). 9 and 11, and XI (3). 11–12 with Lact. *Mort. Pers.* 8. 1–2.

3 M. Zahariade, "The Halmyris Tetrarchic Inscription," *Zeitschrift für Papyrologie und Epigraphik* 119 (1997), 228–36; Rees (2004), 19.

4 The publication of Galerius' Heraclea letter (*AE* 2002. 1293) makes him a more plausible issuer for the anonymous Tymandus text often attributed to Diocletian (*Monumenta Asiae Minoris Antiqua* IV. 236).

5 For the abdication, I very much follow the interpretation of Barnes (1996), 544–6.

6 But note a unique pair of milestones from Heraclea/Perinthus recording Diocletian as *divus* along with Constantius and Galerius (*AE* 1998. 1180–1).

Simon Corcoran

Further Reading

T. D. Barnes, *The New Empire of Diocletian and Constantine* (Cambridge, Mass., and London, 1982)

T. D. Barnes, "Emperors, panegyrics, prefects, provinces and palaces (284–317)," *Journal of Roman Archaeology* 9 (1996), 532–52

A. K. Bowman, "Diocletian and the First Tetrarchy, AD 284–305," *Cambridge Ancient History*, vol. 12, 2nd edn (Cambridge, UK, 2005), 67–89

S. Corcoran, *The Empire of the Tetrarchs: Imperial Pronouncements and Government AD 284–324*, 2nd edn (Oxford, 2000)

S. Corcoran, "Galerius's Jigsaw Puzzle: The Caesariani Dossier," *Antiquité Tardive* 15 (2007)

W. L. Leadbetter, *Galerius and the Will of Diocletian* (London and New York, 2008)

R. Rees, *Diocletian and the Tetrarchy* (Edinburgh, 2004)

S. Williams, *Diocletian and the Roman Recovery* (London and New York, 1985)

XI

Constantine

Noel Lenski

Between Augustus and Justinian, no emperor ruled as long as Constantine. Arguably, apart from these two, no other emperor had as profound an impact on the Roman world either. Constantine's establishment of a new imperial capital at Constantinople, his creation of a distinctive and lasting architectural heritage, his revisions to Diocletian's new administrative apparatus, his restructuring of the army, his introduction of a new coinage system, and his initiation of a new dynasty and new style of dynastic rule all had a major impact for centuries to come. More than anything else, however, his conversion to Christianity and his persistence in championing his new religion inside the empire and beyond its frontiers provided the impetus that vaulted this religion to the forefront of world history. It is certainly possible to conceive of a western world that might have come to be dominated by Christianity without the arrival of Constantine, but it is impossible to deny that he both hastened its appearance on the world scene and left his indelible stamp on its history and the history of the world through his conversion.

Background

Constantine was born near the Balkan city of Naissus (modern Nish in Serbia), most likely in AD 272. In his childhood the soldier emperors Aurelian (r. 270–5) and in turn Probus (r. 276–82), both also from the Balkans (ancient Illyricum), managed to rescue the empire from a lengthy period of civil war, economic turmoil, and barbarian invasions. When Constantine was approaching adolescence, the emperor Numerian (r. 282–4) was murdered by his praetorian prefect while returning from a military expedition into Persia. Numerian's murder was avenged by the commander of the imperial guard, also from Illyricum, who was then proclaimed emperor under the name Diocletian on November 20, 284.

By the time Diocletian came to power, the Roman empire had become quite accustomed to control by co-rulers, emperors who took on one or more imperial colleagues for increased security. Its territory and possessions were vast and in the third century had proved too unwieldy for a single emperor to govern. To solve this problem, and also to help cement a dynasty in place and thus reduce the chances of usurpation, a mid-third-century emperor would, when possible, proclaim his son or sons as co-emperor(s). Although Diocletian had no sons, he wisely chose to follow this trend and name a co-ruler in the person of his friend and fellow former guardsman Maximian in 285. The tradition of imperial co-rulership had generally distinguished between the title *Augustus*, given to an emperor with full powers, and that of *Caesar*, which entailed a grade of authority subordinate to that of the *Augustus*. Although Diocletian appointed Maximian as *Caesar* in 285, he thought it necessary or advantageous to promote him to equality with the title *Augustus* one year later. The two *Augusti* faced the challenges of empire, particularly the relentless waves of barbarian invaders, together for seven years, but in 293 they chose to appoint two further co-rulers as *Caesars*: Diocletian chose as his junior colleague Galerius and Maximian selected Constantius Chlorus. Like their superiors, both were from Illyricum and both former guardsmen. Constantine was the son of the latter. Constantius' lofty distinction will no doubt have created certain expectations in Constantine about his future.

Moderns have coined the term "tetrarchy" ("rule of four," from the Greek), to characterize the imperial system devised by Diocletian. They have also noted that the system, often referred to as a "college" of emperors (from the Latin for "club"), retained elements of dynastic co-rulership characteristic of the earlier third century. In public art and monuments, the emperors regularly appeared in unison and with uniformly schematic visages; in public declarations the *Augusti* referred to one another as "brothers" and to their *Caesares* as "sons"; and, in public ceremonies the tetrarchs knotted their families together with the bonds of marriage, Galerius marrying Diocletian's daughter Valeria and Constantius Chlorus Maximian's stepdaughter Theodora. This last arrangement came at the expense of Constantine's mother Helena, who may have been married to Constantius Chlorus or may, some sources indicate, have simply been his concubine. Whatever the case, Helena was put aside in favor of the princess. This blow will surely have forced Constantine to acknowledge that his ambitions for power, though not unfounded, would not go uncontested, above all because Theodora quickly began producing offspring of her own by Constantius. Constantine was thus obliged to prove himself worthy of rule in the fashion most appropriate for a late Roman emperor: fighting on the battlefield. This he did under Galerius, in whose army he fought in both Persia and the trans-Danubian territory of the Sarmatians. In these conflicts he gained combat experience and prepared himself for a life of military engagement.

Early Ambitions and Accession

Constantine's first chance to ascend the throne arose on May 1, 305 when, for the first time in Roman history, the emperors voluntarily abdicated. In orderly fashion, the *Augusti* Diocletian and Maximian turned over power to their *Caesares* Galerius and Constantius Chlorus, who were now elevated to *Augusti*. With the apparent intention of maintaining a "tetrarchic" system, Galerius and Constantius immediately appointed new *Caesares* of their own. If Constantine was expecting to fall into this role, he will have been sorely disappointed, for Galerius appointed his nephew Maximinus Daia while Constantine's own father – probably under considerable pressure from Diocletian as well as Galerius – promoted a certain Severus. Both new *Caesares* certainly fit the profile of their tetrarchic predecessors, for both hailed from Illyricum and both had served as and commanded soldiers. Yet dynastic concerns had clearly played a role in Maximinus' promotion, giving Constantine all the more reason to bridle at having been passed over despite his own military experience, Illyrian background, and dynastic connections.

Indeed, Constantine was probably still chafing, when only a matter of months later, glimmerings of a second opportunity for power arose. In late 305 Constantine's father, now preparing a war against the barbarian peoples of northern Britain, petitioned Galerius to send Constantine west from the eastern court in order to aid him in his military campaigns. With great ambivalence, Galerius consented one evening but then retracted his permission the following morning – too late, for Constantine had already departed. Legend has it that, anticipating pursuit by Galerius' henchmen, he hastened west using imperial post horses, and that when he arrived at each posting station he selected the fittest mount and then killed or lamed the rest to slow the pursuers sent by Galerius to recall him. Whether or not the story is true, it does offer an accurate reflection of the level of Constantine's ambition. He thus reached his father in Boulogne before the end of the year and accompanied him on his mission to Britain. There, after successful engagements over the summer of 306, Constantius fell ill, and late in July he died. Far from the centers of power and freed from the strictures of the three remaining tetrarchic colleagues, Constantine and his father's army seized the moment by proclaiming Constantine full *Augustus* on July 25.

This did not sit well with Galerius, Diocletian's successor as the strongest member of the tetrarchic college. Nevertheless, considering that Constantine was a world away and was supported by an army more loyal to Constantius' son than to the protocols of the tetrarchy, Galerius yielded to reality and acknowledged Constantine's proclamation. He insisted, however, on his demotion to the rank of *Caesar*. Constantine wisely consented, at least for the moment, and moved over into Gaul, where he established himself in the strategic center of Trier, from where he would rule (with some periods in Arles) for the next decade.

Meanwhile, in Rome, another dynastic claimant was no less discontented with the tetrarchic transfer of power in 305. Maxentius, the son of the former *Augustus* Maximian, was just as ambitious as Constantine and, when he learned that the latter had assumed the throne in succession to his own father, persuaded the praetorian guards in Rome to proclaim him emperor, on October 28, 306. At this Galerius drew the line and ordered Severus, now *Augustus* in the west, into Italy to suppress Maxentius' usurpation. Maxentius, meanwhile, had engaged the support of his father Maximian, who had abdicated only with reluctance and under pressure from Diocletian. Not surprisingly, Maximian resumed the purple and, together with his son, succeeded in persuading Severus' troops – whom he had commanded until recently – to desert. Severus was captured and soon thereafter executed. Infuriated, Galerius took the field himself and descended into Italy against Maxentius. Once again, however, Maxentius was able to outmaneuver his opponent by encouraging his soldiers, camped before the formidable walls of Rome, to desert. In point of fact, Galerius, like many of the later emperors of "Rome," had never actually seen the city before his march against Maxentius. He and his men were thus somewhat overwhelmed by the twelve-mile circuit of walls standing twenty feet high which stood between them and victory over Maxentius. In a desperate plea to retain their loyalty, Galerius permitted his men to abandon the siege and convinced them they could make up for the spoils they had hoped to win sacking Rome by granting them permission to plunder Italy instead on their return eastward. Galerius was thus forced for the second time to permit a dynastic ruler to remain on the throne: the traditional attractions of dynasty were proving a more powerful force than the more novel system of tetrarchic collegiality.

Maxentius had been granted a reprieve, but by no means an acquittal. Though Galerius had been forced to admit discomfiture, he continued to regard Maxentius as a usurper and public enemy. Nevertheless, he left the job of removing Maxentius to another. Constantine would soon rise to the challenge, but only after allowing Maxentius enough room to set the stage for his own demise. In the initial phase of his emperorship, Maxentius had done a tremendous job of currying favor among the imperial guards, the masses in Rome, the people of Italy, and his own imperial father. Gradually these allies began to peel away in the face of his failure to live up to the exigencies of rule. Early in his reign, Maxentius quarreled with Maximian and eventually drove his father into the open arms of none other than Constantine. The latter had already allied himself to Maximian in 307 by marrying his daughter Fausta – in keeping with the tetrarchic trend of cementing imperial alliances with marriage bonds. When Maximian was expelled from Italy by Maxentius, Constantine was thus delighted to receive the older man as a co-ruler. This split with his own father weakened Maxentius' authority considerably, especially in Africa, where the vicar (a high-level representative of the praetorian prefect) Domitius Alexander broke into open revolt. Because north Africa supplied much of the grain that fed the Roman masses, this uprising caused food shortages in the capital, and, even after it was suppressed, riots broke out which Maxentius brutally suppressed with his guards. His situation was thus growing more precarious by the day.

On November 11, 308, Galerius had summoned the legitimate tetrarchs to a conference in the city of Carnuntum (Petronell in modern Austria) and there, in the company of the great Diocletian, hammered out arrangements to firm up the wobbly imperial college. First on the agenda was the election of a replacement for the western emperor Severus. Rather than agreeing to the promotion of Constantine to *Augustus* in the west and choosing a new *Caesar* for him, Galerius pushed strongly for the immediate appointment as full *Augustus* of another one of his confidants and fellow Balkan soldiers, Licinius. In addition, Maximian was ordered to abdicate once again, and the condemnation of Maxentius as a usurper was reaffirmed.

After several more years of fighting against the barbarian peoples along the Rhine, in 312 Constantine was finally ready to take on Maxentius. In the summer of this year he assembled a crack force, including a number of Frankish barbarians he had recently recruited as auxiliaries, charged over the western Alps, and made a sweep across northern Italy, securing Susa, Turin, Milan, Verona, and Aquileia. In so doing, he sealed off northern Italy and defeated

Maxentius' advance forces under the general Ruricius Pompeianus. Lightning quick and boldly decisive on the battlefield, Constantine wasted no time in marching on Rome that same season. There Maxentius waited, apparently content to fall back on the strategy of forcing his opponent into a lengthy and precarious siege, such as he had used against Severus and Galerius. With this in mind, Maxentius had cut the bridges over the River Tiber into the city, including the Milvian Bridge which lay directly on Constantine's route. Nevertheless, when Constantine was just a few miles north of the city on the Via Flaminia, Maxentius reversed his strategy upon hearing from his diviners that "the enemy of Rome would perish that day" (Lact. *Mors. Pers.* 44. 8) and chose to exit Rome and engage Constantine in open battle. To sally forth he had to construct a temporary boat bridge across the Tiber alongside the truncated Milvian Bridge. Meeting Constantine's forces in battle to the north of Rome at a place called Saxa Rubra, Maxentius and his men were roundly defeated and put to flight. When they reached the Tiber and attempted to hasten back over the shaky boat bridge, it gave way and many, including Maxentius, tumbled into the river and drowned. His body was recovered from the water and its head removed and paraded into the city the next day by Constantine's victorious army. The citizens of Rome, by now utterly disaffected with their erstwhile champion, greeted Constantine with jubilation.

Conversion

In the buildup to the Battle of the Milvian Bridge, Constantine is reputed to have had a vision that would become the pivotal event in his long reign. Unfortunately, our two best sources for what happened are disappointingly brief and seem to contradict one another. Lactantius, who served as a tutor to the emperor's son and who wrote his treatise *On the Deaths of Persecutors* (*Mort. Pers.*) around 315, reports:

> Constantine was advised in a dream to mark the heavenly sign of God on the shields of his soldiers and then engage in battle. He did as he was commanded and by means of a slanted letter X with the top of its head bent round, he marked Christ on their shields. Armed with this sign, his army took up its weaponry. (44. 5–6)

Eusebius, who composed his *Life of Constantine* shortly after the emperor's death in 337, reports an account which is clearly related, but differs on important details:

About the time of the midday sun, when day was just turning, he said he saw with his own eyes, up in the sky and resting over the sun, a cross shaped trophy formed from light, and a text attached to it which said, "By this conquer." Amazement at the spectacle seized both him and the whole company of soldiers which was then accompanying him on a campaign he was conducting somewhere, and witnessed the miracle. He was, he said, wondering to himself what the manifestation might mean; then, while he meditated and thought long and hard, night overtook him. Thereupon, as he slept, the Christ of God appeared to him with the sign which had appeared in the sky and urged him to make himself a copy of the sign which had appeared in the sky and to use this as protection against the attacks of the enemy. (1. 28. 2–30. 1)

Eusebius goes on to recount how Constantine himself had reported this story to him – in a conversation which scholars date to 325 – and claims that the emperor had shown him a copy of the battle standard he fashioned in response to the dream. Both accounts thus have circumstantial credibility and both authors appear to have been close enough to Constantine to have spoken with him about what happened. Yet Lactantius describes only a dream vision while Eusebius reports the observation of some celestial sign prior to the dream.

The situation is complicated still further by our knowledge that Constantine is also reported to have experienced a celestial vision in 310, a vision which contemporaries associated with the sun god, Apollo.[1] Indeed, from this date forward until 325 a solar deity under the Latin name Sol Invictus (the Unconquerable Sun) appears with great frequency on Constantine's coins and in imperial art. It is thus hard not to conclude that Constantine believed a vision of light appeared to him in the heavens, but that our interpretation of this vision is clouded by variances in the reported accounts. Perhaps the best resolution to the problem – though not all agree the problem is soluble – has been proposed by Peter Weiss (2003): Constantine had a midday vision in 310 whose description accords well with a documented atmospheric phenomenon called a "solar halo"; because he was still pagan at the time, he interpreted this as a sign from Apollo or some related sun god; Constantine was, nevertheless, a religious seeker who had displayed serious sympathies for Christianity even from the first years of his reign; when, shortly before his battle with Maxentius, he had a dream telling him that the heavenly vision had been from Christ, he converted and emblazoned the shields of his men with the sign he had seen, the chi-rho (☧, a monogram of the first two letters of Christ's name in Greek); by the time he met Eusebius, more than a dozen years later, these two experiences – vision and dream – could be collapsed into a single, abbreviated, continuous narrative of conversion.

However we choose to interpret the specifics of the sources for his conversion, we have good evidence that its effects were real and immediate. In the first year following the Battle of the Milvian Bridge, Constantine granted special exemptions from mandatory government service to Christian clergy and offered Christian churches a share in imperial revenues. He also began playing a role in resolving the heated disputes that had arisen in the church in the wake of the Great Persecution, a series of ruthless attacks on the Christian church that began in 303 and continued, at least in the eastern empire, down to 313. To be sure, Christian persecutions had been initiated on numerous occasions by local and even imperial authorities ever since the first century AD. Nevertheless, Diocletian and his fellow tetrarchs, who were, as we have seen, notoriously systematic, conducted persecutions that were so widespread, so long-lasting, and so thoroughgoing that they rightly merit their designation. The Great Persecution had wrought havoc on individuals, families, cities, and private property. It had rent communities asunder both by pitting non-Christians against their Christian neighbors and by arousing resentment within the embattled Christian churches themselves. Seeing this turmoil, Constantine's father had given only halting support to the persecutions in his sphere of influence in the far west. For his part Constantine, who had witnessed the start of the Great Persecution at first hand in the east, adopted a policy that reflected the leniency of his father. Almost immediately after assuming the throne he granted freedom of worship to all in his western realm. His efforts at healing the rifts created by the persecutions began in earnest, however, only after his conversion and the defeat of Maxentius. It was at this point that he began actively displaying his favor to the church and extending his efforts on its behalf into the realms of his fellow emperors.

The Great Persecution had weighed quite heavily on north Africa, where a number of Christians had eventually given in by surrendering church property, denying their faith, and at times sacrificing to pagan gods. Those north Africans who had abided by the faith unwaveringly – and suffered for it – were understandably resentful toward others who had not. Troubles arose when the rigorists began denying authority to those clergy who had been ordained or consecrated by leaders who subsequently lapsed. These same rigorists began creating their own clergy distinct from that recognized by the leadership in Carthage, a division which ushered in bitter disputes over the control of congregations and of church property. This split, known as the "Donatist" schism after an important early rigorist leader named Donatus of Casae Nigrae, was already in full spate by the time Constantine gained control of Italy and Africa from Maxentius in 312. It came to the emperor's attention almost immediately after his victory, for his offer of exemptions and emoluments to the church leadership raised the question of who precisely the legitimate leaders were. In an attempt to settle these disputes, Constantine called for the creation of two church councils, the first in Rome in the autumn of 313 and a subsequent one in Arles in 314. Both found against the hard-line Donatists, though neither succeeded in putting a definitive end to the controversy, which continued to roil well into the fifth century. Regardless of the outcome of this particular episode, however, Constantine had openly displayed his allegiance to the church, not merely as its benefactor, but as an active arbiter of its disputes.

Disintegration of the Tetrarchic System

Constantine even began promoting his new faith outside the imperial territory he himself controlled. To understand how this might have been, one must examine further developments in the tetrarchic system of joint rule. By the time Constantine defeated Maxentius in 312, the tetrarchic system of Diocletian was in free fall. The conference of Carnuntum in 308 had left four recognized emperors in place: Constantine in the west, Licinius in the Balkans, Galerius in Anatolia, and Maximinus in the east. When Galerius died of a degenerative bowel disease in 311, rather than appoint a successor and round out the imperial college once again to four, the remaining three began bickering. Maximinus precipitated this squabble by engaging in a land grab through which he added Anatolia, formerly occupied by Galerius, to his sphere of authority. Moreover, angered by Licinius' precipitous promotion to full *Augustus*, Maximinus also had himself proclaimed *Augustus*. For his part, Constantine had been styling himself *Augustus* since late 307, and in the years after his defeat of Maxentius in 312 he took to advertising himself as the *Maximus Augustus*, a clear claim to superior authority. No longer a cooperative collection of paired junior and senior colleagues, then, the imperial college had devolved into a group of three rival and competing *Augusti*. In order to leverage his central geographical position in this power triangle, Licinius needed to ally himself with either Maximinus or Constantine. Given Maximinus' brazen aggression in 311, Constantine made the more obvious choice, so Licinius met him in early 313 in the city of Milan and there the two cemented their alliance by overseeing a marriage between Licinius and Constantine's half-sister Constantia.

Licinius also agreed to subscribe to a decree granting freedom of worship to Christians in his realm and providing for the restoration of property Christians had lost in the Great Persecution. Now termed the "Edict of Milan," this 313 agreement was part of a growing trend toward the acceptance of Christianity as a legitimate religion. The trend had surely begun with Constantine's recognition of Christians at the start of his reign, but it had also been fostered by the formerly rabid persecutor Galerius who, shortly before his death, had issued an "Edict of Toleration" granting freedom of worship to Christians throughout the east as early as April 311. After Galerius' decease, Maximinus ignored the edict and revived the persecutions one final time. His refusal to follow the trend, however, contributed to his demise. Constantine's and Licinius' mutual support of the Edict of Milan was at least in part designed to fire a warning shot across Maximinus' bow: the other two *Augusti* were now defending Christians, even to the extent of using Maximinus' persecutions as a reason to undertake war against him.

In the end, however, it was Maximinus who brought war to Licinius. Even while the latter had been in the west negotiating with Constantine, Maximinus attempted to steal a move on him by marching across the Bosporus and into Licinius' territory of Thrace. On returning east, Licinius faced his rival head-on in a series of battles beginning near Adrianople (now Edirne, on the border of Turkey and Bulgaria), where Maximinus suffered defeat. Licinius then moved eastward into the Taurus Mountains of Cilicia; here Maximinus was again routed, eventually losing his life at Tarsus (in southern Turkey) late in 313.

The tetrarchy was thus reduced to a dyarchy: two rulers, both *Augusti*, both with equally expansive territories, and both, for the moment at least, allies. The attractions of supremacy were, nevertheless, too great to permit one to abide the other for long. Once again it was the question of co-rulers and successors that brought the issue to a head. In a complicated incident very poorly attested in the sources, Licinius and Constantine became embroiled in a dispute over the appointment of a relative of Constantine's, a certain Bassianus, as *Caesar*. Licinius seems to have suborned Bassianus, who was eventually executed by Constantine. Tensions continued to rise when Licinius began desecrating statues of his colleague along the border between their territories, and eventually full-scale war erupted in 316. Ever the military genius, Constantine defeated his rival at a major battle near the city of Cibalae (Vinkovci in modern Serbia). Nothing daunted, Licinius retreated eastward over the River Save toward Thrace, where he was worsted in two further engagements. A consummate escape artist, Licinius managed to flee after each defeat with just enough troops to hold Constantine at bay and force him to a stalemate. By the end of 316 both sides were weary of war and so opened negotiations, which dragged on into early 317. From these Constantine emerged as clear winner, gaining control of the central Balkans while Licinius, who had during the conflict promoted a co-ruler in the person of a general named Valens, was forced to hand over his new partner for execution. Both sides did, however, win new imperial colleagues, but, unsurprisingly, dynastic ones: Constantine appointed his teenage son Crispus and his infant son Constantine II as *Caesares* and Licinius appointed his one-year-old son Licinius as well.

Although these arrangements bought five more years of peace, troubles began brewing once again in 322 when Licinius refused to advertise Constantine's successful campaigns against the Sarmatians (a trans-Danubian barbarian people) on his coinage. After Constantine encroached on Licinius' territory in 323 to suppress a threat from the Goths (another trans-Danubian people), tensions once again erupted into civil war. Starting out as he did from the central Balkans, Constantine had a much better chance of eliminating Licinius in this war than in the previous one, provided he could gain control of the Propontis, the fast-flowing channel that separated Europe from Asia. With this in mind, he deployed his son Crispus – very much like his father in being a military genius – with a fleet to the Hellespont, the southern opening of the Propontis. Constantine then moved on Licinius, smashed his army at Adrianople and then overcame its remnants with a siege at the city of Byzantium, on the Bosporus. Once Crispus had neutralized Licinius' fleet and gained control of the Propontis, Constantine mounted a crossing into Asia just north of Chalcedon. There Licinius, having retreated in order to regroup his ragged forces, engaged Constantine in a final battle near the city of Chrysopolis on September 18 and was decisively defeated. He managed to escape one final time with a tiny force to Nicomedia where his wife, Constantine's half-sister Constantia, negotiated for his life and the life of their son. Father and son were both stripped of their powers and sent to Thessalonica as prisoners, where they suffered execution shortly thereafter on suspicion of treason. In practice, then, from fall 324 Constantine ruled the entire empire alone.

Final Years

It is only natural that Constantine's concerns and style of rule changed somewhat after he acquired sole power. This trend was apparent even before that point in measures he took to secure the imperial succession of his dynasty. He had already been ruling conjointly with his two sons Crispus and Constantine II since early 317. These had only ever been promoted to *Caesar* and were thus explicitly denied the authority to legislate or conduct imperial affairs without the approval of their father. Shortly after gaining control of Licinius' eastern holdings, Constantine increased the number of *Caesares* to three by adding his third son, Constantius II, to their numbers on November 8, 324. Nothing could have made it clearer that he was no longer following the tetrarchic model of co-rulership, which, as we have seen, deliberately avoided the promotion of dynasts. To be sure, Constantine was building on tetrarchic precedent by creating a college of emperors – even four emperors – who shared power; but the members of this college were exclusively blood relatives, and Constantine regularly emphasized his own superiority within this group by continuing to style himself *Maximus Augustus* in imperial propaganda. His arrangements thus fit much more closely the organic model of shared family rule prevalent in the mid-third century than the sterile schematization of Diocletian. Constantine's desire to formulate a dynastic consortium became even more pronounced in the years that followed: although Crispus was killed in 326 (under circumstances described below), in 333 Constantine appointed his fourth son Constans *Caesar*, and in 335 he appointed two nephews, Dalmatius and Hannibalianus, respectively as *Caesar* and "King of Kings and of the Pontic Peoples." At his death in 337, then, Constantine left a college of five co-rulers, all blood relatives – an unwieldy number and hardly a formula for cooperation, as will become evident below.

Constantine's style of rule also changed in that his abundant stable of dynastic successors provided him with a ready pool of commanders on which to draw for the conduct of military campaigns. Military conflicts did not cease with the elimination of Licinius, not even civil wars. In 334 a civil uprising on the island of Cyprus was led by an official named Calocaerus. Rather than suppress Calocaerus himself, however, Constantine dispatched his half-brother Dalmatius, father of the similarly named *Caesar*, to do the job. And the years after 324 also witnessed a number of foreign wars. Constantine had already engaged the Franks and Alamanni along the Rhine in the first decade of his reign, and the Sarmatians and Goths along the Danube after he moved his capital to Serdica, beginning in 317. After 324, similar conflicts continued, but Constantine began to rely ever more heavily on his sons to do the work of fighting. When in 332 the formidable Goths – the same people who would sack Rome in 410 – attacked the neighboring Sarmatians, Constantine deployed Constantine II to drive them into submission. Two years later, when the Sarmatians themselves fragmented in the wake of a civil war, Constantine II again played a key role in resettling them south of the Danube. Finally, when the Persian Shah Shapur II overran Armenia on the eastern frontier, Constantine deployed his nephew

Hannibalianus and his son Constantius II to contain the problem. Only after negotiations broke down and a major war loomed did Constantine mobilize an expedition which he planned to lead into Persia personally in 337. It was in the process of marching eastward on this campaign that he expired.

A New Capital

Constantine was also able to reshape the empire in the wake of his defeat of Licinius by creating a new and decisively important capital at the site of Byzantium, which he renamed Constantinople after himself. Byzantium sits on a narrow peninsula, approachable by land only from the west, and is thus unusually easy to defend. Its location on the Bosporus rendered it the most important connecting point between Europe and Asia, its access to the sea on three sides made it easy to supply, and its proximity to the Danube gave it strategic importance in an era when Rome's northern frontier demanded growing vigilance. Constantine was thus more than provident to have begun reconstruction of Byzantium as a new capital. To be sure, Rome had long lost its status as the exclusive seat of imperial power. By the mid-third century, emperors were generally compelled to pass most of their reigns away from Rome in their struggle to suppress the persistent incursions of the barbarian peoples on the frontiers. The tetrarchs followed suit by rarely visiting Rome. Indeed, Diocletian and his comrades quite deliberately embellished other provincial cities as capitals, including Antioch, Nicomedia, Sirmium, Thessalonica, Milan, and Constantine's early favorite, Trier. Yet the renaming and reconstruction of Byzantium was different, for it entailed capital investment and the bestowal of honors on a scale previously unheard of.

Constantinople was given a formidable fortification wall on its western side, an imperial palace adjoined to an extended hippodrome, a massive bath complex, a huge circular forum with a monumental column in porphyry, and, not surprisingly, a series of churches, including the mausoleum church of the Holy Apostles where Constantine would be buried. Constantinople was also endowed with an imperial mint, an imperially funded grain supply, and a senate whose members enjoyed privileges like those of the senators of Rome. Little wonder, then, that by the time it was dedicated on May 11, 330, Constantinople was already being referred to as a "Second Rome." It would continue to rival the traditional capital for the next century, and after the sacks of Rome in 410 and 455 and the collapse of western Roman rule in the late fifth century it would supplant Rome as the capital of the empire.

The Byzantines, who referred to themselves as *Romaioi*, were thus made the inheritors of Roman political and cultural traditions which they helped preserve for all future generations. They maintained this role as the continuators of the Roman tradition down to 1453, when Constantinople was finally overrun by the Ottomans.

Building Program

Constantinople was hardly the only city affected by urban renovation and construction under Constantine. Much as one could follow his sweep from west to east in the relentless pursuit of territorial acquisition, one could also trace his building program from west to east as a reflection of the changes in his architectural priorities and the development of his architectural tastes. At his first capital in Trier, Constantine's most enduring structure was a massive new imperial audience chamber, referred to by architects as an *aula palatina* (palace hall) or *basilica* (royal hall). This type of structure, already common in Roman architecture since the republican period, had by late antiquity taken on a distinct form: a large, open, rectangular hall, often with a vaulted ceiling and always with an apse opposite the entrance from which an emperor could hold court. This very form recurs in imperial palaces at a number of tetrarchic "capitals" and villas, making Constantine's Trier basilica stand out not so much for its unique form as for its massive scale. Even more massive was the basilica near the Forum in Rome, which Maxentius had begun and Constantine completed after winning the city from his rival in 312. In contrast with the Trier basilica, which still stands intact thanks to its conversion into a Christian church, the Basilica of Maxentius and Constantine in Rome is in ruins, albeit ruins whose scale and relatively good state of preservation still reflect the magnificence of this three-aisled structure and its elaborately coffered ceilings.

If Constantine was not unique in constructing such imperial basilicas, he certainly is unique in having adapted this architectural form to suit the needs of the growing Christian church. The first evidence of this can be found in Rome, where Constantine authorized the construction of the first known imperially funded cathedral in history, the Lateran Basilica. Begun shortly after his victory at the Milvian Bridge, the Lateran was designed to serve as the cathedral church of the bishop of Rome (the pope), a role it continues to play down to the present.[2] The plan of Constantine's Lateran reflected the form of the basilica: a large rectangular hall culminating in an apse at one end. Its open interior, however, was widened out with two rows of

Constantine

columns on either side that articulate the space into five aisles. This allowed the building to accommodate large crowds of worshippers, for Christians held their ceremonies in interior spaces, in marked contrast with most of their pagan contemporaries whose worship tended to occur outdoors. A similar plan was followed in another of Constantine's Roman churches, the original Constantinian basilica of St Peter, begun in the early 320s on the Vatican hill across the Tiber from the walls of the city. The reason this church sat outside the city was that it was designed to enclose the tomb of St Peter which, like all grave sites, was placed beyond the walls. Almost all of the many other churches built by Constantine at Rome similarly memorialized Christian martyrs and were therefore also located outside the city walls. Furthermore, most of these followed a common architectural pattern, with a floor plan that closely resembled the shape of an ancient circus course. Six such "circiform" churches have been identified in and around Rome, one from archaeological remains discovered less than two decades ago. It is thus strange that this architectural form does not appear to have spread beyond Rome or even beyond the reign of Constantine. Instead, Constantine built a variety of churches in the cities of the empire which reflected a degree of experimentation to be expected when one is inventing a whole new class of buildings. Moving eastward, the church of the Holy Apostles he constructed in Constantinople seems to have joined a circular mausoleum (a common enough form in earlier periods) to a sanctuary in the shape of a cross. This latter, completely new, form would gain common currency in Byzantium. The cathedral he built for the eastern capital of Antioch, by contrast, had an octagonal plan, yet another form that caught on in subsequent religious architecture, especially in the Levant.

An octagonal structure also encased the cave in Bethlehem where Constantine's mother Helena believed she had found the original birthplace of Christ. This discovery occurred in the wake of a journey to Palestine that Helena undertook in the late 320s in hopes of rediscovering the places made sacred by the life of Jesus. Helena's visit to Palestine seems to have been part of a larger project of reclaiming the Holy Land for Christians that Constantine realized in the last decade of his reign. Chief among the places on which he lavished attention were the sites believed to have been the location of Christ's crucifixion and, nearby, his burial. Over these Constantine ordered Macarius, bishop of Jerusalem, to build an elaborate complex with a basilica, much like those he had built in Rome, opening onto a courtyard, which in turn gave way to a circular shrine built to surround the tomb of Christ, the Holy Sepulcher. Prior to Constantine there is very little evidence of Christian pilgrimage to or interest in Palestine. After his reign, by contrast, the Holy Land became a destination for pilgrimage and a locus of architectural patronage by emperor and subject alike. Added to this interest was the discovery – in legend attributed to Helena, but in fact first attested only in the 350s – of what was believed to be the cross on which Christ was crucified. This most sacred of all Christian relics became the focal point of veneration for Christian pilgrims for centuries to come, and soon became an object of fierce contention between Byzantium and its Persian (and in turn Muslim) neighbors. Out of Constantine's interest in the sacred geography of Palestine, then, arose the rivalries for control of the Holy Land which boiled over into the crusades and continue to seethe in world politics even up to the present.

Administrative Measures

Constantine had a lasting impact on administrative and military structures. In this arena, much of the ground had been prepared by his tetrarchic predecessors, who had devised a new and more hierarchically sophisticated system than had existed earlier. The empire had long been divided into provinces, which had grown from about twenty-five in number under Augustus to almost fifty by the third century, mostly through the division of existing provinces into smaller ones. Diocletian continued this trend to the extent that nearly one hundred provinces are attested by the end of his rule. Such provincial "calving" continued under Constantine and throughout the fourth century. These smaller provinces Diocletian had grouped into twelve larger administrative units called "dioceses," over each of which he had placed a new official termed a "vicar" (literally a "deputy"). The vicar had responsibility for financial administration and particularly the collection of taxes under a new system through which Diocletian introduced standardized units for laborers and land. The vicar was, as his name implies, "deputized" to the praetorian prefect, an officer whose post had existed since the days of Augustus and who had served almost as the emperor's vizier, with administrative, judicial, and military responsibilities.

Constantine kept much of this tetrarchic administrative system intact, but he also made important modifications. He relieved the praetorian prefect of military responsibilities and some financial and legislative controls, giving him time to focus instead on the collection and redistribution of taxes. Furthermore, while it had not been uncommon for a single emperor or pair of emperors to have two praetorian prefects at a time, by the time of his death Constantine had multiple prefects (as many as five) working simultaneously, an arrangement which would continue throughout late antiquity. To perform functions that had been shed by the praetorian prefects, Constantine promoted the imperial quaestor, a long-standing office, to chief legal advisor and created the "count of the imperial funds" and the "count of royal estates," charged with the management respectively of the money supply and the vast array of imperial properties. Finally, it is likely though not certain that he instituted the post of "master of the offices," an official charged with a variety of responsibilities, including supervision of the imperial secretariats and of the newly created imperial guards, the *scholae palatinae*, which replaced the old praetorian guards whom Constantine disbanded in 312.

Diocletian had also altered earlier structures by removing military authority from most provincial governors, who had up to that point commanded armies in addition to managing administrative responsibilities. These military roles he reassigned to new officers called *duces* ("dukes") who could focus solely on the military problems of the province or combination of provinces to which they were assigned. By stripping praetorian prefects of their military authority, Constantine created a need for a similar substitute at the very highest echelons of command. He filled this gap with a new kind of officer called the "master of the soldiers." One or two such generals were assigned to each *Augustus* or *Caesar*. They were given command over military divisions which also underwent considerable transformations under the tetrarchs and Constantine. The Roman army had grown rather sclerotic in the relative peace of the second century AD when the traditional legions of around 5,000 men each had settled into massive, permanent, fortified cities along the main frontiers. As troubles began to brew in the third century, emperors had difficulty mobilizing these units without leaving gaps in the frontier defenses. To solve the problem they often detached smaller units from the legions and increasingly turned to the creation of crack mobile regiments not attached to any fixed base. Diocletian had continued this trend and had become especially fond of dispersing smaller detachments into more numerous fortifications spread widely across the frontiers. For his part, Constantine focused primarily on increasing the size and strength of his mobile forces. These he divided into small paired regiments of 1,000 men or fewer and classed as *palatini* (imperial mobile troops) and *comitatenses* (non-imperial mobile troops). The garrison troops earlier dispersed along the borders (often referred to as *limitanei* or "border troops") he kept, but these were now supplemented with his much larger mobile army, which was capable of moving quickly to hotspots or undertaking offensive expeditions. Here again Constantine was not so much innovating as building on successful models already pioneered in the past. In any event, he increased the total size of the imperial army from 400,000 to as many as 600,000 effective troops, more than twice what it had been in the first century AD. To accomplish this Constantine turned increasingly to non-Roman recruits drawn from the very barbarian peoples with whom he regularly fought. Here again, he continued a process begun in earlier centuries, but brought it to new heights. The long-term effects of this reliance on barbarian military manpower, some would argue, were a simultaneous empowerment of barbarian might and a weakening of Roman self-reliance.

Financial Reorganization

Constantine tackled the problem of inflation and currency depreciation that had plagued the empire since the mid-third century. Not surprisingly, Diocletian had attempted the same, introducing reforms to the coinage system and above all promulgating an elaborate Prices Edict in 301 that dictated precise legal limits on the amount one could charge for any of several thousand goods or services. Diocletian's law was in fact so complicated and restrictive that it proved to be a colossal failure and had to be abrogated shortly after it was issued. Constantine's solution to the inflation problem was much less grandiose but ultimately more successful, at least from the perspective of the wealthy ruling class. In 309, faced with a shortage in his gold supplies, Constantine reduced the weight of the standard gold coin (called the *aureus*) from about 5.4 grams to 4.5 grams and renamed the unit the *solidus*. His object was surely not to implement a major economic reform but rather to increase the number of gold coins he could mint out of a limited bullion supply. Ultimately, however, the introduction of the *solidus* had a profound economic impact, primarily because, after creating this smaller gold coin, Constantine transformed it into the primary unit of exchange in his domains. By minting large quantities of *solidi* and insisting that taxes, fees, and fines be paid in this new denomination rather than the silver coin traditional since the third century BC, he introduced a shift from a silver to a gold standard, with lasting effects for centuries to come.

To guarantee the success of this reform, Constantine melted down the treasuries of pagan temples – filled with gold coins and objects – and reminted these as *solidi*; this was at once a deliberate blow to the traditional religions and a huge infusion of gold into the monetary economy. It allowed him to issue his new gold-based currency in large enough quantities to guarantee wide diffusion and give it staying power over time. This in turn created a degree of economic stability that endured through the fourth century in the west and down to the sixth century in the east. However, because a single *solidus* amounted to several months' wages for the average laborer, Constantine's reform also served to concentrate economic power in the hands of the very wealthiest people who could afford to deal in gold. While these enjoyed a new prosperity, the lower classes – the vast majority of the population – witnessed a dramatic deterioration in their buying power as the base metal coins (bronzes) in which they were forced to deal inflated wildly against the new gold standard. Even so, the profound and lasting impact of the *solidus* (pl. *solidi*) can be witnessed even today in the survival of the name in Romance languages, for example in the Italian *soldi* (the generic word for "money") and the French *solde* ("pay").

Religious Reforms

The many structural, administrative, military, and financial reforms introduced by Constantine were thus sweeping, significant, and enduring.

Nevertheless, if there is any one arena where he can be said to have had a crucial impact on world history, it is in the realm of religion. Many of the effects of Constantine's religious policy have already been discussed, for there is no easy way to separate out religion from politics or administration in the ancient world. This is doubly true of his reign, since he regarded himself not just as a ruler but as a religious visionary and the agent of God's plan on earth. Time and again he refers to himself as the "servant of God" in extant documents (Euseb. *Const.* 2. 29. 3, 55. 1, 71. 2; cf. *Tric. Or.* 7. 12), a sobriquet that allowed him to cast himself simultaneously as humble slave and exalted leader.

We have seen that Constantine began privileging the Christian church within months of defeating Maxentius by granting exemptions from mandatory service to clergy, by calling two councils to examine the Donatist dispute, and by pushing for freedom of worship and the restitution of properties confiscated during the Great Persecution. His grant of revenues from imperial domains to Roman and African churches in the months after the Battle of the Milvian Bridge was eventually extended across the empire. This amounted to imperial financing for Christianity, making it into something of an official religion. Constantine took further steps down this road, beginning in the mid-310s, when he granted authority to bishops formally to manumit slaves and to adjudicate civil suits. The combination of these powers and privileges turned bishops into an elite, which, by the end of the fourth century, had come to dominate local government and even to play a significant role in politics at the imperial level.

We have also seen already that, when he reached Rome in 312, Constantine was almost instantly confronted with the problem of the Donatist schism that had pitted rigorist Christians from north Africa against their better-connected though less stalwart counterparts, in a dispute over which group could claim legitimate control of "the church." Similar troubles awaited Constantine when he gained dominion over the eastern empire in 324. This time, however, the issue was not so much the after-effects of the Great Persecution – though this too was at play – as a doctrinal dispute over the very nature of Christ. The see of Alexandria, the powerful Egyptian port city, had broken out in open dispute when a suburban priest named Arius had asserted that Christ had not existed from all eternity but had been created by God the Father and was therefore in some sense subordinate to him. This assertion, whatever its theological merits or demerits, provoked open hostility between Arius and his bishop Alexander and soon spilled over into neighboring provinces in the east. Upon learning of the controversy, Constantine sent a letter scolding both parties for prying into questions he felt were better left unasked; when it became clear that his reprimand alone would not suffice to quell the bickering, he called for a church council to be held in 325. The council convened at the city of Nicaea, just east of the Bosporus, in May that year with about 300 bishops in attendance. Constantine apparently played an active role in its debates and eventually lent his support to a creed that proclaimed Christ both "uncreated" and "of the same nature as God the Father." All present signed on, with the exception of Arius and two bishops, all of whom were exiled. The creed the council produced, now called the Nicene Creed, represents a statement of faith and doctrine that is still recited in Christian churches across the world today. By becoming directly involved in the discussion and playing a decisive role in the council's decisions, Constantine had gone well beyond the role he played in organizing the Donatist councils in the west. Like the Donatist dispute, however, the Arian controversy long outlived Constantine's efforts to suppress it. Indeed, it flared up again even before Constantine's death, having been given new vigor when the emperor opened negotiations with bishops favorable to Arius and eventually recalled Arius himself. Ultimately, Constantine was baptized by the "Arianizing" bishop Eusebius of Nicomedia as he lay on his deathbed.[3]

Constantine's conception of his role in religious history is perhaps nowhere more clearly attested than in the statement he made to a group of bishops, apparently during the Council of Nicaea, that, "You are bishops of those within the Church, but I am perhaps a bishop appointed by God over those outside" (Euseb. *Const.* 4. 24. 1). The precise meaning of these words continues to puzzle scholars, but taken in their broadest sense they imply that he felt some mandate to care for potential Christians, be they his subjects living outside the church or those people, especially Christians, living outside his empire but in need of his protection. Not surprisingly, Constantine acted on both fronts. With regard to those outside the empire, he appears to have played a role in spreading Christianity in the territory of the Goths and certainly in that of the Georgians of the Caucasus region and the Aksumites of Ethiopia. He also undertook his final expedition against the Persians with the ostensible motive of defending those Christians inside Persian and Armenian territory against whom the Shah had begun a persecution. Although his death prevented Constantine from completing this military action, the expedition clearly represented something of a proto-crusade and thereby set the standard for subsequent military action by Christian rulers against those perceived to be suppressing the faith.

With regard to those non-Christians within his realm, Constantine also made efforts to "minister" to them in a fashion that would encourage conversion. He regularly heaped scorn on the Jews in public pronouncements and saddled them with legal restrictions unless they chose to convert. Pagans, whose sacrifices he found particularly repugnant, he also hemmed in by restricting their modes of divination, confiscating their temple treasuries, and even destroying some of their places of worship. There is much dispute about whether Constantine also issued a law forbidding blood sacrifice – the central ritual act of pagan worship. Unfortunately, there is too little evidence to resolve it definitively. We certainly have evidence pointing in this direction, though there is also good evidence that such a law – if it ever existed – was not aggressively enforced. Quite the contrary: Constantine showed favor to many prominent pagans throughout his reign and even gave indications, lasting down to the end of his rule, that he continued to look favorably on certain aspects of pagan belief. Above all, Constantine's fascination with the sun god (Apollo/Sol Invictus) never fully abated, to the extent that he was willing to portray himself on coins in close association with this pagan deity until 325, long after his conversion. Indeed, he was even so bold as to have erected a statue of himself with the attributes of the sun god on a porphyry column in the center of his new forum in Constantinople as late as 330.

Strange though it seems to modern sensibilities, then, Constantine managed simultaneously to project the image of the devout Christian and that of the crypto-pagan down to his dying days. Whether this was motivated by realpolitik in a world where pagans still constituted the vast majority of the population, or by some deeper psychological ambivalence, we can no longer say. Whatever the case, it would not be long before more active measures began to be taken against paganism, and by the end of the fourth century we can fairly say that pagans suffered persecutions on a scale similar to those endured by Christians less than a century earlier, albeit without nearly as much bloodshed.

Succession

We have already seen that, by the time he died, Constantine had appointed no fewer than five successors, each assigned a specific territorial sphere, to replace himself. These included his sons Constantine II, who ruled over Britain, Gaul, and Spain; Constantius II, over the eastern empire; and Constans, over Italy and Africa. In addition, Constantine had appointed his nephew Dalmatius to rule in the Balkans and Hannibalianus to rule Pontus and Armenia, which Constantine had hoped to recapture from Persia. Immediately after he expired on May 22, 337, these arrangements unraveled. The army, apparently in collusion with Constantine's natural successors, executed Dalmatius and Hannibalianus together with most of their living relatives. This purge, which would be remembered bitterly by one of its few survivors, the future emperor Julian, should not perhaps surprise us, given Constantine's own record of family murder earlier in his reign. For reasons still shrouded in mystery, in 326 Constantine had ordered the execution of his own son Crispus, the son of his first wife Minervina, who had played such an important role in his victory over Licinius. Accounts transmitted in the pagan sources indicate that Crispus was murdered on suspicion of attempted rape of the empress Fausta, Constantine's second wife and thus Crispus' stepmother. More likely, Fausta herself dreamed up the charge as a way to eliminate a rival to the succession of her own sons, Constantine II, Constantius II, and Constans. If so, Fausta paid dearly for her misdeed when Constantine turned on her and had her executed as well, by suffocation in an overheated bathchamber. Kin murder was thus not unheard of in Constantine's house. Nor did it cease with the executions of 337. Already in 340 Constantine II began to quarrel with his younger brother and the two eventually wound up in open warfare. In the event, Constans defeated and killed Constantine II. In 350 Constans was himself executed by the usurper Magnentius, an event that left only Constantius II to avenge his murder. In order to be in a position to accomplish this, Constantius II named his cousin Gallus (one of the two survivors of the 337 family massacre) *Caesar*. Magnentius had scarcely been defeated, however, when Constantius ordered Gallus' execution and, shortly thereafter, appointed his half-brother Julian as *Caesar*. When, in 360, Julian had himself proclaimed *Augustus* against Constantius' will, Constantius prepared to make war on his cousin and was prevented from doing so only by his death in 361. Julian lasted only a further two years before being killed in battle in Persia and thus bringing to a close Constantine's dynasty.

At least in part because of the trauma he suffered upon the execution of his immediate family in 337, Julian was quite unwilling to promote his uncle's political and religious program. Upon being proclaimed full *Augustus*, Julian openly declared himself an "apostate" from the Christian faith and began the process of attempting to restore the empire to its pagan roots. Dramatic though his efforts were, Julian's premature death ensured that he did not succeed in turning back the clock on the Christianization of the empire. Indeed, after nearly fifty years of Christian emperors, Julian's apostasy did little more than provoke his Christian successors to accelerate the suppression of pagan religion and thus complete the process of Christianization that Constantine had begun.

Constantine thus actualized his personal religious conversion into a major factor in the history of the Roman empire. Given that his dramatic life story, filled as it was with ambition, intrigue, and uncanny good fortune, worked itself out on the world stage, it is little wonder that he very quickly came to play an important role in legend. We have already seen that the attention he and his mother Helena paid to the Holy Land generated a legend that Helena herself had discovered the true cross on which Christ was crucified. Though we have good evidence that what people believed to have been the "True Cross" had already turned up by the 350s, the first testimony linking its discovery to Helena dates only to the 390s. The credibility of this legend is thus strained. By the fifth century another legend had arisen that Constantine had been a rabid pagan who was miraculously cured of leprosy by Sylvester, pope of Rome, and chose to be baptized early in his reign by his healer. This seems to have been a pious forgery invented to cover up the fact that Constantine's baptism was actually performed at the end of his life at the hands of an Arian. This notwithstanding, the Sylvester legend spawned yet another regarding the so-called "Donations of Constantine," according to which the emperor bestowed on Sylvester and all subsequent popes supreme authority over the Christian church and political control over Rome, Italy, and all the west. Though the "Donations" were used to justify papal hegemony in matters ecclesial and temporal from the eighth century onward, they were proved to be a forgery in the fifteenth century, an epoch which saw the beginning of Constantine's deflation from saint back down to ruler and sometimes even to scoundrel.

The fact is that a figure as monumental and pivotal as Constantine is bound to attract the attention, positive and negative, of subsequent generations. Even today the popular book and feature film *The Da Vinci Code* portrays Constantine as a prominent player in its elaborate, and quite legendary, version of the development of world Christianity. Constantine was, by any measure, a larger-than-life figure whose story has been and will be told and retold by each generation.

Notes

1   *Latin Panegyric* 6. 21. 4–5, best accessed in the translation of Nixon and Rodgers (1994), 248–50.
2   St Peter's at the Vatican became the pope's residence only in the fifteenth century; the Lateran remains the pope's official cathedral as bishop of Rome.

3   Late Roman emperors usually took baptism at the end of their life so as not to encumber their souls with sin – especially through having to order wars and executions – after receiving this expiatory sacrament.

Further Reading

T. D. Barnes, *Constantine and Eusebius* (Cambridge, Mass., 1981)

A. Cameron and S. G. Hall, *Eusebius' Life of Constantine: Introduction, Translation and Commentary* (Oxford, 1999)

N. Lenski (ed.), *The Cambridge Companion to the Age of Constantine* (New York, 2006)

C. E. V. Nixon and B. S. Rodgers, *In Praise of Later Roman Emperors: The Panegyrici Latini, Introduction, Translation and Commentary* (Berkeley, 1994)

P. Weiss, "The Vision of Constantine," *Journal of Roman Archaeology* 16 (2003), 237–59

XII

Justinian

James Allan Evans

Background

About 470, while the emperor Leo I (r. 457–474) ruled in Constantinople, three peasants from upper Macedonia, seeking escape from grinding poverty at home, set out on foot for the capital with only some toasted bread wrapped in their cloaks for food. Two of them, Zimarchus and Dityvistus, had Thracian names, but the third, Justin, bore a Latin name, and his home town was Bederiana (near modern Skopje), where people spoke Latin rather than Greek and the church owed allegiance to Rome. On reaching Constantinople they enrolled in the Excubitors, a new corps of bodyguards which Leo had founded to counterbalance the German troops in the city, whose primary loyalty was to Aspar, the all-powerful Master of the Soldiers. Aspar was himself an Alan, and hence of Iranian rather than German stock but, like the German federates, he adhered to the Arian heresy. While this barred him from the imperial office itself, it did not prevent him from being the power behind the throne. There already was a corps of palatine guards, the Scholarians, which Constantine I had created to replace the old praetorian guard, but over the years they had become more ornamental than effective, and Leo wanted troops in his Excubitors who could fight. Most of the enlistees were Isaurians from Asia Minor, famed both as stonemasons and as fighting men, but while Justin and his companions were not Isaurians, they were ideal recruits: sturdy youths, inured to hardship. We hear no more of Zimarchus and Dityvistus, but Justin would rise through the ranks until he became Count of the Excubitors and eventually emperor, laying the pathway to power for his nephew and adoptive son, Justinian.

Aspar was murdered in 471 and the power of the German federates eliminated in a massacre that gave Leo the sobriquet Makelles, the "butcher." But the bloodbath freed Constantinople from the grip of the barbarian warlords who had already emasculated the western Roman emperors and would terminate the imperial office in the west only five years after Aspar's fall. In history books, 476 is a crucial date, marking the end of an era, but to contemporaries it must have appeared only as another vicissitude to befall the Roman empire, which continued to exist in the hearts and minds of its citizens. The city of Rome had been sacked twice, once in 410 and again in 455, and it was now only a magnificent museum recalling its imperial past, with its sprawling palace on the Palatine hill ready to receive the western emperors, though they had long since deserted it, first for Milan and then, in 402, for Ravenna. But the eastern emperors survived: when the warlord Odoacer dethroned the last western emperor, Romulus Augustus, he dispatched the imperial insignia to Zeno in Constantinople, with the message that the empire needed only one emperor. The status of *rex* ("king") would satisfy him, as well as the ancient title of *patricius*, "patrician," which Constantine I had revived, and which was used thenceforth of a person holding high office at court. Zeno's response was non-committal, and in 490 he encouraged the Ostrogoth Theodoric the Amal to invade Italy and destroy Odoacer. It fell to Zeno's successor, Anastasius, to regularize Theodoric's position, recognizing him as *rex*, and ruler of Italy. Theodoric appropriated one-third of the land to support his Ostrogothic followers, and the Italians who owned the great estates in Italy became a little poorer, but Roman and Goth lived side by side peaceably enough until Justin succeeded Anastasius to the throne.

In the eyes of the Romans in Italy, their legitimate ruler was the eastern emperor, but Theodoric had no reason to be apprehensive about their loyalty, for Anastasius was a heretic, which dampened their commitment. The stumbling block was the Chalcedonian Creed, adopted by the Council of Chalcedon in 451, but hewing close to the dogma of pope Leo the Great. It defined Christ as of two natures, one human and the other divine, remaining separate. This was a creed that was perilously close to the heresy of Nestorius, who taught that Christ possessed both perfect divinity and perfect humanity, which remained separate. Yet it was defended stubbornly by Rome, so much so that it came to be identified with Rome's supremacy. In the prefecture of Oriens, however, stretching from Constantinople to the Euphrates, it was generally detested, though there were islands of support, particularly in Palestine. It was particularly abominated by the Christians whose native tongues were neither Latin nor Greek: in Egypt, the Copts were anti-Chalcedonian, and so were the Syriac-speakers in Oriens. Christianity had given back their identity to these non-Greeks who had been submerged first by Hellenistic culture and then by Rome, and behind their resistance to the Chalcedonian Creed lurked separatist aspirations.

The common label for the anti-Chalcedonians is Monophysites – "single-nature believers" – but it was not applied to them until long after Justinian was dead and, convenient though it may be, it gives the erroneous impression that the anti-Chalcedonians were united with a single credo. They were not. Under Justinian, two main groups emerged. One was the Miaphysites, believers in a single nature; their spokesman was Severus, whom Anastasius had appointed patriarch of Antioch. They never denied Christ's human nature, but, following the doctrine of the great Cyril, patriarch of Alexandria in the early fifth century, they held that the two natures were fused within Christ to form a single divine nature. Their theological descendants form the present-day Monophysite churches in Egypt and the Near East. The second branch was more extreme: called variously Julianists, Phantasiasts, Gaianists, or Aphthartodocetists, they denied Christ's human nature and taught that he was all divine, to such an extent that Christ's flesh was always incorruptible.

The emperor Zeno had attempted to find common ground. He issued an edict of unity – a *Henotikon* – which was composed by the patriarch of Constantinople, Acacius. It was acceptable to most of the Miaphysites, but pope Felix III condemned it, and the "Acacian Schism" that resulted split the churches of Rome and Constantinople from 484 until Justin's accession. Anastasius, who supported the *Henotikon*, had to tread carefully, for the Balkans and the royal city itself were largely Chalcedonian. In 512, a mob almost drove him from his throne when he introduced a coda to the liturgy of Hagia Sophia with a whiff of anti-Chalcedonianism about it, and next year, Vitalian, the commander of the barbarian mercenaries in Thrace and a Chalcedonian partisan, rose in revolt to force him to yield to the pope's non-negotiable demands. Vitalian was finally routed, but when Anastasius died he was still lurking in his native province of Scythia Minor at the Danube river mouth, awaiting another chance to strike.

The Accession of Justin

During a midsummer night of 518, Anastasius died while a storm raged and lightning struck the imperial palace: a fitting end for the heretical old emperor, or so the Chalcedonians thought. The senate, patriarch, and high officials in the government gathered in the palace to choose the next emperor, while outside, in the Hippodrome, a great crowd assembled and waited impatiently. No obvious successor was at hand – Anastasius had a nephew, Hypatius, with a long, thoroughly undistinguished military career, but he was in Antioch, and the stage was set for a power struggle. The chamberlain Amantius, who coveted the throne but as a eunuch did not qualify, backed his domestic, Count Theocritus, and entrusted a sum of money to Justin to make the necessary bribes. Justin spent the money, but the choice fell not upon Theocritus, but on Justin himself, who began his reign by putting Amantius and his clique to death. Now about sixty-five years of age, he appeared in the *kathisma* high above the crowd in the Hippodrome and received the acclamation: "Justinus Augustus, *tu vincas!*" His wife Lupicina, once a slave purchased by Justin, who then freed and married her, took the name Euphemia, which was more suitable for empresses than Lupicina, which was common among whores. Her choice was significant, for it was in the church of St Euphemia outside Chalcedon that the church council had gathered in 451 to adopt the Chalcedonian Creed. Justin and Euphemia both were determined to end the Acacian Schism. Equally determined was Justinian, Justin's sister's son, who was still, at this point, a *candidatus*, one of the forty white-uniformed soldiers attending the emperor. Justin had seen to it that Justinian got the education that he himself lacked, and contemporaries, looking back on Justin's reign, were to consider it merely a prelude to Justinian's. But Justinian's progress to power was not completely smooth.

The Chalcedonians quickly consolidated their victory. A synod met in Constantinople ten days after Anastasius died, and restored the Councils of Nicaea, Constantinople, Ephesus, *and Chalcedon* to the tablets that were read aloud to the congregations during the eucharist. Severus, the anti-Chalcedonian patriarch of Antioch who had been Anastasius' protégé, was deposed and narrowly escaped to Alexandria. Three invitations went from Constantinople to pope Hormisdas, one from John Cappadox, the patriarch, the second from Justin, and a third, more peremptory in tone, from Justinian. Three and a half months later, they reached Rome. The pope declined to come himself, instead dispatching a delegation with instructions not to debate theological quiddities, but accept only capitulation. The patriarch John was unhappy, for the pope demanded abject surrender, but Justin and Euphemia were ready. On Maundy Thursday, March 28, 519, as Justin, the senate, and the clergy looked on, John signed the papal *libellus* rejecting the *Henotikon* that Zeno and Acacius had crafted. Though Justinian was unaware of it, he and his successor Justin II would seek in vain for a replacement.

Hormisdas then demanded the suppression of the anti-Chalcedonians, and Justin did not hesitate. Monks were driven from their monasteries, stylite saints were forced down from their pillars, and bishops in Oriens were ousted from their churches. The persecution was confined to the clergy, but henceforth, if the anti-Chalcedonian laiety were to receive the sacraments, they would have to take them from the hands of Chalcedonian clergy. Justin did not extend the persecution to Egypt, though the pope urged him on, for Egypt was Constantinople's breadbasket, and Justin, old soldier that he was, knew what the consequences of a grain shortage in the capital would be. Egypt became a haven for anti-Chalcedonians. There, at least, their lives were safe.

Vitalian was recalled to the capital, and in the church of St Euphemia he pledged Justin his allegiance. In return he was made a patrician, appointed an army commander in Constantinople, and promised a consulship in 520. He seemed a possible successor to old Justin. But in his consulship year he was assassinated, thus removing a rival to Justinian, who was suspected of having plotted the assassination. Next year, Justinian would inaugurate his own consulship with extravagant celebrations. He was now a *magister militum praesentalis*; within his residence, the Hormisdas Palace, he was building the basilica to Sts Peter and Paul, and requested the pope for relics of Sts Peter, Paul, and Lawrence to add to its sanctity. It would commemorate the end of Acacian Schism and the victory of the Chalcedonians.

Yet he cannot have felt secure. Justin and the former slave who was now his empress remained upstarts in the eyes of the old senatorial elite, and Justinian himself remained an outsider, even though he had the right education. Constantinople was full of monuments celebrating the good old House of Theodosius. Moreover, at this time, one of its richest and most distinguished members, Anicia Juliana, the daughter of a western Roman emperor and a scion of the Theodosian House through her mother, was building a palace church dedicated to St Polyeuctus – the largest and most splendid church in Constantinople until Justinian built Hagia Sophia, which still stands in modern Istanbul. St Polyeuctus was a calculated challenge to the new regime, and it may have been Justinian's determination to create his own coterie, untouched by the disdain of Constantinople's old families like Juliana's, that led him to identify with the Blues, the fans of the charioteers who raced the chariots of the Blue faction.

The factions were the production companies that organized the races in the great Hippodrome that flanked the imperial palace, as well as supplying entertainment in the theaters and in the Hippodrome itself, where dancers and acrobats diverted the crowd between the races. The colors of the racing teams, Red, White, Blue, and Green, came from the Circus Maximus in Rome, though by this time the Reds and Whites no longer had their own stables, but were junior partners of the Blues and Greens. The aficionados sat, each

The Church of Saints Sergius and Bacchus, now the little Ayasofya Mosque in Istanbul. Saints Sergius and Bacchus may have been the church used by the anti-Chalcedian whom the empress Theodora sheltered in the Palace of Hormisdas.

in their own bloc of seats, in the Hippodrome opposite the *kathisma*, where the emperor took his place. It was the Blues and the Greens in particular that attracted Constantinople's young men: they affected a Hunnic appearance, with untrimmed beards and mustaches, pony-tails at the backs of their heads but shaven foreheads, and they wore loose-sleeved garments to accommodate their presumably impressive biceps. Blue and Green gangs made the streets of Constantinople unsafe at night, and Justinian was blamed for encouraging the violence, for when Blues attacked Greens they could count on his support if they got into trouble with the law. The Green response was fierce. Men of property became nervous; some thought it prudent to cancel debts owed to them and others manumitted their slaves.

The historian Procopius, to whom we owe much of what we know about the factions, thought the gang rage was irrational, with no rhyme nor reason. Modern historians have attempted a better explanation. One hypothesis, now generally abandoned, suggested that the Blues represented the Chalcedonians and the Greens the anti-Chalcedonians. That, however, will not do: the anti-Chalcedonian emperor Anastasius was a Red, and the empress Theodora was a perfervid fan of the Blues, though she was anti-Chalcedonian. So the Blues and Greens do not seem to have been divided by theology. Another theory has it that the gangs were the city militia, and it is true that when Antioch was captured by the Persians in 540, it was the Blue and Green gangs that put up the most vigorous defense, continuing to fight even after the regular army had fled. However, they were an ad hoc militia, fighting without armor and using stones and sticks as weapons. The best explanation is that given by Edward Gibbon and recently restated by Alan Cameron: these gang members were semi-employed young men coping with the testosterone rush of youth, easily politicized but without any consistent political or theological policies.

Justin seems to have been unaware of how extensive the street violence was. Procopius (*Anek.* 8. 1–6) calls him a stupid donkey, blind to the misdeeds of Justinian. But eventually the hooligans went too far, and murdered a respectable citizen within Hagia Sophia itself. Justinian was ill, and the palatine officials seized the chance to inform Justin, who responded by ordering the prefect of the city to restore order; the prefect in turn acted vigorously, with an even hand. When Justinian recovered he tried to have the prefect put to death, but the best he could do was to exile him to Jerusalem, and after 523 the street violence abated. When Justinian became co-emperor with Justin in 527, they issued a decree mandating law and order throughout the cities of the empire; street violence was to be suppressed whether those responsible were Blues or Greens. But Justinian remained a Blue.

Theodora

It was during this period, while street violence was peaking, that Justinian met the woman who became his wife and partner in power. For Theodora's early career we are dependent on Procopius of Caesarea, who produced an unpublished diatribe at the same time as he was finishing his *History of Justinian's Wars*, putting in it all the scandal and venom that he did not dare publish. In the early seventeenth century a copy turned up in the Vatican library, and though there were doubts about its authenticity – its portrayal of Theodora fitted the papacy's opinion of her almost too well – nowadays it is generally accepted as a genuine work of Procopius, reporting scandal with a basis in fact, even if not all the details are true.

Theodora was the second daughter of the bearkeeper for the Green faction, who tended the bears used for acrobatic acts and wild-beast fights. He died suddenly, leaving three children, Comito, Theodora, and Anastasia. His widow, a woman of resource, remarried immediately, hoping that the Green faction would make her new husband its bearkeeper; but it was the prerogative of the head ballet dancer of the faction to make the choice, and he selected another candidate who had given him a generous bribe. Theodora's little family was left destitute. Her mother dressed her daughters as suppliants and, when races were next held in the Hippodrome, she had them kneel before the Green section of the bleachers and beg for mercy. But the Greens had none to give. However, the Blues had just lost their bearkeeper too, and they took pity on the three young girls and employed their stepfather.

As soon as they were old enough, the widow put her daughters on the stage. She had little choice, for she herself belonged to the despised *demi-monde* of the theater. Actresses were held in such contempt that the clergy refused them the sacraments unless they were on the point of death, and even then priests were instructed to make certain that an actress who begged for the last rites really was on the point of dying, for if she recovered, she could never return to the stage. Actresses and the daughters of actresses could not abandon their profession except for the holy life of a nunnery, for the shows had to go on, and the masses had to be amused. Probably Theodora's mother put her daughters on the stage because she had been a *mima* – a mime actress – herself.

Comito rapidly became a star, and Theodora made her debut as her elder sister's attendant; then, once she was old enough, she became a *mima* herself. Procopius claims that she had no talent, that she could neither dance nor play a musical instrument, but had a quick wit, and that her interpretation of the myth of Leda and the Swan was notorious. Like most actresses, she was a part-time prostitute, and gave birth to an illegitimate daughter whose name is lost, as well as, according to gossip (which is likely untrue) a son. Eventually she escaped: an official named Hecebolus took her with him when he went to Cyrenaica as governor, but soon tired of her and left her to find her own way home. She reached Alexandria, where the city was full of anti-Chalcedonian refugees fleeing from Justin's persecution, and there, it seems, she was converted. One tradition has it that she met the patriarch of Alexandria, Timothy III; certainly she later regarded him as her spiritual father. She was not baptized, but she may have become a catechumen. At any rate, she became a convinced anti-Chalcedonian and remained one for the rest of her life.

From Alexandria she went to Antioch, where she met a dancer with the Blue faction, Macedonia, who lived a double life: she not only performed on the stage, but was a secret agent for Justinian as well (*Anek.* 12. 28–32). Finding Theodora downcast and depressed, she tried to comfort her, predicting that her fortune would change. Then Theodora remembered that only recently she had had a dream that she would come to Constantinople and there marry the Lord of the Demons, who would supply her with untold wealth. This story bears the stamp of Theodora's denigrators, but there is probably a germ of truth to it. It seems likely that Macedonia recruited Theodora into Justinian's secret service, and that is how Justinian first met her.

There are other, more flattering stories about Theodora's early career, for she is still revered in the Monophysite churches of the Near East which vigorously reject Procopius' tale. In any case, by 521 Justinian and she were living in the Palace of Hormisdas close by the Imperial Palace – when Justinian became emperor, he joined the two with a covered passageway – and Theodora was already known as supporter of the anti-Chalcedonian cause. At Justinian's behest, Justin made her a patrician. But the empress Euphemia disapproved. She objected strenuously to a marriage between Justinian and Theodora, with her anti-Chalcedonian beliefs and her disreputable background – and a bastard daughter into the bargain! But Euphemia died about 523, and without her Justin was malleable.

There was still a law to be circumvented, for Constantine I had banned marriage between actresses and senators. But Justin smoothed the way with an edict that allowed repentant actresses to marry whomsoever they wished, and made it unnecessary for actresses with patrician rank to get the emperor's approval (*Cod. Just.* 5. 4. 23). The edict must date to 524, and the marriage of Justinian and Theodora followed shortly thereafter.

The aged Justin's health was failing. An old wound was troubling him, and, not without reluctance, he made Justinian co-emperor on April 1, 527, crowning him and Theodora in the Great Palace before presenting them in the Hippodrome for the populace to acclaim. Four months later Justin died, and Justinian became sole emperor.

The Early Years in Power: The Age of Optimism

The first decade of Justinian's reign was a period of extraordinary achievement. Less than six months after his accession, on February 15, 528, he initiated his great codification of the law, followed by the *Digest* and the *Institutes*, a textbook for law students, which was followed by a second edition of the *Codex*. Sixteenth-century legal scholars would designate the whole achievement the *Corpus Iuris Civilis*, which is its title today.

Having reformed and codified the law, Justinian turned next to reorganizing the administration. On the eastern frontier the war with Persia, which had broken out again in 525, ended in a draw, and in 533 the two evenly matched empires entered upon a peace which was intended to last for ever. Next year, Justinian's great general Belisarius led an expeditionary force against the Vandal kingdom in Africa and overthrew it; then, in 536, he began the conquest of the Ostrogothic kingdom. The Great Palace in Constantinople was in a buoyant mood in 536: Justinian voiced a hope in one of his laws that God would let him recover the lands which the indolence of former emperors had let slip away. (*Nov.* 30. 11. 2). Rome fell to Belisarius without a blow before the year's end, thanks to the cooperation – or, from the Gothic perspective, the treachery – of pope Silverius. The fall of Rome was followed by a great siege that lasted more than a year, but it ended in defeat for the Goths, and in 540 Belisarius entered Ravenna.

The triumphs were mingled with setbacks. In January 533, rioting in Constantinople almost forced Justinian and Theodora to leave the Great Palace in flight. The destruction of the Vandal kingdom proved to be only the first step in the pacification of Libya. The Berbers were restive, and not until 547 did the Byzantines, led by an able general and administrator, John Troglita, defeat the insurgents. The year 540, when Belisarius returned from Italy, bringing with him the Gothic king as a prisoner, also saw a foray of Huns and Sclaveni from across the Danube River almost reaching Constantinople, spreading panic among the citizens who cowered behind the great Theodosian Walls which still stand in Istanbul. In the east, the shah of Persia, Khusro, broke the "Endless Peace" after only seven years and invaded the provinces of Oriens, destroying the city of Antioch. Imperial prestige in the east was shattered.

Nor was there theological peace. Justinian and Theodora had tried hard to find a new *Henotikon* acceptable to Chalcedonian and anti-Chalcedonian alike, and Theodora had one almost within her grasp, when it was shattered by the obduracy of pope Agapetus. Agapetus would win Dante's praise in his *Paradiso* for his sanctified intransigence, but Christendom would never be so close to consensus again.

Then, in 541, bubonic plague broke out in Alexandria and next year it reached Constantinople. The empire faced a future with diminished taxation revenues and undiminished expenses. But the buoyant decade of the 530s is worth a closer look, for it is the period when Justinian hoped to achieve great things and, to some extent, succeeded.

The Codification of the Law

The first step was to set up a commission chaired by John the Cappadocian to draw up a new code. John acted efficiently; a year later the first edition of the code appeared. Then in 530 another commission, chaired by Tribonian, a brilliant, if corrupt, jurist, set to work on the *Digest* (in Greek, the *Pandects*), which collected and organized the legal opinions of past Roman jurists. This was a prodigious work: 1,528 books were read and excerpted, and the result was a monument to Roman juridical talent. It was published at the end of 533, and the same year saw the appearance of the *Institutes*, a manual for the instruction of lawyers. By now it was clear that the *Codex Justinianus* was already outdated, and a new edition was produced. This is the edition that we have; the first edition produced under John the Cappadocian's supervision is no longer extant.

Legal education was reformed. The *Institutes* was not merely a textbook; it had the force of law and could be cited in the courts. Legal education was concentrated in Beirut and Constantinople; the law schools in Alexandria, Caesarea, and Athens were closed, and after Beirut was devastated by an earthquake in 550, the school there never reopened. The curriculum was also reformed: students henceforth completed five years of study before they might purchase their togas and plead cases in court. The importance of Latin faded. Legal education had been its last stronghold in the eastern empire; it was the language of the *Corpus*, and Beirut, which had been founded by Augustus as a colony for his veterans, still retained a reputation for elegant Latin. But Greek was the language of the streets, and Justinian's laws issued after 535 – his *Novellae Constitutiones* – were written in Greek unless they were addressed to Latin-speaking subjects in Italy or Africa.

Justinian planned to make a collection of his new laws – his *Novels* – but never did. An unofficial collection in Latin appeared, dating to shortly after 555, for it contains no laws later than that date. The fullest collection appeared in the reign of the emperor Tiberius II (578–82). The third collection is the so-called *Authenticum*, with 134 *Novels*, the latest of which dates to 556. It contains literal Latin translations of the original Greek texts, and was probably made for use in Italy when the empire was trying to restore civil society there after the havoc of the Gothic War. The *Code*, the *Digest*, the *Institutes*, and the *Novels* make up the corpus of Justinian's laws, and they are a magnificent salute to the Roman genius for jurisprudence.

The Suppression of the Heterodox

In Justinian's mind the division between the orthodox and the heterodox was a division between right and wrong. Heterodox sects included the Hellenes, as the pagans were called, Jews, Samaritans, and various Christian heretical groups such as the Montanists, Julianists, Ophites and Arians. The law did not treat all of them equally: Judaism was still a "licenced religion" and Justinian left its legal position unchanged – in Palestine, archaeology shows that there was a synagogue-building boom during his reign. But in Justinian's mind, Judaism was as much a heresy as Arianism, and the Jewish communities were wary. Samaritanism, like Judaism, enjoyed a protected status, but the Samaritans were loved by neither the Christians nor the Jews. A Samaritan revolt in 529 was suppressed without mercy: Procopius writes that most of the farmers around his home city of Caesarea in Palestine were Samaritans before the revolt, and afterwards so many of them had been killed or enslaved that their farms were left untilled and their taxes had to be paid by their Christian neighbors (*Anek.* 11. 30). But it was the pagans who were given no quarter.

Justinian's first law (*Cod. Just.* 1. 5) against the heterodox dates to the first year of his reign, and he followed it two years later with a sweeping edict against the pagans, outlawing sacrifice again, and restating and strengthening the various penalties prescribed for them. In that year Justinian's anti-pagan zeal escalated into a witch-hunt (Malalas, 18. 42, 47), and another outburst of persecution in 545–6 swept another throng of teachers, lawyers, and doctors into its net. Pagans were still to be found, however, especially in the provinces. In 542, while plague was raging in Constantinople, Justinian sent John of Ephesus, anti-Chalcedonian though he was, to the provinces of Asia, Caria, Lydia, and Phrygia in Asia Minor to weed out the Hellenes, and John claimed to have destroyed numerous temples, idols, altars, and sacred trees, and to have built ninety-six churches.

One casualty of Justinian's anti-pagan zeal was the Neo-Platonic Academy in Athens. John Malalas (18. 47) is our only source for the closure of the Academy, and he reports merely that, in 529, Justinian sent to Athens a decree forbidding non-Christians to teach philosophy or interpret the law. The Neo-Platonic Academy's connection with Plato's Academy was tenuous, but it did represent a link with pagan intellectual tradition, and the year 529 has acquired symbolic status as marking the end of the classical intellectual tradition. The ruins of a house (Building Chi) on the south slope of the Acropolis has been identified as the "House of Proclus," where the "diadoch," that is, the head of the Academy, lived, and it shows some evidence of hasty abandonment. Yet contemporary writers were curiously silent about the closure. The historian Agathias (2. 30. 3–4), who continued Procopius' work, tells a tale of how seven philosophers, among them Damascius, the last diadoch, visited the shah of Persia, for they had heard that he was a philosopher king. They were soon disillusioned, and returned. Agathias fails to connect this tale with the closure of the Academy; nevertheless his report has given rise to a tale that the philosophers ousted from Athens traveled to Persia, hoping to find a less chilly climate there, and were disappointed. The evidence for the closure of the Academy is slender; yet it is not unlikely that it faded out when 'Building Chi' was abandoned, for it is hard to believe that Justinian would overlook this intellectual center of paganism, when elsewhere pagans were persecuted. At any rate, by midcentury Athens had lost its last remaining export, philosophy, and lapsed into obscurity.

Peace with Persia

On Justinian's eastern frontier, the Roman and Persian empires faced each other. The rivalry between the two went back to the third century, when the Persian Sassanid dynasty replaced the Parthian Arsacids, and neither was strong enough to gain a decisive victory. In 525 war broke out again, and two brilliant young army officers made their appearance: Sittas, who married Theodora's sister, Comito, and Belisarius, who married Antonina, Theodora's crony and another who had risen from the *demi-monde* of the theater. They first appear leading two raids into the Persian-controlled sector of Armenia. On the second they suffered defeat, but nonetheless Belisarius was appointed commander of the troops in Dara, a great fortress on the Euphrates which Anastasius had built in violation of an old treaty. Belisarius' *assessor* (legal secretary) was Procopius, from Caesarea in Palestine, to whom we owe most of our information, both good and bad, about Belisarius and his wife. Sittas was equally capable, and his connections at court were impeccable, but he lacked a press agent like Procopius, and was killed in a skirmish in 538 before he made his mark on history.

In 530 Belisarius defeated a much larger Persian force outside the walls of Dara: the first time in 109 years that a Roman army had won a victory over the Persians. In the same year, the Master of Soldiers in Illyricum, Mundo, a Gepid prince who had cast his lot with Justinian, defeated Bulgar marauders in the Balkans, and Justinian marked both victories by erecting an equestrian statue of himself in the Hippodrome. Belisarius' reputation soared. But next year he almost lost it, for he led an army to defeat at Callinicum on the Euphrates, at least partly – though Procopius does his best to exculpate him – through his own mismanagement. He was recalled to Constantinople. Mundo took over his command temporarily, and Sittas took charge of the overall defense of the eastern frontier. However, Belisarius' luck held; when the *Nika* riots broke out next year, he was in Constantinople – whereas Sittas was not – and it was the loyalty of his bodyguard that saved Justinian's regime.

The *Nika* Riots

According to two sources (Theophanes, 181. 32–184. 2; *Easter Chronicle* R776, p. 620), the *Nika* riots were prefaced on Sunday, January 11, 532 by a remarkable dialogue in the Hippodrome between the emperor in the *kathisma*, speaking through a herald trained to project his voice, and the Greens in their bloc of seats, uttering their grievances in a rhythmic chant led by a precentor. The Greens protested that Kalopodius the *spatharius*, or guard of the imperial bedchamber, was doing them wrong. We cannot identify him, but a eunuch from Armenia, Narses, was *spatharius* at this time, and "Kalopodius" ("pretty-foot") might have been his nickname. The Greens cried out: "Would that Sabbatius had never been born, to have a son who is a murderer!" (Flavius Petrus Sabbatius was Justinian's father.) A murder had been committed, the twenty-sixth in a string of killings, and the Greens believed that Justinian was implicated. The Blues in their seats now rose to Justinian's defense. "It is you who are the only murderers in the Hippodrome!" they told the Greens. The dialogue ended with the Greens walking out, cursing the bones of the Hippodrome patrons.

That evening the city prefect, Eudaimon, who was holding some gangsters, both Greens and Blues, ordered the execution of seven who had been convicted of murder. But the executioner was incompetent; his scaffold broke and two convicts, a Blue and a Green, tumbled to the earth, still alive. Then from the nearby monastery of St Konon the monks rushed out, rescued the convicts, and took them for asylum into the church of St Lawrence. The prefect put the church under guard.

At the races again the following Tuesday, Justinian, high in his loge, faced the Blues and Greens, both imploring him to show mercy. But he remained silent as one race followed another – twenty-five were held in a day. Then, at the twenty-second race, the Blues and Greens cried in unison: "Long live the merciful Blues and Greens!" They had united to become a mob, with a watchword, "*Nika!*" – "Conquer!" The riots had begun.

That evening, the mob demonstrated outside the city prefect's headquarters and, getting no response, killed the guards, released the prisoners who were there, and set the building ablaze. The fire spread down the main street to the church of Hagia Sophia and burned it to the ground. Justinian's first reaction was to appease; he tried to hold races again but the mob was out of control, and the center of the city, including the monumental entrance to the imperial palace known as the "Brazen House," was now in flames. The mob demanded the dismissal of three unpopular ministers: Eudaimon, the urban prefect;

Tribonian, the quaestor of the sacred palace, who was working on the *Digest* at this time; and the praetorian prefect of diocese of Oriens, John the Cappadocian. Justinian promptly replaced them with men who had the respect of the senators, and his choice showed where he thought the riot was getting its support. The old Constantinople elite disliked Justinian, with his appetite for reforms, and hated Theodora, the former striptease *artiste* who now insisted that senators prostrate themselves before her as well as before Justinian when they were granted audiences. But Justinian's appeasement only fed the appetites of the rioters. They now wanted to overthrow the regime.

The situation was critical. Justinian could not count on the loyalty of the troops in the capital, and the palatine guard was more ornamental than effective. But Belisarius had his bucellarii, a corps of elite soldiers attendant on a general, and supported by him even though they were regular troops. They attempted a sortie from the palace, but in the narrow streets of Constantinople they were no match for the rioters. The mob now was determined to be rid of Justinian. On Thursday evening, January 15, it rushed to the palace of Probus, a nephew of the old emperor Anastasius, determined to make him emperor, only to find that Probus had prudently withdrawn from the city; so it burned his palace. Fires continued to rage for the next two days, and Justinian, fearing the senators who had taken refuge in the imperial palace with him, ordered them to return to their own mansions and defend them. Two of them, Hypatius and Pompeius, were nephews of Anastasius, and they begged to stay. But Justinian, now in a state of paranoia, was obdurate.

On Sunday, Justinian appeared in the imperial loge and tried to appease the mob in the Hippodrome. There were a few cheers, for Narses had been seeding the crowd with bribes, but they were drowned out, and Justinian retreated. By now the mob had learned that Hypatius was at home, and it determined to crown him. He was dragged to the Oval Forum where, at the foot of Constantine's Column, a golden chain was placed on his head. At first Hypatius was reluctant, but then a rumor spread that Justinian had fled, and he began to feel the lure of the imperial purple. He let himself be taken to the Hippodrome and displayed in the imperial loge to the cheering crowd below.

Procopius (*Wars* 1. 24, 25–38) describes this moment of crisis with all the literary skill he can muster. In the senate house facing the Oval Forum, a senator named Origines, otherwise unknown, urged caution. In the imperial palace, there was panic. Justinian's advisors, including Belisarius, John the Cappadocian, and Mundo, who had paused at Constantinople on his way to a new posting in Illyricum and commanded a corps of Herulians, counseled flight, and Justinian was ready to go. Then Theodora arose, full of steely resolve. The others could leave, she said. But as for herself, she would not live to hear herself no longer being addressed as empress, for she liked the old proverb, that kingship made a good winding sheet.

Theodora's great scene was a product of Procopius' imagination, but this much is no doubt true: It was Theodora's courage that saved the day. Justinian ordered Belisarius to lead his troops along the passageway connecting the palace with the *kathisma*, and take Hypatius from the rear. But the guardsmen at the doorway into the loge refused Belisarius entry and he returned to the emperor, who told him to try again, taking his men across the smoldering ashes of the "Brazen House" and into the *kathisma* by an outside entrance. There, too, he was blocked; so he ordered his troops to draw their swords and assault the mob in the Hippodrome. Mundo, meanwhile, entered the Hippodrome by the gateway through which smashed chariots and the cadavers of their horses and charioteers were removed, and his Herulians fell gleefully upon the mob. Estimates of the dead ranged from 10,000 to 30,000.

Law and order was restored. Anastasius' nephews, Hypatius and Pompeius, were put to death, and their bodies cast into the sea, but when they were washed ashore Justinian allowed them to be buried in the family mausoleum. Later, Theodora would find a husband for her illegitimate daughter in Anastasius' family. The power of the old senatorial elite that despised Justinian and Theodora was broken, but Justinian had no wish for vengeance. The city core of Constantinople had been burned out, but the fire had cleared the area for Justinian's building program: only forty-five days after the *Nika* riots, the construction of the great domed church of Hagia Sophia began on the site of the incinerated basilica that Theodosius II had built. The levers of power were now in Justinian's confident hands.

The Reconquest

The *Nika* riots had proved Belisarius' loyalty, and he was the natural choice to lead the offensive against the Vandal kingdom the next year. There was little enthusiasm for it in the emperor's court, for many recalled the ill-fated armada sent against the Vandals in Africa sixty years earlier, commanded by the brother-in-law of the emperor Leo. Had it not been for his yearning to succor the Catholics in Africa, whom the Vandals, themselves Arians, were persecuting, Justinian might not have ventured on the expedition. As it was, he took no great risk: Belisarius' expeditionary force numbered only about 18,000 men. Three years later, when he invaded Italy, his army was just half that.

Belisarius' convoy of troop transports and fast warships reached Africa before the Vandals knew of their approach. The Vandal kingdom fell after two battles: the first was a victory at the Tenth Milestone outside Carthage, which the Byzantines entered the following day. Three months later Belisarius won another victory, and the Vandal king, Gelimer, fled to the Berbers, or Moors, as the Byzantines called them, in Numidia: there the Byzantines beleaguered him on a mountaintop for three months that would prove terrible for Gelimer, who was unused to the hardships of a siege. Finally he surrendered.

Belisarius returned to a hero's welcome in Constantinople, bringing with him Vandal prisoners, including Gelimer, and the treasures of the kingdom, though he surreptitiously held back a portion for himself. In his honor, Justinian revived the ancient Roman ceremonial of the triumph, adapted to a Christian empire, and appointed him consul for 535. Though the Byzantines were only dimly aware of it, Africa was not pacified; the Vandal kingdom had collapsed, but now the Byzantines had to deal with the Berbers.

Justinian had good grounds for attacking the Ostrogothic kingdom in Italy, for the Ostrogothic king, Theodahad, had killed Amalasuntha, the daughter of Theodoric, and Italy seemed ready to fall like a ripe apple into Justinian's hands. Belisarius conquered Sicily easily in 535, and the next year he crossed the Strait of Messina and moved north. Naples stood siege briefly, but Theodahad sent no help, and in disgust the Goths replaced him with a more warlike leader, Witigis. But the Franks, encouraged by Justinian, were threatening to invade Italy from the north, and Witigis thought that mollifying them was of more immediate importance than the defense of Rome. So, taking an oath of allegiance from pope Silverius, he left a small garrison in the city and hurried north, both to placate the Franks and to legitimate his own kingship by marrying Amalasuntha's daughter, the last of the Amals. When Belisarius approached, the Romans, following the counsel of the pope, opened the city gates.

Witigis realized he had erred. He returned to Rome and laid it under siege. Belisarius had only 5,000 troops, but for more than a year he defended Rome, and eventually, in mid-March 538, the Goths gave up. But the war went on, the devastation of Italy continued, and when Belisarius eventually took Ravenna, treachery was his collaborator: he allowed the Goths to believe that if they surrendered Ravenna, he would cast off his allegiance to Justinian and revive the western Roman empire with himself as emperor, ruling in partnership with the Goths. The Goths yielded Ravenna as agreed; but shortly afterwards Belisarius sailed off for Constantinople with the royal treasury and the Gothic royal family. The Goths realized bitterly that they had been gulled, and looked for a new king.

Belisarius found the court in crisis and his reception was chilly. Only recently a barbarian raid from across the Danube had menaced Constantinople itself. The shah of Persia had invaded the eastern provinces, taking and destroying Antioch. The Gothic treasure that Belisarius brought was welcome, but Justinian would have been content to allow the Goths a kingdom north of the Po River, where it would serve as a buffer for central Italy. Belisarius, feeling underappreciated, was dispatched to the eastern frontier, to hold Persia in check.

Then bubonic plague broke out in Egypt in 541, reaching Constantinople the next year. We have a description of it, modeled on Thucydides, by Procopius (*BP* 2. 22. 1–39) and another by John of Ephesus which survives in the *Chronicle of Zuqnin* (*anno* 855, Seleucid era). The bacillus causing plague is borne by fleas carried by rodents; the black rat, now almost extinct, is blamed for the Black Death of the mid-fourteenth century and may also have been the carrier for the Justinianic plague, but there is no proof of this. Justinian's was an age when men believed that devils walked the streets, disguised as humans, fixing their intended victims with hard stares. There were frequent reports of bronze boats crewed by headless creatures moving swiftly over the sea at night toward a new port, spreading pestilence. Justinian himself fell ill, and though he recovered, these were anxious times: when Theodora learned that Belisarius and an officer on his staff had been discussing the succession, she ordered them back to Constantinople. Belisarius' property was confiscated and he feared for his life. Finally she relented out of consideration for Antonina, and Justinian yielded to the general's request to return to Italy, all the more readily because he offered to recruit the necessary forces himself.

When Belisarius reached Ravenna, he found the situation worse than he imagined. The Goths had chosen a new king, Totila (Baduila, on his coins) who had swiftly driven the Byzantine officers to take refuge in fortified towns. For the next four years, Belisarius would struggle to maintain his position in Italy while Justinian remained unmoved by his pleas for reinforcements. Finally, he sent his wife Antonina back to Constantinople to try to get Theodora's support, for Justinian would listen to his wife. But before Antonina reached the capital, Theodora died, and Antonina had nowhere to turn. She asked Justinian to recall Belisarius, and he agreed. Justinian could find no fresh troops for him, yet in 552 he could dispatch an army to Spain, led by Liberius, a civil servant over eighty years old, to support a pretender to the throne in the Visigothic kingdom, thus carving out a Spanish province for the empire. Eventually Justinian dispatched Narses to Italy, with more than adequate troops, and in 552 this force smashed an outnumbered Gothic army at a place called Busta Gallorum. Some mopping up remained to be done, but when Justinian died in 565 Italy was impoverished but secure. Three years later, the Lombards invaded.

Theological Stalemate

Justinian had supported Justin's pro-Chalcedonian policy; yet when he married Theodora, he was making an anti-Chalcedonian his partner. Contemporaries marveled: were they disagreeing by design? Or was there a sinister motive? Once Justinian and Theodora became emperor and empress and moved into the Great Palace, Theodora transformed their previous residence, the Hormisdas Palace, into a refuge for displaced anti-Chalcedonian holy men; and not only did Justinian allow it, he sometimes accompanied her on her regular visits to receive the blessings of her anti-Chalcedonian saints. No doubt it was at her urging that the persecution was suddenly relaxed about 531, and Justinian turned instead to dialogue. Chalcedonian and anti-Chalcedonian leaders, monks and churchmen alike, were summoned to the Hormisdas Palace for conversations. Severus, the exiled patriarch of Antioch who was the acknowledged leader of the Miaphysites, was invited, but declined; yet many anti-Chalcedonians did come, leaving the desert places where they had found refuge. The conversations lasted a year and culminated in an inconclusive three-day debate. For the Chalcedonians, one of the six bishops who spoke was Anthimus from the see of Trebizond, though he preferred to live in Constantinople, and for some reason, Theodora noticed him. When Epiphanius, the patriarch of Constantinople, died, she saw to it that he was chosen as his successor.

Then Severus arrived from Alexandria. He had refused Justinian's invitation at first, but now he braved a midwinter voyage to come to Constantinople. There was a reason: the pope of Alexandria, Timothy III, was on his deathbed and they faced the issue of who his successor would be. Severus' Miaphysitism had been losing ground to the Aphthartodocetism taught by Severus' erstwhile friend Julian of Halicarnassus, who had also found refuge from persecution in Egypt. Severus foresaw a struggle ahead for the soul of Egyptian Christianity. Once he reached Constantinople, Theodora arranged a meeting between him and Anthimus and the two men discovered that there was little difference between their doctrines. They agreed upon a common creed.

The rift between east and west, between Chalcedonian and anti-Chalcedonian, seemed on the verge of healing. To be sure, the patriarch of Antioch was appalled, and so were the Chalcedonian monasteries in Palestine, but the patriarch of Jerusalem was flexible. Everything depended on Rome.

There, pope John II had only recently died, and his successor was a scion of a Roman noble family, Agapetus, whose views were unknown. But not for long. Belisarius' army was poised to invade Italy, and king Theodahad sent Agapetus to Constantinople to intercede. Once there, Agapetus wasted little time pleading for the Ostrogothic king. Instead he destroyed the covenant of Severus and Anthimus.

At first Justinian blustered and threatened, but Agapetus remained unafraid, and at last, after Anthimus refused to admit the two natures of Christ as defined at Chalcedon, Justinian abandoned him. Severus escaped to Egypt with Theodora's help. Anthimus disappeared. Justinian thought that Theodora was keeping him concealed in a "safe house" somewhere, and did not press the search for him, but even he must have been surprised when, after her death, Anthimus emerged from the women's quarters in the Great Palace, where Theodora had kept him hidden away from prying male eyes. Yet Justinian greeted him respectfully and did him no harm.

Agapetus then used the few days left to him cleansing Constantinople of anti-Chalcedonians. But the tongue with which he had excoriated Anthimus and Severus intumesced until it dangled out of his mouth. Attempts to lance the swelling failed, and in April 536 he died in agony. The way was clear for a new pontiff, and the papal nuncio in Constantinople, Vigilius, was eager for the office.

In Alexandria, too, the death of pope Timothy III, whom Theodora used to call her spiritual father, unleashed an outburst of religious passion. Theodora's chamberlain, who was on the spot when Timothy died, saw to it that the dying pope's secretary, Theodosius, was chosen as his successor, but at his enthronement an Aphthartodocetist mob burst into the cathedral, forcing Theodosius to flee for his life, and installed a deacon named Gaianus instead. Theodora, with the acquiescence of Justinian (who was secretly pleased to learn that the anti-Chalcedonians were quarreling among themselves), sent Narses with a force of 6,000 to dislodge Gaianus and restore Theodosius. But the Gaianists fought back, and the street battles between them and Narses' troops continued until autumn 536, when Narses gave up and returned to Constantinople with Theodosius. During this period, Belisarius with only 5,000 troops was defending Rome, which was under siege by a vastly greater army of Goths.

The Roman papacy was a greater prize. Vigilius agreed with Theodora to lift the excommunication of Anthimus if she helped him become pope, and set out for Rome with great expectations. But when he arrived, he found a pope already chosen: Silverius, the son of the pope Hormisdas with whom Justin had negotiated the end of the Acacian Schism. Yet Theodora was not to be thwarted. Rome was now occupied by Belisarius' army, and his wife, Antonina, was one of Theodora's agents. Antonina trumped up a charge of treason against Silverius, and he was hustled out of Rome to die of starvation in exile. Vigilius took over.

But once Vigilius held the papacy, he reneged. Rome's opposition to any compromise on the Chalcedonian Creed was too entrenched for Vigilius to modify it. He evaded and equivocated, but, in the end, Theodora accepted the bitter truth that Vigilius would not annul the excommunication of Anthimus, who remained hidden in the women's quarters of the Great Palace.

The "Three Chapters" Controversy

Meanwhile Justinian wore the nights away discussing the fine points of theology with his coterie of favorite religious scholars. One of these, Theodore Askidas, suggested Justinian's next move to narrow the rift in Christendom. Chalcedonians and anti-Chalcedonians alike demonized Nestorius. Yet the Chalcedonian Creed also defined a two-nature doctrine that was so close to Nestorianism that even Nestorius himself found no fault in it. The Council of Chalcedon had accepted three ex-Nestorians – Theodore of Mopsuestia, said to be Nestorius' teacher, Theodoret of Cyrrhus, and Ibas of Edessa – into communion, thereby providing ammunition for the charge that Chalcedonianism and Nestorianism were different labels for the same doctrine. Justinian, at Askidas' suggestion, resolved to remedy this error by condemning these ex-Nestorians from the previous century, and in 544 he issued his "Three Chapters" edict, condemning three things: the person and writings of Theodore, some writings of the theologian Theodoret, and a letter of Ibas to a Persian bishop. This set off a titanic struggle with pope Vigilius.

It was a contest that the pope could not avoid, for Justinian was claiming the right, as emperor, to amend the Council of Chalcedon's judgment by condemning long-dead churchmen, and the other patriarchs watched to see what Rome would do. Menas of Constantinople countersigned the edict, with the proviso that he could withdraw his signature if Vigilius did not also countersign. Zoilus of Alexandria did likewise. Vigilius procrastinated. But Justinian was prepared for harsh measures: in November 545, a few days before a second Gothic siege of Rome began, a detachment of Byzantine troops arrested Vigilius while he was saying mass and took him to Sicily, where he stayed for over a year before continuing to Constantinople for a warm greeting from Justinian and Theodora. But the warmth was illusory. The bishops of the west expected Vigilius to head the battle.

Vigilius put up a long, strenuous fight, but in the end he was forced to yield. He must always have been an unsure champion, for, like most Latin bishops, he was not bilingual. His Greek was not fluent enough for him to read the writings that Justinian was condemning, and when the patriarch Menas had some passages translated for him, he recognized that they were heretical, and that the condemnation was justified. He would have liked to find some middle ground, but his vociferous Latin bishops, especially those from Africa, would not let him retreat. When the Fifth Ecumenical Council opened in Hagia Sophia in May 553, Vigilius did not attend, but issued a *Constitutum* condemning the writings *attributed* to Theodore and Theodoret. Perhaps, he hinted, the attribution was wrong? Justinian would have none of it and the Council condemned him. Finally, early next year, he surrendered. He was by now a sick man, and he died on his way back to Rome, where he was refused burial in St Peter's basilica. Justinian got what he wanted. But as far as the anti-Chalcedonians were concerned, the "Three Chapters" dispute made no difference.

An anti-Chalcedonian hierarchy was already being built. Just as bubonic plague was breaking out, al-Harith, the emir of the Ghassanid tribe of Christian Arabs, vital allies who guarded the south-east frontier for the emperor, visited Constantinople and while there asked Theodora for bishops to minister to his people; they were anti-Chalcedonians, and Justin's persecution had deprived them of clergy. Theodora approached Theodosius, the patriarch of Alexandria, who was now in comfortable exile in Constantinople, but recognized by the Miaphysites as their leader, and he consecrated two monks, Theodore, as metropolitan of Bostra and Jacob Baradaeus as metropolitan of Edessa. It is the latter whom the Jacobite church regards as its founder. Baradaeus spent little time in Edessa, where he would have been arrested; instead he went from place to place, consecrating clergy to serve the anti-Chalcedonians. The imperial police tried to catch him, but he was a master of disguise, and always eluded them. By the time Justinian died there were two parallel churches: the Melkites (from the Syriac word for "king"), controlled by the emperor and centered in the cities, and the anti-Chalcedonians, with their strength in the countryside monasteries, ministering to non-Greek-speakers.

Justinian's Last Years

Justinian lived on for seventeen years after the death of Theodora, his ally as well as his adversary in religion, whom he described in one of his *Novels* as "our most pious consort given us by God." Raids by proto-Bulgar tribes and

Slavs still harried the Balkans almost every year; in 559, an incursion by the Kutrigurs threatened Constantinople itself, and in desperation Justinian called out of retirement his old commander Belisarius, who managed to ambush them with a scratch force and put them to flight. Still, Justinian did his best to defend the Danube frontier and there were no permanent Slavic settlements south of it until after his death. He continued his building program everywhere except in Italy, and his new churches, forts, and public amenities drained the treasury. Antioch, which the Persians had destroyed in 540, was rebuilt. In 558, the same year that the plague returned to Constantinople to cut down a new crop of victims, the dome of Hagia Sophia, which had been damaged by a great earthquake the previous December, collapsed; it was rebuilt, and reconsecrated on Christmas Eve 562. Also in 562, the long war with Persia ended with a treaty which assigned Persia a yearly subsidy of just over 400 gold pounds, and about the same time a new enemy from the steppes, the Avars, reached the Danube and asked for land to settle on, in Dobruja at the river mouth. Their khagan, Baian, got a subsidy but no land, and for the time being he remained quiescent.

Under the surface there was discontent. Street violence in Constantinople between the Blues and the Greens was on the increase again. In November 562 a plot to murder Justinian was uncovered, and Belisarius was implicated. Justinian put him under house arrest, but seven months later he dropped the charges. Much later, an anonymous fourteenth-century romance would relate how Justinian blinded Belisarius and left him to beg at the crossroads, but the historical Belisarius died in his bed only a few months before Justinian.

The old emperor pressed on with his quest for orthodoxy. In 563 he made a pilgrimage to the shrine of the Archangel Michael at Germia, near modern Ankara. During his long reign he had never stirred more than a few miles from the royal city, but now some impulse led him to consult the Archangel. Whatever it was, on his return he discovered the true faith at last: it was Aphthartodocetism. Toward the end of 564 he issued an edict proclaiming Aphthartodocetism the orthodox faith. The patriarchs were appalled, but Justinian was in no mood to trifle. Eutychius, the patriarch of Constantinople, was packed off to a monastery and Justinian was preparing tough action against the other patriarchs when he died in his sleep. His successor, Justin II, revoked the edict.

It had been a long reign – forty-seven years, if we count Justin's reign as part of his, as his contemporaries did. Edward Gibbon's verdict on it was that Justinian's only lasting achievement was his laws, but Gibbon's standards were high. Only Augustus and Constantine could claim more lasting achievements than Justinian. He presided over a last flowering of the

Roman empire: a period of literary, artistic, and architectural achievement that few ages can equal. The early years of optimism, when everything seemed possible, were brought to an end by the plague, which continued periodic visitations. By 600 the population of the empire is estimated at 60 per cent of what it had been a century earlier. Justinian's aims were lofty, but the times did not smile on him.

Further Reading

R. Browning, *Justinian and Theodora* (London, 1987)

A. Cameron, *Cambridge Ancient History*, vol. 14, 2nd edn (Cambridge, UK, 2000), 63–258

J. A. S. Evans, *The Age of Justinian: The Consequences of Imperial Power* (London and New York, 1996)

J. A. S. Evans, *The Empress Theodora: Partner of Justinian* (Austin, Tex., 2002)

G. Greatrex, "The Nika Riot: A Reassessment," *Journal of Hellenic Studies* 117 (1997), 60–86

M. Maas (ed.), *The Cambridge Companion to the Age of Justinian* (Cambridge, 2005)

J. Moorhead, *Justinian* (London, 1994)

Glossary of Roman Terms

assemblies Groupings of the Roman citizens convened to carry out specific tasks.

auxiliaries Elements of the Roman army made up of non-citizens, distinguished from legionaries, who were citizens.

bucellarii Units of soldiers in the late Roman and Byzantine empire, supported not by the state but rather by an individual general or governor.

censor Magistrate in charge of public morality, most importantly in monitoring the citizen list and the rolls of the senate. In the imperial period the emperors discharged the duties of the censor.

centurion The commander of a legionary "century," consisting originally of 100 men but by the imperial period of 80.

cognomen The third element of a Roman name, sometimes reflecting a supposed ancestral physical attribute, sometimes a title granted to mark an achievement.

cohort An operational unit of the Roman army; there were ten cohorts to a legion. The term is also used of independent units of the auxiliaries.

colony/*colonia* Originally a settlement of Roman citizens, usually veterans. Later the status could be conferred on other towns as a mark of distinction.

consul The senior Roman magistrate. Two were elected at a time for a period of a year.

denarius Silver coin, worth 4 sestertii.

dictator A magistrate elected during the republic in an emergency. He would hold office for six months.

diocese One of twelve large administrative units into which the provinces were grouped at the end of the third century, each headed by a *vicarius* of the praetorian prefects.

donative A distribution of cash to mark a special occasion.

duces Military commanders. In the later empire *duces* assisted the governors of provinces and, after Diocletian's reforms, the *vicarii* of dioceses.

equestrian Member of an order originally related to service in the cavalry, latterly of citizens with a property qualification of 400,000 sestertii. Although not eligible for the Roman senate, members of the order (also known as knights) played an important part in the administration of the empire in the imperial period, and held certain key offices, such as the prefectures of Egypt and of the praetorian guard.

excubitors A palace guard corps, raised by the emperor Leo, to offset the influence of Germans in the imperial army.

freedman A former slave who has been granted his freedom. Often the freedman would stay in the service of the household where he had been slave.

imperator During the republic a victorious general would be acclaimed as *imperator* (commander) by his troops. In the imperial period commanders served as the emperor's legates and the salutations that followed their successes became the prerogative of the emperor.

imperium The power to command, assigned for a fixed period to magistrates of a certain rank.

iuridici Senior officials in the provinces with broad activity in judicial matters, operating independently of the governor.

knight *See* equestrian.

legate A broad term with three common meanings: (a) an individual assigned a particular task; (b) the commander of a legion; (c) the governor of an imperial province.

legion The major operational unit of the Roman army, consisting of between 5,000 and 6,000 men, all Roman citizens, under the command of a legate appointed by the emperor.

magister memoriae ("master of memory") Important official in the later empire, who drafted and issued imperial decisions and responded to appeals.

magister militum ("master of the soldiers") A post created by Constantine, its holder selected from the senior military commanders within the empire.

maiestas *See* "treason law."

nomen The central element of a Roman name, indicating the holder's *gens* or family.

pater patriae ("father of the fatherland") In the republican period this title was granted first to Cicero for exceptional service to the state. In 2 BC it was conferred on Augustus, who considered it his most significant honor and initially refused it. Tiberius seems never to have accepted the title officially. Even Caligula delayed accepting it.

patrician Member of a select branch of the Roman aristocracy that controlled power in the early republic. The status could only be passed down within the family for most of the republican period, but as the numbers fell new grants of patrician standing were made by Julius Caesar and his successors.

plebeian Originally, member of the lower order of citizens who were not patrician. By the imperial age there were several prominent and distinguished plebeian families.

plebeian tribune Magistrate originally charged with protecting the plebeians against the patricians. During the republic the tribune was powerful, because of his right to veto and to initiate legislation, while the person of the holder was sacrosanct. Under the empire the importance declined and the office became a routine stage between the quaestorship and praetorship.

pontiff Member of one of the four priestly colleges of Rome. The pontifex maximus was the senior priest (*see* "supreme pontiff").

praenomen The first element in the name of a Roman man, the "given" name. There was a very limited number of such names.

praetor The senior magistrate after the consuls. His main task was to preside over the courts.

praetorian guard The imperial guard, originally consisting of nine cohorts, under the command of a prefect or pair of prefects.

prefect This term meant basically "the person placed in charge," and could have a range of applications, both military and administrative. The more significant military ones were (a) the commander of an auxiliary unit or of the fleet; (b) camp prefect, second-in-command to the legionary legate and commander of the troops in the legate's absence; and (c) commander of the praetorian guard and of the fire service (*vigiles*). The key administrative prefects were the governor of Egypt and the prefect of the grain supply. All those prefectures were held by equestrians. The ancient office of city prefect (*praefectus urbi*) was held by a senator of consular rank. By the late republic his duties were largely ritual, but his functions were revived by Augustus, and he was given responsibility for maintaining order in the city and commanding the city police (the *cohortes urbanae*); he was allowed to exercise summary justice in dealing with minor criminal cases and gradually assumed responsibility for more serious cases. In the late empire he wielded considerable power.

proconsul The senatorial governor of a "public" province, chosen by lot.

procurator A highly flexible term. It is used of a private agent or bailiff on an estate. From Claudius on, the term is used of administrators of small districts like Judea. There were also procurators who oversaw financial business relating to the imperial properties within the provinces, some of whom eventually assumed official administrative duties, as "provincial" procurators, in subordinate roles to the governors, in both the imperial and senatorial provinces. The position was held by equestrians or freedmen.

propraetor The governor of a province with the rank of praetor. Legates (governors) of imperial provinces held this rank, so as to be outranked by the consular authority of the emperor.

protectores Soldiers who belonged to one of the branches of the imperial guard in the later empire, appointed for their service and proven competence.

province The term initially referred to the sphere of competence of a magistrate but acquired a more geographical character, defining individual external territories governed by Rome. Following the Augustan settlement external provinces were of two types. "Imperial" provinces, in the unsettled part of the empire, housed Roman legions and were administered by governors appointed directly by the emperor. Some smaller districts were governed by equestrians with the rank of procurator from Claudius on (the title of prefect is usual earlier). Egypt was a major imperial province in its own class, governed by an equestrian prefect. "Public" provinces, in the more stable areas, with rare exceptions did not house legions. Public provinces were governed by proconsuls, men of the senatorial class elected by lot.

quaestor A magistrate who by virtue of this office became a member of the senate. The duties were often financial.

rescript Written answer by an emperor to a legal query.

Secular Games A festival that marked the end of one era (*saeculum*) and the beginning of another. It was held on April 21, the traditional birthday of the city.

senate The senior governing body of the Roman state, made up of ex-magistrates of at least the rank of quaestor and of others deemed worthy by the censor or by the emperor. Under Augustus the number was approximately 600, each with an individual census rating of 1,000,000 sestertii.

sestertius The highest-value base-metal Roman coin, made of an alloy of zinc and copper. It is used by the Romans as the basic unit to express monetary values, with the symbol HS.

supreme pontiff (*pontifex maximus*) The senior priest of Rome. From 12 BC the office was held by the emperor.

toga The traditional public dress of Roman men, made of fine white wool. Boys wore the *toga praetexta* with a purple border. At about fourteen, they put this aside for a plain white version, the *toga virilis*, in a ceremony that marked the transition to manhood. The wearing of the toga *praetexta* was resumed by those entering into curule magistracies.

treason law The laws against *maiestas* were the chief source of dread and resentment in the imperial period. From Augustus on they provided protection against verbal abuse and slander (such protection also existed under the republic, though it was never invoked). An insult to the emperor or a member of his family was an insult to the state.

treasury The state treasury was housed in the Temple of Saturn on the Capitoline hill. It was used also as a depository for senatorial documents.

tribunician authority Emperors did not hold the office of tribune of the plebeians, but they were granted the tribune's authority (*tribunicia potestas*) and his sacrosanctity. This authority was in many ways the foundation of the imperial position, and emperors dated their accession from the time of its bestowal.

triumph The procession led by a commander, after a major victory, through Rome to the Temple of Jupiter on the Capitoline hill, accompanied by war booty and prisoners of war. In the imperial period the triumph was restricted to members of the imperial family.

triumphal regalia Legates of the emperor could not celebrate personal triumphs and their victories were recognized by the right to wear the garb of the triumphator.

vigintiviri Holders of the minor offices often assumed by individuals on the first rung of an administrative or political career.

Index

Note: page references in *italic* indicate illustrations

322 *Index*